PAT ROBERTSON

PAT

AN AMERICAN LIFE

ROBERTSON

David John Marley

ROWMAN & LITTLEFIELD PUBLISHERS, INC.
Lanham • Boulder • New York • Toronto • Oxford

ROWMAN & LITTLEFIELD PUBLISHERS, INC.

Published in the United States of America
by Rowman & Littlefield Publishers, Inc.
A wholly owned subsidary of The Rowman & Littlefield Publishing Group, Inc.
4501 Forbes Boulevard, Suite 200, Lanham, Maryland 20706
www.rowmanlittlefield.com

PO Box 317
Oxford
OX2 9RU, UK

British Library Cataloguing in Publication Information Available

Library of Congress Cataloging-in-Publication Data

Marley, David John, 1967–
    Pat Robertson : an American life / David John Marley.
      p. cm.
    Includes bibliographical references and index.
    ISBN-13: 978-0-7425-5295-1 (hardback : alk. paper)
    ISBN-10: 0-7425-5295-0 (hardback : alk. paper)
    1. Robertson, Pat. I. Title.
    BV3785.R595M37 2007
    269'.2092—dc22
    [B]   2006100537

Printed in the United States of America

♾™ The paper used in this publication meets the minimum requirements of American National Standard for Information Sciences—Permanence of Paper for Printed
Library Materials, ANSI/NISO Z39.48-1992.

～ CONTENTS

∾ PREFACE

"A man who cannot seduce men cannot save them either."
SØREN KIERKEGAARD

P EOPLE love to make fun of Pat Robertson, and apparently with good reason. He seems like a throwback to the days of wild televangelists like
Jimmy Swaggart and Jim Bakker, when TV was rife with men with thick
southern accents claiming to speak for the almighty. When Robertson made
unusual statements, such as his call for the assassination of Venezuelan president
Hugo Chavez or his claim that Israeli prime minister Ariel Sharon's stroke was an
act of God, he became an easy target. However, we need to take Pat Robertson
seriously.

American society has a tradition of belittling those with whom it disagrees.
We compared Adolf Hitler's mustache to Charlie Chaplin's and we mocked
Osama Bin Laden as just another Muslim Fundamentalist. We were wrong both
times. The media's mocking attitude toward Robertson tells the nation to not
take him seriously. Besides being arrogant, it is a huge mistake. While Robertson is not a terrorist, or even half as threatening as most people make him out
to be, he has repeatedly used people's low opinion of him for his benefit. He beat
sitting vice president George H. W. Bush in the 1988 Iowa caucuses due in part
to Bush's low opinion of the televangelist. He was instrumental in the mid-1990s
Republican resurgence, which came after he was blamed, and mocked, for Bush's
defeat in 1992. Robertson's Christian Coalition led the Republican takeover of
Congress in 1994, and although they have never been close, Robertson's leadership of the Christian Right helped elect George W. Bush. After the 2004 presidential election, pollsters and scholars claimed that the Republican Party had

become America's first religious party. A big part of the reason that one political party became identified with evangelical Christianity is Pat Robertson.

When he ran for president in 1988, Robertson said that America should follow the biblical example of the year of jubilee in which all debts were canceled every fifty years. He said this would free third-world nations from grinding poverty and help make the world freer and safer. He was mocked for proposing such a radical idea, yet nearly twenty years later Bono and Pope John Paul II were nominated for the Nobel Peace Prize for suggesting the same thing. That is the danger in writing someone off as a crackpot. By stereotyping him, the world has missed the enigma that is Pat Robertson. He is ahead of his time and decades behind it almost simultaneously.

The most important reason that Robertson should be taken seriously is that no matter what the mainstream thinks, he still matters to millions of people: people who vote. To belittle him is to mock millions of evangelicals and Fundamentalists who feel increasingly attacked by a hostile nation. Robertson is more than happy to use this to his advantage. How can a religious group claim to be oppressed when its membership consists of millions of white middle-class Americans and the president of the United States? Robertson makes the claim with a straight face thanks in part to newspaper editorials that compared his comments to the war-mongering rants of the president of Iran. Robertson says radical things because he knows it energizes his constituency, and the more he is publicly vilified, the more his minority-under-attack-thesis appears to be true. The more he is put down, the more the rest of America is taught to ignore him, the more power he is able to muster.

After nearly forty years on the air, Robertson is still watched by millions on his daily religious talk show *The 700 Club*. Many Americans struggle to understand him just as they struggle to understand evangelicalism. While he seems foreign to some, a large percentage of evangelicals see him as their spokesman. He is not a fiery preacher with an outlandish personality. His show is modeled after Johnny Carson's *Tonight Show*, welcoming and entertaining. He presents a different side of conservative Christianity to the world. This has brought him success, which brought him power, which brought trouble.

To understand Robertson—and what he says and why he acts the way he does—you must study the entire story of his life. He grew up in a world of power and prestige, then renounced it to follow a spiritual calling. Eventually he went back to the political world that he had been born into. Robertson is also interesting because he has spread himself across so many areas of life. His success as a broadcaster, which made him millions, was enough to make him famous. His Christian Broadcasting Network, which started almost literally from nothing, eventually became more popular than MTV. CBN was using satellite and cable to reach a wider audience years before some major networks were. Robertson has also made significant contributions to American evangelicalism. When he entered the community of Charismatic Christians, they were at the fringes of evangelicalism. Through his TV ministry and the notoriety of having a famous father, he was able to give the movement legitimacy. Since the mid-1980s he has made his greatest impact in the political arena. He led an initially successful presidential campaign and went on to form the Christian Coalition, one of the most politically influential groups in recent American history. In Robertson's story we can follow some of the major themes of American life since the 1960s. From the rise of conservative politics, to the struggles within American evangelicalism, to becoming accepted by society again, Robertson has played an important role in recent American history.

This story is not one of an unencumbered rise to power. There were many compromises and enemies made along the way. Although Robertson was raised in a world of power, he arrived at the top a significantly different person than when he began. In the end, the infamous scandals that destroyed the ministries and lives of his competitors in the late 1980s touched Robertson as well. He was more than willing to use his considerable wealth and power to do some ethically questionable things, but instead of buying prostitutes or air-conditioned doghouses, he bought political power. While his own struggles were not as salacious as others' had been, they were just as serious. How he has managed to keep his image clean in the public eye and even expand his empire is a testimony to the strength of his will, and it makes for a great story.

There are numerous people that I would like to thank for their help. First of all I must thank my dissertation director Leo Ribuffo. I always appreciated his guidance and support for my topic. I moved across the country to work with him, and I found that his advice was always scholarly and brutally honest. During my time in graduate school I was also fortunate to work with Dewey Wallace, who helped me refine my ideas and put them in the broader context of American religious history. During the summer of 2004 it was my honor to work with Alan Wolfe at the Boisi Center for Religion and American Public Life at Boston College. His seminar, sponsored by the National Endowment for the Humanities, gave me the time to put the finishing touches on the book. I also appreciate the help provided by the staff of Rowman & Littlefield, especially my editor John Loudon and his assistants Sarah Johnson and Sarah Stanton. In addition, Erin McGarvey and my copy editor Luann Reed-Siegel were also very helpful. They are all very patient people.

I would like to thank the following libraries for allowing me access to their many valuable materials. The library staff at Boston College, American University, the Library of Congress, the Ronald Reagan Presidential Library, Vanguard University, Washington and Lee University, George Washington University, and

California State University, Fullerton were always helpful. A very special thank you is reserved for Regent University and especially their director of Special Collections, Donald Gantz. The research facilities of the Institute for the Study of American Evangelicals and the Billy Graham Center at Wheaton College, the Americans United for the Separation of Church and State, and People for the American Way were also generous in their assistance. Megan Lee, first of the Ronald Reagan, then the Richard Nixon Presidential Library was always helpful. I also would like to thank Angell Vasko at CBN and Pat Robertson for allowing me to be the first person who was allowed access to his presidential campaign materials.

There were a number of individuals who helped me in myriad of ways. Some of them read chapters, took my unsolicited emails, or helped keep me focused on my goals. My thanks go out to Alexandra Kindell, Paul McGraw, Kirk Borkman, Terry Lindvall, Mark Santangelo, Allida Black, Elizabeth Leonard, John Wilson, Mike Wilson, Eric Patterson, Jerry Camery-Hoggatt, Larry Eskridge, Felix Posos, Jeri South, Ronald Wells, Richard Pierard, Gordon Bakken, Ronald Rietveld, Lawrence deGraaf, Muriel Atkin, James Oliver Horton, Tony Clifton, and my fellow skippers at the world-famous Jungle Cruise at Disneyland. I would especially like to thank Quinn Schroeder for providing me with housing during my many research visits to Virginia Beach. Thanks are also due to my diligent student research assistants, Sarah White and Iman Mahli.

My family was a constant source of love and support during the entire process. I wish to thank my parents, Erla Curtin and Ronald Marley, my brother Larry, my sister Linda Fern, and their families for their help. A very special thanks goes out to my uncle Terry Wolfsen who opened his home to me when I moved to Washington, D.C., and also fixed and re-fixed my computer over the years. He was a constant source of encouragement and help. The time I spent working on this project was given new meaning thanks to the arrival of my daughters Olivia and Isabelle. My girls may have missed the years that their daddy struggled as a graduate student, but they get to be around for the student loan payments.

Finally, I dedicate this work to my wife Debbie. She left the warm beaches of Southern California for Washington, D.C., and supported me while I visited libraries and conducted interviews. I can never thank her enough for all that she has done. This project would have been impossible without her love and support.

CHAPTER 1

SENATOR'S SON

C HILDREN of congressmen often live in a world of privilege, the best private schools, spacious homes, luxury hotel suites. For the first seven years of his life, Marion Gordon "Pat" Robertson lived in this world of power and prestige. Robertson, born March 22, 1930, remembers a life of waiting for the Good Humor ice cream truck and playing stickball in the streets with his brother A. Willis Jr., usually called Taddy, who was six years his senior, and the neighborhood kids.[1] It was his older brother who gave Robertson the nickname "Pat." Taddy enjoyed patting his baby brother's cheeks while saying "pat, pat, pat." Robertson's parents thought the name was cute, and it stuck. As a baby he was "obviously defenseless to protest, but later in life I felt that 'Marion' sounded a touch effeminate and 'M. Gordon' sounded affected, so I continued to be Pat."[2]

Due to the regular income that being in political office provided, Robertson's family was relatively untouched by the Great Depression. His father's $10,000 a year salary as a representative, a "modest sum" as Robertson called it, paid for both a cook and a maid. Such a standard of living was rare in Depression-era America. Originally the Robertsons lived in Washington, D.C., near Georgetown, in the exclusive neighborhood off Foxhall Road. Eventually the family moved across the Potomac River to Alexandria, Virginia.

Politics was in Robertson's blood from the start. In fact, he joked that his first two words were "mama" and "daddy" and his third was "constituent." Young Pat Robertson visited his father, A. Willis Robertson, in his Capitol Hill office where he served as the representative from Virginia's Seventh District. While there he watched his father debate, and he had the chance to meet famous congressmen and other politicians in New Deal–era Washington. The Robertson men would then adjourn to the members-only dining area and have lunch.

While Robertson was able to enjoy a life largely unaffected by the Depression, World War II changed the situation.

When war broke out in Europe, Washington, D.C., quickly filled with soldiers and bureaucrats. The city changed, and crowding became worse. Representative Robertson decided to move his family from Alexandria back home to Lexington, deep in Virginia's Shenandoah Valley. Even today, the ghosts of the Civil War hang heavy in the town. The idea of the lost cause and young men dying for their beliefs is an almost palpable presence. Despite some modern buildings erected on the outskirts, the city remains much the same as it has been for decades. Limited by geography and history, Lexington is a town where collective memory reaches back generations. It seemed a world away to Pat Robertson, who had just completed the fifth grade.

Lexington was established by Scotch Irish immigrants in 1777. The town was named in honor of Lexington, Massachusetts, the birthplace of the Revolutionary War. Notoriety came to the city by way of its two major colleges, both originally exclusively for men. Washington College was spared the torch by Union soldiers during the Civil War, in honor of the nation's first president. After the war Confederate general Robert E. Lee became president of Washington College, and after the general's death in 1870, the name was changed to Washington and Lee University. The Lee family is buried there, along with the general's favorite wartime companion, his horse Traveler. Robertson, like so many white southern boys before him, idolized the general. "He was a magnificent gentleman who was held up to me as being more or less the ideal man. . . . He was particularly a model of what a Southerner would consider chivalry."[3]

Next door to the university is the Virginia Military Institute (VMI), the training ground for generations of warriors from Virginia. Stonewall Jackson was president of VMI before the Civil War. During the war, the cadets fought an advancing U.S. Army and watched as the school was burned to the ground.

The Robertson family traces its descendants for over one thousand years from the Norman conquest of Britain to English kings and the founders of the Virginia Colony. In his mother's heritage Pat Robertson claims links to two presidents (William Henry Harrison and Benjamin Harrison), Winston Churchill, and John Armistead, a member of the Virginia House of Burgesses in colonial Williamsburg.[4] Robertson's mother constantly reminded him of his heritage. "Her whole approach," he recalls, "was to convince me that I was born for leadership, that she had great expectations for me."[5] Living in Lexington, this lesson was reinforced daily.

Pat Robertson's father, Absalom Willis Robertson, gave his son the lifelong love of politics. Willis, as he was called, was the son of a Baptist preacher and married Gladys Churchill soon after he graduated from the University of Rich-

mond in 1908. He practiced law but was almost immediately drawn into politics. By 1916 he was serving in the Virginia State Senate.[6] In 1932 he went to
Congress, where he had a reputation as a fiscal conservative and avid conservationist.[7] His conservative politics ran him afoul of two very powerful men in
Washington. One was President Franklin D. Roosevelt; the other was his fellow
congressman from Virginia, Senator Harry Byrd, who ran the state's Democratic political machine.

Willis Robertson was tied for first place among Democrats who opposed
the New Deal legislation of the Roosevelt administration. One historian notes
that Willis voted against FDR about 65 percent of the time.[8] Even when the rest
of his state delegation voted for federal projects favorable to their state, Willis
voted against them when he felt they were not economically feasible. His determination to vote against any program that would add to the nation's debt was
equaled only by his decision to go against Harry Byrd's Democratic party
machine. Robertson was nominated by the party to be Virginia's junior senator
in 1946 to fill a vacancy after Senator Carter Glass died. Robertson was chosen
over Byrd's objections because state party leaders felt that he was able to win
elections without being tainted as a machine politician. Robertson remained in
the Senate until he was defeated in the 1966 Democratic primary. Neither Harry
Byrd nor Robertson faced a Republican challenger from 1950 to 1964, a testimony to the now-forgotten southern hatred of the Republican Party and the
strength of the Democratic party machine.[9]

The elder Robertson was a tall, athletic man who looked years younger than
his age. This was reinforced when he decided to run for reelection at age seventy-
eight. When he lost his bid he was the third oldest man in the Senate. During
his tenure he was an avid conservative, voting against such New Deal plans as
the Social Security Act in 1935 as well as the Great Society–created Department
of Housing and Urban Development. Senator Robertson also signed the Southern Manifesto in 1956, which asked southern states to fight the federal government's intervention on behalf of the growing civil rights movement. Willis was
the grandson of a Confederate captain who had died at the Battle of Gaines Mill
in 1862, and his southern heritage was the hallmark of his tenure in office. While
in the House, he was on the powerful Ways and Means Committee. As senator
he sat on the Foreign Relations Committee and served with Joseph McCarthy
on the important Banking Committee. Senator Robertson was an avid hunter
and conservationist. Much of his work was spent preserving lands used by
migratory birds and passing laws to help states fund conservation efforts. He
also wanted to create a national fish hatchery so sport fishermen would always
have a plentiful supply. Senator Robertson was understandably one of the busiest
men in Washington, D.C., and he rarely had time to travel down to Lexington
to visit his family.

On the rare weekends that he was home, Senator Robertson had the aura of celebrity about him. One neighbor recalled that when he did come home, he would walk around the neighborhood with his hunting dogs, which would knock over every trash can they came to. He had a home built in 1925 for his family on the edge of town in Lexington, which stands to this day. When it was built it was considered to be a mansion by the locals, and it is still imposing in the upper-class neighborhood that has grown up around it. Behind the house was an unfinished railroad line. All that had been completed was the digging of the bed; the track was never laid. This ditch filled with water in the summer and became a small wildlife sanctuary, which remained until, despite Mrs. Robertson's protests, it was paved over and became Highland Avenue. Across this ditch stood the town's high school, since converted to an elementary school.

Robertson's mother was described as an unusually beautiful woman, who strongly disliked the social scene of Washington, D.C. Robertson remembers his mother continually turning down invitations to the White House and embassy parties. Since the senator spent so much time away from home starting when Robertson was ten and his brother was nearly grown, it was only natural that Pat was closer to his mother. By all accounts she was a dutiful mother, if at times a bit overprotective. Both of the Robertson boys had long hair with big Shirley Temple curls. During the summer Mother Robertson pinned their hair up so it wouldn't get tangled as the boys explored the woods beyond the house. A neighbor girl recalled that the two Robertson boys were picked on for their long hair by the other boys. When Senator Robertson returned to Lexington he marched his sons to the barber. The boys seemed relieved.

Senator Robertson was apparently concerned that his sons did not appreciate how fortunate they were. Robertson recalls that "in our lives we didn't experience the Depression."[10] When Robertson was thirteen he spent the summer on a relative's farm, where he learned the value of hard work. Working from 6 AM to 9 PM some days, he was paid $15 a month for harvesting potatoes, chopping wood, and feeding the livestock.[11] The senator wanted his boys to learn the value of hard work and the importance of being careful not to waste money.

Gladys Robertson was religiously devout, and became more so the older she got. She donated to many local charities and wrote letters to evangelists like Kathryn Kuhlman asking her to pray for her children's salvation. Kuhlman said that she treasured the letters because they asked for prayer for Pat and his father.[12] These religious contacts led to the Robertsons' introduction to a young Billy Graham, who years later recalled that the senator was one of the first people to introduce him in Washington, D.C., during his first crusade there in 1952.[13] Despite her deeply held beliefs, church attendance for the rest of the family was casual; it was more of an assumed social obligation. In fact, Robertson admits that although he joined the Southern Baptist Church, just like the rest of his friends, it meant little to him.[14]

During his childhood, racial discrimination was the law of the South, yet this was apparently another issue that was never a conscious issue for young Robertson. In his official biography, Robertson recalls playing with his white friends and playing baseball with the black children, who lived on the other side of town. Robertson nonchalantly writes that when summer was over the black kids went to their school, and he and his white friends went to theirs. This more than anything else demonstrates how widespread segregation was, and how little it seemed to affect young whites. Robertson's official biography contains many references to his dealings with blacks while a child in pre–civil rights era Virginia, yet there is not a single mention of segregation, or his father's role in supporting Jim Crow laws.[15]

Robertson attended well-funded white public schools in Lexington after attending private schools in Washington, D.C. When his penchant for mischief got him in trouble, he was sent to military school. Robertson attended McDonough School in Baltimore for a year in 1943 and returned to complete high school in Lexington. After one more year of troublemaking, his parents sent him to the McCallie School in Chattanooga, Tennessee. The college preparatory high school had a military program in addition to its academics. While there he blossomed academically in history, English, and French and graduated in 1946. Since Robertson's primary interest was in history, he majored in it while at Washington and Lee University.[16]

The university had an active social scene. Until 1984 the school was strictly a men's college, and on the weekends, the young men visited the local women's colleges, such as nearby Mary Washington College. Lexington was still a fairly small town and the young people only had a few acceptable places to hang out. The town's two five-and-dime stores were popular hangouts. The most popular place was McCrum's Drugstore, which had tables and a soda fountain. While Robertson was a freshman, the girls who came into town on the weekends from the local colleges stayed on the second floor of the Lee Hotel, but by the time he was an upperclassman, the popularity of cars made it easier to get back and forth.

While in college, Robertson lived at home, which was about two miles from campus. During his freshman year the young men of the university were told that "nobility obligates," an idea that Robertson claimed was one of the most important things he ever learned. His father gave him an allowance of $40 a month, which he spent largely on parties and "lavish" living. Robertson remembers "stumbling home with whiskey on my breath and seeing my mother's face, she was always praying."[17] While he did not participate in student government, he was involved in the social scene. Among his friends at school were the great-grandson of Robert E. Lee and the son of Supreme Court chief justice Fred Vinson.[18]

Robertson was a good student, making Phi Beta Kappa during his junior year and graduating with almost straight As. After four years of scholastics and fraternity parties he graduated in 1950. However, before he could head off to make his fortune, war broke out in Korea, and Robertson joined the Marine Corps.

Robertson was one of the first graduates from Washington and Lee to volunteer for military service when the Korean War erupted. While his father was proud to see his son enlist, he was concerned for his safety. Senator Robertson wrote General Lemuel Shepherd asking that his son not be sent to combat immediately after his basic officer's training was completed. The senator had written about his ability to get favorable military assignments for people without it appearing on their records.[19] It appears that he performed this service for his own son. Shepherd wrote to Senator Robertson about his son's progress, and the senator wrote letters to the secretary of defense recommending the general for Marine Corps commandant. The series of letters between the two men mostly consisted of the senator expressing his happiness that his son was not being sent into combat.[20] While there is no evidence that Pat Robertson asked for special treatment, his father was actively working on his behalf. Earlier biographies of Pat Robertson assume that it was merely his name recognition that helped him in the Marines, but the records now indicate otherwise. If, however, Robertson wanted to avoid combat, joining the Marine Corps was an odd decision. He did not join the National Guard; instead he joined the one branch of the military that is most likely to be sent into harm's way.

After going through basic training, Robertson was sent to Asia, along with the rest of his unit. When the ship reached Kobe, Japan, Robertson disembarked, and his compatriots went on to Korea. Senator Robertson had received word several days earlier that his son was to be taken off the ship before reaching Korea. Years later Congressman Pete McCloskey, who had traveled to Korea with Robertson, charged that he had used his father's influence. McCloskey said, "[M]y single distinct memory is of Pat with a big smile on his face . . . telling us that his father had gotten him out of combat duty."[21] Other Marines recall Robertson sending at least two telegrams to his father while aboard ship. One believes that at least part of the telegram was in code. In Japan Robertson worked as an assistant adjutant, and his job included regular trips to Korea to deliver classified codes. He performed his duties well, even if they were not terribly demanding. His wartime friends, including future Virginia senator John Warner, gave him the nickname "Division Liquor Officer."[22] Robertson was in charge of what he euphemistically calls "class 6 ordinance, which was cases of liquor for the officers. . . . I got blind staggering drunk on a mountain in Korea called the punch bowl on a cold winter night celebrating New Years."[23] Robertson has referred to his service alternately as "active duty" and "combat duty," but what is clear is that the fraternity party boy was not changed by his experience in Korea.

Robertson was disheartened by his experience in Korea, later stating, "I knew we were fighting a no-win war. Politically in the U.S., the citizens were in no way supporting the war. . . . I thought it was the greatest folly I'd ever seen to waste our energy, our lives, and our money for a situation that was pointless."[24] He is, however, still proud of his military service. Next to the door of his office at CBN headquarters, Robertson displays the medals and citations he earned while in the Marines.

Upon returning to the States, Robertson was accepted into Yale Law School. While there his grades dipped, and his official biography claims that his studies there left him embittered at the Supreme Court for their perceived blatant disregard for the Constitution. Robertson himself commented that he was asked to read what scholars, lawyers, and others had said about the Constitution, but he was never asked to read it himself.[25] Perhaps the most significant event that occurred in his life at this time was meeting his future wife.

Dede Elmer was a Yale nursing student who met her future husband at a sorority party to which the law school men had been invited. While trying to light some candles for the party, Dede caught her hair on fire, and Robertson came over to help her out. They quickly left the party and went to a campus beer hall to get better acquainted.[26] Robertson immediately hit it off with the Irish Catholic girl from Ohio. After a year and a half of dating, Dede became pregnant and Robertson proposed marriage. The expectant couple traveled from Connecticut to Elkton, Maryland, which at the time was the quick marriage capital of the East Coast. Elkton had seen such celebrities as Glenn Miller, Debbie Reynolds, and Martha Raye drop in for fast marriages. The city, just south of the Delaware border, was a popular stop for couples from states with restrictive marriage license rules.[27] Dede and Pat were secretly married on August 27, 1954, and their first child, Tim, was born in November of that year.[28] The story of their unexpected pregnancy was kept a family secret until 1987 when Robertson ran for president. For decades the Robertsons maintained that March 22, 1954, was their wedding day and the date remained unchallenged until reporters discovered the couple's marriage certificate in 1987. In the years following the quick marriage the young Robertson family steadily grew. Daughter Elizabeth was born two years after Tim. Next came Gordon, a year and a half younger than his sister. Their last child, Ann, was born four years later when the family was in Norfolk starting their television ministry.

After graduating from Yale, Robertson took and failed the New York Bar Exam. His wife was still finishing nursing school in New Haven, and Robertson took a job in New York City with W. R. Grace Company, which was heavily involved in shipping at the time. The company was happy to hire a son of a U.S. senator, even if he couldn't practice law. The job required him to travel to Peru, Bolivia, and Brazil, where he became concerned about the morality of selling trinkets to impoverished Indians.[29] Robertson kept himself busy working long days and used the experience to plan for a business that he would one day own, although he was still unsure of exactly what it was that he wanted to do.

The Robertsons lived in a cottage that was attached to a larger house in Staten Island. Their home was small, and Dede spent her days taking care of their young son while Robertson worked long hours in Manhattan. Robertson was unhappy and restless, and according to Dede was constantly pacing, going from Tim to the fridge to the window, always a flurry of activity.[30]

A new business opportunity arrived in the name of the Curry Sound Company. The company, which was developing a new type of speaker, was the brain-child of two of Robertson's law school friends. He quit W. R. Grace and became a partner, buying a third of the stock. They had advertisements published and were looking toward profitability when it was discovered that it would require more research to fix some technical problems.[31] In the midst of all of this, another problem was brewing within Robertson's soul.

The Robertson household had been a nominal Christian home; church attendance was irregular and their faith was relevant only on Easter and Christmas. Robertson had led a wild life of women and drink, and even while married he and Dede continued to go to wild parties and tried to become part of the New York City social scene. They also stayed involved in politics. In 1956 Robertson supported Democratic presidential nominee Adlai Stevenson and chaired the 1956 Elect Stevenson Committee for Staten Island.[32] However, he found social life and politics unsatisfying and tried various things to fill the emptiness that he felt. He was an adult now, and his life was supposed to have followed a path of success and adventure. The senator's son had led a life of privilege and found it lacking. His decision on how to change things was a characteristic that remained a part of his personality for the rest of his life. He boldly took a step and only later took the time to count the cost.

Notes

1. Pat Robertson, interview by author, tape recording, Virginia Beach, Va., May 25, 2000.

2. Pat Robertson, "Origins of His Nickname," www.patrobertson.com/FastFacts/nickname.asp (accessed June 24, 2006).

3. John B. Donovan, *Pat Robertson: The Authorized Biography* (New York: Macmillan, 1988), 15.

4. Donovan, *Pat Robertson*, 5.

5. Donovan, *Pat Robertson*, 8.

6. David Edwin Harrell Jr., *Pat Robertson: A Personal, Religious, and Political Portrait* (New York: Harper & Row, 1987), 11.

7. Willis Robertson was named the sportsman of the year by *Field & Stream* magazine in 1926.

8. Ronald Heinemann, *Depression and New Deal in Virginia* (Charlottesville: University of Virginia Press, 1983), 141.

9. J. Harvie Wilkinson, *Harry Byrd and the Changing Face of Virginia Politics, 1945–1966* (Charlottesville: University of Virginia Press, 1968), 212.

10. Donovan, *Pat Robertson*,11.

11. Donovan, *Pat Robertson*, 12.

12. Kathryn Kuhlman radio show, circa 1972. Billy Graham Center (BGC).

13. Billy Graham, speech at Amsterdam 1983. July 17, 1983. BGC.

14. Harrell, *Pat Robertson*, 8.

15. Donovan, *Pat Robertson*, 7.

16. Harrell, *Pat Robertson*, 21.

17. Kuhlman show, circa 1972. BGC.

18. Harrell, *Pat Robertson*, 22.

19. April Witt, "Robertson Fighting for Honor," *Virginian-Pilot*, April 12, 1987.

20. The papers of A. Willis Robertson are held by the College of William and Mary. The collection forbids any quotation from the letters that deal with a living person.

21. Associated Press, "Robertson's Father Wrote General," circa early 1987.

22. Harrell, *Pat Robertson*, 25.

23. Kuhlman show, circa 1972. BGC.

24. Donovan, *Pat Robertson*, 23–24.

25. Donovan, *Pat Robertson*, 25.

26. Dede Robertson and John Sherrill, *My God Will Supply* (Lincoln, Va.: Chosen Books, 1979).

27. Marshall Berdan, "Elkton Marry-Land," *Washington Post*, February 13, 2002.

28. Harrell, *Pat Robertson*, 26.

29. Harrell, *Pat Robertson*, 28.

30. Robertson and Sherrill, *My God Will Supply*, 20.

31. Harrell, *Pat Robertson*, 28.

32. Hubert Morken, *Pat Robertson: Where He Stands* (Grand Rapids, Mich.: Revell Co., 1988), 21.

CHAPTER 2

CONVERSION

R OBERTSON's uneasiness with his life was matched by his mother's concern for his soul. She was unhappy with his sudden marriage to Dede,
especially since she was a Catholic and was from the North.[1] Dede did not
match her expectations for the son of a U.S. senator, and she feared that even his
casual church attendance was going to lapse as he tried to find a career in New
York City. She was also not pleased when her son visited her in Lexington to
announce that he was thinking of joining the ministry. He thought that this would
please both his parents, since his grandfather had been a Baptist preacher. As far
as Mother Robertson was concerned, he had not had the religious conversion necessary to dedicate one's life to God's service.

At his mother's constant urging Robertson made a date to meet with a traveling evangelist named Cornelius Vanderbreggen, whom she financially supported, who like Pat had been a Marine. The two men met in an upscale
Philadelphia restaurant, and Robertson was amazed at how this man opened his
Bible and spoke of Jesus as an actual person. He later said, "I wanted to hide
under the table, he even gave the waiter a Bible tract."[2] Vanderbreggen told
young Robertson that his view of Jesus as merely an ethical teacher was not good
enough. It took time for Robertson to get over the initial embarrassment; he
tried to end the conversation by telling the evangelist that he was entering the
ministry as soon as his business deals were settled. Vanderbreggen continued to
ask personal questions about his faith. Eventually Robertson admitted, "All of
my experiences with God so far had been religious, not spiritual."[3] They talked
for hours, and Robertson left that meeting with his life forever changed.[4]

That evening Robertson came home and announced that he had become a
born-again Christian. Dede Robertson had no reaction at first. She later wrote
that she "couldn't believe her ears." Her husband claimed that he finally knew

Jesus; she protested that she thought that they already did.[5] It was months before his wife realized the depth of his conversion. Soon Robertson told his wife that he planned on entering the ministry and that he felt called by God to sell his share in the electronics company.

Dede was worried about her husband's decision to work for some church but then reflected, "Maybe we had better start going to church to see what it's all about."[6] Over the course of the next few weeks the couple tried a Baptist, a Moravian, and an Evangelical Free church. During all of this time, they maintained their social lifestyle, not fully realizing the commitment that a career in the ministry would entail.

The religious conversion didn't decrease the growing tension in the household; instead, it increased tenfold. Robertson became more obsessed day by day with his new faith. The week before their second child was due, Robertson went on a church retreat, telling Dede that it was just something that he had to do. Dede was understandably furious and contemplated moving back to Ohio; but her parents had retired and moved to Lebanon, and her siblings were too busy to help her out. "I was really stranded," she recalls.[7] Her mother flew from the Middle East to be there for the delivery of their first daughter, Elizabeth. She also complained constantly about her son-in-law who had two college degrees and no job. Robertson recalls that his mother-in-law "never liked me. Having felt that Dede should have married a Catholic—a wealthy one."[8] She considered her son-in-law to be immature and self-centered. When Pat worked as a volunteer for a Billy Graham crusade, Dede did as well, if only to spend more time with her husband.[9]

In the fall of 1957 Robertson entered the Bible Seminary of New York (renamed the New York Theological Seminary in 1966), where he eventually earned a Master of Divinity degree.[10] The Robertsons moved to Queens so they could be closer to the school and the church where he was assigned to work. Dede was still angry at her husband. She later admitted to attacking and needling him constantly, to try to pry him away from his new faith.

The basic theological assumption of the seminary was that all truth could be discerned from the Bible. The school had been founded in 1900 by Wilbert White, who believed that the Bible should be the central focus of a theological education. White was a proponent of a systematic study of the Bible, called the inductive method. Students were taught that through careful study and prayer they could understand God's message in any section of scripture. White taught that there were three "laws of the heart," which, when followed, allowed true believers to understand the Bible. The first was "the law of prayer," which claimed that if a believer is in constant prayer while studying the scriptures, God will reveal the truth. The second law states that the Holy Spirit has been given to Christians so that they understand God on a deep level. In the final concept, "the law of our spiritual nature," White taught that believers should feel confident that if they are in prayer and study diligently, the spirit will guide their study and bring them to the correct conclusions.[11] This style of study has been the cornerstone of Robertson's belief system ever since. His 1982 book *The Secret Kingdom* was based upon the assumption that there are truths and powers that are hidden within scripture that merely need to be discovered. This method did not require the use of Greek or Hebrew, focusing instead on the individual's ability to connect with the Bible and with God. It is popular in many evangelical and Charismatic groups, such as the Intervarsity Christian Fellowship, because it is easy to use. It is also easy for people to come to radically different conclusions about the same passage since it relies on an individual's work alone.

Robertson was impressed with the scripture study skills that he was taught, which he referred to as textual criticism. Originating with liberal Protestant churches in the late 1800s, it had melted into the conservative seminaries by the 1950s. Simply put, textual criticism is a way to better understand the author and intended audience of a biblical passage. While liberal seminaries mostly used this skill to attack the idea of biblical inerrancy, conservative seminaries used the same tool to come to the opposite conclusion. Textual criticism implies a knowledge of biblical languages, and use of commentaries of renowned scholars, in an effort to understand what the author of a particular section of scripture meant when they wrote it. This is not the method of inductive study. Since his time in seminary, Robertson has become a more serious student of the Bible, even if he relies on the easier to use inductive method.

In addition to studying the Bible, he also took classes in soteriology, eschatology, and the major church doctrines. Robertson has always been fond of eschatology, the study of the end times, so it is no surprise that he was particularly proud of the A+ he got in a class on the book of Revelation. Church history was also a major emphasis. He studied the origins of the church and the works of men like St. Augustine and the Nicene Fathers.[12] Another aspect of his training included working in a local church as an assistant. His work at the church kept him so busy that he was unable to hold a regular job. As a result the young Robertson family's income was so low that Senator Robertson claimed them as dependents on his 1957 income taxes.[13]

Outside of the classroom, Robertson began to examine the lives of famous American evangelists. He remembers, "I probably studied John Wesley as much as anyone. I had his journal and read it extensively."[14] He also read about American evangelists Dwight Moody and Charles Finney. Robertson was particularly impressed by Finney, reading and rereading his autobiography and his collected letters several times. Finney was the great evangelist of the Second Great Awakening, and he is widely considered the first professional evangelist. Finney had been a lawyer before his own conversion and he preached the Gospel to thousands across the country. Finney was also a moral crusader; while president of Oberlin College, he made it the first in the United States to accept blacks and one of the first to accept women.[15] Robertson took many lessons from Finney, who had been master of the media in his age. At this point in his life, Robertson had no intention of becoming an evangelist, and certainly not one who would be as popular as his hero Charles Finney.

More significant than his study of evangelists, Robertson began to search for a more dynamic relationship with God. He studied the scriptures, which contained miracles, and wondered why the same things couldn't happen today. He encountered other students at the small seminary who felt the same way. They began meeting at 6 AM for prayer sessions that sometimes lasted hours. Eventually a female student from Korea named Su Nae Chu joined the group. She told Robertson and the others about her experiences in Korea and the revival that was sweeping her homeland. She claimed that the revival was empowered by Christians praying in tongues.[16] This experience, also called *glossolalia*, is the defining experience of the Pentecostal and Charismatic movements. The first record of Christians speaking in tongues is found in the New Testament book of Acts, where Jesus' disciples are filled with the Holy Spirit and begin to speak in languages unknown to them. In the Bible, tongues were used to preach the Gospel to others in their own languages. The modern Pentecostal movement began in the early twentieth century due to the work of Charles Parham in Topeka, Kansas.[17] Some early Pentecostals went around the world as missionaries in the mistaken belief that the Holy Spirit would allow them to speak the language of wherever they ended up. In the modern manifestation tongues serve as a way to exhort fellow believers, reveal special messages from God, and as a simple act of worship.

The group prayed earnestly for this in filling of the Holy Spirit, and slowly each member of the group began to speak in tongues, except Robertson. The prayer and Bible study sessions continued, but Robertson never had the experience, which his wife thought was both loud and disturbing.[18] Finally, Robertson spoke in tongues during a moment of crisis. After a long day at school, Robertson came home to discover that his son Tim was running a high fever and was unconscious. In desperation both parents knelt at Tim's bedside and prayed for a miracle. Robertson recalls, "Suddenly I was aware of the love of God enfolding him, and the power of God going through him. He opened his eyes and murmured 'mommy, I gotta go to the bathroom.'" He knew that God had just healed his son. In the joy of the moment, he began to thank God for the miracle. "It was in this moment that I became aware my speech was garbled. I was speaking in another language."[19] The experience that he had struggled to receive for months had finally come to him in his own home.

Robertson had undergone tremendous changes in a span of two years. One personality trait remained the same with the pre- and postconversion Robertson: his drive and determination to be successful in whatever field that he chose to work in. If anything, his drive was increased by his conversion, since this new religious fervor had made him work even harder. For a man who had such a strong desire to work hard, no matter what he was working at, evangelical Christianity was a perfect match.

Evangelicalism, although now almost synonymous with the Christian Right, is actually one of the oldest and most popular religious movements in American history. Its American roots can be traced to the 1730s with the religious revival known as the Great Awakening. Traveling evangelists preached a Christianity that was focused on an individual's relationship to God. This relationship was more important than church attendance or adherence to a single denomination. This idea was best summarized by evangelist Gilbert Tennant's 1740 sermon "The Danger of an Unconverted Ministry." Tennant shocked colonial churches when he encouraged true Christians to do whatever it took, including changing denominations, to find a church where the Gospel was preached.[20] It was this focus on the individual, and the responsibility of Christians to spread the Gospel, that allowed evangelicalism to grow. Historian D. G. Hart writes that the movement owes its success to its rejection of church hierarchies and formal church structures.[21] Another term for these early evangelicals might be Revivalists, since the movement's central emphasis was on preaching their message. Evangelicals enjoyed great success and a grip on American popular culture until after the Civil War when a new liberal theology made its way over from Germany. In the late 1800s, denominations were split in a theological struggle over the nature of the Bible. The liberals, also called Modernists, eventually controlled the major seminaries and Protestant denominations, while the conservatives, called Fundamentalists, left to start their own churches.

Modern Evangelicalism is the descendant of Fundamentalism, but despite their similarities, there are significant differences. The term *Fundamentalist* is used to describe people who are both theologically and culturally conservative and comes from a series of books, *The Fundamentals*, which were published in 1912. Those volumes sought to answer the charges of the liberal wing of Christianity, which was taking over most universities, and defend the basic, or fundamental, beliefs of the church. The books were written by leading conservative theologians and were more intellectual than just about anything one is likely to find in a Christian bookstore today. Fundamentalists hold to biblical inerrancy and to social mores that were in vogue in pre-industrial America. Fundamentalism is not just a religious belief; it is a way of life and looking at culture. Many of its social views were adopted at a time when conservative Christians were near the bottom rung of American society. As a result there was an intense hostility to popular culture. This uneasiness with the world meant that they tended to outlaw things like drinking, dancing, and going to movies, activities that besides their moral concerns were too expensive for most Fundamentalists to engage in. A popular Fundamentalist refrain went, "I don't drink, dance, chew, or go with girls that do." They were hostile to culture and defined themselves by what they didn't do more than what they did. This movement became so hostile to anything that smelled of liberal theology that it even rejected social work (helping the poor, etc.) since those activities had been taken over by liberals. The event is known as "The Great Reversal" and was an attempt by Fundamentalists to focus exclusively on spiritual issues.[22]

During the 1940s the term *evangelical* came into heavy use by those who wished to separate themselves from the negative image that Fundamentalism had acquired. It is this version of Christianity that has been the fastest growing religion in America for the past one hundred years. While maintaining most of the central theological tenets of Fundamentalism, evangelicals are less culturally reclusive or exclusionary. Where Fundamentalists have withdrawn from society, evangelicals engage it and participate in a wide variety of cultural activities. Evangelicals try to make a culture that is both modern and Christian. While their theology is conservative, like that of the Fundamentalists, they are not afraid to adapt what is not dictated by the scriptures. So while there may be compromises on Sabbath laws, rock music, and dating practices, issues like the role of women in the church, homosexuality, and abortion are unlikely to be adapted based on trends in American culture. Evangelicals are also likely to be committed to education, although they still tend to believe in the biblical version of creation over Darwinism. Significantly, there is no political belief that is essential to evangelicalism. Some religious conservatives, most notably William Jennings Bryan, were famous for their political liberalism.[23] The idea that evangelicalism demands political conservatism is testament to the power that the Christian Right has had over the movement for more than thirty years. Evangelicalism lacks a central denomination or leader and has no unifying creed. Historians of American religion have been rightly amazed by the coherence one finds in the movement despite the absence of what has been central to earlier denominations.[24]

When Robertson converted, he did not merely return to the Southern Baptist Church of his youth; instead he joined the most "spirit-led" wing of the evangelical movement. While he usually attended Baptist churches, he looked for churches that were Charismatic, a form of Pentecostalism. Pentecostal churches became widespread in the United States in the early 1900s and were primarily concerned with exercising "spiritual gifts," especially *glossolalia* or speaking in tongues. The movement was based on the search for a movement of God after sanctification. These believers wanted a second blessing, an in filling of the Holy

Spirit, which they teach is primarily evidenced by speaking in tongues. The central tenets of the Pentecostal-Charismatic movement are all based on an individual's experience: baptism in the Holy Spirit, *glossolalia*, and the exercise of other spiritual gifts. *Glossolalia* was not the only evidence of spirit baptism; a poll taken in 1980 revealed that only one-sixth of Charismatics have actually spoken in tongues.[25] The same poll estimated that there were as many as twenty-nine million Charismatics in the United States. Many Pentecostals and Charismatics also practice faith healing and believe that they can hear directly from God. These "words of knowledge" as they are called, are a central part of the Charismatic experience. There is also a tendency to try to use the Bible to predict future events and make sense of the modern world.[26] The critical problem with a movement known for an emphasis on experience over doctrine is that it is open to abuse or infamous offshoots like the Appalachian snake handlers.

The Pentecostal movement had grown so large by the 1960s that it began to gain acceptance in several Protestant denominations and even the Roman Catholic Church.[27] A Charismatic is one who practices the same spiritual experiences as a Pentecostal, but does so while remaining in their own church.[28] So while Robertson returned to the Southern Baptist Church, he was a Charismatic Southern Baptist. This put him at odds with the majority of the people in his denomination. Some prominent Baptists, such as Jerry Falwell, who is not a Southern Baptist, considered the practice of *glossolalia* heretical. Besides remaining in their own denominations, Charismatics are by definition more diverse than Pentecostals, who have historically remained separated from other Protestant denominations.

For most of his career, Robertson has not mentioned speaking in tongues very often. On *The 700 Club* his Charismatic beliefs find expression in the prayer session that ends each broadcast. It is during this section of the show that Robertson and his cohosts regularly have "a word of knowledge," which they believe are messages from God. These messages range from prophecies to encouragements. More often than not they relate to viewers' physical needs and proclaim God's healing touch.

There was a significant upside to Robertson's new religious affiliation. The Charismatic movement is ecumenical, and this allowed him to make contacts with people from a myriad of denominations. This has also given him the freedom to take elements from many branches of Christianity. Robertson has said, "[A]s far as the majesty of worship, I'm an Episcopalian; as far as a belief in the sovereignty of God, I'm Presbyterian; in terms of holiness, I'm a Methodist . . . in terms of the priesthood of believers and baptism, I'm a Baptist; in terms of the baptism of the Holy Spirit, I'm a Pentecostal. So I'm a little bit of all of them."[29] So while preachers such as Falwell and Jimmy Swaggart kept mostly to their own denominations, Robertson was able to create a large circle of friends. This has allowed him a larger sphere of contacts and influence than any Protestant religious leader of his time except for Billy Graham, who was also very ecumenical in his outlook.

During his seminary training Robertson's commitment to his faith deepened, and this only led to more tension with his wife. While on vacation in Ohio with her children, Dede Robertson called home to check on her husband. She discovered that their phone had been disconnected, and when she called the forwarded number, she learned it was the house of family friends, Dick and Barbara Simmons, who were living in a New York City slum in Bedford-Stuyvesant. The Simmons had moved into an old brownstone that had been vacant for years, while he pastored a local church. Robertson informed his wife that he had sold most of their furniture, giving the $400 he had raised to the ministry World Vision, and moved them all into one room of his friend's apartment. The most valuable possession that he kept was their car, a seven-year-old DeSoto.[30] Dede was horrified; not only had her husband completely upset their lives again, but this time she feared that he was putting his family in danger. A few months earlier, she had actually visited the house that Pat had moved them into and returned home in tears. At the time she called the house "the filthiest, ugliest, most germ infested place I've ever been in." She had even said, "I'll never go back. Never. I'll tell you one thing, if I were Barbara Simmons, I'd walk out for good!"[31]

To Dede's credit, she came back to New York instead of staying in Ohio as her family had suggested. When she married the son of a U.S. senator, she could never have imagined that he would graduate from Yale Law School then choose to live in poverty in a slum. Her dreams of living the good life in New York City had vanished, yet she decided to endure the radically different circumstances that she found herself in. Pat had turned down the pastorate of a prosperous church in Manhattan's East Side for a slum in Bedford-Stuyvesant because he felt God's call. The Robertson family of five lived in a communal apartment where they shared one and a half rooms.

In the midst of all of this, Dede finally had the kind of religious experience that her husband had undergone. For a vacation Robertson decided to take the family to a Bible camp for a week. Dede attended a service there while her husband babysat. She later wrote, "I sensed a ploy on his part, but I accepted nevertheless because it meant getting out for a few hours."[32] When the altar call was given, she was too proud to go forward, but she did decide to become a better Christian. She also refused to tell anyone, especially her husband. Dede even stayed home on Sunday while Robertson went to church. Her silence was broken a month later when Robertson confronted her about what happened at the camp meeting. He had sensed her change. From that point on, their marriage troubles smoothed out. Historian David Harrell writes, "For the first time in her life, Dede acquiesced peacefully to her husband's spiritual wanderings, although she despised living communally in the slums."[33] She would not have to endure that particular hardship for long, because soon her husband's entrepreneurial spirit would move them to Virginia.

Notes

1. John B. Donovan, *Pat Robertson: The Authorized Biography* (New York: Macmillan, 1988), 41.

2. Kathryn Kuhlman radio show, circa 1972. Billy Graham Center (BGC).

3. Pat Robertson, *Shout It from the Housetops* (Astoria, N.Y.: Logos International, 1972), 24.

4. Robertson, *Shout It from the Housetops*, 21.

5. Dede Robertson and John Sherrill, *My God Will Supply* (Lincoln, Va.: Chosen Books, 1979), 21.

6. Robertson and Sherrill, *My God Will Supply*, 32.

7. Robertson and Sherrill, *My God Will Supply*, 22.

8. Robertson, *Shout It from the Housetops*, 38.

9. Robertson and Sherrill, *My God Will Supply*, 23.

10. David Edwin Harrell Jr., *Pat Robertson: A Personal, Religious, and Political Portrait* (New York: Harper & Row, 1987), 35.

11. DiAnna Paulk, "How to Do Inductive Bible Study," www.pathlight.com/inductive.htm (accessed June 2, 2006).

12. Pat Robertson, interview by author, tape recording, Virginia Beach, Va., May 25, 2000.

13. Donovan, *Pat Robertson*, 46.

14. Pat Robertson interview.

15. For more on Charles Finney see Charles Hambrick-Stowe, *Charles G. Finney and the Spirit of American Evangelicalism* (Grand Rapids, Mich.: Eerdmans, 1996).

16. Robertson, *Shout It from the Housetops*, 47.

17. Vinson Synan, *The Holiness-Pentecostal Tradition: Charismatic Movements in the Twentieth Century* (Grand Rapids, Mich.: Eerdmans, 1997), 89.

18. Robertson, *Shout It from the Housetops*, 62.

19. Robertson, *Shout It from the Housetops*, 63.

20. Sydney E. Ahlstrom, *A Religious History of the American People* (New Haven, Conn.: Yale University Press, 1972), 271.

21. D. G. Hart, *That Old Time Religion in Modern America: Evangelical Protestantism in the Twentieth Century* (Chicago: Ivan R. Dee, 2002), 14.

22. George M. Marsden, *Fundamentalism and American Culture* (Oxford: Oxford University Press, 1980), 85.

23. Michael Kazin, *A Godly Hero: The Life of William Jennings Bryan* (New York: Knopf, 2006).

24. George M. Marsden, *Understanding Fundamentalism and Evangelicalism* (Grand Rapids, Mich.: Eerdmans, 1991).

25. Harrell, *Pat Robertson*, 107.

26. Margaret Poloma, *The Charismatic Movement: Is There a New Pentecost?* (Boston: Twayne Publishers, 1982).

27. Synan, *The Holiness-Pentecostal Tradition*, 216.

28. Synan, *The Holiness-Pentecostal Tradition*, 254.

29. Harrell, *Pat Robertson*, 102.

30. James Frasca, "The Preachers Kids," *Port Folio Weekly*, August 26, 1997, 16.

31. Robertson, *Shout It from the Housetops*, 74.

32. Robertson and Sherrill, *My God Will Supply*, 25.

33. Harrell, *Pat Robertson*, 34

CHAPTER 3

THE $70 NETWORK

W
HILE Robertson was on a visit back home to Lexington, Virginia, his mother showed him a letter she had received from his high school friend George Lauderdale. In the postscript, Lauderdale mentioned that a TV station in Norfolk was up for sale, and wondered if Robertson could do anything with it as a Christian ministry. The two had been corresponding for months since Lauderdale had left the pastorate of a Lexington church to preach on a television station in Portsmouth, Virginia. He had moved his family across the state and worked odd jobs to pay the bills while he used the TV station to spread the Gospel. The station had suddenly shut down in August 1959, and Lauderdale was out of the TV preacher business. When the owner asked if he wanted to buy the station, he thought of his old friend Pat Robertson.[1] After the conversation with his mother, Robertson ran into Lauderdale on the streets of Lexington. He had driven from Norfolk that evening after receiving a vision. He told Robertson that the station was for sale for around $300,000.

Initially Robertson was not interested. He had no idea how to run a TV station, nor did he have money or a way to raise any. Still, the thought seemed to stick in his head. He had the opportunity to preach on the radio while visiting Lexington, and his wife thought that he was a natural at it. Robertson toyed with the idea and contemplated the cost.

According to Robertson he walked through a field near his childhood home and prayed for God's direction. He prayed about what kind of offer to make and "an immediate figure came to mind. It was $37,000."[2] He decided to write the owner of the station and make an offer. The owner, Tim Bright, wrote back telling Robertson that he wanted $50,000 for the station and all the equipment or just $25,000 for the equipment alone. Dede suggested he fast and pray about whether to stay in Brooklyn and start a rescue mission or buy the Norfolk station. Robertson locked himself in the Presbyterian church where he worked and prayed and fasted for seven days.[3] It was during this time that he felt the confidence to pack the family's belongings into a small trailer and move back home to Virginia.

Robertson explains his decision in strictly spiritual terms. "The Lord told me to buy a station, I didn't own a TV set. My kids were excited, they thought I was buying a TV. They were disappointed that it was only a station."[4] This seemingly random decision to enter into an expensive venture in an area in which he had no experience was not unusual for Robertson. His entire life was marked by ideas that should have been disasters, but ended up working. In his career he hired people who appeared totally unprepared for their jobs, then ended up doing better than anyone could have expected. He also made business decisions on the spur of the moment. Not everything he did turned to gold, but his propensity for risk taking generally served him well. Without any idea how he was going to start, Robertson moved his family from New York City to the Hampton Roads region of Virginia to start the nation's first full-time Christian TV station. Before he could begin, however, Robertson had to cut a deal with the station's owner and find a way to pay for it, and find a place to live.

The Robertsons crossed the Chesapeake Bay on a ferry with all of their worldly possessions packed into their 1953 DeSoto and the trailer it pulled. When Dede told her husband that she was happy to be leaving dirty New York City, he stayed silent; she soon discovered why. Norfolk was the major East Coast port for the U.S. Navy and was at the time the living definition of a seedy harbor town. Trash lined the streets, and strip clubs and industrial sites littered the city. They briefly stayed at the home of a friend of George Lauderdale's until they found an apartment of their own. Their first residence in Virginia was a three-bedroom, two-story apartment, the nicest place that the couple had lived in four years. They moved in without paying a security deposit, which was fortunate since the Robertsons had less than $40 to their name. Since they didn't have a regular source of income, they relied on their parents for help. Dede finally convinced her husband to let her work at a local hospital, while he went about trying to buy the TV station.[5]

On their first day in Norfolk, the Robertsons drove down Spratley Street to see the station they planned to buy. The building was next to Scott's Creek, which was actually a tidal basin of Norfolk harbor. The tide was out as they drove toward the broadcast building and the smell from the harbor was overpowering. Neither of them had actually seen a TV station before and they were underwhelmed to say the least. The small, one-story brick building had been empty for months. The station had gone off the air in 1959. Due to its proximity to the harbor, moisture had ruined much of the sensitive equipment, and vandals had broken in. Glass, papers, and rats were everywhere. The young couple walked in and looked at the debris covering the floor. Robertson looked at his wife and said, "All that I can say is that God has to be in this if it is ever going to be turned into something useful."[6] Their next step was to find the station's owner.

Tim Bright, the owner of the defunct station, owed RCA approximately $40,000 and he was willing to sell the entire station for that amount. He seemed confident that Robertson would have the proper connections because of his father. The story, as Robertson tells it in his autobiography, is reminiscent of the biblical story of Moses before Pharaoh. Robertson repeated the $37,000 figure, while the owner told him that the tower alone cost him $100,000.[7] An exasperated Bright even asked if Robertson would just ask his father to buy it so they could stop haggling over the lower price. Robertson then made the owner fire up the station to make sure the equipment still worked. When they started the transmitter, fire leapt up the tower's power lines.[8] A week later the two men signed the deal while sitting in Bright's car. Robertson purchased the station for $37,000, but it was going to be quite some time before he would be able to get the studio ready to broadcast. The purchase price of the station was already well beyond his means. While the million-dollar deals of his later years show a shrewd business sense, this early move was a combination of faith and naiveté.

To put it mildly, Senator Robertson was displeased with his son's decision to start a TV ministry, which could prove both embarrassing and costly. The elder Robertson even had his staff prepare a report on how badly UHF stations fared.[9] More than anything else the senator was afraid that his son would embarrass him in his home state. Robertson recalls that his father "thought I was going to disgrace the family [and that] this was a fool's errand. He wanted me to be an appropriate minister at some church."[10] The senator even went as far as to call many of his son's friends, to see if they could talk sense into him, but to no avail.

Robertson used his legal training to draw up the incorporation papers of the new station, which he called the Christian Broadcasting Network (CBN), and applied to the Federal Communication Commission (FCC) for a renewed broadcasting license. He also started a corporate bank account. He walked into the Norfolk branch of the Bank of Virginia and deposited $3, which was the station's first contribution. After getting the account and paying for the checks, which cost $6, CBN was $3 in debt on its first day of existence.[11] While Robertson took the bank's kindness as a sign from God, it also showed the advantage of being a senator's son. It would be more than a decade before the network managed to stay on solid financial ground.

Robertson was busy with the negotiations and starting CBN, but he still needed to find a source of regular income. Through the help of friends, he was able to preach at local churches for a small honorarium. One evening he was paid $5. On another occasion the church had nothing to give, but a church deacon offered his help in any way he could. When Robertson found out that the man sold farm supplies, he asked for soybeans. A few days later the man delivered a seventy-pound bag of soybeans to Robertson's apartment. While the man considered soybeans to be good only as animal feed, the Robertsons made great use of the gift.[12] Dede Robertson's autobiography, *My God Will Supply*, contains several recipes using soybeans, which she believed could be God's "tribulation food."[13]

The FCC approved a provisional broadcast permit for Robertson's new station WTFC (Television for Christ) in the fall of 1960. Originally, Robertson planned to run the station only eighteen hours a week, during prime time. An acquaintance from New York gave Robertson $8,000, but this did not make much of a dent in the repairs that were needed at the station.[14] Donations, mostly from friends, slowly came in, and the final $500 needed to pay off the mortgage was received just minutes before the first broadcast on October 1, 1961. Soon the local Norfolk paper was publishing puff pieces on the new "Television for Christ," noting that it was being run by a senator's son. WTFC was the first television station in the country to have more than 50 percent of its content be religious programming. It was also one of the first to be totally dependant on gifts from viewers.[15]

One of the reasons that religion, especially evangelicalism, has flourished in America is that religious groups have taken advantages of new forms of mass media to reach an ever wider audience. During the second Great Awakening, Revivalists used newspapers and pamphlets to spread their message, which was made possible by cheaper printing costs.[16] Some of the first radio broadcasts in the 1920s were religious, as Catholic and Protestant churches hoped to reach an even greater audience. In 1928 the National Broadcasting Company (NBC) set up a committee with the help of the Federal Council of Churches (renamed the National Council of Churches in 1950). This committee was given the task of allocating time for religious broadcasts for Protestant groups. The result was that only mainline churches were given airtime, and Fundamentalist and evangelical churches were excluded. This was to be expected since the council predominantly consisted of theologically liberal churches, and most evangelical groups refused to associate with the group. There was, however, convincing evidence that the council actively sought to keep evangelicals off the air. They even went so far as to sign contracts with stations across America that forbade the broadcasting of any religious program except those approved by the council.[17] These contracts kept religious programs from even being allowed to purchase airtime on those stations. Allegations that the Federal Council of Churches was conspiring to keep evangelicals from even being allowed to buy airtime were made—but never proven—during a Senate hearing in 1947.

In response to their exclusion from the free airwaves, the National Association of Evangelicals, founded in 1942, formed the National Religious Broadcasters in 1944.[18] The goal of this new group was to help promote radio (and later TV) ministries by theologically conservative Christians. As radio networks grew, they either gave away free airtime to select groups or sold it to anyone who could pay.[19]

When television began to become popular in the early 1950s TV networks were required to donate free airtime to religious programming in order to maintain their licenses, just as radio stations had. And as was the case with radio, evangelicals were largely kept out of TV due to the influence of the National Council of Churches. These early religious TV shows were more like documentaries and discussion groups because it was felt that simply filming a preacher would not be interesting enough. These formats were more expensive than filming a church service, but this was irrelevant to the shows since they were not paying for airtime.[20]

In 1960 the FCC changed the regulations and decided that time that was sold was just as valid as time freely given, as long as the requirement for public interest programs was met.[21] This ruling was met with disbelief among the more liberal mainline churches, and joy among evangelicals and Fundamentalists, who had by and large been excluded from this free airtime. When the playing field was leveled in 1960, many of the mainline shows quickly disappeared, and theological conservatives like Pat Robertson, Oral Roberts, and others took their place.[22] These new TV ministries were used to having to ask for money, and they were well prepared for this new world of free-market televangelism. Since they could not afford expensive production efforts, they relied on filming sermons, which proved to be a good way to grab the attention of a TV audience.[23] While radio had made some preachers famous, television would make them stars. The first TV preachers were Rex Humbard, who began broadcasting in 1952, and Oral Roberts, who followed him in 1955. Some preachers realized that the way to avoid the conflict of airtime was to buy stations outright. The key problem, which Robertson found out, was that TV is an incredibly expensive medium, and it is difficult to start a TV ministry and raise the money needed to sustain one for any significant length of time.

By mid-1962 the Robertsons were again on the move, this time to nicer living accommodations. Local businessman Fred Beasley gave Robertson $100 a week so he could leave his part-time job at a local church and focus full time on CBN. Beasley also gave the Robertsons a new home to live in, which was two blocks from the station. The house was in good condition, but the neighborhood was rough.[24] The family settled in the best that they could and waited for better times.

As a strictly religious station CBN was different from the outset. Since it was not run by people with any media experience it stumbled for years before it developed a professionalism that allowed it to prosper. Originally, the network consisted of Robertson, his wife, and a few volunteers. They quickly realized that they needed outside help. The network's first paid employee, Neil Eskelin, had a master's degree in communications and had turned down jobs from ABC and CBS while searching for a Christian ministry to work for. Eskelin was offered $50 a week, but had to settle for $10 his first week when the ministry only brought in $8. He recalls, "[We] didn't have any money, so we were in the back room, praying for burnt out tubes. Pat and I spent a lot of time just cleaning the floors."[25] Eskelin claimed the local newspaper, the *Virginian-Pilot*, refused to publish the station's broadcast schedule since the station's signal was so weak that it only went out about eleven miles.

In its first year the station had a budget of $550 a week.[26] One day a sailor stationed in Norfolk toured the facilities. He noticed the dirty floors and volunteered to clean them. When he showed up the next day, he was put behind a camera filming Dede's show. A decade later this ex-Navy man helped CBN get on the air in Minneapolis, Minnesota, where he also set up their counseling center.[27]

CBN's WTFC station was broadcast on UHF channel 27 and had a very limited range. It produced a "class A" signal that reached eleven miles and a "class B" signal that went eighteen miles. This meant that the signal could only reach sections of Norfolk, Portsmouth, Virginia Beach, and Hampton. From the outset the station was set up to take calls from the community for prayer requests and to accept donations. One of the station's first counselors remembered that there were six phone lines and no calls coming in. "During commercial breaks, Pat kept asking the counselors to pray for someone to call. We got a call from someone from Williamsburg, VA, which was supposedly outside of their range. She could see the show, even though it was blurry." They stayed on the air while she drove to the station at 2 AM for prayer.[28]

One evening during a broadcast of a show for the deaf, a rat got into the equipment and electrocuted itself and took the audio equipment with it. Since it was a show for the deaf, Robertson and Eskelin decided to run the show all night, while they tried to replace the broken equipment. This incident resulted in the first Associated Press story on CBN. Eskelin also starred in the first children's show on CBN, *Mr. Pingo and His Pals*, which featured him and a little toy bear.[29]

The entire process lacked sophistication, and many of the early programming decisions were strange, yet the station began to flourish. Robertson asked his children for advice on what kinds of shows to put on the air. For a time, his daughter Elizabeth was the unofficial station programmer. "Between her and her friends, I had sort of an 'oooh and ahh meter'," Robertson recalls. "If they liked the show, I put it on the air and ratings went up 400 percent in a matter of a month."[30] In the years before local ratings, Robertson could only tell how popular shows were by the kinds of feedback and pledges that the station received.

In addition to the television station, Robertson later purchased a radio station, which he named WXRI (XRI being the first part of *Christ* in Greek). The station broadcast religious programming, music, and commercials, which made money. The profits from the radio station were funneled to the struggling TV station. In 1974 Robertson hired Scott Ross, a former secular disc jockey, to play Christian rock music. The idea of Christian rock music was still controversial as many believers still thought of rock as the devil's music. The fact that Robertson encouraged it shows both his boldness and eye for marketing. The show was syndicated across the country and brought in more revenue.

Ironically, a young married couple who would one day gain infamy by destroying the credibility of all televangelists saved the struggling CBN: Jim and Tammy Faye Bakker. Robertson's network and programs had always been different than those of most of his contemporaries; however, Robertson continually crossed paths with the Bakkers during his career. At times they helped CBN, at other times they competed for airwaves and donations. Their story is interesting for the Bakkers both saved CBN and later helped send the entire genre into chaos. Robertson was never as close to other televangelists as he was with the Bakkers, which made their eventual falling out all the more painful and embarrassing.

There was a children's show on CBN, and the Bakkers, who had been traveling evangelists, were asked to fill in for a couple of shows. Soon after, Robertson asked Jim and Tammy Faye, who were then twenty-five and twenty-two respectively, to star in a children's puppet show called *Come On Over* in 1965. The Bakkers used CBN as a catapult for their career. The show was soon renamed *The Jim and Tammy Show*. It featured Jim in front of the camera, with Tammy Faye working the puppets. Many of their ideas were taken from secular children's shows. Tammy created her most popular character "Susie Moppet" by melting off the ears of a Porky Pig doll and gluing a blond wig to its head. Another puppet, Allie, was an alligator suspiciously similar to Ollie on the popular *The Kukla, Fran and Ollie Show*. The show also featured the puppets Zippy the mailbox and Charlie the Happy Christian.[31] In a September 2000 interview on NBC's *Today Show*, Tammy admitted to using the puppets to tell her husband things that she could not say in private. They were her way to confront her husband and make her wishes known. This merely added to the energetic feeling on the set, helping *The Jim and Tammy Show* become CBN's most popular program. Eventually one out of every five dollars that CBN received was spent on the show. The Bakkers had an ease in front of the camera that Robertson lacked, so they naturally came to have a greater share of the airtime.

Robertson and Jim Bakker tell different stories about the origins of *The 700 Club*. In early 1963, years before Bakker's arrival, Robertson had a telethon for the upcoming year. He asked for seven hundred people to pledge to give $10 a month to meet the $7,000 monthly budget. These people would be called "faith partners" and members of *The 700 Club*.[32] In the fall of 1966 another *700 Club* telethon was underway, with Jim Bakker as host. The show featured faith healings and emotional testimonies. The telethon was very successful, and by the end of the week, Robertson decided to make the show a regular part of CBN programming.[33] The show was broadcast each weeknight at 10 PM with Bakker as the original host and Robertson often cohosting and doing other segments of the show. It has been the cornerstone of the network ever since.

CBN was a loosely run organization for years and *The 700 Club* was no exception. Shows would run long or change topics when participants felt called by God to do something else. For example, one evening in 1972 Bakker was signing off *The 700 Club* broadcast. When the ending theme music tape jammed, the national anthem tape was played, and it jammed as well. Bakker walked back into the studio and told the television audience that God did not want them off the air. Robertson recalls that Bakker said, "All the people who want to find Jesus as their savior call in now, and 35 people did, then they signed off."[34] Bakker's leading by the spirit soon became routine and he created a unique (and highly emulated) style of raising money. Bakker was a dropout from North Central Bible College, an Assemblies of God school. He was not polished like Robertson, but had charisma and was able to help keep the station afloat. Bakker could connect with the audience in a way that Robertson couldn't. In this regard, Bakker was more of a classic television preacher than Robertson.

The format of *The 700 Club* is different from that of any other religious TV show. Most other ministry shows are filmed in a church, at a regular Sunday church service, or special revival meetings. Their format is similar to that of a church, and the preacher is always the central focus of the show. *The 700 Club* uses a talk show format that has more in common with a morning news program or NBC's *Tonight Show* than most other televangelist shows. The show features news, testimonies of salvation, stories of healing, and tips on healthy living and personal finance. The show usually consists of taped news features anchored by Robertson's cohosts, who ask him for an analysis of the topics. The show begins with the news and then moves to more spiritually based topics. The latter half deals with family and parenting issues and the regular feature of faith healings that are the hallmark of the show and the thing that gave Robertson the most trouble with the secular press during his 1988 presidential campaign. This format allowed Robertson to try to distance himself from the other televangelists and refer to himself as a "religious broadcaster" and at other times as just a "businessman." It is doubtful that he could have made those claims with any credibility had he been involved in the more traditional type of TV ministry that erupted in scandal in the late 1980s.

Eventually the Bakkers' popularity began to cause friction between them and Robertson. Jim and Tammy Faye were selling record albums, children's books, and Susie Moppet dolls, but none of the money went to CBN. The Bakkers "were willing to eat beans and struggle" in order to save money for fancy things. Jim went out and bought a large black Cadillac, but Robertson didn't care for it. "He suggested the car belonged to the Mafia, not a minister, Bakker replaced it."[35] By early 1969 the Bakkers could afford an expensive waterfront home, which only deepened the imagined and real distance between themselves and their coworkers. In the fall of 1971, Robertson hired Jerry Hortsmann as a producer, and he clashed with Jim immediately. Hortsmann did an audit of the network and discovered that Jim and Tammy Faye were making more money per week than anyone else, including Robertson. As journalist Charles Shepard writes, "Hortsmann was troubled most by the Bakkers' perks," including allowances for housing, clothes, babysitters, and roses for Tammy Faye. Hortsmann considered the Bakkers to be fake; Tammy Faye claimed that he put the couple through "three years of torture."[36]

The Bakkers' relationship with Robertson was strained at times. When Bakker refused to work a night shift at WXRI radio, Robertson threatened to fire him and then fined him $100.[37] In response Bakker quit and stormed out of the office. He came back a few days later and apologized, and Robertson paid the fine out of his own pocket. Despite this and other periodic blowups, the two men needed each other. Robertson liked the attention that flowed to his station, and Bakker liked both the fame and money. As the years progressed a serious struggle developed between the two men. It came to a head in 1972 when they fought over who was the most important person at the network. Still, for all of the tension the chemistry worked. By the dawn of the 1970s, CBN was finally on a firm financial foundation. The station that was started with $70 was by 1970 pulling in $1 million a year; the figure doubled to $2 million in 1972.[38]

Even though the station was taking off, life for the Robertson family was precarious at times. After two years living rent free in the house Fred Beasley had donated it was time to move. The quaint toughness of the neighborhood they had been living in turned dangerous. One day their eldest son Tim was attacked by some older boys. A few days later an arsonist set fire to their toolshed, but firemen arrived before it spread to the main house. Soon afterwards, Beasley called again and offered them a house on the grounds of Frederick College in Plymouth. They moved into the new house in August 1964. Dede thought the house looked like a southern plantation mansion, but it was barely big enough for their family that had now grown to six. For nineteen years the family lived rent free in the large house in Portsmouth. Other supporters pitched in, and a local car dealer even gave Robertson a Lincoln.

Besides working at CBN, Dede focused on raising the children and also worked at Tidewater Community College as a nursing instructor. Some of the Robertson children had a harder time than others adjusting to life with an increasingly famous father. Both Tim and Gordon attended their dad's alma mater, the McCallie School, even though it had dropped its military program in

1970. But while Tim excelled, Gordon rebelled. "I spent a great deal of time try-ing to prove that I was not Pat Robertson's son," Gordon said.[39] Eldest daugh-ter Elizabeth remembers being horrified at being driven to school by her father in a van that had *The 700 Club* emblazoned on its sides. She usually asked to be let out a few blocks from school. "I saw the struggle of the early years, and the ridicule, especially locally. He was not accepted until I was grown."[40] The youngest daughter, Ann, often neglected to tell people who her famous father was: "it creates expectations and there's a higher standard to live up to." By all accounts, the Robertsons were dutiful parents even as Pat found himself spend-ing more time at the station.

The first pieces of Robertson's future empire had slowly fallen into place. Robertson had the station, a stable family, and a growing following. What was missing was most surprising considering his later career—politics. Robertson had decided to focus on the ministry even as his father remained powerful in the Senate. For a man who later became known for his political aspirations, Robertson kept his early work on CBN essentially free from politics. In a 1964 interview Dede Robertson reported that her husband was "quite interested in politics."[41] However, that interest was rarely shown on TV. The best example of his political ambivalence was in 1966 when Senator Robertson came up for reelection, and was in for the fight of his political life.

Willis Robertson, a Democrat, had been criticized for his timid support of Republican Dwight Eisenhower in 1952, even from fellow senator Harry Byrd's newspaper, the *Winchester Star*. There were rumblings in the party again in 1960 but the senator was able to stop a challenge before it grew.[42] When Byrd won reelection at age seventy-seven, this gave Robertson, who was two weeks older, hope to run again. In early November 1965 a sickly Harry Byrd suddenly announced his resignation from the Senate, and was dead a year later. As soon as he heard about Byrd's sudden retirement, Willis Robertson, who was on vaca-tion in North Carolina, announced that he would still run again in 1966.[43]

As is usually the case in an election where one party dominates, the real competition came during the primaries. For decades whoever won the Demo-cratic primary easily won the general election. In 1966 Willis Robertson was challenged by William Sprong of Portsmouth, where ironically Pat Robertson was living at the time. Willis Robertson, who had been in Congress since 1932, narrowly lost the primary. The Robertson family blamed low turnout caused by bad weather for the elder Robertson's loss, but the election had the largest pri-mary turnout in Virginia history. Newspaper reports also blamed a boycott of Robertson by the Conservative Party for his defeat.[44]

In his 1972 biography *Shout It from the Housetops*, Robertson states that God would not allow him to campaign for his father. He felt that he had been called to the ministry and not to politics. He writes that the Lord told him,

"[Y]ou cannot tie my eternal purposes to the success of any political candidate . . . not even your own father."[45] Robertson's distaste of politics was palpable. He made it clear that serving God precluded work in politics. Robertson had decided to follow a life in the ministry and build his television empire. He had come to accept what many conservative Christians had thought for most of the twentieth century: the world was only becoming increasingly evil, and Christians should concentrate on saving souls and not on political activism. In fact, later on Robertson said that his father's defeat was a gift from God. He writes, "His soul was far more important than his seniority in Washington." Lyndon Johnson, he claims, had already begun to "taint the federal government with the easy morality and arrogance."[46] For Robertson there could be no turning back; it was Christ or Caesar. His television network was expanding to Atlanta, New York, and even out west. Robertson was too busy to think about politics, let alone take an active role.

Robertson's main link to the world of politics was severed when his father passed away from a sudden heart attack on November 3, 1974, at age eighty-four. After leaving the Senate, Willis Robertson worked for the World Bank until he retired around the time his wife died in 1967. The elder Robertson spent the last six years of his life back at the family home in Lexington, Virginia. The senator's funeral was held before a large audience at the Virginia Military Institute. After his father's death, Robertson felt that he was able finally to get out from his shadow.[47]

Now that he was free from having to consider the political implications of his actions, he was able to pursue new avenues for his ministry. He toyed with the idea of starting a Bible college, and tried to expand CBN and its flagship show, *The 700 Club*, across the nation. With all of these goals to strive toward, there could be little time for political commentary, much less activism. Now that he was free from such a direct political bond, he could turn his full attention to CBN.

In the early 1970s the Christian Broadcasting Network was still growing, with the energetic and charismatic Jim Bakker hosting the nightly show *The 700 Club*. As the popularity of the show increased, so did the revenue the network received. By 1972 CBN was pulling in $2 million per year; however, while the network finally appeared to be on solid ground, its troubles with state and federal governments were just beginning. As the network progressed and added affiliates, it became increasingly difficult to fill the time with strictly Christian fare. From the outset CBN played films with moral themes, but in 1974 a decision was made to broadcast more secular programming in order to increase advertising revenue. Old reruns of *Lassie* and *Dobbie Gillis* were broadcast to bolster network ratings and income. This move toward profit was based on several considerations. First of all, the Bakkers' self-merchandising demonstrated that it was easy to make a lot of money in Christian broadcasting by selling yourself as the product. To this end the network had begun in 1971 to buy commercial time on various stations around the nation to show *The 700 Club*. This cost money, not entirely offset by the increase in revenues from these new markets. By showing family-friendly reruns, CBN could raise money to pay for these ventures, and for buying new stations.

The tactic worked, and by early 1972 *The Jim and Tammy Show* was also syndicated to other stations around the country. In April Robertson bought his second television station, WRET, in Charlotte, North Carolina, which began to broadcast CBN programming twenty-four hours a day. The potential audience grew rapidly from an estimated sixty-four million viewers in 1974 to 110 million a year later. However, all of this growth came at a price. Tension between Robertson and Jim Bakker continued to mount. They were both leaders, and Bakker repeatedly tried to run things his way, only to be thwarted time and again by Robertson. CBN producer Jerry Hortsmann had pressured the Bakkers into giving up many of their perks, and whenever their arguments became heated, they turned to Robertson, who always sided with Hortsmann.

The behind-the-scenes tension finally made it on-screen during election night 1972. Bakker was hosting *The 700 Club* while Robertson occasionally gave vote tallies of the Nixon–McGovern race. "The interruptions annoyed Bakker. . . . It seemed that Pat was being insensitive to the workings of God."[48] A week later, Bakker left CBN for good. It was clear that CBN was Pat Robertson's network, and although Bakker was the star, he was not in charge. The Bakkers were local celebrities. They rode on the CBN floats in Virginia Beach parades, many of which won first place for decoration.[49] However, celebrity was not enough to take the network from Robertson. For his part, Robertson is to this day almost totally silent on the issue of Bakker's resignation and Bakker's own version suffers from a serious case of revisionism.

In his 1976 autobiography *Move That Mountain*, Bakker claims that he woke up one day and was told by God to resign from CBN. As Bakker tells it, their house was miraculously sold and they were on their way to greener pastures. His book never mentions any conflict with Robertson and makes it appear as if nothing was ever amiss between the two, but that was not the case. The Bakkers had put their house up for sale months before his vision and were looking to leave Virginia Beach. Bakker and Robertson came into conflict later as they tried to expand their rival television empires and began to compete for limited airwave space and donor support.

When the Bakkers left CBN Robertson took over the reins of *The 700 Club*, which he hosted continuously thereafter. The decade of the 1970s, which began with the groundbreaking on a new facility in Virginia Beach, ended with millions of viewers and donations focused on an increasingly large operation. In 1974 a twenty-four-hour counseling center was opened and took half a million calls. Robertson took CBN into the new field of cable television in 1975 and became one of the first basic cable stations. This allowed the network to hold its first simultaneous broadcast of telethons. All of these advancements were expensive, and the more secular format of the network allowed CBN to survive. In 1975 CBN made $28.3 million, and yet it was not enough to pay for the expanding empire. The network was able to make it back into the black in 1976.[50] Robertson credits the success to two things: the network's support of Israel and its decision to start giving money away to local and international Christian ministries. In 1978 he created Operation Blessing, a ministry of CBN that gave millions to the poor in America and around the world. By 1987 the ministry had a budget of $50 million a year and claimed that only 1 percent went to overhead.[51]

On October 6, 1979, the massive new CBN International Headquarters building was completed. The building housed the new studio and broadcast facilities for *The 700 Club* and all of the other CBN original shows. The building blends into the campus of Christian Broadcasting Network University, which has arisen around it (see chapter 9). White columns, four stories tall, stand at the entrance to the cruciform-shaped structure. Each arm of the building houses a large soundstage. In front of the building is an eternal flame, which begs comparison (some say intended) to that at President Kennedy's grave in Arlington National Cemetery. The building was dedicated in a gala televised fireworks-filled ceremony featuring a keynote address from Billy Graham. CBN continued to thrive and contributions grew. So did trouble with various state and local governments.

The first problem for the network arose in Massachusetts when the state sued CBN and Robertson after it determined that more than 50 percent of the programming on CBN-owned station WXNE was not religious in nature. In the suit the state sought the financial records of CBN. In response Robertson announced that he was spinning off his TV stations into a new company, CBN Continental Broadcasting. According to Massachusetts sources this move was designed to keep CBN finances a secret.[52]

Robertson had made other moves to avoid taxes, some closer to home. He moved the network's operations out of Portsmouth when the city challenged his tax-exempt status as a church. In 1970 the Portsmouth city council held a private meeting with Robertson and demanded that he pay taxes on CBN's holdings in the city, which totaled $208,630. The tax bill on the television and radio broadcast buildings was $4,696 a year.[53] In the late 1960s Robertson moved the bulk of CBN's operations to the neighboring city of Virginia Beach, making it the third Hampton Roads city to have CBN as a resident in ten years. The network bought a few hundred acres, and purchased more in the late 1970s. Initially relations between the network and the city were much more congenial than they had been with either Norfolk or Portsmouth. Eventually the new city began to take an interest in Robertson's activities and declared that CBN was not a church, and was therefore not tax exempt. At first Robertson wrote an angry letter in which he told the city council that he supplied the city with hundreds of jobs and that "you don't shoot Santa Claus." He later agreed to pay $450,000 a year in property taxes. These cases were just a hint of things to come, especially after his presidential campaign. For the time being his greatest struggle was with his fellow televangelists.

Robertson had never met Jerry Falwell, or several other famous men whose names were often mentioned in the same breath as his. As the 1970s progressed, it became clear that Robertson had the fastest growing and most solid television ministry. Falwell and Oral Roberts had smaller operations, and Jimmy Swaggart did not gain national prominence until the early 1980s. The one person Robertson came into conflict with most often was the man whose career he had helped launch, Jim Bakker.

After leaving CBN, Bakker traveled to California where he briefly worked with Paul and Jan Crouch as they set up what became the Trinity Broadcasting Network (TBN). Although Tammy Faye Bakker and Jan Crouch shared an affinity for huge wigs and grotesque amounts of makeup, their husbands did not always work well together. Despite some personality conflicts, Bakker was able to help launch TBN by using tried-and-true formulas. The first thing he did was start *The PTL Club* (Praise the Lord or People That Love), a talk show based on *The 700 Club* format. Just like he had done at CBN, Bakker shared the hosting duties, this time with Crouch. Bakker also began broadcasting old episodes of *The Jim and Tammy Show*, copies of which a sympathetic employee had sneaked out of CBN headquarters. Bakker's illegal broadcasting of his old shows infuriated Robertson. He demanded that Bakker stop immediately, and he ordered CBN to destroy all copies of the show. Robertson also stopped re-airing the show on CBN and its affiliates. He was no longer going to give Bakker free publicity.[54]

Jim and Tammy Faye Bakker finally had another show and network of their own. *The PTL Club* featured the charismatic Bakker begging for money while Tammy Faye sang and cried on almost every show. Bakker wanted to be in charge of TBN, but the less charismatic Crouch owned the equipment, and arguments over who was in charge were common. Even though they shared the on-air duties, Bakker was the president of TBN while Crouch was the chairman of the board. According to Crouch, Bakker eventually led a failed coup in an attempt to gain total control of the network.[55] After several closed-door shouting matches, Jim and Tammy Faye Bakker were on the move again, this time to Charlotte, North Carolina. Just as he had done at CBN, Bakker took some of the staff with him, and had evidently spent considerable time trying to win supporters. Bakker was determined to run things his own way, but his plans caused him to run afoul of his old boss Pat Robertson.

Bakker and Robertson had a gentlemen's agreement not to compete with each other for television time, fearing that the competition would allow stations to charge more. The problem with this agreement was that Robertson already had a presence in many of the largest markets, such as Los Angeles, New York, and Boston. Bakker was quick to try to move into those markets, and this angered Robertson. Bakker received a letter from Robertson about their competition on September 15, 1977. Considering that Bakker was already involved with ethical problems that were not publicized for another ten years, Robertson's words of warning were prophetic. Bakker had been making extravagant claims, and Robertson was calling him on it.

As you requested when you telephoned, I insured that none of our people were making any overtures whatsoever which would conflict with the airing of the "PTL Club" on Channel 36 [WRET] in Charlotte, and we have not in any way moved to cause any inconvenience to you in your plans.

You can imagine my shock when I learned today from an officer of Channel 18 [in Charlotte] that members of the "PTL Club" have approached [a station official] with a specific request to purchase the time that the "700 Club" has been buying on their station.

This was reminiscent of an incident a year or two ago when we specifically refused to accept your affiliate in Savannah, Georgia, because we did not feel it was ethical, and within weeks our kindness was repaid by your attempt to take away our Orlando affiliate and your entry into the Hartford market which played a part in ruining a transfer of license which we had been working on at great expense for some months. Now this new evidence of duplicity, coupled with recent purchases either in competition with us, or on the same station as we are on, make me question seriously your financial wisdom, your ethics, and your truthfulness.

I might add that the outrageous claims about your satellite project to be on the air by the end of April, "the first ever to broadcast twenty-four hours a day,"—when you knew an April date was impossible and you also knew that CBN had already done what you were claiming—were patently false and misleading. You know that a satellite project can cost up to $6 million and that the only market for yours now is a tiny part of the US cable industry, because your project is in direct competition with CBN which already is covering the market, yet you continue to make untrue claims about it to the public. This is a totally uncalled for waste of the money of God's people merely for the purpose of gratifying your personal ego and unbelievable competitive spirit.

Jim, God does not bless falsehood, and the Bible says He resists the proud. This competitive spirit and financial wastefulness has brought

about many of the troubles you are now in. Unless you face reality and ask
God's forgiveness, He is going to bring you down. God is speaking to you
through things that are happening. I pray that you will get His message.[56]

Bakker was never publicly critical of Robertson, but their competition continued. Even though they had battled and continued to do so for the next decade,
Robertson owed a debt of gratitude to Bakker. Despite his personal excesses and
ethical failings he was able to help build a secure foundation for CBN.

The 700 Club needed another charismatic personality to balance Robertson, but not someone as egocentric as Jim Bakker. The answer came in 1975
when Ben Kinchlow joined the show as a regular cohost. As a younger man,
Kinchlow had been a fan of Malcolm X and looked forward to the coming conflict between whites and blacks. After his conversion, he returned to his home
state of Texas and began a ministry that worked with drug addicts. His work
brought him to the attention of the staff of CBN, and he was invited to Dallas
to appear as a guest. He agreed, even though he had never heard of The 700
Club. Kinchlow thought nothing more of the experience until he was invited to
CBN headquarters in Virginia to appear on the show again.

At the studios, he was told to take his place on the set and was horrified to
learn that Robertson was in Israel and he was the host of the show. He recalls,
"[T]hat was my second appearance on television ever and I was the host—for
two hours. I don't remember who the guests were, or what we talked about. I
am certain that I was awful."[57] After that appearance he was put in charge of
the counseling center in Dallas, and eventually moved to Virginia Beach to be
Robertson's cohost.

Kinchlow, like Bakker before him, served as a perfect foil to Robertson's blue
blood upbringing and was asked to become a regular in 1975.[58] They were a perfect pair. Robertson, tall, white, and a former U.S. Marine, and Kinchlow, tall,
African American, and a Vietnam War protester, worked well together. He
quickly became almost as popular as Robertson, but without the drama and
competition that marked Robertson's relationship with his previous cohost.
What is significant about Kinchlow's job on The 700 Club was that at the time,
there were few African American television hosts, and CBN's biggest audience
was white southerners.[59] Robertson took another risk, and it paid off. With this
successful partnership, CBN was assured continued growth into the next decade.

Although the first part of the senator's son's life had followed the expected
course, Pat Robertson's conversion to Christianity had changed everything. He
renounced his wealth and privilege and lived a life that horrified his family and
former friends. Even though Robertson had changed his religious worldview,
he remained the same person. His determination to make something of himself
and his competitive nature were merely moved to the religious arena. This drive

led him to make his ministry as successful as possible. During the 1970s Robertson made CBN into not just the largest Christian network, but one of the largest networks in the United States. While he attempted to stay strictly in the spiritual world his own nature would not allow it. Although he was horrified by the crimes of Richard Nixon, it was the possibilities he imagined when fellow evangelical Jimmy Carter ran for office that brought him once more into the political realm.

The early 1970s were a struggle for Pat Robertson. His network was still experiencing growing pains; its survival was anything but a certainty. From all outward appearances, Robertson's life seemed to be stuck in the backwater of televised religion. The notoriety of being a senator's son had faded and it appeared that all of the sacrifices of the early days of CBN had borne little fruit. To Robertson, however, things looked entirely different, but even he would have been surprised had he known what his world would look like in ten years time. The 1970s, derided as a time of stagflation and political corruption, were quite the opposite for Robertson. In ten short years, CBN grew to reach tens of millions with its cable and satellite broadcasts. A Christian graduate school rose up among the antennae and trees of the CBN compound, but most importantly, Robertson found himself the guest of presidents at the White House. His family, used to having to scrape by, was flush with cash and finally lived in their own home. In 1970 however, all of these things were years away and Robertson had a long path ahead of him.

Notes

1. David Edwin Harrell Jr., *Pat Robertson: A Personal, Religious, and Political Portrait* (New York: Harper & Row, 1987), 48.

2. Pat Robertson, *Shout It from the Housetops* (Astoria, N.Y.: Logos International, 1972), 82.

3. Robertson, *Shout It from the Housetops*, 102.

4. Kathryn Kuhlman radio show, circa 1972. Billy Graham Center (BGC).

5. Dede Robertson and John Sherrill, *My God Will Supply* (Lincoln, Va.: Chosen Books, 1979), 118.

6. Robertson and Sherrill, *My God Will Supply*, 115.

7. Robertson, *Shout It from the Housetops*, 111.

8. Robertson, *Shout It from the Housetops*, 112.

9. Harrell, *Pat Robertson*, 50.

10. *The 700 Club* twenty-fifth anniversary show, circa 1986. Regent University Special Collections (RUA).

11. Robertson, *Shout It from the Housetops*, 117.

12. Robertson, *Shout It from the Housetops*, 108.

13. Robertson and Sherrill, *My God Will Supply*, 86.

14. Harry Nash, "He Gave Up a Career in Law," *Norfolk Ledger-Star* [Va.], May 14, 1966.

15. Ella Hixson, "Television for Christ Granted Construction Permit," *Virginian-Pilot*, November 4, 1960, 31.

16. For the use of new media by religious groups during the early 1800s see Nathan O. Hatch, *The Democratization of American Christianity* (New Haven, Conn.: Yale University Press, 1989).

17. Jeffery Hadden and Anson Shupe, *Televangelism: Power and Politics on God's Frontier* (New York: Henry Holt, 1988), 47.

18. R. Laurence Moore, *Selling God: American Religion in the Marketplace of Culture* (New York: Oxford, 1994), 247.

19. Jeffery Hadden and Charles Swann, *Prime Time Preachers: The Rising Power of Televangelism* (Boston: Addison Wesley, 1981), 79.

20. Moore, *Selling God*, 247.

21. Steve Bruce, *Pray TV: Televangelism in America* (London: Routledge, 1990), 30.

22. Hadden and Shupe, *Televangelism*, 49–52.

23. Moore, *Selling God*, 247.

24. Robertson and Sherrill, *My God Will Supply*, 130.

25. *The 700 Club*, twenty-fifth anniversary show.

26. Hixson, "Television for Christ," *Virginian-Pilot*, November 4, 1960.

27. *The 700 Club*, twenty-fifth anniversary show.

28. *The 700 Club*, twenty-fifth anniversary show.

29. *The 700 Club*, twenty-fifth anniversary show.

30. James Frasca, "The Preachers Kids." *Port Folio Weekly*, August 26, 1997.

31. Charles Shepard, *Forgiven: The Rise and Fall of Jim Bakker and the PTL Ministry* (New York: Atlantic Monthly Press, 1989), 37.

32. Robertson, *Shout It from the Housetops*, 178.

33. Robertson, *Shout It from the Housetops*, 204.

34. Kuhlman show, circa 1972. BGC.

35. Shepard, *Forgiven*, 42.

36. Shepard, *Forgiven*, 46.

37. Robertson, *Shout It from the Housetops*, 198.

38. "Robertson Empire Reaches Heavenward," *Virginian-Pilot*, August 6, 1978.

39. Frasca, "The Preachers Kids," 19.

40. Frasca, "The Preachers Kids," 19.

41. Teresa Edge, "Woman behind the Man," *Virginian-Pilot*, March 12, 1964.

42. George Kelly, "Drums for Robertson," *Virginian-Pilot*, May 30, 1965.

43. "Robertson to Run for Reelection," *Virginian-Pilot*, November 12, 1965.

44. Wayne Woodlief, "Robertson Blames Defeat on Apathy," *Norfolk Ledger-Star* [Va.], July 15, 1966.

45. Robertson, *Shout It from the Housetops*, 180.

46. Robertson, *Shout It from the Housetops*, 180.

47. Pat Robertson, interview by author, tape recording, Virginia Beach, Va., May 25, 2000.

48. Shepard, *Forgiven*, 47.

49. Jim Bakker with Robert Paul Lamb, *Move That Mountain* (Plainfield, N.J.: Logos International, 1976), 65.

50. "Robertson Empire Reaches Heavenward."

51. John B. Donovan, *Pat Robertson: The Authorized Biography* (New York: Macmillan, 1988), 156.

52. John Fiakla and Ellen Hume, "Pulpit and Politics: TV Preacher, Possibly Eyeing the Presidency Is Polishing His Image," *Wall Street Journal*, October 17, 1985.

53. Bill Trask, "Broadcaster, City Confer on Taxes," *Virginian-Pilot*, April 30, 1970.

54. Shepard, *Forgiven*, 53.

55. Paul Crouch, *I Had No Father but God: A Personal Letter to My Two Sons* (Santa Ana, Calif.: Trinity Christian Center, 1993), 87–90.

56. Shepard, *Forgiven*, 84–85.

57. Ben Kinchlow with Bob Slosser, *Plain Bread* (Waco, Tex.: Word Books, 1985), 220.

58. Associated Press, "CBN Co-Host Shrugged Off Radical Views," *Lynchburg News* [Tenn.], August 7, 1986.

59. Kinchlow, *Plain Bread*, 221.

CHAPTER 4

HIGH HOPES AND
JIMMY CARTER

C LYDE Wilcox writes that the Christian Right has gone through three major phases in the last seventy years. The first phase lasted from the 1930s to the 1940s and was a time of political retreat, although anticommunism was still a major concern. The second phase went from the end of World War II until the late 1960s. This was the heyday of evangelical anticommunism. The third and most famous phase, the New Christian Right led by Jerry Falwell and Pat Robertson, started in the early 1970s.[1] Wilcox sees continuity in the movement in the third phase, but a closer inspection reveals two distinct elements at work. While most religious leaders wanted political influence, they remained outsiders. Falwell never ran for office; he just wanted access to the Oval Office from time to time. Phyllis Schlafly, a highly successful Christian Right activist, based her headquarters in St. Louis and only rarely traveled to Washington, D.C. Pat Robertson gave the movement an entirely new twist, a more politically savvy attempt to get power on its own. The direction that the Christian Right took under his leadership made sense given Robertson's upbringing in a political, not primarily religious, world.

Although Falwell and Robertson came from different waves of the movement, they have a common history in regard to political action. Like many conservative Christians of their era, they opposed Christians' participation in the political world. In 1964 Falwell preached a sermon entitled "Ministers and Marches" where he denounced those who were called to preach the Gospel but who instead got involved in the civil rights movement. Both Falwell and Robertson had renounced politics, and it took the excess of the Nixon years, *Roe v. Wade*, and the hope of Jimmy Carter to bring them back to the political limelight.

The scandals that consumed the Nixon administration had a powerful effect on evangelicals. Some, like Billy Graham, felt used and repelled by the political world. In 1976 Graham said that he opposed "organizing Christians into a political bloc."[2] The famous evangelist admitted that he had learned "the hard way" to avoid politics. In that spirit he announced that he was not going to endorse any candidates in the 1976 elections.[3]

The Christian Right has never been monolithic in its beliefs, goals, or leadership—this is a result of the fractured nature of evangelicalism itself. Unlike other religious movements, evangelicalism is not a denomination, but a religious belief encompassing many theologically conservative Protestant Christian denominations. The various wings of the Christian Right are also the result of its birth. It is a mighty river of a political movement that is the result of thousands of small streams across the nation that finally merged.

Even though it is often portrayed as a male-dominated patriarchal movement, in its early years the Christian Right was energized by female leaders. During the late 1960s a series of battles took place, most famously in Anaheim, California, and St. Albans, West Virginia, over the teaching of sex education in public schools. These protests were usually led by concerned mothers, and their experiences led them to take up the banner of family values (although the term was not widely used then) to combat the Equal Rights Amendment (ERA). The first famous leader of the Christian Right was Phyllis Schlafly, who made it her life goal to defeat feminism by using its benefits. While pro-ERA groups picketed the homes of state legislators, Schlafly had her followers bring home-baked bread to the same politicians. The ERA was finally declared dead in the early 1980s due largely to her work.[4] Schlafly's success, Watergate, Jimmy Carter, and the *Roe v. Wade* decision all worked to turn conservative Christians into a politically motivated army.

Robertson had been upset by the *Roe* decision, the push for the ERA, and the general lack of morality that he claimed was epitomized in the counterculture. Still, it was Watergate that compelled him to speak about politics on the air. In 1974 Robertson spoke "with fear and trembling and calling upon our president to . . . confess his sins before the Lord."[5] Robertson thought that many Christians had voted for Nixon due to his religious beliefs. "Instead there was an arrogant palace guard, misuse of government process, illegal contributions, enormous slush funds, tax evasion, bribes, coverup, perjury."[6] The scandal had changed his mind; Robertson began to realize the importance of commenting on the political life of America. He felt it was his duty to present a Christian viewpoint to the crisis every day, and not just on election night. While the scandal unfolded, Robertson began to present his views on domestic and international politics almost daily.[7] He said, "I couldn't support him after I heard the tapes."[8] He had rediscovered his taste for politics, and this interest only grew with the candidacy of Jimmy Carter.

Robertson illustrates how many people in the evangelical camp felt about Jimmy Carter, and how those feelings changed over time. In fact, Robertson can even be seen as a model of their politicalization. Carter raised expectations among evangelicals, and their disappointment with him and the Democratic Party in general can still be seen today. On a surface level, Carter and Robertson had much in common; both were Southern Baptist Democrats who were socially conservative, and they were about the same age. They also had both served in the military during the Korean War. Carter had made great political use of his faith, and the nation was hungry for such a man. Although Carter used his beliefs to the greatest extent possible, he also tried to live out what he talked about.

By the early 1970s there were approximately seventy-five million evangelicals in America; they represented about 40 percent of all Protestants.[9] Carter made a concerted effort to reach this group that was still hesitant to participate in politics. He had been a regular Sunday school teacher at his home church in Plains, Georgia, for many years, and the media descended on the small town to see him teach. He often returned home from the campaign trail to teach when it was his turn. Carter taught a men's Sunday school Bible class and covered such topics as love, justice, faith, salvation, and the return of Christ.[10]

At home and on the campaign trail, Carter talked about his faith. He often mentioned his prayer life, stating that he had prayed more during the four years he was governor of Georgia than during the rest of his life combined.[11] Although it was not the central issue of his campaign, he did make sure that it was always there on the sidelines. Presidential candidates in later years who publicized their religious beliefs had an easier time than Carter, because in 1976 the media was unsure about how to talk about his faith. There was much that the media never understood about Carter's religion. What is surprising is the lack of understanding demonstrated by Pat Robertson. He assumed a great many things about the presidential candidate, and this was a large part of the reason that he would later be unhappy with Carter. Historian Leo Ribuffo sums up the attitude of many evangelicals when he writes that they "paid scant attention to Carter's theology and overlooked political differences to embrace him as one of their own."[12] This was certainly the case with Robertson, who made leaps of faith about Carter's theology and how it would influence his politics.

In 1951 H. Richard Niebuhr published *Christ and Culture*, and it has since been viewed as one of the most insightful studies of the many ways in which Christians have dealt with the issue of integrating their faith and culture.[13] Niebuhr outlines five basic ways in which Christians see the relationship between Christianity and human culture. The positions range from the liberal "Christ of Culture" to the conservative "Christ against Culture." Therein lies the dilemma that Carter faced; while he could be considered a member of the centrist "Christ and Culture in Paradox" group, many evangelicals were not. The majority of evangelicals, Pentecostals, and Fundamentalists were, like Pat Robertson, ardent members of the "Christ against Culture" group. It is their belief that culture is totally corrupt and to be allied with God requires believers to be hostile to the world.

Up until the time he ran for president in 1988, Robertson held a very adversarial attitude about society and the role that Christians should play in it. The problem was not just that this was Robertson's view of the world; it was also a belief held by most evangelicals, and he assumed that Carter was in the camp as well. This ideological conflict caused most of the trouble that Robertson had with Carter and led to his eventual disillusionment with the president.

Some of the theological issues that separated Carter and Robertson were significant. While they were both Southern Baptists, Carter was no Charismatic. They both opposed abortion, but Carter was willing to, and did, compromise on the issue, while Robertson refused to give any ground. They also differed intellectually in their approach to religion. While Robertson focused on the Bible almost exclusively, Carter quoted Reinhold Niebuhr and Søren Kierkegaard. It was on issues such as human rights and eschatology that the greatest discrepancies arose. To Robertson, communism was the ultimate evil, the enemy of God, and had to be stopped at almost any cost. His rhetoric took on an almost crusadelike quality. Carter, on the other hand, thought that the world would be a better place, and communism would be less attractive, if he supported those governments that treated their people humanely. Eschatology was the dividing point, for it played a central role in Robertson's understanding of the world. While Carter kept his views on the end of the world publicly vague, Robertson's were a matter of public record. In their 1976 interview Carter mentioned that the founding of Israel in 1948 was a fulfillment of prophecy; Robertson took this as a sign that their eschatology was similar, which was not the case. Robertson assumed that as fellow Southern Baptists, they had much in common, and that commonality in religion would hopefully translate into a similar political outlook. Unfortunately, Robertson assumed that since they used a similar religious vocabulary their theology and politics were much closer than they actually were.

The first glimpse of this coming conflict between Carter and evangelicals was broadcast nationwide. Late in the campaign of 1976, Robertson and his crew from *The 700 Club* made the trip to Plains, Georgia, to interview Carter. The two men were amiable and the interview seemed to be a success, but there were clues of the coming storm. When Robertson later criticized Carter, he complained most bitterly about the broken promises that Carter made in the interview.

The interview was filmed on the porch of Carter's home in Plains. The first question that Robertson asked Carter showed his mindset about America and the role of Christians in it. He asked the candidate why a good country boy would want to leave his home for the turmoil of Washington. Although Robertson had returned to the idea of Christians playing a role in society, he was still wary of people becoming too involved. This was an example of his "Christ against Culture" presuppositions.

Robertson asked the candidate about how big and active government should be in the life of the average American. In response, Carter talked about the need for the family and the church to take up the slack that would be created by the smaller government that he envisioned. "One of the reasons that we have begun to rely much more heavily on the government to provide our needs is because of the destruction of relationships within the family or within the church," Carter said.[14] The future president then talked about the limits of the federal government's ability to help people and the fact that it cannot always meet people's expectations. In an interesting twist, it was Carter, not Robertson, who focused on the role and importance of the family. The governor stated that since families had failed, the government had stepped in. Although he realized that government could not legislate morality, he could try to model it in his own life. "The president needs to set an example, not only himself, but the members of his family." These comments were evidently lost on Robertson, even though he had seemed agreeable to a politician committed to less government.

Halfway through the interview, Robertson asked Carter if he would appoint people to his cabinet who would serve as "Godly counsel." Carter commented that it would be wrong for him to select appointees on the basis of their religion. However, they should have "a commitment to the principles expressed to us by God." As he spoke about qualifications, Robertson said "amen" and made approving sounds. When Carter said that he would work with people who were not Baptists, Robertson said "certainly." When Carter stated that he would hire people who believed in "unselfishness, truthfulness, honor, a sense of compassion, even if they were not Christians," Robertson was silent. This was to become the basis for the first and most common complaint that Robertson had with the new president.

Almost as important to Robertson as having the right type of Christians in government was the nation's relationship with the Soviet Union. Modern evangelicalism had consistently seen communism as one of the biggest threats to the world. Pat Robertson in particular attached a great deal of eschatological meaning to the USSR. Because it was the key to the end times for him, it was natural that Robertson asked Carter, a fellow evangelical, how he planned to deal with the Soviets. In almost every question on foreign policy and especially in a question about detente, Robertson hinted at the answers that he was looking for.

On Israel, however, Carter was closer to Robertson, even stating that the formation of modern Israel in 1948 was the fulfillment of biblical prophecies. As the twenty-minute interview concluded, Robertson asked Carter to do a promotion for an upcoming television revival on the need for prayer. The interview was, on the whole, not that different from many others that Carter had done during the campaign. The greatest distinction was that both men had shared beliefs, and each was trying to stake out the ground where he felt average evangelical Christians were. Although the meeting was amiable, there was an undertone of expectation on Robertson's side that went unexpressed and unfulfilled.

Much of what Robertson hoped Carter would be as an evangelical president is found in the questions that were asked. Although Robertson is usually connected with family values and other domestic issues, it is foreign policy that interested him the most. That interest was evident in his questions to Carter. Of the twelve questions asked, four dealt with religion, three with foreign policy, and only two with domestic issues with the second question a follow-up to the first.

The three foreign policy issues were all very specifically worded. While many commentators expected Robertson to focus on America, his politics, heavily influenced by his eschatology, led him elsewhere. That is the main reason that Robertson turned against Carter. An analysis of his newsletter, *Pat Robertson's Perspective*, shows that he wanted a strong president who would keep the Soviets at bay. Robertson would have been, it seems, quite content had Carter acted with the same kind of rhetorical vigor that Ronald Reagan later showed. By the time that Carter started an arms buildup and sanctions against the Soviet Union, Robertson had been at least tacitly hostile to him for more than two years.

More than any other event it was the presidency, or more accurately Robertson's expectations of a born-again Christian presidency, that fueled his return to politics. Although Robertson publicly vacillated, privately he became increasingly convinced that evangelicals had to play a larger role in politics. Years after presidential candidate Carter's appearance on *The 700 Club*, Robertson said, "I thought it would be wonderful to have a man who was a born again Christian as president."[15]

In 1987, as he was launching his own presidential campaign, Robertson was asked about his views on Carter. His answers on *Larry King Live* demonstrated how he really felt and the consistency of his conservative outlook. "I supported him in the primary, but I interviewed him . . . several days before the election, and after that experience I voted for Gerald Ford. I was unimpressed."[16] However, in later interviews he claimed to have helped Carter win the Pennsylvania primary.[17] While some conservative Christian leaders, including Jerry Falwell, made it clear that Carter was not the kind of leader that the nation needed, according to his writings in *Perspective*, Robertson was at least willing to let Carter try to prove himself.

As the election neared, conservative Christian publications began to warm to Carter. *Christianity Today* published an editorial on whether or not Christians should vote for Christians. Although Carter did not deserve votes just due to his faith, "Christians surely have a right to expect more from those who profess belief."[18] This is an example of the double standard to which Carter was held. Many evangelicals thought that Carter owed the election to them, and they were the most vocal opponents when they became disappointed in him.

Carter owed his victory to many groups, but evangelicals took much of the credit for themselves. Both Ford and Carter had managed to draw their respective parties' typical constituents, but Carter was able to pull enough evangelicals out of the Republican camp to make the difference. In the 1976 election Ford garnered 9.6 million evangelical votes, and Carter won 6.4 million, a gap of only three million. That distance seems to belie the surge of conservative Christian support for Carter until it is examined in context. In 1968 Richard Nixon had beaten Humphrey by 7.2 million evangelical votes, and in 1972 he beat George McGovern by an extraordinary ten million.[19] Jimmy Carter was able to cut into this formerly Republican stronghold and take two-thirds of their votes. This proved to be the margin of victory.

Both the new president and his coreligionists were flush with victory. Jerry Falwell, although not a supporter of Carter, toured every state capital with his university's choir for his "I Love America" rallies. *Newsweek* magazine proclaimed 1976 the "Year of the Evangelical," and conservative Protestant churches started to experience even faster growth.[20]

The hope of Carter's presidency so energized Robertson that after the 1976 election, he began to send a newsletter called *Pat Robertson's Perspective* to contributing members of *The 700 Club*. His intent in writing this newsletter was to "track the progress of world events under the presidency of a Christian."[21] The newsletter covered politics and finances, and also had a healthy dose of end times prophecy from Robertson himself. Among his numerous predictions was that the Soviet Union would take over all of Africa by the mid-1980s. In 1979 he predicted that a worldwide depression and nuclear war would occur by 1982. In one issue, he predicted that God would financially bless Christians just before the world collapsed, just as God blessed the nation of Israel before they fled Egypt. This newsletter was mailed out to tens of thousands of Christian Broadcasting Network (CBN) supporters, but when Robertson ran for president in 1988 several journalists had a hard time finding copies and his campaign was not forthcoming with them.

The newsletter served as both a gauge of Robertson's support for Carter and a window through which to see what many evangelicals thought about the state of the nation. Before Carter took office, most evangelicals were excited about voting for one of their own kind, and Robertson was no exception. Although he had been a lifelong Democrat, it is more accurate to say that Robertson has always been politically conservative. He changed parties in the early 1980s, but never his political ideology. Robertson held the mistaken belief that Carter was just as politically conservative as he was. Once a man of faith, like Carter, made his intentions and beliefs clear, it was often the case that others would read what they wanted into them.

The newsletter was sent to all financial supporters of CBN and *The 700 Club*. The newsletter had the look and tone of a privately typed letter with the important sections of the four-page journal underlined. The monthly letter dealt with familiar themes in each issue, usually the Middle East, the Soviet Union, and personal finance, in that order. *Pat Robertson's Perspective* was written in an easy to read format. It did not contain a deep analysis of topics, but was intended to get Robertson's points across to a friendly audience. Interspersed among these topics, the Carter administration was discussed, dissected, and later reviled.

Robertson mailed out his *Perspective* once a month and then, in 1979, once every two months. He stopped writing the newsletter in 1982, and did not start again until after he ended his presidential campaign in 1988. In the forty issues sent out during the Carter administration, there were thirty-nine comments about the president. Twelve were positive and twenty-seven were negative or at least wary. Roughly half of the complaints that Robertson had with Carter were based on religious issues. These can be divided into two categories. The first problem, according to Robertson, was the lack of evangelical Protestants in the Carter administration. Second, because there were so few "born-again" Christians in government, America's foreign policy had been compromised and the world was racing toward destruction: the battle of Armageddon was close at hand. These written comments often were buttressed by his commentary on *The 700 Club* broadcast.

As the Carter administration progressed it became more unpopular with Americans in general and evangelicals in particular. The problems of energy, inflation, and the Iranian hostage crisis sank his presidency. It stands to reason that Robertson would become more critical as the years progressed, yet the opposite was the case. In 1977, Robertson made nine negative comments; in 1978, eleven; then in 1979, six. Robertson made only one negative comment during Carter's final year in office. Robertson had attacked Carter so heavily during the first two years, there was little left to gain in continuing the assault. He had made his points about the president's religious isolation and broken promises. In short, he had given up on Carter and was waiting for the end of his term. In the premiere issue of *Pat Robertson's Perspective*, Robertson tried to show the danger facing the new president. The secular media had found Carter to be a mysterious person, and Robertson echoed this belief in his first newsletter. "Christians must pray earnestly for Jimmy Carter."[22] Noting that Carter owed his election to Christians, it also announced that he had "ignored the wishes of Evangelicals," and made appointments from Robertson's arch nemesis, the "eastern establishment." It was this group more than any other that Robertson hated. In fact he often attacked them and their supposed head David Rockefeller. In not selecting evangelical Christians to be in his cabinet, Carter had shown the first sign of compromise with the fallen culture that Robertson had warned him to avoid. He wondered why "there can't be someone other than a single enor-mously wealthy family who picks our officials for us." Years later Robertson com-mented, "We were talking to him (Carter), recommending people for his cabinet and it turned out that his hands were tied, he was under the control of the Council on Foreign Relations and the Trilateral Commission."[23]

As the year progressed, Robertson took the president to task for the Panama Canal treaty, his energy policy, and tax reform. Interestingly enough, it was the Bert Lance affair that brought about the greatest amount of sympathetic com-ments. Lance was Carter's budget director and was forced to resign after Con-gress questioned loans he had made to himself while president of the National Bank of Georgia.[24] Robertson pointed out that Lance was the only evangelical high in the administration besides Carter. Robertson declared that this scandal brought the administration "to a crossroads," and that it was a symbol of the deeper struggle between good-hearted Christians and the Eastern establishment. It was very hard to please Robertson, for in the same paragraph, he criticized the president for protecting the "wrongdoer" for so long and then for letting him go. Allowing Lance to resign had left the president in a state of "dangerous isolation . . . from acceptable counsel."[25]

From Robertson's point of view the danger that the president faced was seri-ous. Since Carter had been removed from any Christian influence, Robertson feared that the president would quickly become susceptible to disastrous deci-sions. Chief among Robertson's fears was the issue that was closest to his heart, Israel. The Jewish nation was the center of all of his end-of-the-world scenar-ios. Now that Carter was isolated from other Christians, the Soviets would be allowed to join the new peace process in the Middle East. At first he heavily crit-icized Carter for asking the Soviets to lend a hand in the negotiations. Robert-son later cleared the president in April 1978, when he wrote that it was Zbigniew Brzezinski's fault, and this Soviet initiative "was not cleared with (Hamilton) Jordan or Carter for political implications."[26] This, according to Robertson, was just one of the warning signs of the things to come, now that Carter had been left without conservative Christian advisors.

The Georgian's second year in office produced the most comments, both positive and negative, from Robertson. They dealt with everything from the per-sonal life of Hamilton Jordan to the creeping socialism of national health insur-ance. The year started off much as the last one had, with hope for the president, but warnings that things were more likely to go wrong. Stating that the admin-istration was a combination of elements, "inept, Machiavellian . . . liberal, con-servative, blessed by God,"[27] Robertson wondered which of these would ultimately come to dominate. In 1977 Robertson focused mostly on foreign pol-icy and the Christians in government issue; during the next year he focused on the budget and the growing economic crisis. Of course a close second to all of this was the lack of Christians in the government. Evidently Robertson did not count United Nations ambassador Andrew Young among the believers, for he held him out for particularly harsh criticism for his tolerant attitude toward both the Palestine Liberation Organization and Cuban soldiers in Angola. Young had touched upon Robertson's two greatest fears: the growth of Soviet-communist influence in the third world and the security of Israel. To his mind, one was dangerous to America on a geopolitical level and the other was dangerous to the world on a spiritual–eschatological level.

Some works, such as *With God on Our Side* by William Martin, give great significance to the White House Conference on Families in 1980 and the fallout thereafter.[28] While it is true that many evangelicals were put off by the entire affair, it did not receive a single mention from Pat Robertson in his *Perspective*. Perhaps this is because he had already written off the administration, but that in itself does not fully answer the question. During the Carter administration, Robertson was still largely unknown outside of the evangelical world. It was not until the first term of the Reagan administration that he gained the notoriety that he held for the next twenty years.

During 1978, Carter received a great deal of praise for mediating peace talks between Israel and Egypt. Robertson also praised the president for what would become the Camp David accords. Robertson claimed that Carter was so successful because he was a man of faith and was able to appeal to a Muslim and a Jew on that basis. Another reason was that by helping to bring peace to the region, he was helping to fulfill biblical prophecies. Robertson stated repeatedly that Israel must join with Egypt before the final world battle could take place. This helps to explain how Robertson could both praise the peacemaking of the president and also applaud the sale of fighter jets to Israel, Egypt, and Saudi Arabia.[29]

Aside from favorable comments on Middle East peace and his personal religious beliefs, Robertson found little positive to say about Carter in 1978 and beyond. The most common complaint during those years was about Carter's budget and the state of the economy. *Perspective* had long been predicting an economic slowdown in the late 1970s followed by a total worldwide collapse by 1985. What Robertson saw in the budget priorities of the Carter administration only fueled the fears of what he was predicting. Early in the year, he harangued the president for failing to keep such campaign promises as reducing the budget deficit, controlling spending, and cutting the size of the federal government. Robertson complained that over fifty-two thousand new federal jobs had been created. He also attacked the newly proposed Departments of Energy and Education, just as his father had strenuously opposed the creation of new government agencies. In later years it was the Department of Education that Robertson singled out as the ultimate sign of a government gone too far. However, in 1978 all he said on the subject was that it was a sign of Carter's broken promises. "It is obvious," Robertson wrote, "that there has not been any serious move to control and simplify the vast federal bureaucracy, as was promised in Carter's campaign rhetoric."[30]

For all of his focus on the federal budget, in the March 1978 *Perspective* Robertson spent several paragraphs on a scandal that, in his eyes, made the Lance affair seems tame. Robertson wrote that controversy surrounding an attorney in Pennsylvania would cost Carter the 1980 election. According to Robertson, the president had broken another campaign promise when he used the Justice Department for his own political purposes. He accused the president of yielding to pressure and removing a Republican U.S. Attorney for Pennsylvania. The attorney, David Marston, was investigating several supposedly corrupt Democratic politicians. According to Robertson one of the men under investigation asked Carter to remove Marston, and the president complied. Robertson stated that "the entire matter reflected a lack of candor . . . which took us back to the sordid pre-Watergate days. It will serve to weaken Mr. Carter's future moral leadership, and it was a serious blunder."[31] The matter was a good deal more complicated than Robertson let on, but he was able to get away with an exaggeration due to President Carter's poor handling of the firing.[32] As the year progressed the comments only became more harsh. The president had made a fatal error and broken a serious pledge when he refused to surround himself with conservative evangelical Christians.

The April 1978 issue was one of the harshest in its assessment of Carter. It also contained one sentence that may well sum up Robertson's entire problem with the president. He wrote, "It is abundantly clear that Carter did not select his cabinet or key aides from the ranks of 'born again' Christians."[33] This central problem led, in Robertson's mind, to many others. A lack of evangelical Christians meant that the president was relying too heavily upon the Rockefeller Eastern establishment. This in turn meant that America was being run by people who had put their own economic interests above the nation's.

Other hostile statements followed. After mentioning the drop in the polls that the president had experienced, Robertson blamed it on his failure to keep his campaign promises. The president's "speeches show a considerable lowering of expectations to reflect the loss of power of his administration."[34] Robertson said that the president had a "fatal flaw"—no charisma. In short, he lacked "a sense of greatness," and he was "honest and decent, but unsuited for his task."[35] Robertson, never one to be subtle, ended that issue with a quote from Psalm 1. The first of the six quoted verses was "Blessed is the man that does not walk in the counsel of the ungodly, nor stands in the way of sinners, nor sits in the seat of the scornful."[36] Robertson called it a "word for the President."

However, even if Carter had brought more evangelicals or simply other Christians into the cabinet, they probably would not have met with Robertson's approval. Robertson was very critical of Andrew Young, who certainly had the religious credentials to count as "godly counsel." It was in the important field of foreign policy that Young had angered Robertson. He was also dismayed with what he called "the shenanigans of Hamilton Jordan and some of the other things that were going on. . . . I was disgusted."[37] Still other members of the administration also caused him concern. He claimed that Health and Human Services secretary Patricia Harris was an avowed enemy of Christianity. In a speech at Princeton University she had said, "Any attempt to Christianize America would be dangerous for democracy." Robertson also quoted her as claiming that humanism had to defeat Christianity in the nation. While her comments had been directed at the Moral Majority, Robertson was willing to use them to forward his own agenda.[38] Fear of a secular humanist threat was something that he developed in the mid-1980s as a conspiracy with the Illuminati at the center, but the idea was still embryonic. Robertson was disappointed by all of these actions; and through them, he discovered that Carter was not the type of evangelical Christian that he had taken him to be.

Robertson had refused to speculate about the election, and there are only two issues where he mentioned specific candidates. In March 1979 he made the first comments about the coming election and some of the Republican challengers—Ronald Reagan, John Connally, and Phillip Crane. Interestingly, he was the least enthusiastic about Reagan. While conceding that Reagan had a large lead in the polls, Robertson thought he was too old, and had a "lack of intellectual depth," which would hinder his campaign.[39] Robertson wrote, "Reagan has the largest lead; Crane the best mind; and Connally would make the strongest president."[40] In a brief description of each man, it was clear that he favored Crane, who was a Christian. It was also in this issue that Carter received his harshest treatment. While stating that the president was "personally devout, his administration comes through as so repugnant to many Christians. . . . [He has] offended the very Christian groups who were his ardent champions."[41] The status of Robertson's ministry prevented him from openly endorsing a candidate, yet his apocalyptic visions, combined with his constant attacks on the Carter administration, made his opinions clear.

In an issue that was written just before the November 1980 presidential election, but mailed out soon afterwards, Robertson gave a detailed account of what he thought about a possible Reagan presidency. In the two-page section, Robertson did not mention religion at all. The comments all referred to the capable people that Reagan would hopefully bring back into government, and the strong anti-Soviet attitude that he would bring to the White House. Robertson even predicted that Reagan would do little to change the government. From the size of the bureaucracy to the budget for the welfare state, he felt the new president would maintain the status quo. This was a startling admission from someone who supported Ronald Reagan over Carter. Groups like the Moral Majority had staked their claim with Reagan, and the new Christian Right was publicly taking credit for his victory, yet in the early months, Robertson was unwilling to predict a change in the nation's course. This early analysis is especially interesting in that Robertson later said that Reagan was the greatest president of the twentieth century. His reticence to have much faith in Reagan and his rhetoric is directly attributable to the four-year disappointment that he had with Carter. If an evangelical did not make the nation stronger, then surely Reagan, a casual Christian at best, would not do any better.

After the Carter era most evangelicals became much more deliberate about basing their voting behavior on political issues, not religious ones. That is why even though neither Ronald Reagan nor George H. W. Bush acted to end abortion, or any significant element of their social agenda, they continued to receive widespread support from many evangelicals. Their movement toward Carter in 1976 was based more on the novelty of voting for one of their own kind than politics. Carter's election was a matter of pride for many.

For a man whose early life was steeped in politics, Robertson was still surprisingly naive at times. His criticisms of Jimmy Carter showed that even though religious conviction was important to him, rhetoric was more important. That is why evangelicals swung so heavily back into the Republican fold. He never understood who Carter really was and his disappointment was based on that misconception. The secular press also failed to understand Carter, but for the most part they did not feel the same sense of abandonment that Robertson and many evangelicals did. The most lasting lesson that he learned was that it was more important to agree with a candidate's political ideology than his religion. A marginal Christian who fought communism was better than a devout Christian who was "soft" on leftists worldwide. Robertson took that lesson to his campaign in 1988, and later to the Christian Coalition. From the Carter era on, conservative politics, not conservative religion, was the defining ideology for the Christian Right. This can be seen in how they spread their concerns into other areas like tax cuts and the Star Wars missile defense system, something that was not easy to find biblical support for.

Robertson's hopes for a Christian-controlled America had been dashed because he did not understand who Carter was. In 1976 he was willing to give Carter a chance if not his vote. His unrealistically high hopes for an evangelical presidency had led to disappointment. He realized that religious conviction did not mean a single form of political action. Robertson discovered that he could ally himself with people of different religious beliefs if they held the same political convictions. In the early 1970s, Robertson had no dealings with Mormon politicians like Utah's senator Orrin Hatch, yet by 1980 the senator's conservative political pedigree was all that mattered. Meanwhile on *The 700 Club* Mormons were still portrayed as a dangerous cult. While Ronald Reagan made many of the same type of Christians-in-government promises that Carter had, Robertson never criticized Reagan for failing to live up to the promise. The Carter years had allowed Robertson to bridge the gap between his religious beliefs and political interests. The genie was out of the bottle, never to be put back in.

The evangelical world was deeply affected by Jimmy Carter. As shown by Pat Robertson, conservative Christians' involvement in politics increased dramatically as the 1970s progressed. Their leadership was much more cynical and willing to bend in order to sit at victory's table. Still, the 1976 election was significant for several reasons. It was the first time in over fifty years that evangelicals had demonstrated their political power, and it was the first time that they were able to make a credible claim that they were the margin of victory for a candidate. It was also the last time that the majority of politically liberal and conservative evangelicals were united behind the same candidate. Carter's support from evangelicals, while still significant for a Democrat, slipped in 1980. In 1976 Carter received about 43 percent of the white Protestant vote. In 1980 that percentage slipped to a still significant 31 percent. In both elections, the Republican candidate received more that 50 percent of the evangelical votes.[42] Most conservative evangelicals voted for Reagan and the liberals for John Anderson. Carter's support among white evangelicals is even more impressive when it is compared to the 2004 presidential election, where 78 percent of them voted for George W. Bush.[43]

The era left Robertson a changed man. He was becoming increasingly wealthy, his network was growing, and so was his power within evangelical circles. He became convinced that conservative Christians had a role to play in politics, and that God just might let them run the nation.

Notes

1. Clyde Wilcox, "The Christian Right in Twentieth Century America: Continuity and Change." *The Review of Politics* vol. 50, no. 4 (Fall 1988): 659–81.

2. "Politics from the Pulpit," *Newsweek*, September 6, 1976, 49.

3. "Politics from the Pulpit," 49.

4. For an excellent history of the role of women in the early Christian Right see Ruth Murray Brown, *For a Christian America: A History of the Religious Right* (New York: Prometheus Books, 2002).

5. David Edwin Harrell Jr., *Pat Robertson: A Personal, Religious, and Political Portrait* (New York: Harper & Row, 1987), 175.

6. Associated Press, "Rev. Robertson Urges Repentance by Nixon," *Virginian-Pilot*, May 3, 1974.

7. Harrell, *Pat Robertson*, 175.

8. Pat Robertson, interview by author, tape recording, Virginia Beach, Va., May 25, 2000.

9. Paul Lopatto, *Religion and the Presidential Election* (New York: Praeger, 1985), 37.

10. Wesley Pippert, ed., *The Spiritual Journey of Jimmy Carter: In His Own Words* (New York: Macmillan, 1978), 153.

11. See Jimmy Carter interview, *The 700 Club*, August 26, 1976, and Perry Deane Young, *God's Bullies: Power Politics and Religious Tyranny* (New York: Holt, Rinehart and Winston, 1982).

12. Leo Ribuffo, *Right Center Left: Essays in American History* (New Brunswick, N.J.: Rutgers University Press, 1992), 218.

13. H. Richard Niebuhr, *Christ and Culture* (New York: Harper & Row, 1975).

14. Jimmy Carter interview, *The 700 Club*, August 26, 1976. All interview quotes are from this source. Regent University Special Collections (RUA).

15. Pat Robertson interview.

16. *Larry King Live*, April 23, 1987, CNN.

17. Pat Robertson interview.

18. "Should Christians Vote for Christians?" *Christianity Today*, June 18, 1976, 12.

19. "The Evangelical Vote for Carter," *Fides et Historia*, John Patterson, June 1986.

20. "Born Again! The Year of the Evangelical," *Newsweek*, October 25, 1976.

21. Harrell, *Pat Robertson*, 177.

22. Pat Robertson, *Pat Robertson's Perspective*, February 1977.

23. Pat Robertson interview.

24. Peter Carroll, *It Seemed Like Nothing Happened: America in the 1970s* (New Brunswick, N.J.: Rutgers University Press, 1990), 213.

25. Robertson, *Pat Robertson's Perspective*, October 1977.

26. Robertson, *Pat Robertson's Perspective*, April 1978.

27. Robertson, *Pat Robertson's Perspective*, January–February 1978.

28. William Martin, *With God on Our Side* (New York: Broadway Books, 1996), 168.

29. Robertson, *Pat Robertson's Perspective*, September–October 1978.

30. Robertson, *Pat Robertson's Perspective*, March 1978.

31. Robertson, *Pat Robertson's Perspective*, March 1978, 3.

32. Myra MacPherson, "Marston, after the Massacre," *Washington Post*, January 26, 1978.

33. Robertson, *Pat Robertson's Perspective*, April 1978.

34. Robertson, *Pat Robertson's Perspective*, April 1978.

35. Robertson, *Pat Robertson's Perspective*, April 1978.

36. Robertson, *Pat Robertson's Perspective*, April 1978.

37. Pat Robertson interview.

38. Denis Collins, "TV Evangelist Snags Reagan, but Not Everyone Down Home," *Washington Post*, October 4, 1980.

39. Collins, "TV Evangelist Snags Reagan."

40. Collins, "TV Evangelist Snags Reagan."

41. Collins, "TV Evangelist Snags Reagan."

42. Gerald Pomper et al. *The Election of 1980* (Chatham, N.J.: Chatham House Publishers, 1981), 71.

43. Kevin Phillips, *American Theocracy: The Peril and Politics of Radical Religion, Oil, and Borrowed Money in the 21st century* (New York: Viking, 2006), 195.

CHAPTER 5

PROPHET OF POLITICS
AND DOOM

J IMMY Carter's presidency had a huge impact on Robertson's thinking, and this change came about as his power in the evangelical world was on the rise. Although Robertson had high hopes for the potential role of Christians in politics, he still had reservations about his own political involvement. At this point in his life he faced an inner struggle between his religious calling and his inherently political nature. In the 1960s the fervor of his newfound beliefs and his hectic schedule at the Christian Broadcasting Network (CBN) helped him to clearly separate these two worlds, but the borders became hazy in the late 1970s. As his network grew and the Christian Right began to take an active role in America, Robertson was pulled toward politics and new theological concepts. He began to make his presence known in Charismatic circles and stepped onto the political stage for the first time. More significant than his actions, Robertson's theology was changing to allow Christians to become more involved in the affairs of the secular world. At this point in his life, Robertson was flirting with ideas that were extremely controversial while he increasingly warned of the world's upcoming day of judgment.

A sign of Robertson's growing influence in the Charismatic community was the central role that he played in a doctrinal controversy in the mid-1970s. Since the Charismatic movement, like most elements of evangelicalism, does not have a central leadership, there is a constant struggle to maintain orthodoxy and banish heretics. As is the case with most religious movements in their infancy, there can be a wide variety of concepts. Eventually the group grows to the point where it becomes necessary to draw boundaries in an attempt to define itself. The Charismatic movement had grown to the point that it was becoming an active part of the larger evangelical world, and some of its unusual ideas began to stand out.

The Shepherding movement was one such idea. Founded by a group of four ministers in Fort Lauderdale, Florida, who had taken over the publishing duties of the magazine *New Wine* in 1970,[1] it sought to bring order to the Charismatic movement by creating a regimented system of discipleship. Their ideas became enormously popular since, by definition, Charismatics remained in non-Pentecostal denominations and many felt isolated. This shepherding concept was designed to foster unity and allow believers to grow in their faith. What sounded like an innocuous and historically based attempt at discipleship quickly took a dangerous tone. The Ft. Lauderdale pastors taught that people needed to enter into "covenant relationships" in which they vowed to live in submission to their leader. It was the role of this shepherd to help each of his disciples find his or her role in the church.[2] The shepherd was to guide, but the line between guiding and controlling was blurry.

Some Charismatic leaders, such as Demos Shakarian, the founder of the Full Gospel Businessman's Fellowship, were concerned about the Shepherding movement from its inception, while most others, like Pat Robertson, came around slowly. The movement continued to grow throughout the 1970s as it gave out more than 4.5 million copies of its magazine, sold thousands of books and tapes, and held yearly conferences.[3] This rapid growth also helped bring about its sudden downfall, which was led by Robertson himself.

In the summer of 1975, two of Robertson's former CBN employees told him of their troubling experiences with the Shepherding movement. According to the two men, their Shepherd required that he have approval over every aspect of their lives, from vacations to buying a car or a house. They also had a few others contact Robertson and tell him of their experiences as well. Robertson was told that the Shepherding meetings had dealt almost exclusively with relationship issues, and rarely spiritual matters. The couple told Robertson, "[T]here was very little talk about the Lord and seldom did we even talk about the Word."[4] These comments were confirmation of rumors that he had heard earlier, and that was enough for him. He took the accusations so seriously that he flew several of the disaffected people to Virginia Beach to formally write out their complaints. For most of his life Robertson was disdained as a hothead, someone who makes seemingly random statements. This story shows how seriously he can take important issues, and how careful he is to avoid legal traps.

In May 1975 Robertson publicly lashed out at the movement. He denounced the group's leaders and told those who were part of these groups to leave them immediately. He then ordered that copies of any CBN tapes that featured any of the leaders from Ft. Lauderdale were to be destroyed immediately. In June he sent an open letter to the most prominent of the leaders, Bob Mumford, in which he mentioned the stories of abuse that he had heard and advised that he agree to a meeting with those opposed to him to discuss the charges.[5]

The floodgates opened up on the Shepherding movement once Robertson's letter became public. Soon others, including evangelist Kathryn Kuhlman, denounced the movement and barred the leaders from speaking at major Charismatic conferences. Robertson's suggested meeting eventually happened in August 1975. One historian refers to the meeting as "the shoot-out at the Curtis Hotel." Mumford was apparently dismayed when Robertson appeared with a large stack of what looked like legal briefs.[6] The two sides never saw eye-to-eye, and the meetings proved pointless and even embarrassing for the entire Charismatic movement.

Robertson stuck to his guns, and the Shepherding movement went into decline. Their magazine *New Wine* shut down in 1986, and in 1989, Mumford publicly renounced his teachings.[7] Robertson remained concerned about the movement. A 1985 book, *The CBN Ministry Handbook*, which was taken from guides used by CBN telephone counselors, has a section on how to advise people to leave Shepherding groups. It describes the groups as "religious dictatorships" that put people in "spiritual and mental bondage."[8] This was the first time that Robertson had flexed his muscles in doctrinal issues, and his ability to cripple the Shepherding movement shows just how powerful he had become.

While Robertson was publicly attacking one questionable religious movement, he was embracing another. In the late 1970s, Robertson began to preach ideas taken from Rousas John Rushdoony, the father of Dominion theology, also known as Reconstructionism. Although Robertson later publicly repudiated the man and his teachings, his ideas were influential and Rushdoony was a guest on *The 700 Club* several times in the 1970s and 1980s. Reconstructionist theology remained both outside the evangelical mainstream and the public's attention until George W. Bush became president in 2000. Suddenly, critics of the Christian Right were quick to claim that almost every evangelical was a Reconstructionist. While these accusations obviously had a political motive, they were based in truth. To understand Robertson's relationship to the movement, it is critical to first understand Reconstructionist theology. Then both Robertson's words and actions will make more sense.

Rushdoony is often called the father of Reconstructionist theology. He was a Fundamentalist theologian with degrees from Berkeley and the Pacific School of Religion, and created the Chalcedon Institute in 1965. The theological movement that he became the chief apologist for was developed by Westminster seminary professor Cornelius Van Til, a student of Gresham Machen. The Dominion/Reconstructionist movement has been led by intellectuals who have published literally hundreds of books since the 1960s in attempts to gain converts. They take the passage in Genesis where God gave man dominion over the

earth and interpret it to apply to Christians. There are five key ideas of the movement. First is a belief in salvation by faith, since only those who are saved can
change society for the better. Second is "the continuing validity and applicabil-
ity of the whole law of God," which includes the laws of Moses. Next is an optimistic eschatology, which predicts that Christians will bring about the millennial
era of peace. The fourth idea is a belief that the Bible is self-authenticating as
God's word and superior to human reason. The final key belief is that civil government is one of several types of equal forms of government established by
God. This means that church and family governments cannot be intruded upon
by the civil government.[9]

In 1973 Rushdoony wrote the epic work on Reconstructionist theology with
his study of the Ten Commandments entitled *The Institutes of Biblical Law*. The
book begins by criticizing the commonly held Christian belief that the new
covenant established by Jesus meant that believers were no longer bound by the
laws set down in the Old Testament. "If the law was so serious in the sight of
God that it would require the death of Jesus Christ . . . it seems strange for God
then to proceed to abandon the law!"[10] Basing his arguments on the Bible, early
church fathers, and even Plato and Homer, he argues that Christians have been
given the responsibility to bring God's law to the entire earth. Only Christians
can establish peace, because they have both the authority of Jesus and the power
of God. For Rushdoony, conversion is one way to spread the Christian dominion, but coercion is also a viable option since it will allow God's law to be
enforced. Christians were supposed to rule the entire earth using God's laws,
and he warned his readers not to try to further their own political goals, but to
establish God's laws. According to Rushdoony, there is no telling what it might
take for this to occur. "God's order required the fall of Rome, not its peace. Many
Christians prayed for Rome, and rightfully so; they sinned when they limited
God's work to the framework of the empire."[11]

As it applies to America, "the distinguishing mark of a dominionist is a
commitment to defining and carrying out an approach to building a society that
is self-consciously defined as exclusively Christian, and dependant specifically
on the work of Christians, rather than based on a broader consensus."[12] Rushdoony has said, "[L]ike the Puritans, we seek to assert the crown rights of Christ
the King over all of life."[13] Perhaps his most controversial idea is that only evangelical Christians should be allowed to hold positions of power in government,
and that they were designed to rule the world. "According to biblical law, all basic
powers except the death penalty are given to the family. . . . A resurgent Christianity is taking (these rights) back from the state."[14] The more radical elements
of the movement favor replacing public schools with Christian ones and limit-
ing voting rights exclusively to evangelical Christians.[15] One Reconstructionist
claimed that God's law is paramount, therefore majority rule in a democracy

can never be allowed to supersede God's laws.[16] Robertson clearly believed that only observant Christians had a role in government, as exampled by his questions to Carter about having Godly counsel in the White House.

How have these ideas impacted Robertson? Is he a Reconstructionist? These questions are essential to answer so that his later political moves can be understood. In April 1980, CBN ran a weeklong series on psychology and philosophy, and their effects on the modern world. Rushdoony was the special guest that week and the following exchange reveals his views on Christians and government.

> RUSHDOONY: Hegel said God was the state and all political philosophies are based on his teaching, and we are in a battle between God and Caesar.
> ROBERTSON: What is going to happen?
> RUSHDOONY: The government has to crush Christian schools. The government comes in to schools declaring they are there for the children. The IRS case did us a great favor; it made Christians realize that they are in a war, and that someone is shooting at them.
> ROBERTSON: We could see Christianity growing and everybody coming to Christ.
> RUSHDOONY: Here are the attacks to the church. The IRS case, the national labor relations board trying to unionize Christian teachers and parochial schools. Pastors have been arrested for starting day care centers.[17]

Although Robertson later claimed he never bought into Rushdoony's ideas, the fact that he was a regular guest on *The 700 Club* during the late 1970s and early 1980s suggests otherwise.

Another piece of evidence that shows that Robertson was a proponent of this type of thinking is shown by his hiring of Herbert Titus at Regent University. Robertson would not have brought in such a vocal Reconstructionist to be the academic dean, then dean of the law school, if he did not agree with the movement. Titus also helped Robertson with at least one of his books, *Answers to 200 of Life's Most Probing Questions*, which promoted some of the basic ideas of Dominion theology.[18] When asked about Titus, Robertson said, "[H]e is a very creative thinker, I was always intrigued to talk to him, because I'm a lawyer. In my opinion it [Reconstructionist theology] would have made a very interesting speculation in a class about legal theory. But for an administrator it was not a good thing. He was very narrow minded and had a very narrow definition of what a Christian is."[19]

In 2006 Kevin Phillips wrote that "for all practical purposes, Robertson is a Christian Reconstructionist."[20] Such statements do not explain the complexity of Robertson's thoughts on the issue. While it is clear that he was attracted to many of the ideas of Reconstructionism, his experiences during the 1988 election and his early work with the Christian Coalition led him to rethink his stance. By the 1990s any interest he had in Reconstructionism was clearly a secondary part of his theology. As detailed in chapter 17, Robertson eventually purged Titus and other Reconstructionists from Regent University. While he might occasionally say things that resonated with fans of Rushdoony, Robertson's Baptist roots showed when he praised religious pluralism and demonstrated his willingness to work with politicians like Utah senator Orrin Hatch, a Mormon. Robertson's hopes that Christians will hold sway over the government are based on the democratic idea of majority rule. If religious conservatives are the largest single group of Americans, their ideas should naturally find expression in the nation's laws. Dominionists do not view democracy as God ordained, especially if it keeps his law from being enacted.

In recent years Reconstructionists such as Gary North have claimed that this movement has deeply penetrated evangelicalism. North goes so far as to claim that most Protestants are "for the most part unaware of the original source of the theological ideas that are beginning to transform them."[21] One journalist even claims that the Southern Baptist Church's leadership was dominated by adherents to Rushdoony's philosophies.[22] Certainly it appeared that by the time that George W. Bush took office many evangelicals, Fundamentalists, and Charismatics were espousing such doctrines. Many leaders of the Christian Right perhaps unknowingly adhere to the movement's basic tenets, and many outsiders do not understand conservative Christianity.

The problem with most discussions of evangelicalism and Reconstructionism is a lack of attention to the overlapping circles of their beliefs. These groups use the same phrases and believe many of the same things, but their differences are significant. They both may believe that God gave mankind dominion over the earth, but they have totally different understandings of what that implies. They also express a desire to have a government based on what they see as biblical principles, although their methods to obtain that goal are radically different. Most significantly, evangelicals tend to believe that it is possible to work with those of other faiths, or no faith, as long as their political and social goals match. Ralph Reed's work in attempting to bring Catholics and Jews into the Christian Coalition is a perfect example. A deeply important difference between the two groups is that Reconstructionists are Calvinists, and the vast majority of evangelicals are Arminians.[23] The Pentecostals trace their spiritual heritage to John Wesley, the founder of the Methodist Church and an ardent Arminian. Calvinists believe that God has predestined those who will join his kingdom. It is impossible to resist if you have been chosen, and there is nothing one can do to work toward salvation. Arminianism teaches that faith alone is not sufficient, but must be accompanied by good work. An important distinction between them is that Arminians believe that anyone can be saved, so it is extremely important to preach the Gospel. For Calvinists this evangelical impulse is not as important since God will save whom he wills.

There are a number of obstacles to determining the influence of Reconstructionism on the Christian Right and evangelicalism. First, Reconstructionists like North enjoy claiming that its ideas are widespread because it obviously benefits his cause. At the same time, liberal groups are tempted to make evangelicals appear more threatening in order to mobilize their own constituencies. Finally, the biggest problem is that the average evangelical has more than likely never heard of Rushdoony, North, or Reconstructionism. A good indicator of this is the recent phenomenal popularity of the *Left Behind* book series. These books are based on an eschatology that is premillennial, while Reconstructionism requires a strict adherence to a postmillennial return of Jesus. This is a significant difference, and one that can be seen as a reliable way to test the extent to which modern evangelicalism is steeped in Rushdoony's ideas.

As mainline Protestant churches became more theologically liberal in the late nineteenth and early twentieth centuries, some conservative churches began to promote eschatological ideas, some of which were as old as the earliest days of the church. These ancient ideas were given a new twist with the addition of premillennial dispensationalism, which soon became the predominate theme in conservative Christian theology. Dispensationalism, which became popular in the United States through the work of John Darby in the mid-nineteenth century, is a belief that the earth has experienced six dispensations, or time periods, in which God had a covenant with mankind.[24] Darby taught that the world was awaiting a seventh and final dispensation with the physical return of Jesus.[25] Premillennial dispensationalism holds that Jesus will return just prior to the start of the final age, which will be a thousand-year peaceful reign of Jesus on earth. These ideas became increasingly widespread as the twentieth century progressed. The practical effect was that many Fundamentalist Protestants began to see the future as a time when the world situation would be worse and Christians would be persecuted.[26] This theology allowed conservative churches to back away from social involvement, since it was deemed to be pointless. Many conservative churches preached these ideas, but it was one man who took this idea and popularized it for a new generation of evangelical Christians—Hal Lindsey.

Lindsey was the author of a best-selling book of the 1970s, *The Late Great Planet Earth*. Like the *Left Behind* books, Lindsey's book is a retelling of the Book of Revelation, the last book of the Bible, which foretells the end of the world and the return of Jesus to Earth. The central thesis of Lindsey's book became gospel for preachers of the end times: Things are going to get much worse in the world before the end arrives. At some unknown point in time, God would remove all Christians from the earth in an event called the rapture. Once all of the Christians were gone the tribulation, a time of intense suffering while the Antichrist rules the earth, will commence. After a few years, Jesus will return with all of his followers, to begin a thousand-year reign of peace on earth.

Besides the end of the world stories, Lindsey's book taught another important lesson: Although evil will triumph, it will only be for a short while, so evil can be fought and beaten. Moreover, it should be fought at every turn. Men like Billy Graham, Jerry Falwell, and Pat Robertson constantly used the ideas of Lindsey in their books and sermons. The major impact of Lindsey's book was the spread of premillennial dispensationalism, which is the most popular form of apocalyptic belief in the United States.[27] This led many evangelicals and Fundamentalists to study world events and read the New Testament looking for predictions of the earth's demise. This in turn led many conservative Christians to become even more involved in the political realm.

While the majority of evangelicals believe in the premillennial return of Christ, Robertson does not. He is unique among televangelists because he believes that Christians will live through the tribulation. In the mid-1980s he wrote, "[T]he Bible teaches two comings of Jesus. One was his birth, and the second will be his coming again in triumph. There is no third coming for a secret rapture."[28] While he did believe that Christians must live through this horrible time, he believes that God will protect his followers just as he protected the Jews in Egypt during the plagues. He does believe that Jesus will return after a seven-year period of tribulation and not before, as most evangelicals believe. In recent years Robertson has made it clear that he still holds onto a post-tribulation eschatology; an example of this is his 2003 book, *Bring It On.*[29]

So what does all this mean for Robertson and his politics? He saw the necessity for Christians to influence government and pray that the time of tribulation is delayed. One scholar describes Robertson's stance as schizophrenic, believing that the world will get worse but it is important for Christians to be politically involved regardless.[30] What is clear is that during the 1970s and 1980s Robertson was supportive of some of the key ideas of Reconstructionism, even as he disavowed the more radical aspects. He was never as enamored with the theology as his critics charge. Both his many statements disavowing Rushdoony's thinking and his rejection of postmillennialism are solid evidence. Finally, Robertson is an Arminian, as are most evangelicals. In his book *Answers to 200 of Life's Most Probing Questions*, he presents a balanced view on the importance of both faith and works. He clearly sides with Arminianism when he writes that it is possible to lose "the assurance of salvation" if you continue to live in a sinful manner.[31]

If there was one thing that is clear about Robertson's theology in the late 1970s, it is his belief that the end times were at hand. His writings became more apocalyptic than at any time before or since. Perhaps it was a combination of his reading of scripture and his pessimism about the political condition of the United States. Vietnam, Watergate, economic stagflation—even a Christian president like Jimmy Carter couldn't stem the tide. It was during this period that he made some of the most radical predictions of his career.

Robertson repeatedly referred to the end of the world and the violence and destruction that he feared were lurking just around the corner. During the Carter administration he became obsessed with his idea of a coming conflict with the Soviet Union. This fear, coupled with what he perceived as Carter's weak foreign policy, began to grow as the 1980 election drew near. He still attacked the president for his lack of Christian counsel, but his fear of Armageddon was paramount.

Early in 1979 Robertson predicted that Iraq and Syria would merge into one nation and that all of Israel's neighbors (except Syria) would join into peace agreements with her. This would lead the Soviets to attack Israel; the ultimate battle could only be months away. Robertson wrote that due to biblical prophecies he was "armed with the certainty of these future events."[32] At any moment the world would be drawn into war.

In Robertson's rhetoric at the time the belief that it was more important than ever to have conservative evangelical Christians in charge—people who, like him, could see the future in the Bible and "know the moves in advance"[33]— occurs over and over. Robertson predicted that by the mid-1980s Russia would "move to capture Africa" and cut off Europe's oil supply. This in turn "will undoubtedly bring about a nuclear war . . . [and] Russia will be destroyed as a world power" through the intervention of God.[34] This was Robertson's vision of the fulfillment of Ezekiel 38 and 39, which many evangelical Christians interpreted to predict the invasion of Israel by the Soviet Union.

The year 1980 brought a special seven-page issue of *Pat Robertson's Perspective* called "Prophetic Insights for the Decade of Destiny." Out of all of the issues that were printed from 1977 until 1982, this was the most eschatological and the most frightening. Robertson saw two worldwide trends that had increased since 1967: the growth of humanism and a Christian spiritual awakening. It was during the 1980s that he predicted these two forces would wage a final spiritual war, just as the nations of Earth were preparing to fight. In 1988 Robertson was widely lambasted as a crackpot and a fear monger; this one issue of *Perspective* alone would have furnished his opponents with an amazing amount of material. According to his calculations, by 1980 the Antichrist was at least twenty-seven years old. Also, based on his understanding of the Old Testament, the battle of Armageddon would start in 1982, and seven years of intense suffering would follow. These were going to be "nightmare" years and whoever was elected president in 1980 would "be faced with a challenge more grave than that which has faced any world leader in modern history."[35] After seven pages of these end-of-the-world warnings, Robertson concluded by reminding his audience that "times will be terribly hard, but we will survive."[36] Such rhetoric sounds similar to the warnings of religious leaders like Jim Jones or David Koresh who led their followers to commit mass suicide. However, Robertson's comments were meant to be encouragement, not a tool to control the minds of his followers. He urged people to get involved politically at every level. His call made sense because it was exactly what he was preparing to do.

In 1978 Robertson made his first foray into politics, and he did so as a Democrat. The Senate seat once held by A. Willis Robertson was again up for grabs, and Pat Robertson supported Norfolk businessman G. Conoly Phillips. There were nine men running for the party's nomination, and Phillips was the least known. Thanks to Robertson, however, he was able to walk into the convention at Williamsburg with enough delegates to place him third. One journalist wrote that this was the first time Robertson used his "invisible army" tactics that served him so well during his 1988 campaign for president.[37] The senator's son turned televangelist gave a rousing speech in support of his candidate. He predicted that the party would heed the desires of the nation's fifty million evangelical Christians because they were a "sleeping giant."[38] Phillips did not win the nomination but remained a close friend of Robertson and even sat on the board of his university. That convention was Robertson's last involvement in Democratic Party politics. It had been the party of evangelicals when he was a young man, but those days were gone. Years later he would say that he never left the Democratic Party, it left him. Robertson was right: At least politically he could not go home again.

As the 1980 presidential election neared many evangelicals uneasily viewed political activity. The best example of this cautious marriage of born-again religion and politics is the 1980 Washington for Jesus rally. The event was promoted as nonpartisan; however, when hundreds of thousands of evangelical Christians and their leaders descend on the nation's capital in an election year, there were obvious political ramifications.

The rally was held on April 29, 1980, a date chosen by Pat Robertson because it was on that day in 1607 that the first permanent English colony was founded in the future United States.[39] The rally was originally planned by local Norfolk area pastor John Gimenez, who told Robertson of his idea of having a prayer meeting on the steps of the Capitol. About six months later Bill Bright, the founder of Campus Crusade for Christ, had a similar vision and joined forces with Robertson, who had now taken a leading role in planning the rally. The three men sent out thousands of letters and set up meetings across the nation in hopes of bringing one million people to the rally.[40] It was one of the first times that Charismatic Christians Robertson and Gimenez teamed up with non-Charismatic evangelical Bill Bright.

As much as they tried to claim that the event was politically neutral, favor for the Republican Party was there at the inception, and continued to grow. In a letter mailed to pastors explaining the rally's goals and focus, Gimenez explained how God told him to plan the event. He explained a vision of David and Goliath, and to him, the evangelical Christians were clearly playing the role of David. "Even as David aimed at Goliath's head and slew him, so we have to go to the capitol—the head of government—where unrighteousness is being legislated."[41] The scriptural base used for the meeting was 2 Chronicles 7:14: "If my people, who are called by my name will humble themselves and pray and seek my face and turn from their wicked ways, then I will hear and forgive their sins and heal their land." This was, ironically, the verse that Jimmy Carter had planned on using for his 1976 inaugural address, but he thought it was too sectarian and harsh and chose another verse. The stated goal of the rally was to "call God's people to repentance," a seemingly simple plan until one asks what they needed to repent for, and why Washington, D.C., was the place to make such a spiritual show of force. If, as Gimenez wrote, "unrighteousness is being legislated" while the president and Congress were controlled by Democrats, did this mean that their rally would support Republican candidates? This was what many people feared was the real reason for the meeting. It was also what others hoped for.

On the day of the event, approximately two hundred thousand people showed up at the mall, although the official Washington for Jesus tally put that number at four hundred thousand. Most prominent evangelical leaders of the time spoke at the meeting. Besides Gimenez, Robertson, and Bright, speakers included Jim Bakker, Robert Schuler, James Robison, and a host of other leaders, each talking on the theme of bringing the nation back to God. Ten years later, Robertson claimed that the event was both nonpartisan and responsible for Reagan's victory in 1980 and shifting the Senate toward the Republicans. The reason for these GOP victories was a revival that had swept across America due to the rally.[42]

Notable absentees at the event included Billy Graham, who thought the meeting was too political, and Jerry Falwell, who was busy organizing the Moral Majority. Falwell had been holding patriotic rallies around the nation to coincide with the Bicentennial. He was approached by secular New Right leaders Richard Viguerie and Paul Weyrich, who convinced him to form the Moral Majority in 1979. This group was the focal point of the Christian Right actions in the late 1970s and early 1980s. When looking for someone to run the group, Viguerie and Weyrich purposely neglected to talk to Robertson. He had seemed to want nothing to do with politics. Weyrich had also considered having James Robison lead the Moral Majority, but Robison was only willing to lend money and support to a committee; he had no interest in running the organization.[43] Falwell was more than willing to adjust his agenda to fit that of his new coworkers, and the Moral Majority was born. Through this group, Falwell was able to join the ranks of religious leaders like Billy Graham, who were able to meet with the nation's leaders and give counsel. What Falwell discovered was that access to power did not necessarily equal having power.

There were other Christian Right political organizations that were founded about the same time. One of the most important was the Religious Roundtable. The organization, started by Ed McAteer, was designed to be another interest group for the Christian Right. Robertson was an original member in 1979, but quickly lost interest in the group. In August 1980 he spoke at its national convention, which featured Republican presidential candidate Ronald Reagan. However, a month later, Robertson's opinion of the group soured, as did, perhaps, his role as one of fifty-six council members. Publicly Robertson said that he did not want to take away from preaching the Gospel.[44] He also thought that the council had interfered with such events as the Washington for Jesus rally and given it an unacceptably political tint.[45] He realized the problems that were bound to arise when politically naive evangelicals got involved with secular politicians. He had stepped down publicly, but privately he remained active.

Robertson is always a man of action, and he soon began his next adventure; the pursuit of political power in its own right. Within months of leaving the Religious Roundtable, Robertson announced the formation of his own group: the Freedom Council. Its announced goal was to teach Christians how to be involved in politics. In many ways the council was the precursor of the Christian Coalition. The council was not a direct mail organization, like the Moral Majority, focusing instead on lobbying in Washington, D.C., and grassroots organizing. For the first few years of its life the council focused on voter education and communicating with the Reagan White House. However, around 1984 it gradually became a covert arm of Robertson's presidential campaign. Robertson's political foes commented that the council was always a front for his presidential ambitions. Was Robertson planning on running for office as early as 1980? Probably not, but he was intent on being a power broker rather than a pawn.

The first phase of the New Christian Right was in full swing by 1980, and Robertson was still unsure what role he should play. He did not want to appear to be a pawn as Falwell did, or to be one of many in a group like the members of the Religious Roundtable; he wanted to be his own man. He was content to grow his own empire and wait for a time when he could have a political group that he could run. Fear of an imminent tribulation only encouraged him to become more involved in every aspect of life, from promoting CBN, to electing conservatives, to trying to keep the evangelical movement theologically pure. Always a man of action, Robertson was unlikely to remain politically sidelined for long.

If the first phase of the modern Christian Right movement, the part led by Falwell, was about gaining a political voice, the second phase, led by Robertson, made its goal political power in its own right. The inspiration for this was

Ronald Reagan, a strong conservative who placated the Christian Right better than the evangelical Jimmy Carter ever could. However, Robertson was disappointed by Reagan as well. He was both disheartened and energized by Reagan's presidency. Once Robertson realized that access to power was not enough he would spend the next fifteen years trying to get it on his own terms.

Notes

1. Vinson Synan, *The Holiness-Pentecostal Tradition: Charismatic Movements in the Twentieth Century* (Grand Rapids, Mich.: Eerdmans, 1997), 264.

2. S. David Moore, *The Shepherding Movement: Controversy and Charismatic Ecclesiology* (London: T&T Clark International, 2003), 57.

3. Synan, *The Holiness-Pentecostal Tradition*, 265.

4. Moore, *The Shepherding Movement*, 93.

5. Moore, *The Shepherding Movement*, 95.

6. Moore, *The Shepherding Movement*, 99–100.

7. Synan, *The Holiness-Pentecostal Tradition*, 266.

8. Christian Broadcasting Network, *The CBN Ministry Handbook: Biblical Solutions to Everyday Problems* (Wheaton, Ill.: Tyndale, 1985), 218.

9. Gary North and Gary DeMar, *Christian Reconstruction: What It Is, What It Isn't* (Tyler, Tex.: Institute for Christian Economics, 1991), 81–82. Also see H. Wayne House and Thomas Ice, *Dominion Theology: Blessing or Curse?* (Portland, Ore.: Multnomah Press, 1988), 17.

10. Rousas John Rushdoony, *The Institutes of Biblical Law* (Nutley, N.J.: Craig Press, 1973), 4.

11. Rushdoony, *The Institutes of Biblical Law*, 777.

12. Bruce Barron, *Heaven on Earth? The Social and Political Agendas of Dominion Theology* (Grand Rapids, Mich.: Zondervan, 1992), 14.

13. Russell Chandler, "Leaders Assail 'Moral Bankruptcy of Humanism and State,'" *Los Angeles Times*, March 29, 1986.

14. Chandler, "Leaders Assail 'Moral Bankruptcy of Humanism and State.'"

15. Kevin Phillips, *American Theocracy: The Peril and Politics of Radical Religion, Oil, and Borrowed Money in the 21st Century* (New York: Viking, 2006), 243.

16. North and DeMar, *Christian Reconstruction*, 122.

17. *The 700 Club*, April 16, 1980. CBN, Regent University Special Collections (RUA).

18. Pat Robertson, *Answers to 200 of Life's Most Probing Questions* (New York: Thomas Nelson Publishing, 1984), 224.

19. Pat Robertson, interview by author, tape recording, Virginia Beach, Va., May 25, 2000.

20. Phillips, *American Theocracy*, 215.

21. Phillips, *American Theocracy*, 243.

22. Phillips, *American Theocracy*, 244.

23. North and DeMar, *Christian Reconstruction*, 62.

24. George M. Marsden, *Fundamentalism and American Culture* (Oxford: Oxford University Press, 1980), 46.

25. Sydney E. Alhstrom, *A Religious History of the American People* (New Haven, Conn.: Yale University Press, 1972), 810.

26. Paul Boyer, *When Time Shall Be No More* (Cambridge, Mass.: Harvard University Press, 1992).

27. Daniel Wojcik, *The End of the World as We Know It; Faith, Fatalism, and Apocalypse in America* (New York: New York University Press, 1997), 7.

28. Robertson, *Answers to 200 of Life's Most Probing Questions*, 156.

29. Pat Robertson, *Bring It On: Tough Questions. Candid Answers* (Nashville, Tenn.: W Publishing Group, 2003).

30. Barron, *Heaven on Earth?* 115.

31. Robertson, *Answers to 200 of Life's Most Probing Questions*, 57.

32. Pat Robertson, *Pat Robertson's Perspective*, March 1979.

33. Robertson, *Pat Robertson's Perspective*, March 1979.

34. Robertson, *Pat Robertson's Perspective*, March 1979.

35. Robertson, *Pat Robertson's Perspective*, March 1979.

36. Robertson, *Pat Robertson's Perspective*, February–March 1980.

37. Garrett Epps, "Voices of '88," *Washington Post*, February 14, 1988.

38. Donald Baker, "The Politics of Piety," *Washington Post*, June 11, 1978.

39. Press Release, "Q&A with Pastor John Gimenez," Washington for Jesus rally. RUA.

40. Jeffery Hadden and Charles Swann, *Prime Time Preachers: The Rising Power of Televangelism* (Boston: Addison Wesley, 1981), 128.

41. Press release, Washington for Jesus rally.

42. Pat Robertson, *The New Millennium* (Dallas, Tex.: Word Publishing, 1990), 93.

43. Paul Weyrich, interview by author, tape recording, Washington, D.C., August 16, 2000.

44. Robertson, *Pat Robertson's Perspective*, September 1980.

45. Frederick Talbott, "Pat Robertson Backs away from Politics," *Virginian-Pilot*, September 30, 1980.

CHAPTER 6

THE REAGAN MIRAGE

O N the surface, the evangelical community's response to the beginning of Ronald Reagan's presidency appeared eerily similar to its initial reaction to that of Jimmy Carter. Both men had claimed to be conservative Christians, and as presidential candidates both had promised to put many conservative Protestants into office. Evangelicals had largely abandoned Carter for Reagan in the 1980 election, and if anything, their hopes were higher with Reagan due to his conservative social views.

Ronald Reagan quickly became the darling of the Christian Right during the 1980 presidential campaign, even though sitting president Jimmy Carter was himself an evangelical Christian. Reagan advocated prayer and the teaching of creationism in public schools. In August 1980 he spoke at the national convention of the Religious Roundtable, a group led by fifty-six prominent evangelical and Fundamentalist religious leaders. The future president's speech before the organization became one of the most quoted stories in the history of the Christian Right. While Reagan was being driven from the airport to the convention center in Dallas, Texas, Pastor James Robison, a televangelist and rising star of the Christian Right, prepped him on what he should say. Since the Religious Roundtable was officially nonpartisan, it could not endorse candidates, but it was suggested that Reagan make the statement, "I know this is nonpartisan, so you can't endorse me, but I want you to know that I endorse you."[1] Reagan loved the line, and he received an enthusiastic response when he repeated it to the twenty-five hundred people in attendance. The quote became a signal to many politically conservative evangelicals and Fundamentalists that Reagan was with them in heart and soul.

The 1980s was the defining decade for Pat Robertson. While the previous twenty years had been a time of growth for his television ministry, in the 1980s all of his hard work began to bloom. He went from a TV preacher who was only recognized in his own world to a national celebrity. Robertson also began the climb from comfortable businessman to multimillionaire. While there were many televangelists who appeared poised to make the jump to a higher level of fame and influence, by the end of the decade it was clear that Robertson was the only one who had been able to take center stage and stay there.

The earliest and still popular conception of the Reagan era is that it was the high-water mark for the Christian Right, and they went into decline after 1988; however, the opposite is true. It is best to view the Reagan administration as a period of growth in which the Christian Right enjoyed a high profile but had little tangible success in politics. While the president spoke of his personal dislike of abortion and the need for prayer in public schools, he was unwilling to expend any of his considerable political capital to move those issues forward. Many Christian Right leaders realized that being granted a meeting with the president was no substitute for having their agendas made into law. As one anonymous Reagan administration official put it, "[W]e want to keep the Moral Majority types so close to us they can't move their arms."[2] For religious conservatives the Reagan era was a time of photo opportunities, kind words, and little else.

When the politically expedient mythology is stripped away, it is clear that Reagan's presidency had a twofold effect on the Christian Right movement. First, it demoralized those like Jerry Falwell who realized the limits of political pressure groups. By the mid-1980s Falwell largely withdrew from politics and only occasionally commented on current events. The second and more powerful effect was on men like Pat Robertson, who was also disappointed with Reagan but took the opposite route. Robertson realized that the only way that conservative Christians could be effective in politics was to hold office on their own. Eight years of frustration with Reagan led Robertson to run for president in 1988. The Christian Right had never been the margin of victory for Reagan, in either 1980 or 1984. If Robertson wanted to get his views across, it would have to be from a position of power. Robertson's campaign led to the creation of the Christian Coalition, which was the pivotal factor in both the Republican takeover of the House of Representatives in 1994 and the election of George W. Bush in 2000.

Robertson had such high hopes for Reagan's presidency that he finally returned to the realm of politics, this time for good. Reagan had made a series of promises to evangelicals during the 1980 campaign, and it was expected that he would live up to them. Perhaps the most controversial was Reagan's comment that he would appoint evangelicals to his administration in proportion to their numbers in the population. Reagan's inner circle showed no interest in following through on the president's impossible promise. Besides, there were not enough evangelicals with government experience to fill the 20 to 40 percent of the openings. Robertson never showed any anger at Reagan for this failure to hire theologically conservative Christians. Reagan never made the promise to Robertson personally as Carter had done, and so he had little reason to feel personally lied to.

Perhaps the biggest blow to the Christian Right during the Reagan era occurred soon after the president was shot in March 1981. Senate majority leader Howard Baker and White House chief of staff James Baker made a joint announcement that as long as the economy of the nation was in turmoil, social issues would be put on the back burner. They referred to social issues as both "collateral" and "emotional" and claimed that the GOP was united in this view.[3] The next day Reagan gave an interview for the *Washington Post* where he said nearly the same thing.[4] For many evangelicals, this was a sign that the Republicans only wanted their votes. Paul Weyrich, the founder of the Moral Majority, was incensed. He believes that this was the most serious single blow that religious conservatives faced during the Reagan years.[5] Weyrich called a special meeting of Christian Right leaders, and Robertson was there. Weyrich told the group that Reagan would not have won if it had not been for their help. Several senators owed their victories to the Christian Right as well, and thanks to their efforts the Republicans controlled the Senate for the first time since 1954. The Christian Right was valuable but was being taken for granted.

Weyrich recalls saying, "[C]ould you imagine if the Democrats had won and they issued a statement saying Civil Rights legislation has to go on the back burner?"[6] When other Christian Right leaders were not convinced, Weyrich pressed the issue. "You have to show righteous indignation over this and you can't just take it. You have to say, 'Sorry this isn't acceptable.'" When he finished speaking, the other leaders treated him as if he had leprosy. "They told me to calm down and give these people their due," he recalls.[7] Christian Right leaders had surrendered to Republican Party political persuasion while they were still celebrating their victory.

Another sign of their lack of real influence came when White House deputy chief of staff Michael Deaver was quoted in the *Washington Post* as saying that the only way the leadership of the Christian Right could get into the building was "by the back door." Deaver ran into Jerry Falwell when he was about to visit Reagan, and he begged Falwell not to mention his statement to the president. Falwell did so anyway.[8] Robertson never showed any anger at Reagan for the treatment his coreligionists received. The president's conservative political agenda was enough to keep him quiet.

These events should have demonstrated to both Falwell and Robertson that the Reagan administration was going to be less than forthcoming in all of its dealings with conservative Christians. However, not everyone took these events as bad omens. Some, like Jerry Falwell, spent the eight years that Reagan was in office trying to make good on the promises of 1980. Regardless of what Reagan's advisors said or did, Falwell always expected the president to come through for him. Meanwhile, others like Robertson were friendly to Reagan only so long as their agendas meshed, which did not last for long. An analysis of their correspondence with the president shows that Falwell and Robertson were treated in very different ways.

The volume and general tone of the correspondence between Reagan and Falwell reveals a warm personal friendship. Over the eight years that Reagan was president he received regular letters from the leader of the Moral Majority on a host of issues both important and trivial. Unlike Robertson's, Falwell's letters to the president are rarely critical or entreating. Falwell had spent considerable time and effort working for Reagan in 1980, and he was not about to jeopardize the relationship. While some politicians in Washington, D.C., were refusing to take social issues seriously, Falwell remained silent, hoping that the president would respect his faithful support. While Reagan was appreciative of Falwell's help, the president was hit with criticism from the Left, even though little of the Christian Right agenda was being supported.

Perhaps the best example of what the White House thought of Falwell can be found in a memo to the president written by Assistant for Public Liaison Faith Whittlesey. She was in charge of dealing with religious groups and wanted Reagan to be reminded of how important Falwell had been. Falwell had an appointment to meet with Reagan in March 1983, and as was the case with most meetings, the president was given a briefing memo for the event. The memo contained a bulleted list of accomplishments of Falwell and the Moral Majority, along with other pertinent information. Below this was an interesting comment on Falwell. Whittlesey wrote, "[U]nlike some other national conservative organization leaders, Dr. Falwell has never criticized you or Reagan administration policy. He has been strongly supportive on economic and social issues."[9] Interestingly enough, among the "suggested talking points" for the president was the question of how the administration could "recapture the enthusiasm in the fundamentalist and evangelical community. Clearly their political activism declined between 1980 and 1982."[10] Undoubtedly, Reagan was interested in their support as the 1984 campaign approached.

While Robertson was not as publicly supportive of the president as Falwell was, the Freedom Council was quietly moving the president's agenda forward. Previous studies of Robertson have barely mentioned the Freedom Council, largely because evidence of its activities is scarce and because the council was written off as merely an arm of Robertson's presidential campaign. While it is true that Robertson used the council to forward his own agenda, its first few years were actually spent lobbying the president on a variety of issues. The council was originally an honest attempt by Robertson to involve evangelical Christians in the political process. The Freedom Council's board of directors included Ben Armstrong, head of the National Religious Broadcasters; Beverly LaHaye, who ran the largest evangelical women's group; and Demos Shakarian, the president of the Full Gospel Business Men's Fellowship.[11] The council was not a group of Robertson followers who would blindly support him. However, the Freedom Council's activities from 1981 to 1984 were very different from those in 1985 when Robertson began to consider running for the White House.

The first major piece of lobbying that the Freedom Council focused on was a push for a constitutional amendment allowing the reestablishment of prayer in public school. Senate resolution 199 would have forbidden the state or federal government from interfering in the right to pray on public property.[12] The council lobbied Congress to support the prayer amendment and sent pamphlets to churches and religious leaders around the country that contained specific information on how to contact Congress and how to phrase their letters. There was also a request for donations to help promote the amendment.[13] The president's support for the amendment was restrained to say the least. He only supported it publicly three times: once during his weekly radio address, before a meeting of the National Association of Evangelicals, and once in a rose garden ceremony attended by Jerry Falwell. Behind the scenes however, Reagan was unwilling to actively push for passage of the amendment.[14]

In addition to phone calls and letters to Congress, Robertson made an appearance before the Senate Judiciary Committee in August 1982. His testimony began with a recounting of his version of the history of the United States as a Christian nation (a conservative evangelical Protestant nation at that). Robertson blamed the American Civil Liberties Union (ACLU), which he claimed was formed "to defend Bolsheviks." He spent the bulk of his time discussing various attacks on religious freedom. He also criticized religious leaders who appeared before the committee to denounce the amendment: "These church officials do not speak for the rank and file of the American people."[15] Robertson ended his comments by claiming that since 94 percent of Americans believed in God, it was Congress's duty to support the amendment.

Despite his speech and the work of the Freedom Council, the amendment was doomed to failure. Robertson, however, was able to make this loss a gain for his political agenda. Within months of the final defeat of the amendment, Robertson was using it as a fund-raising device. In a letter sent out in early 1984, Robertson wrote that politicians did not fear evangelicals because they believe that Christians "have the shortest memory of any group of people in the United States."[16] Robertson then listed recent events that he claimed were part of an attack on religious liberties that was being led by "our elected officials."

The Freedom Council did not limit its activities to fighting for the prayer in school amendment. It attempted to start grassroots organizations in each congressional district. Using the motto "prayer, education and action," the council's stated goals were to "educate believers on the Christian history of our nation, on our civic responsibilities, and on our Christian alternatives to obstacles to religious freedom."[17] To this end the council spent most of its time fighting local battles, focusing on religious freedom, home schooling, and prayer in school.

Members of the Freedom Council received "Backgrounders" and "Special Briefings," which were newsletters detailing both national and regional activities of the organization. The council also sponsored and distributed position papers written by experts. Some were written by constitutional lawyers, and one was even written by Franky Schaeffer, son of famous evangelical philosopher Francis Schaeffer.[18] The White House liaison for religious affairs, Faith Whittlesey, appeared at the 1984 Freedom Council meeting and brought with her a message from President Reagan. The letter pledged the president's continued support for the prayer in school amendment.[19] The following day Carolyn Sundseth, also a White House liaison, spoke before the six hundred Freedom Council leaders present. Sundseth also presented a letter from President Reagan that praised the Freedom Council for its work.[20]

While the Freedom Council was doing clearly legal political education work across the country, by mid-1984 the council's leadership had started down the slippery slope of questionable political involvement. In May 1984 the White House sent a series of questions about President Reagan's religious beliefs to Freedom Council leader Ted Pantaleo. The questions were in anticipation of the 1984 presidential election, and the council provided answers for Reagan to use. The questions related to Reagan's use of religion in a pluralistic society and, tellingly, why he did not seem to be so personally religious.[21] The first question was "How can the president be so outspoken on religious subjects, when in his own life he is not a church attender?" The Freedom Council answered that question with another question: "How does so powerful and recognizable a public figure enter into congregational worship destroying the experience both for himself and for others?" The memo went on to suggest that Reagan's staff hinted it was the president's fear that people would think he was "exploiting Christianity to impress people or to rally Christian votes." The memo ended by stating that Reagan was helped in his spiritual growth by entertainer Pat Boone and the pastor of the president's former church in Bel Air, California.[22] The fact that an outside group had to help the White House answer the question of Reagan's casual church attendance is a sign of how poorly the White House understood the Religious Right. It also shows how badly the Christian Right needed Reagan to appear to be a conservative Christian. As shown in this case, Christian Right groups were willing to supply the White House with religious terms, then use those terms as proof of the president's faith. Clearly by this point politics was more important to many Christian Right leaders than religious beliefs.

The White House's desire to garner the support of Christian Right leaders was demonstrated in January 1984 just days before the annual National Religious Broadcasters meeting in Washington, D.C. James Baker and Edwin Meese were scheduled to have a meeting with several prominent evangelical leaders. Both Jerry Falwell and Pat Robertson were invited, and had they attended it would have been their first meeting. They both decided to send lieutenants instead; however, other prominent religious leaders, including James Draper, the president of the Southern Baptist Convention, had planned to attend.[23] The White House staff's primary concern was something that they listed as not to be discussed in the meeting. Many evangelical leaders were upset over the federal government's treatment of Christian schools' tax-exempt status, and the White House feared a backlash if a meeting with these men was not held. In particular, they pointed out that if the issue was not addressed before the convention, it would become a major topic of conversation. The memo warned, "[L]ook for serious criticism of the administration there if some outreach is not made before then."[24]

During the 1984 campaign, the Christian Right and the Moral Majority in particular appeared to be declining in power. With Reagan's stunning victory over Democrat Walter Mondale it was impossible for any one group to take responsibility for the margin of the president's victory. The last time the Moral Majority basked in power was in 1986 when state and national leaders had one last meeting at the White House. Ironically, the meeting was held in the Old Executive Office Building's Indian Treaty Room, an ironic sign that not all alliances are forever.

Despite all of the outward political turmoil, Reagan and Robertson were on personally friendly terms, much better than Robertson had been with Jimmy Carter. In late 1981 Robertson was asked to join the "Presidential task force on victims of crime." The committee submitted its report to Reagan a year later.[25] While this committee did not relate to his expertise in business or broadcasting, it was an important trophy to Robertson and his followers. Reagan was willing to use the evangelical constituency in ways that would allow them to brag to their own followers, without threatening the alliance of voters that he had worked so hard to create.

Another important trophy for Robertson was that he was able to interview President Reagan for *The 700 Club* on three separate occasions. Reagan first appeared in 1983, then twice in 1985, once in April and September. Reagan was the first sitting president to be interviewed on the Christian Broadcasting Network, and the interviews were rebroadcast several times.

The interviews between Robertson and Reagan covered a wide range of topics. Their April 1985 interview was mostly confined to spiritual questions. Many of Robertson's questions were tinged with eschatology, and Reagan's staff was unsure of how to handle them. Robertson's questions had been sent to the White House in advance and several different answers were worked out.[26]

Robertson asked Reagan how he used the Bible in forming public policy. The president's staff crafted a cautious response stating that the Bible gave broad principles of love for one's fellow man but did not help with specifics. Other questions included "As God looks at America in 1985, what do you think he sees? What pleases him?" Another asked why Washington, D.C., was so resistant to a prayer amendment when the nation seemed to want it passed. Reagan was told to disagree with the notion that Washington was resistant to the prayer amendment, although some individual politicians might be. Finally, and most interestingly, was the debate over Robertson's question about why Reagan no longer referred to the Soviet Union as the "Evil Empire." The first proposed answer reserved the right to use the term when it was appropriate. The second answer demonstrated the thawing of tensions between the two superpowers. It was suggested that the president say that Americans and Soviets were both "children of God and we must all find a way to live in peace."[27] Copies of the interview are held by the Christian Broadcasting Network (CBN) and difficult to obtain, so it is not known if Reagan used these answers. At this point, Robertson still thought that he and Reagan had a lot in common both politically and religiously, but in just a few short months, given the tone of their next meeting, their relationship had changed significantly.

Their second interview of 1985, held in mid-September, dealt primarily with political issues. The majority of the questions that Robertson asked concerned economic issues and taxes. The majority of the questions were so different from the first interview that it seems that they could have easily come from two different men. This second interview is a sign of the change of heart that Robertson had undergone. He no longer expected Reagan to push conservative evangelical Christian goals. Robertson realized that if a religious conservative was going to be in the White House, it was going to be him. At this point he just wanted Reagan to follow a conservative political agenda. However, near the end of the interview, Robertson asked one question out of the blue. He told Reagan that "word reached us that a member of the White House Staff was dispatched . . . to Iran" to help free six American hostages that were held by Iran-backed groups in Lebanon. Reagan was surprised by the question and replied, "I can't really talk about what we are doing." The president's staff issued a statement saying that Reagan's comments did not mean that they were doing anything in Iran at all. In fact, the administration was by then waist deep in what was later known as the Iran-Contra scandal, and Robertson's question and Reagan's reply came up in the Senate hearings. The interview ended cordially with Robertson stating that he believed that the American media were being manipulated by the Soviet Union. This was the last interview Reagan gave for CBN, and it was the last time the two men met before Robertson announced his decision to run for president. Despite the lack of support Reagan had shown for evangelical political causes, Robertson and the president had much in common politically. While Robertson did not get everything on his wish list, Reagan was conservative enough for his tastes. He could console himself with the knowledge that at the very least the nation was headed in the right direction.

One area where Robertson and Reagan's conservative political agendas crossed paths was events in Central America. In 1979 the Nicaraguan right-wing, pro-American regime of Anastasio Somoza was overthrown by leftist rebels called the Sandinistas. Then president Jimmy Carter offered help to the Sandinistas and their leader Daniel Ortega, even as many Republicans feared that they were merely a communist front. When Reagan became president, the aid to the Ortega government stopped and funding for the rebels began. When the new Nicaraguan government appealed to the Soviet Union and Cuba for help, this was taken as proof of the Sandinistas' communist intentions.

The new rebel group, called the Contras, was comprised mostly of former Somoza regime soldiers. The Contras waged a ten-year war against the Sandinista government, killing thousands in their effort to retake power. Reagan's funding of the rebels was perhaps the most controversial effort of his presidency, and it was constantly criticized by Democrats. In 1984 the Democrat-controlled Congress passed the Boland Amendment, which prohibited any federal money from being directly or indirectly given to support the Contras. The Iran-Contra scandal that erupted in 1986 was the direct result of Reagan's staff trying to find secret ways to fund the Central American conflict. In November 1986 a Lebanese newspaper broke the story that the White House had sold weapons to Iran in violation of American law so that Iran would free American hostages held by their allies in Lebanon. The money from the arms sales was funneled to the Contras and their war in Nicaragua.[28]

Years before Reagan began his ill-fated campaign to secretly fund the Contras in Nicaragua, Robertson was doing more than the American government to help the rebels' cause. Besides regularly using *The 700 Club* as a bully pulpit for anticommunism, Robertson gave practical help as well. In 1983 Robertson made a weeklong trip to Central America, where he toured Guatemala, Honduras, and El Salvador. While on his trip he visited a refugee camp in Honduras and talked with Contra soldiers. This visit was broadcast on the Cable News Network (CNN), and Robertson was shown calling the Contras "God's army." This set off minor protests from other religious leaders, including the Catholic bishop of Richmond, who denounced Robertson's statement.[29] A CBN reporter spent weeks in the refugee camps that bordered Nicaragua and reported on *The 700 Club* about the flow of refugees from the countryside and the battles of the Contras.

The next stop was El Salvador, the most controversial nation in Latin America that was supported by the United States. During his four-day visit Robertson met with military leaders and toured the countryside as their guest. When he returned to *The 700 Club*, he tried to give his viewers a different picture of the nation. "The press has shown to the American people a totally false picture of El Salvador, its present and its future," Robertson claimed. Contrary to this picture Robertson claimed, "[T]he left is as much guilty of massacres as the right."[30]

Robertson also visited Guatemala, destabilized by a series of coups and a minor rebel insurgency. Earlier in the year he had written the foreword to a book about Efrain Rios Montt, an evangelical Christian who had led a bloodless coup and ruled Guatemala from March 1982 until August 1983. Robertson had traveled to the country just a week after the coup that brought Montt to power. He praised Montt for ending the death squads and for fighting the communists. Robertson wrote that a combination of Soviet military aid and left-leaning world media had sought to destroy the man and his dreams. Robertson wrote, "The only recourse was prayer," but he did far more than pray for other groups in Central America.[31]

Since the Democrat-controlled Congress prevented the president from giving aid legally to the Contras, Robertson decided to step in. In May 1985 Robertson wrote a letter to the president announcing that CBN was joining with AmeriCares to give a total of $20 million to the Contras. CBN was to give $2 million just for transportation of humanitarian aid material to Central America. Robertson wrote that he hoped the aid would "give hope and encouragement to those in the region who struggle for freedom." He also praised Reagan for his "vision and courage in opposing the spread of totalitarianism" in the Americas.[32]

In 1984 the *New York Times* estimated that conservative American groups had given $17 million in nonmilitary aid to the Contras. The largest donor was CBN's Operation Blessing, which had given more than $7 million. Most of the donations were food, clothing, and shelter for refugees. The materials were shipped to Central America courtesy of the U.S. Navy. The Pentagon was originally reluctant to help ship supplies to the region, until ordered to do so by the White House.[33]

The politically liberal evangelical magazine *Sojourners* reported that Robertson was actually shipping weapons to the Contras. The charge was eventually rescinded when Robertson threatened to sue. While Robertson did not ship weapons to the region, it stands to reason, although there is no corroborative evidence, that the Central Intelligence Agency could funnel more money for arms since groups like Robertson's were handling the humanitarian aid. During his presidential campaign, Robertson called for an invasion of Nicaragua to be led by the Contras but supported and funded by the U.S. government. He told an audience in Miami, "[A]s president I would encourage the formation of a government in exile. . . . I would assist the government of Free Nicaragua to achieve a land bridge into the mainland of Nicaragua itself."[34] Robertson was willing to go further than any other prominent politician in order to stop the spread of communism. That was the luxury of not being in office; he could make officeholders look bad for their inaction and yet not have to do anything himself. In May of 1985 Robertson sent a letter to Reagan and North Carolina senator Jesse Helms, which discussed a poll on aid to the contras that CBN conducted.[35] While the White House was always gracious in response to these types of letters, the administration never used the numbers that Robertson sent.

Another place where Reagan and Robertson's foreign policy aligned was South Africa. In 1986 *The 700 Club* did a series of reports on South Africa and the white government's struggle against the African National Congress. While many socially liberal religious leaders decried the apartheid regime, Robertson openly supported it because he felt that it was a bastion against communism. For Robertson, everything else was secondary to defeating what he saw as the enemies of God. Robertson sent a copy of *The 700 Club* program to Freedom Council's Dick Thompson to have it forwarded to Pat Buchanan, who in turn promised to show it to the president.[36] Reagan's attitude toward South Africa was one of his most controversial foreign policy stands, and Robertson was one of Reagan's few allies on this policy.

If there was something even more telling about the relationship between the president and Robertson than their interview and foreign policy, it was their correspondence. While Jerry Falwell was accustomed to having direct access to the president, Robertson had to settle for back channels and polite refusals. The televangelist communicated with Reagan much more often than he did with Carter. While he rarely visited the White House, as Jerry Falwell did, he wanted to keep in touch. During Reagan's first year in office and into 1982, the letters were restricted to the occasional cordial thank you notes. It was not until June 1982 that Robertson made his first political statement to the president. Robertson wrote to Reagan in support of American ambassador to the United Nations Jeane Kirkpatrick. The next year he wrote repeatedly in defense of James Watt, the secretary of interior. Watt, an evangelical Christian, was one of Reagan's most controversial cabinet appointments. Besides being openly hostile to the environmental movement, he often made outrageous statements that only made him appear more extremely antienvironment. Robertson described him as "a Reagan man," and just one of many victims of "political assassination attempts aimed at your advisors by those who are the enemies of your programs."[37] The letter garnered a two-sentence reply from a Reagan staffer a month later.[38] Robertson continued to write the president on a regular basis. He had hoped that the Reagan presidency would mean access to power when he needed it. However, when Robertson tried twice to cash in on that access he was rebuffed.

CBN opened up a West Coast broadcast facility in July 1982, and to celebrate the city of Corona, California, declared July 9 "Pat Robertson Day." Robertson wrote the White House and asked Reagan to call in during the live broadcast from California. The administration replied that the president could send a telegram. The draft of the telegram is one of the most telling pieces of evidence concerning the Robertson–Reagan relationship. At the bottom of the draft was written, "Should this go as telegram only and on July 8 (one day ahead) to minimize impact?" Next to it, several different hands wrote "yes."[39] Robertson got no call, just a telegram to show on *The 700 Club*. Clearly, the Christian Right was not as important to Reagan as he was to them. The president had taken considerable pains to form a coalition of blue-collar workers (called Reagan Democrats) and moderate Republicans. He was not about to upset that balance by appearing to be too closely aligned with the Christian Right.

Robertson offered no help to Reagan during the 1984 presidential campaign. The bulk of Robertson's letters that year asked the president to attend the opening of CBN University's new library.[40] The library, which cost $13.2 million, was the centerpiece of the growing campus. The building featured huge columns and was built in the same Georgian style as the CBN broadcast building. This was the biggest event in the short life of the school and Robertson was determined to have the president attend.

Reagan and his staff, however, had different ideas. The summer and fall of 1984 were the middle of his reelection campaign, and Reagan was not about to come to Virginia Beach and be photographed with Pat Robertson. In late 1983 and early January 1984, Robertson invited the president to attend the opening ceremonies for the library. Robertson also wrote Attorney General Edwin Meese and requested that he ask the president to attend. In March the dedication was moved to the fall and Reagan was again asked to attend. In the end, it was Ed Meese who was the featured speaker at the library's dedication, and Reagan sent another telegram.[41] From then on, Robertson wrote to the attorney general as often as to the president, although with each year he wrote less and less. It was clear that Reagan wanted votes and little else from Robertson. This caution toward Robertson is interesting considering that he was much more actively partisan then Falwell. Despite constant rebuffs from the White House he worked hard to move Reagan's agenda forward.

Unlike Falwell, Robertson had no problem writing stern letters to the president. His early letters were supportive of people like James Watt and Jeane Kirkpatrick, encouraging to Reagan.[42] The bulk of his letters after 1983 either asked for the president's time or complained about his policies. In 1985 he wrote "with some consternation" about the woman chosen to replace Faith Whittlesey, the White House liaison for religious affairs. Robertson did not explain exactly why he was opposed to Sandy Smoley, the suggested replacement. He only hinted at the problem and delivered a veiled threat, when he wrote to Donald Regan, "[T]he appointment of Smoley would be viewed by the millions of evangelical supporters of President Reagan as a direct affront and repudiation of their support."[43] Other letters that Robertson sent to the president were in the same vein, each one complaining about the administration's choices and direction.

Reagan was unsure how to handle Robertson, and that discomfort only grew as Robertson looked more and more like a Republican presidential candidate. One interesting example of the White House staff's unease with Robertson is shown in a June 1986 letter. The letter is about CBN's support for the Contras, and the first draft is filled with praise for Robertson's support. The letter ends with a quote from the Gospel of Luke about the power of giving. Handwritten notes on the draft show concern about using the correct verse. But the final version, sent in June 1986, is totally devoid of spiritual sentiment. Perhaps this was in response to the secular tone of Robertson's letters. The administration could also have had in mind that Robertson would almost certainly use any letter from the president as a means for fund-raising, and possibly for political purposes.

The final communication between the two men came in 1986 when Robertson intended to announce his candidacy for the Republican nomination in 1988. Robertson sent repeated requests to the White House to set a short meeting or phone call to inform Reagan of his plans. Pat Buchanan was Robertson's point man in the administration on this issue, and he sent Donald Regan several memos regarding it. While Reagan had met with both Vice President George H. W. Bush and former secretary of state Alexander Haig separately to talk about their campaigns, Reagan's staff shut off Robertson completely.[44] One memo stated bluntly, "[S]uch meetings have less to do with respect for the President than with every candidate's understandable desire to see himself on television." The memo also commented on the White House's view of the Reagan–Robertson relationship. "This month is not a particularly good time to emphasize Pat Robertson's close ties to the White House." The staff feared that Robertson's high negative ratings could affect the president.[45] In the end it was suggested that Robertson could pass a message along to the president through Pat Buchanan.[46]

Despite the president's reservations about his connection to the Christian Right, this image was firmly in place in the public mind. Nothing makes this connection clearer than the number of groups that arose during the Reagan era that were a liberal response to the growth of the Christian Right. The most famous anti–Christian Right group, People for the American Way (PFAW), was formed by *All in the Family* creator Norman Lear in 1981. The group found instant popularity, due in large part to the fame of its founder. Americans United for the Separation of Church and State (AUSCS) was founded in 1947 by a loose association of secular leaders and theological liberals who were strongly opposed to the mixing of church and state. Their organization also grew tremendously during the 1980s. Both organizations shared similar goals although they occasionally had different focuses. While the PFAW attacked any conservative group, it spent most of its energy on the Christian Right, especially the Moral Majority in its early years. The AUSCS focused more exclusively on the Christian Right. While both of these groups would have claimed Jerry Falwell as their biggest adversary, as the decade wore on, they increasingly found themselves at odds with Pat Robertson. As they soon discovered he could be a good deal more difficult to deal with than Falwell.

Americans United obtained most of its income from its journal *Church and State*. The magazine's cover often featured caricatures of Christian Right leaders, especially Falwell and Robertson. When Robertson first began to speak on political issues he was regularly vilified by both the AUSCS and PFAW. Robertson, who was not used to having his opinions challenged, regularly threatened to sue both groups for libel. The PFAW even collected Robertson's quotes and used them to show some of his more radical views; among the collection were several statements about People for the American Way. Robertson wrote an angry letter to the PFAW in early 1981. "In the words of the old Negro spiritual, 'Your arms are too short to box with God.' The suppression of the voice of God's servant is a terrible thing! God will fight for me against you, and he will win."[47] AUSCS staff member Robert Boston recalls, "[H]e got really mad. . . . You can't sue for libel if it's true. We knew that we had an absolute defense."[48] Robertson never sued, and after his presidential campaign, he never bothered with such threats again.

Robertson slowly learned to live with the constant attacks from these liberal groups. He began regularly to comment on them and use them to frighten his supporters. Years later he was still vitriolic about them. "Americans United is an ACLU front; Barry Lynn who is the executive director worked for the ACLU," Robertson said.[49] Earlier during a 1986 broadcast of *The 700 Club* Robertson attacked both groups vigorously. "People for the American Way has finally been unmasked as people who are essentially anti-Christian atheists," Robertson claimed.[50] Despite his aggravation at both groups, they did prove to be magnificent foils in his attacks on secular humanists and political liberals. Robertson was able to show his viewers that the bogeymen of secular humanism were real.

In essence these liberal groups became a cottage industry that grew in response to the Christian Right. As much as they disliked Robertson and his kind, they needed the Religious Right to justify their own existence. It is ironic that Robertson and these liberal groups used each other as warnings to solicit donations from their supporters. Robertson could survive without them, but the liberal groups might have had trouble selling their journals without him.

Whether Reagan liked it or not, the Christian Right was inexorably tied to his presidency. Groups like People for the American Way were determined to paint Reagan's conservative politics in as dangerous a light as possible. This meant they had to make the Christian Right look powerful and influential. Their role as power brokers was exaggerated by both right- and left-wing groups because they both used it as a fund-raising tool. Recent studies of the Reagan era have tended to present the Christian Right in a manner that is based more on evidence than on political posturing.[51] For the first time in his career, Robertson's words were carefully watched by people who actively opposed him.

In the final analysis, the Christian Right was not nearly as important to Ronald Reagan as he was to them. He gave them legitimacy in the public square, and they gave him their votes and the status of a living saint. Reagan's feelings toward the Christian Right can perhaps best be summed up in a short memo the president was given in 1981. The note was a list of people for him to call and thank for their support. Three names are listed, two of them obscure political figures unknown to most Americans. The third name is that of James Robison, the man who gave candidate Reagan the famous "endorsement" line in 1979.[52] The first two names were listed without explanation, but next to Robison was a reminder for the president.[53] Robison was a nationally known televangelist who had met with Reagan several times, yet the president needed to be reminded exactly who he was.

Paul Weyrich is more direct in his analysis of the Reagan era and the Christian Right's response to it. "Most of them [Christian Right leaders] wouldn't admit that they were disappointed. . . . [Reagan] was so nice a guy [and] they really didn't want to come to grips with the fact that he basically didn't do anything for them."[54] In 1999 two of Jerry Falwell's lieutenants from the Moral Majority, Cal Thomas and Ed Dobson, wrote *Blinded by Might*.[55] The book tells their side of the story of the Reagan era. They are blunt in their assessment: "Twenty years of fighting has brought us nothing."[56] By the end of the Reagan era, they were both tired of seeking political solutions to what they saw as spiritual problems. Scholars have come to agree with these conclusions. In his recent study of the Reagan era, John Ehrman concedes that "Reagan gave only lukewarm support to the social conservatives."[57] Conclusions such as these were almost unthinkable a few years ago.

All in all, Robertson was disappointed with Reagan on several fronts. Robertson recalls, "[W]hen Reagan was in his second term he got himself in a lot of trouble. He was under intense fire for the Iran-Contra business." For Robertson, this meant that most of his policy goals were not going to be accomplished. "I think Reagan had steam the first couple of years . . . but Democrats got the upper hand and from then on his initiatives began to sputter."[58] During his second term, "things were set in stone, either we weren't getting heard, or being represented, or we didn't think it was necessary to get through to him any more."[59] Robertson had supported two presidents who had said the right things, then compromised and left evangelicals out in the cold. His run for the presidency was a direct result of this disappointment. He had realized that one can only do so much from the outside. To be truly effective he had to control the reins of power.

Ronald Reagan's presidency was hugely inspirational for religious conservatives and continues to be so. While there were many things that he did not do for them, Reagan gave them a sense of belonging. The very fact that the president of the Unites States appeared to agree with the agenda of the Christian Right gave them tremendous power. This gift of rhetoric was inspirational and continues to fuel the modern-day Christian Right. Reagan continues to serve as an example of the limitations of political influence and a reminder that it is better to be in power than be a constituent. Their understanding of this lesson can be seen in their early support of George W. Bush in the presidential campaign of 2000. In the end Reagan's presidency was more important to the Christian Right as a symbol than as an era when they achieved any of their political goals.

Notes

1. William Martin, *With God on Our Side: The Rise of the Religious Right in America* (New York: Broadway Books, 1996), 216.

2. Lou Cannon, *President Reagan: The Role of a Lifetime* (New York: Simon & Schuster, 1991), 316.

3. Bill Peterson and David Broder, "Split in the Senate," *Washington Post*, March 27, 1981.

4. Cannon, *President Reagan*, 318.

5. Paul Weyrich, interview by author, tape recording, Washington, D.C., August 16, 2000.

6. Paul Weyrich interview.

7. Paul Weyrich interview.

8. Martin, *With God on Our Side*, 223.

9. Faith Whittlesey, memo to Ronald Reagan, March 14, 1983. Ronald Reagan Presidential Library (RRPL).

10. Whittlesey memo.

11. Freedom Council letter, circa 1983, RRPL.

12. The full text of the amendment is as follows: "Nothing in this Constitution shall be construed to prohibit individual or group prayer in public schools or other public institutions. No person shall be required by the United States or by any state to participate in prayer."

13. "Support the School Prayer Amendment." Freedom Council pamphlet. RRPL.

14. Matthew C. Moen, *The Christian Right and Congress* (Tuscaloosa: University of Alabama Press, 1989), 134.

15. "Remarks of Pat Robertson, in Support of Senate Joint Resolution 199," August 18, 1982, RRPL.

16. Pat Robertson, Freedom Council fund-raising letter, circa early 1984. RRPL.

17. Freedom Council letter, undated. RRPL.

18. Franky Schaeffer, "The Myth of Neutrality in the Media," Freedom Council position paper, 1982. RRPL.

19. Robert Reilly to Faith Whittlesey, February 15, 1984. RRPL.

20. Draft of Reagan letter to Freedom Council, February 16, 1984. RRPL.

21. Ted Pantaleo to Doug Holladay, May 9, 1984. RRPL.

22. Pantaleo to Doug Holladay.

23. White House unsigned memo, circa January 1984. RRPL.

24. White House unsigned memo.

25. President's Task Force on Victims of Crime, final report, December 1982. RRPL.

26. "Briefing Notes for Wednesday Interview with Pat Robertson," April 23, 1985, RRPL.

27. "Briefing Notes for Wednesday Interview with Pat Robertson."

28. Theodore Draper, *A Very Thin Line: The Iran-Contra Affairs* (New York: Simon & Schuster, 1991).

29. April Witt, "Robertson, Bishop at Odds on Contras," *Virginian-Pilot*, December 15, 1983.

30. "Portrayal of El Salvador Disputed," *Virginian-Pilot*, December 13, 1983.

31. Joseph Anfuso and David Sczepanski, *Efrain Rios Montt, Servant or Dictator?* (Ventura, Calif.: Vision House, 1984), x.

32. Pat Robertson to Ronald Reagan, May 8, 1985. RRPL.

33. Phillip Taubman, "Private Groups in U.S. Aiding Managua's Foes," *New York Times*, July 15, 1984.

34. April Witt, "Robertson Supports Invasion of Nicaragua," *Virginian-Pilot*, circa 1987.

35. Pat Robertson to Ronald Reagan, May 6, 1985. RRPL.

36. Dick Thompson to Pat Buchanan, 1986. RRPL.

37. Pat Robertson to Ronald Reagan, September 28, 1983. RRPL.

38. Joseph Salgado to Pat Robertson, October 24, 1983. RRPL.

39. Draft of Telegram, Ronald Reagan to Pat Robertson, June 29, 1982. RRPL.

40. On election day, Robertson did place ads in several U.S. papers with a quote about communism from Aleksandr Solzhenitsyn. His reasons for doing so are unclear since he repeatedly said that Mondale had no chance of success.

41. Various letters to and from Ronald Reagan to Pat Robertson, circa 1984. RRPL and Regent University Special Collections (RUA).

42. Pat Robertson to Ronald Reagan, various letters, 1981–1983. RRPL.

43. Pat Robertson to Donald Regan, February 25, 1985. RRPL.

44. Patrick Buchanan to Donald Regan, September 15, 16, 1986. RRPL.

45. Mitch Daniels to Donald Regan, September 11, 1986. RRPL.

46. Tod Dawson to Donald Regan, September 15, 1986. RRPL.

47. Pat Robertson to People for the American Way, 1981. PFAW.

48. Robert Boston, interview by author, tape recording, Washington, D.C., April 14, 1998.

49. Pat Robertson, interview by author, tape recording, Virginia Beach, Va., May 25, 2000.

50. Pat Robertson, *The 700 Club*, May 13, 1986. PFAW.

51. For example, see John Ehrman, *The Eighties: America in the Age of Reagan* (New Haven, Conn.: Yale University Press, 2005) and William Pemberton, *Exit with Honor: The Life and Presidency of Ronald Reagan* (London: Sharpe, 1998).

52. Ronald Reagan made an appearance before the Religious Roundtable in 1979. James Robison told Reagan to mention in his speech that although the group could not endorse him, he endorsed them. Reagan used the line, and it was seen as a turning point in evangelical support for Reagan.

53. Memo to the President, October 29, 1981. RRPL.

54. Paul Weyrich interview.

55. Cal Thomas and Ed Dobson, *Blinded by Might: Can the Religious Right Save America?* (Grand Rapids, Mich.: Zondervan, 1999).

56. Thomas and Dobson, *Blinded by Might*, 24.

57. Ehrman, *The Eighties*, 178.

58. Pat Robertson interview.

59. Pat Robertson interview.

CHAPTER 7

THE SECRET KINGDOM

PAT Robertson was empowered by his proximity to power during the Reagan era. One important result of this experience was a change in Robertson's thinking on a number of fronts. The most significant development was a noticeable decrease in both the amount and ferocity of his end times predictions. Gone were the warnings of imminent destruction, and in its place came more subtle warnings of secret societies and conspiracies that were centuries in the making. The one thing that did remain, however, was his interest in Reconstructionist theology. His writings show a man who was willing to take a long-range approach to changing the world, and he wanted to take his loyal Christian Broadcasting Network (CBN) supporters with him.

Many of the books published under Robertson's name have been either ghostwritten or at least cowritten. However, it is unlikely that anyone but Robertson wrote his favorite book, *The Secret Kingdom*, first published in 1982.[1] While he has had more than five books reach the best-seller list, he rarely mentions any of them except this one. Robertson's office walls are adorned with photos of the book's cover and its achievement of reaching the *New York Times* best-seller list. Considering all that he has accomplished, he is unusually proud of this one book. There are several possible explanations for this. First, it could be the only book that he has actually written, or at least mostly written. Second, the book contains his only real contribution to theology.

None of the other books that Robertson has published dealing with political or spiritual issues have been very original. However, *The Secret Kingdom* is different. Robertson expands upon Wilbert White's three laws of inductive Bible study and claims that the scriptures contain several spiritual laws that Christians can use to their advantage. He is careful to steer clear of the more notorious televangelists who were involved in "name it and claim it" prosperity theology. This idea, born and bred among wealthy Charismatic leaders, was that anything that you desire—money, success, physical healing—could be yours for the asking. This idea, which is largely an American phenomenon, is based on Jesus saying "Ask and you shall receive." For example, some evangelists, including Kenneth Copeland, have stated that any Christian who wears glasses lacks the faith to be healed.[2] Robertson is careful to avoid this type of talk, but his book does come very close to that kind of thinking.

Taking a page from Saint Augustine's *City of God*, Robertson writes that there were two kingdoms at work in the world. The natural one is easy enough to see, but it is the spiritual world that provides all of the power. This invisible kingdom is governed by eight rules (expanded to ten in the 1992 edition). According to Robertson, "Jesus had spoken quite precisely about how this kingdom worked. . . . He actually laid down specific principles."[3] As Robertson had been taught at seminary, the Bible contains everything one needs to live a happy life. "The Bible is not an impractical book of theology, but rather a practical book of life containing a system of thought and conduct that will guarantee success."[4] Robertson believes that the reason that so many Christians are unhappy is that they do not know how to use their God-given power, and that Satan has convinced them that he is in control of the earth.

By reminding his readers that Jesus "fully expected us to claim the rights and privileges of our citizenship" in heaven, Robertson tells Christians to take what God had already given them.[5] As the only free being in the universe, God has unlimited power, and that power is available for those who believe. Robertson writes that Jesus allows Christians to have "the same energy and power that prevailed at the creation."[6] The first step in this process is outlined in chapter 3, "Seeing and Entering." In order to have the power of God, one must totally commit to God. While non-Christians could use some of these laws of the kingdom of God, they would only really work well if they are practiced by true believers. Robertson sums it up this way: "Our partnership with God is fulfilled when we speak his word in the power of the Holy Spirit."[7]

What follows is a set of laws that Robertson has deduced from his reading of the Bible. They include the "Law of Reciprocity," which states that if you give, you will receive even greater things. The "Law of Use" asks people to use the abilities that God has given them. For this law, Robertson uses the parable of the talents, where each servant who returned his master's money with interest was rewarded. Robertson explained this law when he was a guest speaker at a Billy Graham conference on world evangelism in 1983. He told an audience of four thousand evangelists that if each person there would win ten converts in one year, and they had ten converts and so on, the world would be entirely Christian in six years.[8]

The Secret Kingdom's other laws include the "Law of Greatness," which promises that those who act as servants of mankind will be rewarded in a multitude of ways. The examples of great people include Mother Teresa. Some of the other people he mentions, such as Henry Ford and Sam Walton of Wal-Mart, are not the best choices. Following the "Law of Honesty" means that stealing one dollar is as bad as taking $35,000, and that those who are honest in little things will be given great rewards. Other laws are self-explanatory, covering perseverance, miracles, and responsibility. The "Law of Unity" promises success to those who live in harmony and seek to join with others who are single-minded. According to Robertson, while God values variety, there can still be harmony.

Most of these laws are innocuous, but there is one ominous one on Robertson's list: the "Law of Dominion." The law states that Christians are supposed to be in control of the world and that God has given them extraordinary power. "Almighty God wants us to recapture the dominion man held in the beginning," and "God wants man to have authority over the earth."[9] Robertson believes that this law has great potential to make the world a better place. "Man, taking his rightful place under God, would subdue the causes of drought and famine. World hunger would cease."[10]

The ideas that Robertson presents in this chapter are essentially the same as Dominion theology, also called Reconstructionism. This theological movement's desire is to establish the United States as a Christian republic that follows all biblical mandates including the death penalty for homosexuals and witches (see chapter 6 of this volume).

Obviously aware of the controversy, Robertson seeks to distinguish his ideas from those of the Reconstructionists. He characterizes their beliefs as "a fairly extreme interpretation of the Scriptures" and notes that while some of their ideas are indeed biblical, their overall view is "mistaken."[11] Recently many people have accused Robertson of being at least secretly in league with the Reconstructionists; however, in *The Secret Kingdom*, he clearly rejects one of their central tenets. There is no way, Robertson writes, that Christians would ever be able to reclaim the earth as the kingdom of God. Man could never usher in the millennial kingdom—that power rested in the hands of God alone.[12] This final point is made repeatedly throughout the book.

While Robertson takes pains to distance himself from Reconstructionist theology, his writing is almost indistinguishable from many of the movement's major ideas. Perhaps it is no coincidence that this book was published the same year that Robertson hired Herb Titus, an admitted Reconstructionist, to be the academic dean at CBN University. While Robertson never went as far as his occasional *700 Club* guest John Rushdoony, he did like the idea of Christians having special rights given by God. Robertson was so pleased with *The Secret Kingdom* that he updated it in the early 1990s and included two new laws, the laws of fidelity and change. If it is debatable that Robertson has changed his mind about Reconstructionism, he clearly has second thoughts about the end of the world, or at least publicizing his views on the topic.

In Robertson's theology, which is similar to that of most other evangelicals, the world will deteriorate as the second coming of Jesus approaches. This had led him to predict a dire future for America and the world. As these events failed to materialize, he revised his dates several times, finally making his prophecies more and more vague. Like many evangelicals, he believed the biblical story of Gog and Magog in Ezekiel 38 and 39 was a prophecy that said the Soviet Union would invade Israel and start the battle of Armageddon. By 1982, however, Robertson was more optimistic about the world's situation; no doubt Reagan's presidency had alleviated many of his fears. Therefore, in late 1982 he ceased publication of *Pat Robertson's Perspective*. There was no momentous announcement, as there had been with the beginning; he simply stopped production. At this point, Robertson was happy enough with Reagan, and was not interested in attacking the president for not having enough Christians in government, as long as he remained politically conservative. While he still believed that the world was going to get worse, he was prepared to engage society and not just wait for the end to come. Instead of pulling back, Robertson was willing to work to push his agenda onto center stage. Such a change in his eschatology could be interpreted as his commitment to Reconstructionism, a political move to prepare himself for the 1988 campaign, or a little of both. It is also possible that his newfound wealth and power had changed him. As humorist P. J. O'Rourke writes, "[M]oney unsaddles the Four Horsemen of the Apocalypse, or anyway, mounts them on donkeys."[13]

In 1985 Robertson published *Beyond Reason: How Miracles Can Change Your Life*, which read like a sequel to *The Secret Kingdom*. The book seeks to "teach some of the basic principles that enable you to understand and experience the flow of God's energy, which moves freely between His Kingdom and our limited, three-dimensional world."[14] The brief work focuses on miracles of physical and mental healing and miracles over nature and personal finances. Keeping in line with Charismatic theology, Robertson claims that there is a "ladder of power and authority" that spans from God to man.[15] The goal of the book is to encourage people to stop focusing on the material world so that they can tap into this spiritual power. The unspoken irony of the book is its emphasis on spiritualism to achieve material benefits.

Each chapter of *Beyond Reason* features stories of average Christians whose lives were altered by powerful miracles. For some it is a miraculous cure from cancer, multiple sclerosis, or drug-damaged brains. Other miracle stories deal with plane flights gone wrong, praying to change a hurricane's path, or prayers to help find oil in Texas. After each story, Robertson summarizes the important steps that each person took. For a woman named Kathy who had both serious arthritis and lupus, healing took fourteen steps of prayer, faith, and commitment to God before she was healed. Chapter 7, "God's Marvelous System of Money Management," is merely a restating of two laws mentioned in *The Secret Kingdom*: the laws of reciprocity and use. The book ends with a section called "A Future Filled with Hope" in which Robertson predicts that mankind will stand "on the threshold of a visitation from God upon our world of such power that seemingly incredible miracles will then seem commonplace."[16] His confidence in the future is a far cry from prophecies of imminent doom that awaited the world. Such an attitude could be interpreted as his Reconstructionist leanings reaching the surface, or his optimism in light of his upcoming presidential run. No matter what lay behind his optimism, it was an interesting change in his thinking.

Another fascinating look into Robertson's mind is found in his 1984 book *Answers to 200 of Life's Most Probing Questions*.[17] The questions are based on those he had dealt with on *The 700 Club* (as is his 2002 book *Bring It On*), and are arranged into twelve general topics. While many of his answers are standard evangelical theology, others reflect his cultural bias and his interesting look at life. He begins the book by answering the top ten questions that the Gallup poll had determined people would ask God if they had the chance. The first question asks why God allows suffering. In his answer Robertson blames Satan and human sinfulness for pain and suffering. His examples of human-caused suffering include alcoholism, which causes thousands of deaths, and Hinduism, which means that the nation of India has "embraced a philosophy which says that rats and cows are sacred," and thereby destroyed its fertile lands and crops, leading to starvation. Other topics include the nature of God and man, salvation, the end of the world, sex, and the role of Christians in government.

In some cases there are contradictions, and in others, Robertson fails to take his arguments to their logical conclusion. For example, in an answer regarding organ donation, Robertson makes a compassionate plea for people to sign up as donors, since the body is merely a shell. However, in a later question about cremation, he answers that it is morally wrong because the body needs to be whole so that it may rise anew at the second coming of Jesus. His real reason for disliking cremation, he eventually admits, is that it is practiced by Hindus and is therefore not appropriate for Christians. In a section on sex Robertson states that oral sex is wrong because it is a selfish focus on the pleasure of one partner and that sex is designed to please both. Robertson does not comment on the obvious, but unasked, question of what to do if one partner cannot please the other sexually. According to his logic, it is sinful for one partner to receive pleasure, but not the other. The Puritans allowed women to divorce their husbands if they were not being satisfied sexually; Robertson does not dare to go that far.

Since Robertson believes in the theology of the secret kingdom, it should not be surprising that he believes that there are consequences for those who do not follow God's laws. Both the Old and New Testaments are filled with stories of sinners who did not repent and were punished. In modern America such images are usually used by fire and brimstone preachers, but unlike Robertson those pastors are not usually on TV. The best example of Robertson's thinking on God's wrath is seen in two related events. In 1998, while on *The 700 Club*, Robertson was commenting on a CBN news story about Walt Disneyworld's "Gay Day" and the city of Orlando, Florida's hanging of rainbow flags in celebration of a gay awareness week. Other groups, such as the Southern Baptist Church, had launched a boycott of all Disney products, since the company granted benefits to same-sex partners. Robertson, while consistently opposed to homosexuality, remained silent, until Orlando's city government's announcement. He predicted that, since public acceptance of homosexuality was a sign that a society was in decline, God was going to pour out his wrath on the city. Robertson said, "I would warn Orlando that you're right in the way of some serious hurricanes and I don't think I'd be waving those flags in God's face if I were you." He claimed that he was telling the city this, not to condemn them, but to save them. He predicted that if they did not repent, "this will bring about the destruction of your nation. It'll bring terrorist bombs, it'll bring earthquakes, tornadoes and possibly a meteor."[18] Robertson's political enemies made sure that his comments received widespread attention. Years later Robertson again appeared on *The 700 Club*, this time with Jerry Falwell, to claim that a horrific event was the result of America's sin of allowing abortion and homosexuality. The event was the 9/11 attacks on the Pentagon and the World Trade Center, and while Robertson would later change his tune, his original comments were perfectly in line with his real thinking.

Notes

1. Pat Robertson, *The Secret Kingdom* (Dallas, Tex.: Word Publishing, 1982).

2. For more on this topic see Stephen Pullum, *"Foul Demons, Come Out": The Rhetoric of Twentieth-Century American Faith Healers* (Westport, Conn.: Praeger, 1999).

3. Robertson, *The Secret Kingdom*, 16.

4. Robertson, *The Secret Kingdom*, 48.

5. Robertson, *The Secret Kingdom*, 37.

6. Robertson, *The Secret Kingdom*, 45.

7. Robertson, *The Secret Kingdom*, 73.

8. Pat Robertson, *Amsterdam '83*, July 17, 1983. Billy Graham Center (BGC).

9. Robertson, *The Secret Kingdom*, 238.

10. Robertson, *The Secret Kingdom*, 243.

11. Robertson, *The Secret Kingdom*, 243.

12. Robertson, *The Secret Kingdom*, 243.

13. P. J. O'Rourke, *All the Trouble in the World* (New York: Atlantic Monthly Press, 1995), 332.

14. Pat Robertson with William Proctor, *Beyond Reason: How Miracles Can Change Your Life* (New York: Morrow, 1985), 20.

15. Robertson and Proctor, *Beyond Reason*, 164.

16. Robertson and Proctor, *Beyond Reason*, 177.

17. Pat Robertson, *Answers to 200 of Life's Most Probing Questions* (New York: Thomas Nelson Publishing, 1984).

18. Thomas Edsall, "Forecasting Havoc for Orlando," *Washington Post*, June 10, 1998.

CHAPTER 8

FROM MINISTRY TO EMPIRE

I F the decade of the 1970s was dedicated to building the physical structure of the Christian Broadcasting Network (CBN), the 1980s were focused on the more ethereal elements of satellite and cable transmissions. Other televangelists were reaching ever increasing audiences as well, and religious broadcasting was becoming an influential voice in evangelicalism. There were so many new operations appearing on TV and radio that the National Religious Broadcasters published a handbook on how to manage a broadcasting ministry.[1] While there was an ever increasing group of TV preachers, they all still stood in Robertson's shadow. During the early 1970s the network used the skills of Jim Bakker to make itself viable; the next decade saw secular, family-friendly programming become the new rocket booster to propel Robertson's small ministry into a multimillion-dollar empire.

The decisions that led to the change were simple but had deep implications. In the final years of the 1970s, CBN began to broadcast old reruns of family-oriented shows like *Lassie*. This expansion in secular shows increased the network's advertising revenue. As a result CBN was able to purchase time on RCA's satellite in 1977, and by 1978 the network was reaching over one million cable viewers. The network was the first Christian ministry to use satellite, which saved them the expense of taping shows and sending them to all of the stations that broadcast *The 700 Club*.[2] Now CBN could broadcast live to America, which it has done ever since. Robertson claimed that by using the satellite he had fulfilled a prophecy from the book of Revelation which said, "I saw another angel flying in the midst of heaven, having the everlasting gospel to preach to those who dwell on the earth."[3] The New Testament records Jesus as prophesying that he would not return until the Gospel had been preached to the entire world; perhaps this was bringing the end time that much closer.

One result of CBN's financial stability was Robertson's desire to expand the types of programs that the network broadcasted. Showing wholesome reruns was one thing, but Robertson wanted to produce "morally uplifting" TV shows. In 1978 he predicted that within a few years CBN would be broadcasting over thirty-two hours of original programming. CBN was working on dramas, situation comedies, and even an evening news show. This was part of Robertson's goal of making CBN "a truly competitive fourth network."[4]

In early 1981 the decision was made to stop broadcasting all religious shows except *The 700 Club*. Previously, viewers could tune into CBN and see Jimmy Swaggart, Oral Roberts, and a host of lesser-known religious personalities; after 1981 the only televangelist they saw on CBN was Pat Robertson. Aside from the obvious business benefits, Robertson hoped to make a bigger impact on nonevangelical television viewers. By showing mostly religious programming, CBN had been "narrowcasting" to a small audience that believed the same things as Robertson did. By developing a more secular appeal, Robertson hoped to increase viewership of *The 700 Club* and reach people who were not going to watch an hour of Jimmy Swaggart or *The PTL Club*. The network began to call itself "The Family Entertainer," and with this change in focus came increased profit.[5] Robertson claimed that "the large audiences drew advertisers who helped pay the bills. The religious programs could speak to much larger audiences than would have been available to an all religious station." He also hoped that since these advertisements now paid CBN's bills it allowed them to make "a much smaller demand for contributions."[6] CBN had gone beyond being a totally viewer-supported ministry to one that mixed donations with revenue raised from commercials. This mix eventually caused trouble with the Internal Revenue Service (IRS).

Robertson did not banish his competition in order to show more reruns of sitcoms from the 1960s; he continued to air original religious content. Instead of puppet shows and religious talk shows, CBN began to air programs that aimed to be both entertaining and evangelical. As the network grew, so did Robertson's desire to produce more interesting shows. In true evangelical fashion, Robertson wrote about the need for conservative Christians to get involved in cleaning up American culture. "Christians should begin to produce top-notch general audience films and TV programs," he wrote in April of 1977.[7] In 1981 CBN debuted the Christian soap opera *Another Life*. This daily show was a typical soap opera in all ways except for the Christian solutions that were presented to the problems the characters faced. Robertson called it a "soap with hope," and the nonunion show was run cheaply, about $4 million per year.[8] The show was originally called *The Life Inside*, and like the original *700 Club* format it did not meet with Robertson's approval. He wanted a show that was not so "stilted and Victorian," as he put it. The show, while never written by Robertson, did have a

Charismatic–Pentecostal influence. In one episode a character dying from liver cancer was suddenly healed and became a Christian.[9] Such healings were similar to those claimed on *The 700 Club*. The show, while popular, proved to be too expensive to maintain and was canceled in October 1984.

One of Robertson's broadcasting ideas was clearly ahead of its time. In the summer of 1985 CBN announced that it would begin airing a nightly news program. This program had been in the planning stages since the late 1970s, but the first episode of the half-hour-long *CBN News Tonight* didn't air until January 27, 1986. The show was hosted by Ben Kinchlow and featured a 900 toll number that viewers could call to voice their opinions on the day's events. The show had been delayed for several years due to the expense of having reporters stationed around the globe. This cost proved to be fatal, and the show was canceled just weeks later in March 1986 due to "lack of interest on the part of advertisers."[10] What made the show groundbreaking was its attempt to give a deliberately conservative evangelical spin to the news. Robertson's program was a predecessor to *The Fox News Channel*, where news is openly given from a conservative perspective.

In 1985 CBN became the nation's heaviest user of toll-free calls, passing American Airlines, a sign that Robertson's strategy to reach out to a wider audience was beginning to work. According to Robertson, in 1981 CBN was on the cable systems of nineteen million people. By late 1986 CBN was reaching thirty-three million people through its placement on over six thousand cable systems across the nation. According to the Nielsen rating system, CBN's viewership jumped 33 percent during October 1986 alone.[11] Robertson appeared to overestimate the size and stability of the network's growth, because by the end of 1986 $25 million was cut from the budget when expected donations did not materialize.

Even though CBN was no longer a small-time operation, the Robertson family remained involved, especially Dede. Even though she taught nursing at Tidewater Community College, and was largely responsible for raising their four kids, she also served on the board of directors at CBN. Most TV ministers have their wives and other relatives on the board, in order to maintain control. However, due to the closeness of their relationship, Dede has reportedly been more than willing to challenge her husband during board meetings.[12] The Robertson children also became involved in CBN to some extent. Tim Robertson followed his father's path into broadcasting, but preferred to remain behind camera. The other three children worked there sporadically, although Gordon Robertson took over cohosting duties on *The 700 Club* in the 1990s.

The burst of growth at CBN in the late 1970s and early 1980s was the result of conflict in the world of religious broadcasting over the nature and size of the audience. The system of ratings created by the A. C. Nielsen Company used by the major networks was of little use to televangelists who were not interested in ratings for advertising purposes. Few if any televangelists were willing to pay for Nielsen's data since it was mostly irrelevant to them. This made it nearly impossible to determine how many people were actually watching these shows. Most ministries were happy to make a guess based on the number of their donors and phone calls.

The claims of these televangelists were shaken in 1981 when Nielsen publicly released its findings. When scholars began to look at the figures, they realized that most televangelists had been greatly exaggerating the number of viewers they had. Exactly how many people watched was still difficult to determine. Some shows like Oral Roberts's were only shown once a week, while *The 700 Club* was shown five days a week. This made it hard to compare them, and to account for people who watched both shows. One report based on the Nielsen survey stated that only thirteen million people watched religious shows weekly; another report from the Gallup organization stated that 37 percent, or about seventy million Americans, watched at least one religious show per week.[13] Still another study suggested that only 6 percent of Americans, or thirteen million people, watched religious programs regularly.[14]

This new study caused a fiery controversy for many reasons. Sociologists Anson Shupe and Jeffery Hadden point out that there were political considerations to be made when discussing the numbers of people who viewed religious television shows. As can be imagined, the televangelists were not happy with this; neither were their opponents. Groups like People for the American Way and Americans United for the Separation of Church and State had claimed that tens of millions were watching and being influenced by these preachers. To suddenly have the number of viewers slashed significantly called these groups' very existence into question.[15]

The other group to make a commotion about the small Nielsen ratings was the leadership of the more liberal and mainline churches, especially those that had been pushed out after they lost their free airtime in 1960. They tried to use the figures as proof that selling TV time to televangelists was not producing shows that met the FCC guidelines of helpful community programming. It was hoped that this would allow the mainstream churches back onto TV and for free. Unfortunately for them, their day had passed. In 1959 paid religious programs accounted for 53 percent of religious broadcasts. By 1977 the number had risen to 92 percent.[16]

Robertson was not happy with any of these figures, especially as he was trying to sell his network as a more secular business. So in the midst of all of this commotion, he sponsored his own Nielsen survey of CBN and other religious broadcasts in 1985. The result was one of the most complete studies of *The 700 Club* and its viewers ever conducted. When his network was young he had relied on his children's reactions to determine what to put on the air. By the 1980s he was the only televangelist to use professional market research techniques so that he could reach a wider audience. When the data from the latest Nielsen survey were announced, it showed that 40 percent of Americans watched at least one religious show per month. The survey also concluded that earlier studies had ignored the growing numbers of viewers on cable TV, and their numbers were 340 percent higher than had been thought. Most importantly, the study showed that over seven million people watched *The 700 Club* each week.[17]

Overall, the rating debate that raged in the world of religious broadcasting only worked to make Robertson's network stronger. His show *The 700 Club* was the most watched religious program, and CBN's move toward secular shows was only making the audience larger and Robertson wealthier.

Along with this growth in secular shows was the explosion of the cable industry. While CBN had been on cable since 1977, the numbers of cable subscribers had remained low, less than five million, until the mid-1980s, when it grew by the millions each year. By 1982 CBN had significantly more viewers via cable than broadcast stations. As a result, Robertson started to sell off the stations. These sales came at the same time as some other TV ministries were selling off their assets due to the recession of the early 1980s. Some media outlets took this as a sign that CBN was weakening, when just the opposite was true. Financially, the network had never looked better. The payrolls depended less and less on *The 700 Club* telethons and more on advertising revenue.

In September 1981 CBN celebrated its twentieth anniversary. President Reagan sent Robertson a telegram congratulating him on being in business for so long. Reagan remarked, "[Y]ou have entered a difficult field and you have done an amazing job. We need the kind of programming that CBN has brought to the nation."[18] *The 700 Club* had a special week of telethons to celebrate the occasion. That same year CBN purchased additional acres in Virginia Beach for the university and broadcast facilities. The ministry now owned 380 acres, more than enough to satisfy its growth into the future. Robertson began to plan for another huge broadcast building, this one to house the daily operations of the CBN's cable channel.

In 1983 Robertson and Kinchlow began to share their cohosting duties with Danuta Soderman, who became the first woman to regularly appear on the show. Soderman had hosted a secular talk show in San Diego, and was looking for something that complimented her faith better. As it was for Kinchlow before her, the path to cohost job at *The 700 Club* was an abrupt one. She was originally hired to be a foreign correspondent for CBN and was told that she would be traveling to places like Israel to interview world leaders. On her first day at the CBN studios, she was informed that she was the new cohost of *The 700 Club*. She was evidently fine with the change of plans, and stayed until Robertson ran for president in 1988.[19] Along with Kinchlow, Soderman proved to be popular with audiences and helped bring a different dynamic to the show. There has been a female cohost ever since.

As Robertson's audience grew so did his political commentary on *The 700 Club*, which occasionally caused him problems. In 1981 Robertson was commenting on an American Civil Liberties Union (ACLU) lawsuit against the state of Arkansas, which had a law that allowed the teaching of "creation science." Robertson claimed that there was something "crooked" about Arkansas attorney general Steve Clark. Clark had given a contribution to the ACLU while he fought their lawsuit in court. Robertson claimed that Clark's contribution was like "bribing a jury." A year later Clark responded with a lawsuit claiming reckless conduct and asked for unspecified monetary damages. Robertson invited Clark on *The 700 Club* to tell his side, but the attorney general would not budge. The suit was settled in October 1983 when Robertson publicly apologized and paid an undisclosed sum.[20]

Robertson took a controversial step into the Middle East when Israel invaded Lebanon in June 1982. Israel's goal was to create a safety zone for the northern border and to try to destroy the Palestine Liberation Organization army that had been shelling cities in northern Israel for years. In response the Israeli army drove through Lebanon and went as far north as Beirut. The army eventually pulled back into a self-proclaimed "security zone" that covered southern Lebanon. The ruler of a Christian Lebanese militia that was in league with Israel allowed CBN to use a TV station and tower in this newly conquered territory. *The 700 Club* could now be broadcast to Israel and the nations surrounding it.[21]

By 1987 CBN was America's fifth largest cable network, and it was estimated that *The 700 Club* was being seen in at least twenty-eight million homes a month.[22] This meant that Robertson himself was being seen by millions of people each week. Even more were tuning into his network without realizing who owned it. Robertson had truly gone beyond the realm of televangelism. He was the head of a major television network. Unlike his colleagues in the ministry world, he even had the rating numbers to back him up. While this distinction was not always believed by the media, the proof came when scandals hit the world of religious broadcasting and show after show went off the air.

While the 1980s were the high point for televangelists, there were significant signs of trouble on the horizon. In mid-1986 both Robertson and Falwell laid off several hundred staff members, and Falwell cut back on his broadcasts. That same year, Rex Humbard, one of the most popular TV preachers of the 1970s, stopped his broadcasting with little fanfare. Humbard's church, the Cathedral of Tomorrow, was the first church specifically built to accommodate broadcast equipment.[23] The world of televised ministries was usually teetering between boom or bust, and rough times had begun to take their toll. Robertson had partially insulated himself from these troubles with his secularization of CBN. For although *The 700 Club* would face financial difficulty during his presidential campaign, it was always buffered from serious harm by the cash cow that was the family-friendly cable channel he had created. CBN began to charge stations to air *The 700 Club* on their networks, which brought in more revenue. The show continued to ask for donations, even as it was making money off of the non-CBN broadcasts of the show. Since the network was bringing in so much cash, Robertson was able to use some of it to fund another one of his dreams: his own university.

Notes

1. Thomas Durfey and James Ferrier, *Religious Broadcast Management Handbook* (Grand Rapids, Mich.: Zondervan, 1986).

2. Pat Robertson, *The Plan* (Nashville, Tenn.: Thomas Nelson Publishing, 1989), 183.

3. Robertson, *The Plan*, 183.

4. "CBN—A TV Network Out to "Create Christian Foment," *U.S News & World Report*, October 16, 1978.

5. David Edwin Harrell Jr., *Pat Robertson: A Personal, Religious, and Political Portrait* (New York: Harper & Row, 1987), 64.

6. Robertson, *The Plan*, 184.

7. Pat Robertson, *Pat Robertson's Perspective*, April 1977.

8. Sandra Boodman, "Another Life: Will a Soap with Hope Make It to the Big Time?" *Washington Post*, May 9, 1982.

9. Boodman, "Another Life."

10. *ADWEEK*, "CBN Cancels 'News Tonight,'" March 31, 1986.

11. *ADWEEK*, "CBN Viewership Jumps," November 17, 1986.

12. Harrell, *Pat Robertson*, 88.

13. Jeffery Hadden and Anson Shupe, *Televangelism: Power and Politics on God's Frontier* (New York: Henry Holt, 1988), 147.

14. R. Laurence Moore, *Selling God: American Religion in the Marketplace of Culture* (New York: Oxford, 1994), 249.

15. Hadden and Shupe, *Televangelism*, 150.

16. Hadden and Shupe, *Televangelism*, 52.

17. Hadden and Shupe, *Televangelism*, 154–56.

18. Ronald Reagan to Pat Robertson, September 30, 1981. Ronald Reagan Presidential Library (RRPL).

19. Jane Harper, "Whatever Happened to Danuta Soderman of The 700 Club?" *Virginian-Pilot*, August 18, 1997.

20. Cindy Schreuder, "Robertson Sued over The 700 Club Comment," *Norfolk-Ledger Star* [Va.], December 9, 1982.

21. The station was abandoned in the fall of 2000 when Israel withdrew to its borders.

22. Harrell, *Pat Robertson*, 165.

23. Hadden and Shupe, *Televangelism*, 123.

CHAPTER 9

ROBERTSON'S UNIVERSITY

I N the late nineteenth and early twentieth centuries, Protestant churches across America split along theological lines. This process had its roots in the secularization of higher education, which became pronounced after the Civil War and was one of the most significant events in American religious history. The cause of the split focused on a debate over the proper way to interpret the Bible. The liberals wanted to remove from the Bible the things that they felt did not relate to modern science, while the conservatives wanted to retain a more literal interpretation of the scriptures. These conservatives wished to hold on to the central, or fundamental, beliefs of the Christian church, hence their name, Fundamentalist.

The conflict between the two camps split denominations, led to pastors being removed from their pulpits, and created a lingering hostility that is still strong today. As religious conservatives appeared to lose the public war they retreated to their own world and created their own institutions. Perhaps the most learned Fundamentalist, although he hated the term, was J. Gresham Machen, who was forced out of Princeton Theological Seminary and started Westminster Theological Seminary in Philadelphia.[1] There were others, like Bob Jones, who took a more extreme path and started schools that were not merely fortresses of Fundamentalism, but also of social conservatism. In Jones's case this included rabid support for racial segregation. Conservative denominations also created colleges to train their next generation of ministers. For example, the Pentecostal denomination Assemblies of God (AG) was founded in 1914 and had over ten Bible colleges across the country by the late 1920s.[2] The AG and religious groups like them had decided that they could no longer trust the public education system to inculcate their children with the values that they considered most important.

Throughout World War II and into the 1970s, these conservative schools flourished, while their acceptance in secular academia grew rather slowly. Most were by the late 1960s regionally accredited, and many were offering graduate programs. By the 1970s these schools branched out and began to teach a wider variety of classes and offer a greater choice of majors. In the meantime, evangelicals once again became a powerful force in American society. With the election of Jimmy Carter in 1976, evangelicalism was in the news again. However, many of its institutions of learning still had a siege mentality.

There are several evangelical Christian universities that have made an effort to influence society, but many were still content to produce citizens for their own world, and not the nation as a whole. Some of these colleges were founded by Fundamentalists, and their self-imposed restrictions on intellectual endeavors left much to be desired. Even a prestigious evangelical university like Wheaton required the faculty to sign a statement of faith affirming such beliefs as premillennial eschatology.[3] Many of the schools held onto strict social rules for years, even decades, after society had moved beyond them. Such things as social dancing or going to movies were banned, and students usually had early curfews. Robertson had attended some of the nation's best schools, and his personal history had an enormous influence on his university, right down to the architecture. He planned to create a different kind of university, and he founded the aggressive educational institution that many expected, and others feared.

Pat Robertson followed in the footsteps of other famous evangelists, like Billy Graham and Jerry Falwell, who started their own conservative Protestant Christian colleges. In Robertson's version of the story, he was sitting alone in a suite at the Disneyland hotel in 1975, when God spoke to him. While eating his dinner of cottage cheese and cantaloupe, he felt the Lord lead him to start a university.[4] Since there were a plethora of academically solid evangelical colleges, he decided to start a graduate school. Three years later, in 1978, the doors of the Christian Broadcasting Network University (CBNU, which was renamed Regent University in October 1989) were opened.

Robertson controlled the content of his network and daily television program. However, a university is much too large and unruly by nature to micromanage, so he did not usually concern himself with day-to-day activities. The struggle was finding religiously conservative scholars who could challenge the liberalism of academia without becoming too extreme themselves. This balance was harder to maintain than he could have imagined.

Hostility toward public and even private secular education has been a staple of the evangelical movement, and Robertson is no exception. His distrust of public education was total. "Satan has established certain strongholds," he once declared on the set of *The 700 Club*. "He has gone after education and has been very successful in capturing it."[5] With comments like those it would be easy to assume that Robertson's would be the most reclusive of institutions. However, Robertson was far too busy to be able to oversee, much less control, every aspect of the university, and what has occurred there is an interesting metaphor for evangelical universities in general.

The central dilemma that has consumed theologically conservative Protestant universities is to what extent should they be separate from what they perceive as secular America. To answer this question, CBNU is a helpful case study. Other Christian denominations and leaders had created places of learning the faithful and like-minded could attend. CBNU has that central component, but it goes one step further. It actively seeks to put its graduates into places of power and influence. On one level, it is part of Robertson's master plan, along with the American Center for Law and Justice (ACLJ) and the Christian Coalition, to reshape America. The coalition and the ACLJ seek to work in the current political arena and change the nation quickly. However, the idea behind CBNU is long term. Robertson has stated that he wanted to raise the next generation of media, government, and policy leaders. During a taping of *The 700 Club*, he spoke of his plans for the nation and his school. "How nice it would be if all three presidents of the major TV networks happened to be trained with master degrees from CBNU. . . . It is possible that superintendents and principals in the major school districts will all have degrees from CBNU."[6] It would take years, perhaps decades, for the university to have a noticeable impact on American society; Robertson realized this and was prepared for the long haul.

There were several major problems that confronted the televangelist in this endeavor. It was not too difficult to find the land since the Christian Broadcasting Network (CBN) had just over 680 acres in Virginia Beach. Still, there were no buildings for the school. The original structures were trailers brought in while construction began. In order to lure faculty members to the new school, Robertson invited over a hundred professors from conservative Protestant colleges around the country. They toured the grounds of the future campus and were offered what were described as "impressive" salary packages. At an evening dinner meeting one prospective faculty member questioned Robertson about the new school's policies concerning academic freedom. Robertson reportedly got angry and said, "[T]hat is the problem with you academics, you run into a theater and yell 'fire, fire!'" A professor of theology stood up and said, "[T]hat is better than you, you run into fire and yell, 'theater, theater!'" The crowd roared with laughter; Robertson was not amused.

Despite the rough beginning he was able to hire several young faculty members to start his dream school. One founding faculty member remembers it this way: "There were no buildings, no library books, I mean there was nothing, not even students."[7] When the first day of classes began in the fall of 1978 there were seventy-six students, seven faculty members, and one chancellor with the money to make his school a "Christian Notre Dame," as Robertson called it. Originally, most of the students were drawn from the viewing audience of *The 700 Club*, but as the school grew, it became a channel for the many Christian colleges that had limited graduate programs.

The problem that proved to be the most difficult for the young school was faculty recruitment and hiring. Originally there was a wide range of personalities. Founding faculty member Terry Lindvall recalls, "[T]here was a Roman Catholic, a Black Pentecostal woman, a Presbyterian cartoonist from *Christianity Today*, Episcopalians, Assemblies of God, so it was a really interesting mix."[8] As the school expanded it was able to hire faculty members with advanced degrees from Harvard, Princeton, and Oxford. Lindvall, himself a PhD graduate of the University of Southern California, commented that as the school grew, its professorial diversity began to shrink. "The original professors were very diverse," he said. "Then people came in who were more sectarian and strident. I call it the Masada complex—we threw rocks out."[9] This reference to the battle between the Roman army and Jewish rebels in CE 77 was a fitting example. Masada was a desert fortress, a sign of futile yet determined resistance. That was the direction in which CBNU appeared to be headed.

Another issue that the new university faced was finances. For its first decade of existence, CBN paid for about 70 percent of the school's expenses, and its endowment was a small $2 million. The problem with relying on CBN for its revenue was clear. The school needed a stable source of revenue, one that would allow it to survive long after Robertson was gone. Indeed, the school remained on a precarious financial footing until 1993 when Robertson gave $107 million to the university as an endowment, which at the time was the largest single gift to a college in American history.[10] The money came from a forced sale of Family Channel stock after an Internal Revenue Service (IRS) investigation into Robertson's claims that his entire operation was nonprofit (see chapter 14). Before this financial windfall the university was supported by the members of *The 700 Club* and could count on getting regular airtime, five days a week, which was an indispensable advertising tool.

The university tried from the beginning to set itself apart from the other colleges around the nation. Its first president was Richard Gottier, the former president of Western New England College. In 1984 Gottier was replaced by one of Robertson's best friends, author Bob Slosser.[11] In its early years, the school focused on communications, and this dovetailed nicely with the change in the CBN/Family Channel as it became more diverse. CBNU added more academic programs as time passed.

Looking around the campus, one cannot help but be struck by the similarities between CBNU and Robertson's alma mater Washington and Lee. Both campuses feature grand columned buildings built in the Georgian architectural style, made of red brick with marble from Indiana. The overall effect was one of grandeur and permanence. But while Washington and Lee is perched atop a hill in the sleepy Shenandoah Valley, CBNU is situated beside the 64 freeway. Even though the campus is engulfed in a virtual forest, the hum of the freeway serves as an ever present reminder that the world is watching. The campus was meant to exude power. Its first building, a combination administrative and classroom structure, was completed for the fall of 1979. As the years progressed other buildings were added.

In the center of the small tree-lined campus is a red brick quad. The chancellor's house is set back beside Robertson Hall, and on another side is the impressive $13 million library, finished in 1984. When people enter the library they pass through a marble lobby with spiral staircases. Above the main entrance is the school's motto, "Christian leadership to change the world." This adds to the sense of permanence and mission that Robertson sought to inject into the school. However, when leaving the library, one used to get another message entirely. Directly across the quad from the library was a sculpture mural of the four horsemen of the apocalypse. Whether or not Robertson and his school would make the impact they hoped for, they still believed the end is near. This visual irony was ended in 2002 when the statue was removed as the campus expanded, but the tension between eschatology and the political process remain.

The 1980s were also a time of growth and change at CBNU. In 1984 the school became fully accredited by the Southern Association of Schools and Colleges, the same organization that oversees William and Mary and the University of Virginia. The campus grew at a faster pace than the television studio that originally dwarfed it. No longer consigned to small portable trailers, the university had classroom and administrative buildings, and work was being completed on the library.

Before the school could send its graduates into American politics, they had to deal with campus politics, which, as any academic can tell you, can be even uglier than a presidential campaign. In early 1986 Oral Roberts University (ORU) in Tulsa, Oklahoma, announced that after years of struggles it was abandoning its pursuit of a law school that could meet American Bar Association (ABA) standards. Roberts offered his entire law school library holdings (totaling 190,000 volumes), twenty-five students, and five faculty members to Robertson, who was planning on starting his own law school at CBNU. Four years prior to this gift, Herb Titus had come from ORU to CBNU to serve as vice president of academic affairs; he was chosen to be the first dean of the new law school. While a professor at the University of Oregon, Titus had been the advisor to Students for a Democratic Society, but his conversion to evangelical Christianity in the early 1970s caused him to abandon Marxism for conservative politics.[12] He was considered to be the most liberal member of the law school, until this conversion. It was at this point that he found out just how far academic freedom could be taken. "I had no academic freedom to teach what I believed to be true.

As long as I was an atheist, I had total freedom."[13] After his appointment as dean in 1986 Titus began to prepare for the arrival of the students and his former colleagues. While the first classes were about to start in the fall of 1987, Robertson hoped that the law school would be the pride of the campus. However, it took years and several ugly public battles before the program began to win respect.

In 1983 the chancellor's home was completed. The house was located just steps from the center of the CBNU campus and the CBN broadcast buildings. For the first time in their married life the Robertsons finally owned a home of their own. The cost of the $350,000 three-story Georgian-style house was paid for half by CBN and half by Robertson himself. When both Pat and Dede die the house will become property of the university. The house featured a large walled yard, a private entrance from the street, and its own security system. Adjoining the house is Robertson's stable of horses. If the overly busy man has a hobby, it is his horses. On his 1986 taxes Robertson reported that his horses were valued between $150,000 and $200,000, although he claimed a loss on breeding fees.[14] In 1986 when he was named one of *People* magazine's most interesting people Robertson dressed up like a cowboy and stood near his favorite Arabian horse for his photo.

By the late 1980s, Robertson, his network, *The 700 Club*, and the university bore little resemblance to the similar enterprises of his contemporaries such as Falwell, Bakker, and Swaggart. The network was bringing in millions of dollars in advertising revenue per month, and Robertson's show had a nightly prime-time slot. The flagship of the network, *The 700 Club*, was a professionally produced show featuring news, interviews, religious discussions, and healings. Only Jim Bakker's *PTL* was close in both popularity and style. However, the Bakkers' daily histrionics kept them firmly in the stereotyped camp of screaming TV preachers. Robertson was an inspiration to some other televangelists. While other televangelists had started schools named after themselves, like Swaggart and Oral Roberts, Robertson put CBNU on a solid footing away from his own fortunes. Swaggart was so inspired by Robertson's success that he began considering creating a cable network of his own. For others, like Falwell, Robertson was the competition. Ironically Falwell and Robertson, the two most famous televangelists of the 1980s, had not yet met each other. Whether he was a role model or competitor to other religious broadcasters one thing was clear by 1985: Robertson was the four hundred-pound gorilla of televangelism and, as was his nature, he wanted to take a step to the next level.

Notes

1. George M. Marsden, *Fundamentalism and American Culture* (Oxford: Oxford University Press, 1980), 192.

2. For a fine study of the history of the Assemblies of God, see Margaret Poloma, *The Assemblies of God at the Crossroads* (Knoxville: University of Tennessee Press, 1989).

3. Alan Wolfe, "The Opening of the Evangelical Mind," *Atlantic Monthly*, October 2000.

4. David Edwin Harrell Jr., *Pat Robertson: A Personal, Religious, and Political Portrait* (New York: Harper & Row, 1987), 80.

5. *The 700 Club*, September 27, 1993. CBN. Regent University Special Collections (RUA).

6. Robert Boston, "Out of Bondage," *Church and State*, September 1991, 5.

7. Terry Lindvall, interview by author, tape recording, Costa Mesa, Calif., February 22, 1996.

8. Terry Lindvall interview.

9. Terry Lindvall interview.

10. Marc O'Keefe, "A Big Cash Infusion for Regent," *Virginian-Pilot*, November 12, 1993.

11. Harrell, *Pat Robertson*, 80.

12. Herb Titus, interview by author, written responses to mailed questions, June 19, 2000.

13. Jack Chamberlain, "Christian Universities Feed Both Mind and Soul," *Greensboro News and Record*, June 4, 1986.

14. Pat Robertson, Financial Disclosure Report, October 1, 1987. Americans for Robertson Archives (AFRA).

CHAPTER 10

༄

TESTING THE WATERS

E XACTLY when Robertson first began to consider running for president is
difficult to pinpoint. Random people at the 1980 Washington for Jesus rally
suggested to Robertson that he would be a great president. As early as 1983
his name had been raised by some unhappy conservatives as a possible alternative
to Ronald Reagan in 1984. Robertson recalls, "[I]t would have been absurd, I never
would have considered it. . . . These so called right wingers are always wanting to
push someone into the arena and watch them slowly burn."[1] This was more fantasy than reality, but the idea seemed to stick in Robertson's mind. Although he
had not published *Pat Robertson's Perspective* in several years, by 1985 it was clear
that his interest in politics was focused on the White House. As Jerry Falwell's star
was on the wane after 1982, there was no religious figure with more political muscle than Pat Robertson. Presidents Carter and Reagan had done an effective job of
using religious rhetoric, but many politically conservative evangelicals were eager
to see one of their own in the Oval Office.

In late 1984 Robertson began to hint to his friends and family that he was
planning on running for president in 1988. Paul Weyrich was in Virginia Beach
for a meeting of the Council on National Policy, of which Robertson was also a
member. He recalls, "[W]e were sitting on the front porch and he told us at that
point he was going to run." Weyrich immediately began to help Robertson find
people who would help run the campaign.[2] He called a young political operative named Marc Nuttle and asked him to consider working for Robertson. Nuttle, whom journalists Jack Germond and Jules Whitcover describe as a "crafty
young veteran of right wing Republican politics," was the strategic thinker of
the campaign.[3] Nuttle had worked as field counsel on the 1984 Reagan–Bush
campaign. He had also worked on several smaller Republican campaigns, as well
as for Weyrich's own Free Congress Foundation. In October 1986, Herbert

Ellingwood of the Justice Department, a personal friend of Attorney General Edwin Meese, resigned his post to work on Robertson's campaign staff.[4]

The first public hint of his intentions came in November 1985 when the *Saturday Evening Post* ran a very positive cover story on Robertson. The article touted his business acumen and featured supportive quotes from many famous conservatives.[5] This article, coming only ten months after Ronald Reagan's second inauguration, was one of the earliest to deal with the 1988 campaign. Robertson had clearly put years of quiet thought into his run.

As soon as Robertson's name began to circulate as a potential candidate the attacks started. One of the first to go on the offensive was Democratic Party chairman Paul Kirk. He realized that Robertson was the perfect bogeyman to frighten the party faithful to donate more money. In a letter intended to make Robertson appear as menacing as possible Kirk described him as the leading contender for the Republican nomination in 1988. Kirk warned that Robertson had the votes of more than twenty-two million people at his fingertips and would be unstoppable unless immediate action was taken. Kirk ended the letter with this postscript: "Don't let 1985 become a year like 1979 when we all said Ronald Reagan can't possibly win. Because when Pat Robertson finishes his scripture reading and begins his televised State of the Union address, it will be too late."[6] Kirk ignored better-known possible Republican candidates like Vice President George H. W. Bush and a host of senators who were considering a run for the White House. Robertson was a great fund-raising tool for the Democrats, even if they did not believe that he would do very well.

While Robertson was still building a staff for a possible presidential run, the long-forgotten Freedom Council was actually doing the most to promote him. Although the council was very quiet after the 1980 election, it was revived in 1984 with a series of large gifts from the Christian Broadcasting Network (CBN). The nascent goal of the council was to offer Christians "a sixth grade level civics course, telling them how to get involved with the political process," according to Marc Nuttle.[7] To this end they held classes on precinct organization and delegate selecting conventions. While the organization was supposed to educate Christians all over America, the group focused its efforts in Michigan, Iowa, and South Carolina, states where Robertson had planned to campaign heavily. The council's training sessions were little more than a front for Robertson's campaign. While the council trained politically naive Christians to jump into the lions' den of politics, CBN was keeping everything afloat financially. According to journalist Michael McManus, CBN had funneled money to the Freedom Council for years. In 1984 CBN donated $821,532, another $939,992 the year after that, and another $3 million in 1986. CBN also gave $3.6 million to a previously unknown group called "The National Freedom Institute," whose address, board, and employees were the same as the Freedom Council's.[8]

The council was originally tax exempt, although donations to it were not tax deductible because the council lobbied Congress on a regular basis. By October 1985 it had a staff of thirty, with several workers in Michigan preparing for the delegate selection campaign the coming year. In 1985 Robertson chose a Weyrich protégé, Dick Minard, to run the Freedom Council. Minard left the council a year and a half later to run the "Draft Robertson for President Committee." By May 1986 the Freedom Council had become a completely tax-exempt organization after it promised the Internal Revenue Service (IRS) that it would not participate in political campaigns.[9] How the council managed this feat while at the same time training Robertson supporters to be precinct delegates was one of the wonders of the 1988 campaign.

The council's status as a tax-exempt charity carried with it certain strings. The most important restriction was against political involvement or endorsement of candidates. Robertson put Bob Slosser, the president of CBN University and a CBN board member, in charge of the Freedom Council after Minard moved on. At its peak it claimed to have about five hundred thousand members and mostly taught people how to be delegates to local political meetings. The meetings were small and not led by a grandstanding national office, as the Moral Majority had been. The nationwide network was based in evangelical churches, with churches and supporter names supplied from the rolls of *The 700 Club*, although the council was rarely mentioned on the program.

Marlene Elwell, a Roman Catholic from Michigan, had been leading pro-life campaigns in her state for years. This activity captured the attention of Pat Robertson, who flew her to Virginia Beach and convinced her to run the Freedom Council in Michigan for the 1986 delegate caucus.[10] Elwell set about training novices how to run for open spots as precinct delegates. Although she had no idea that Robertson was planning on running for president, she was just the kind of person that Robertson needed. She was, however, more than willing to help with his presidential aspirations when the time came.

Robertson traveled across Michigan and to southern states making speeches at Freedom Council meetings. While the group's brochures made no mention of Robertson's candidacy, they did not have to. Most of the five hundred thousand nationwide members of the Freedom Council had been recruited from churches that supported CBN. Pastor James Muffett, who officially led the council's delegate campaign in Michigan, described his work as "mining for gold." Muffett simply called all of the conservative churches in the state and recruited people who already were fans of Robertson.[11] On May 8, 1986, the Freedom Council held a huge rally in Michigan at which Robertson was the featured speaker. After giving a rousing speech on the need for public service, Robertson teased the audience, and made his real intention clear.

"Thousands of people have been asking me to get involved, to be a candidate for president . . . so let me ask you here in Michigan, should I do it?"[12] His question was met with thunderous applause. Robertson made similar appearances at Freedom Council meetings across Michigan, while still maintaining both that the council was independent and that he was unsure if he was going to run for president.

Meanwhile, CBN was giving tens of thousands of dollars a month to the Freedom Council and went even further in February 1986. For the first time in the network's history, CBN sold a copy of its donor list. The buyer was an Arizona businessman, Michael Clifford of Victory Communications (VC). The list was used by his company to invite people to Robertson's 1986 rally in Philadelphia, along with other campaign events. While this list was in VC's possession, it was leased to Robertson's presidential campaign. Americans for Robertson (AFR) staff initially denied that they had used the list until a secret CBN memo detailing the reasons for the lease was made public. The list, described as the best of CBN regular supporters, was added to the ever growing campaign database.[13] AFR staff then clung to the fiction that the address lease was legal because AFR did not get it from CBN, an illusion that the IRS did not accept.

The Freedom Council was not the only Robertson organization at work in the fields of the Midwest. Operation Blessing, the CBN ministry that Robertson credited with saving the network, began to quietly give money to strapped farmers in six midwestern states. The ministry had given out tens of millions to the poor around the world, but its choice to help farmers caused a minor stir. While there had been a drought in the Midwest, and many family farms were going under, Operation Blessing gave an inordinate amount of money to farmers in Iowa, the state that just happened to hold the first election of the presidential campaign.

By October 1986, Operation Blessing had given $213,000 to farmers in Iowa. Meanwhile only $100,000 was given to farmers in the five surrounding states of Kansas, Missouri, Nebraska, and North and South Dakota. A year earlier Operation Blessing had given $25,000 to farmer relief agencies in several states, with the stipulation that the names and addresses of the farmers were to be given to CBN. Some agencies balked and turned down the money.[14] Although CBN claimed that it was pure coincidence that Iowa farmers got more money, few were convinced. In 1985 Robertson's *700 Club* cohost Ben Kinchlow was promoted to executive vice president at CBN and one of his new responsibilities was running Operation Blessing.[15] Within months of Kinchlow's arrival at Operation Blessing, it began to make questionable donations to Iowa farmers. In May 1987, the Robertson campaign issued a press release dealing with family farms in which the 1986 donations to Iowa farmers were claimed to have come from Robertson himself and not Operation Blessing.[16] While the donations did not make national news, they were another reason for the IRS to levy massive fines against CBN after the campaign ended.

Although Robertson has a well-deserved reputation for acting on the spur of the moment, he is also known for his stubbornness. Once an idea gets into his head, he is loath to repudiate it. This attitude has served him well for decades. Most other men would have folded their ministries years earlier had they suffered the same problems as Robertson. Usually this obstinacy has borne fruit; however, it served him poorly in a presidential campaign. Robertson desperately needed a steady source of income and volunteers for his campaign. The CBN mailing list was a good start, but it would not win him the presidency. One day he announced to his staff that his campaign should collect three million signatures on a petition to ask him to run. His staff was dumbfounded. Many, including Marc Nuttle, tried in vain to convince Robertson to abandon the idea or cut the number to the still significant figure of one million. Robertson would have none of it. The desire to get the three million signatures actually cost the campaign more money and time than it was worth. In the end, Robertson's refusal to change his mind cost him dearly. When the campaign ran short on money, right on the heels of his stunning success in Iowa, it was all too clear that they had wasted their efforts. More than anything else, the three million signatures were an anchor around the campaign.

In all, it cost Robertson a little more than ten million dollars to get the three million signatures. The names, in turn, brought in less than it cost to get them. A technique that worked so well for ministries was a miserable failure in the political arena. Massive corporate and personal contributions in the form of "soft money" ads had become popular and widespread by 1988. This made it nearly impossible for a grassroots campaign like Robertson's to raise enough money to compete.[17] Even though Robertson eventually came in second in fund-raising, the $10 million spent on the ego-driven three million signatures campaign diverted much needed funds.

In late 1986, Robertson stated publicly that he would run for the presidency if he received three million signatures urging him to do so. Most other candidates just announced their intentions, formed exploratory committees, conducted polls, and then acted on the information that was brought in. Robertson, however, thought that the three million signatures would be a sufficient call to action on its own.[18] This was Robertson's secret plan for winning the presidency, and he only released this information to select audiences.

While appearing on *Larry King Live* in early 1987, Robertson told the audience that the signatures were needed to lure him away from his job as a broadcaster at CBN. "I wanted to make sure," Robertson said, "that there was a true grassroots movement supporting my candidacy and unless it [the voter support] was there I was very happy to remain a broadcaster."[19] This story was designed to make him sound like a man who was called, like King David, out of the pasture to lead the nation. However, when asked the same question while being interviewed by his old acquaintance Paul Crouch of the Trinity Broadcasting Network (TBN), he gave a remarkably different answer. Instead of a gentle answer about the will of the people leading him, Robertson gave an answer that demonstrated just how much effort had gone into the campaign years before he formally announced.

Robertson looked directly into the camera as he spoke. "If we have the three million [signatures] a couple of things happen. If they are in the right number of states, in the southern primaries and in California . . . it will guarantee us winning the Republican nomination." He went further to show how his simple call for grassroots support was actually an attempt to see if his campaign could garner enough precincts to win the primaries before they had begun. "It will take seven million votes I estimate, nationwide, to win the Republican nomination . . . to get the 1135 plus [delegate] votes which would put me over the top on the first ballot." He went on to list how many popular votes he needed from several key states and concluded by saying, "So that is what the three million means, it means by September, if I have those signatures, I go in as a winner."[20] He probably would have been attacked if he had mentioned that on CNN or other secular media, but in the haven of another Christian broadcaster's domain he showed total confidence.

Robertson needed a mailing list of names of people who would support the campaign financially and physically. Legally he could not use the list of millions who had sent money into CBN to support *The 700 Club*, but he found ways around this. The list that AFR bought in a roundabout way from CBN was the basis of AFR's grassroots fund-raising campaign. The most important reason for the three million signatures was money. Robertson was wealthy, and if he could combine his own money with a significant amount from small donors, he could refuse federal matching funds and its mandatory spending limit. The three million signatures were the key to this plan. Once the list was compiled, the direct mail campaign started. Supporters were asked to send in a onetime contribution of $88 to support Robertson's candidacy. If all three million people had sent that amount, it would have added up to more than $264 million. Even if only one-sixteenth of the signatories donated, about 187,000 people, it would have brought in more than $16.5 million dollars. In essence, the potential donors to Robertson's campaign were going to be *The 88 Club*, a political equivalent of *The 700 Club*. What had worked so well for twenty years in the rough world of television was adapted to American politics. Robertson's idea for a solid list of donors, not just delegate voters, seemed so promising that he pushed the few million dollars he already had into the effort. The potential return in donations by using a tried-and-true formula was too tempting to pass up.

Based on this evidence, it is clear that Robertson intended quite early to run for president. However, few people outside of the evangelical world took notice of him. One evangelical who was able to make others take notice of Robertson was Douglas Wead, who then worked for Vice President George H. W. Bush. Wead warned the Bush team early in 1986 that a major evangelical leader was going to run for president. Although Wead was not sure who it would be, he suspected that it might be Pat Robertson. In order to counter this threat, Wead was given the task of acclimating Bush to the evangelical world. He had Bush read selections from evangelical favorites C. S. Lewis and Francis Schaeffer. Bush also filmed an interview filled with evangelical buzzwords, which was shown only in the South.[21] Wead became a close advisor to Bush when rumblings in Michigan suggested that Robertson was indeed going to run. Michigan's caucus was before Iowa's, and Robertson hoped to put together a small band of victories to launch him into the full campaign. Thanks to the Freedom Council a tremendous army of support was in Michigan to help propel the campaign forward. What they were to learn, however, was that although they had a number of supporters spread around the state, George Bush had the insiders, and that is what it takes to win elections.

The 1988 presidential campaign was unique for a number of reasons, beginning with the Michigan caucus. The New Hampshire state constitution declared that it must be the first in the nation to hold a primary. Still, many larger states were chaffing under a system that allowed such small states to decide the nomination.[22] In response larger states have occasionally moved the dates of their caucus forward; during the 1988 campaign, Michigan was such a state. Michigan had given George Bush a victory over Ronald Reagan in 1980 and the Republican Party regulars there were still loyal to him. With pressure from the vice president, the Republican nomination in Michigan was moved forward, in order to give the Bush campaign a huge boost out of the starting gate.[23] January 29 and 30, 1988, were to be the two caucus days, but the battle for precinct delegates began in mid-1986.

Michigan had perhaps the most confusing rules of the entire presidential campaign, compounded by the fact that the Democrat and Republican Parties operated differently. For the Republicans the Michigan caucus was a multistage process that stretched more than two years. The first step in the process was the election of delegates. After that came the conventions where the delegates voted for their candidates. Two weeks after that came the final phase, the actual caucus voting. To make matters more confusing, the revolving Michigan Republican Party leadership changed the rules and procedures to give their candidate, sometimes Bush, sometimes Robertson or Jack Kemp, the upper hand. What was designed to be an easy victory for the vice president turned into a fiasco that was so chaotic nobody was able to make it work to their advantage.

In order to become a delegate to the state convention one had to be elected from a precinct. This was rarely a problem since in both 1980 and 1984 hundreds of precincts had gone vacant and were later with the party faithful. Unknown to the Bush campaign, however, Robertson was well aware of previous campaigns as well. With the help of the Freedom Council, Robertson began to locate supporters who were willing to run for delegate. The Bush campaign got its first hint of trouble the day the deadline for delegate filing arrived. That evening Bush campaign director Lee Atwater called Douglas Wead several times. Wead's unheeded warning of a secret army of evangelicals had just come true.

Normally three to four thousand people applied to be delegates. By the May 27, 1986, deadline, more than nine thousand people had turned in applications, an increase of 300 percent. About half of that number were Robertson supporters, working under the banner of the Freedom Council. Even if Bush managed to beat Robertson in the August delegate election, it would be by a slim margin, not the huge victory that Michigan was intended to be. The Bush campaign decided that if it could not beat Robertson in a caucus election, it would have to change the rules.

Robertson knew that he was going to have a hard time beating the vice president in Michigan. In 1987 future senator and Department of Energy secretary Spencer Abraham was the head of the Michigan Republican Party during the 1988 campaign and was loyal to Bush. Many conservative Republicans in the state, however, were unhappy with what they perceived to be Bush's liberal leanings and they wanted a conservative candidate to oppose the vice president.

New York representative Jack Kemp was the early favorite of many conservatives. The problem was that he lacked the money and the strength in Michigan to launch a formidable offensive. Robertson had the troops, but not the support of anyone in power. Slowly the Robertson and Kemp campaigns made a pact. In essence their agreement was an "anyone but Bush" movement of conservatives in Michigan. This marriage of convenience had troubles from the start. Neither camp trusted the other and suspicions were always high. The alliance was unusual considering that Bush campaign director Lee Atwater had worked with Kemp's director, Charlie Black, at a large Washington, D.C., political consulting firm. One Kemp advisor stated that "each side felt it could control the other. Our national strategy was that Robertson would not be there in the long run and his people would eventually fall Kemp's way."[24] Robertson's camp, of course, thought much the same thing about Kemp.

The battle in Michigan began to bring much needed publicity to the Robertson campaign, and not all of it was good. A series of articles began to question the legality of the Freedom Council and its relationship to CBN. After Robertson's surprisingly lively battle with George Bush, it became increasingly clear that the Freedom Council had played a large role in Michigan. Robertson had appeared at many of its rallies, and most of his delegates were recruited by the council. An inquiry from the IRS was demanded by other campaigns. Suddenly on September 27, 1986, Robertson announced that the Freedom Council would be shut down effective October 1. CBN University and Freedom Council president Bob Slosser said, "It has become impossible to carry on the organization's activities without its mission being misunderstood and misstated."[25] Two weeks later the *Washington Post* reported that the council and CBN were being investigated by the IRS.

The Robertson message, so carefully crafted on CBN every day, was beginning to spin out of control in the media. The Robertson machine was in full swing, and the undeclared candidate decided that what he needed was a campaign biography. So many people had negative opinions about him, he reasoned that it would be a good idea to tell them who he really was. Since Robertson was so busy with his television network and campaign, he decided to have the book ghostwritten. While it is still impossible to say for sure if any of the other titles with Robertson's name were written by someone else, the writer of the Robertson campaign book later became one of Robertson's most vocal critics.

When the decision was made to hire a ghostwriter, publishing company Thomas Nelson contacted Fuller Seminary professor and author Mel White. White had ghostwritten for Billy Graham and Jerry Falwell and was strongly recommended to Robertson. Robertson wanted White to write a biography that focused on Robertson's life and showed how the 1988 election was America's chance to save the nation by electing him to office. While researching the book, White discovered that most successful presidential candidates did not publish autobiographies. More often than not these books had controversial sections that the candidate failed to notice and made for unwanted press. White convinced Robertson to call the book *America's Dates with Destiny* and have it deal with the many significant events in the life of the nation. Robertson allowed his ghostwriter to determine the important dates and write the book, and promised to review it once it was done. That proved to be the tricky part.

By late 1986 Robertson's life had become a hectic dash from place to place, and his appearances on *The 700 Club* became less frequent; his attention to his empire was similarly sporadic. When White finished the book, he began to chase Robertson around the country in a vain attempt to get the supposed author to read his own work. The task proved to be impossible. White remembers, "[I]t is a sad thing when they don't even want to read the book they have supposedly written."[26] White would fly to a city to meet with Robertson, then sit in his hotel room waiting for him to call. He did this time and time again, and in each instance, Robertson was too busy to meet with him. When they finally did meet again, Robertson suggested that they sit together and read the book aloud. When White said that this process would take several days, Robertson took the manuscript back to his room and promised to review it that night. "The next morning he told me that he had read it and liked it very much," White said. "But I could tell that he hadn't read it."[27] They briefly met two more times to work on the book. The first time, they worked onboard Robertson's private plane during a flight to Los Angeles. The plane landed in Kansas City and White was told to get off to make room for a journalist. He was left in the airport and had to buy his own ticket back home to Southern California.[28]

While White was working on Robertson's book he had another famous client in Virginia: Jerry Falwell. Since he was a ghostwriter, White was obliged to keep mum about the names of his clients; neither Robertson nor Falwell knew about the other. He did, however, talk to both of them about getting together. One day, White was meeting in Lynchburg, Virginia, with Falwell to go over a manuscript. At the end of their meeting Falwell asked White where he was headed next. When White replied Virginia Beach, Falwell told him that he was flying there on his private plane and that White had to come with him. White sheepishly agreed. When the plane touched down at the Tidewater area airport, he was horrified to see Robertson waiting to meet Falwell on the tarmac. Neither man knew about White's ghostwriting for the other, so he sat on the plane until they drove away.[29]

The last time Robertson and White met before the book's publication was in New Orleans. They were walking along the street talking about the book when a pack of dogs appeared out of the darkness, barking, and growling. Although they were behind a fence, the dogs' sudden attack on a poorly lit street surprised Robertson's security team, who quickly carried him into their van, which had been following the men, and drove away, again leaving White to fend for himself.[30] The two men did not see each other again for a decade.

Robertson was less than kind when talking about both Mel White and the book that he wrote. Although it is still available at the CBN bookstore, Robertson has nothing good to say about *America's Dates with Destiny*. "It was a disaster, just a disaster," Robertson recalls. "The only person who made money on it was Mel White. It just didn't sell anything; it just wasn't popular at all."[31] Despite Robertson's claims about the book's quality, it is perhaps the most clearly written book that has Robertson's name attached. The most amazing thing about the book is that it existed at all. Robertson had been so careful about his image and was even more inclined to be so as the presidential campaign neared, yet he never read the book that bore his name.[32] This can only be accounted for by the amazing workload that Robertson had undertaken, and as he spread himself ever thinner, he needed to take huge risks. In this case at least, it paid off in the short run.

There was a good reason for Robertson to publish the book; as the campaign took flight, a series of books came out that tried to explain Robertson and his life. The first was Gerald Straub's *Salvation for Sale*, which offered an insider view of CBN.[33] The book was more of a personal attack on Robertson than an exposé of his empire. Straub sounds like an ex-employee with a grudge, which is exactly what he is. It was not well received; one reviewer even gave it zero stars out of a possible five.[34] Oral Roberts University political scientist Hubert Morken's book *Pat Robertson: Where He Stands* was on the opposite extreme. It was an unashamed apology for Robertson's candidacy with chapter titles like "Prayer: Robertson Supports It."[35] Perhaps unsurprisingly, Morken eventually came to teach at Regent University. There were two other books published on Robertson that were more scholarly. The first, *Pat Robertson: The Authorized Biography* by John Donovan, came out in early 1988 and largely starts where Robertson's 1972 autobiography ended. The best book on Robertson's life prior to 1988 was David Harrell's *Pat Robertson: A Personal, Religious, and Political Portrait*. The book told Robertson's life story through a history of the Pentecostal/Charismatic movement and the Christian Right.

Since Robertson's newest book, *America's Dates with Destiny*, was no longer an autobiography, in late 1986 he decided to reprint his 1972 autobiography *Shout It from the Housetops*. The original intent was to reprint the book in a special edition for CBN's twenty-fifth anniversary. As it was being readied for printing, Robertson's staff presented him with a six-page list of potentially embarrassing items to be omitted or altered. Robertson finally approved a two-page version. The only controversial edit was the deletion of the section where Robertson was told by God to stay out of politics. Robertson allegedly told his staff that his coauthor Jamie Buckingham told him to put the section in the book back in 1972 and that the Lord had never told him to remain out of politics.[36] However, Robertson's denunciation of politics in the first edition was so pronounced that it is highly unlikely that it would have been included without his approval. The media quickly publicized the deletion, yet Robertson kept selling both versions in his CBN bookstore.

By late 1986 it was clear that Robertson was doing everything that a candidate did, but he refused to say that he was running. His staff was in place and the campaign list of his three million supporters was being compiled; all that was missing was an official declaration of his candidacy. However, the exact date of his announcement to run was, like the Michigan campaign, open to interpretation.

There are two versions of when Robertson officially started his presidential campaign. Robertson held that October 1, 1987, was the starting date, while the IRS believed that he became an announced candidate a full year earlier, when he held a huge rally in Constitution Hall in Washington, D.C., on September 17, 1986. While he did not officially declare that he was a candidate in 1986, it was hard to believe that he was anything else.

Constitution Hall was packed with supporters and the media. The theme song from the Sylvester Stallone movie *Rocky* blared over the speakers as

Robertson took the stage. He began the speech by recounting his version of American history, where evangelical Christians held sway over culture and politics. Robertson then announced that the nation was suffering the consequences for abandoning God.[37] Abortion, murder, and the destruction of the educational system were the result. Robertson then outlined his political philosophy: smaller government, rebuilding the nation's industrial might, fighting communism, and creating free markets. The end of his lengthy speech was what brought down the wrath of the IRS. Robertson was talking like a candidate. "Deep in my heart I know God's will for me in this crucial decision and I have his further assurance that he will care for, continue, and enlarge the ministry of CBN which is so dear to my heart."[38] Robertson had clearly made up his mind and was already working toward the nomination. The last paragraph of his speech was as clear a statement of candidacy as he would ever make.

> If by September 17, 1987, one year from today, three million registered voters have signed petitions telling me that they will pray— that they will work—that they will give toward my election, then I will run as a candidate for the nomination of the Republican Party for the office of President of the United States of America.[39]

As much as he later denied it Robertson was clearly a candidate. He was spending millions of dollars compiling his list of three million signatures and tens of thousands of dollars through Operation Blessing. Of all the Republican candidates Robertson started campaigning the earliest, and he was attacked the hardest.

Paul Weyrich had warned Robertson that at some point during the campaign a skeleton would come out of his closet, and he should prepare to deal with it before it became public. Unfortunately for Robertson, he could not have anticipated the first and most damaging allegation. Soon after the Michigan caucus, one of Robertson's Marine Corps associates, former representative Pete McCloskey, wrote a letter to Representative Andrew Jacobs. McCloskey alleged that Robertson had used his father's influence to be stationed in Japan and not Korea. He wrote, "[M]y single distinct memory is of Pat, with a big grin on his face telling us that his father had gotten him out of combat duty."[40] This letter was forwarded to journalists Rowland Evans and Robert Novak, who took Robertson to task for his supposed dishonesty. Robertson was trying to take on the mantle of Ronald Reagan, and this allegation hurt him badly. He was trying to promote himself as a patriot while at the same time denying the charges of cowardice. Worse for Robertson, the charges were difficult to deny out of hand since they boiled down to two men's fuzzy recollections of events that had occurred thirty-five years earlier. Robertson responded to the allegation with a $35 million libel suit against McCloskey and Jacobs. This made Robertson look better, since he was willing to go on the offensive at a considerable personal cost to fight the charges. Even better, the pending court case gave Robertson a good reason to refuse to discuss the matter any further with the press.

The Robertson campaign had weathered its first scandal reasonably well. However, McCloskey's accusations and the lawsuit were particularly damaging, hurting Robertson's ability to present himself as a candidate of the people because he appeared to have used his father's influence. Since he could not expect to be supported by Republican Party regulars, he knew that he had to take his campaign outside the party system and bring it directly to the people. Robertson's style on *The 700 Club* had always had a strong element of populism in it, and his campaign was to take this one step further.

As 1986 drew to a close, Robertson and his campaign staff were cautiously optimistic. There had been some rough battles, and the Bush camp was promising to make things rougher. Still, the campaign had done well in Michigan, and as soon as the three million signatures were in, Robertson's staff assumed it would be easier to bring in more money. The scandal over his Korean War record had been pushed to the back burner and the Freedom Council had done years of solid work in Iowa and the South. Yet however well laid Robertson's plans were, he could not have anticipated the scandals that rocked the evangelical world just as the new year dawned.

As the 1988 presidential primary season dawned, few candidates could claim as many advantages and glaring hindrances as Pat Robertson. He had more on-air television experience than all of the other Republican candidates combined. He had been to forty-four countries and regularly interviewed presidents and prime ministers as a part of *The 700 Club* broadcasts. He was the only candidate with a private campaign plane (Vice President George Bush had *Air Force Two*), and he had a considerable personal fortune (most estimates were around $100 million) to dedicate to his campaign. Robertson had spent a number of years developing a national constituency, and his campaign staff had a detailed plan on how he was going to win the Republican nomination on the first ballot.

However, not since George Wallace ran for the Oval Office had a candidate been the subject of such angry opposition. Robertson was anathema to all liberals and Democrats, and even most Republicans did not consider him to be a serious candidate. He was the only candidate in 1988 (besides Jesse Jackson, a Democrat minister turned politician) who had never held public office. His views on politics were often more cold war in tone than these of his hero Ronald Reagan. Robertson made the claim early and often that it was he, and not George Bush, who was the ideological heir to the Reagan revolution. Although the daily television exposure on CBN was invaluable to him, it also provided a plethora of weapons that his enemies used against him. Robertson had predicted many odd events—for example, that the world would be plunged into nuclear war in 1982—and he believed that his prayers had changed the course of Hurricane Gloria in 1985. His views on the end of the world were enough to discredit him in the secular press, although his political opponents were careful not to press the attacks too far for fear of alienating his constituency. Although Robertson felt he was ready to launch a successful campaign, the late 1980s proved to be one of the darkest and most salacious periods in American religious history.

In 1987 televangelists showed their political muscle when one of their own ran for president. It was also the year that they fell from power almost overnight. The massive televangelist empire was proven to be a house of cards. The collapse was so sudden and widespread that many predicted that the Christian Right was dead and the evangelical movement crippled. Most of the TV preachers who were successful were charismatic men and women who were used to taking big risks. It was also those same qualities that got them into trouble. For Robertson the timing could not have been worse.

The first blow came in February 1987 when Jim and Tammy Faye Bakker resigned from their television ministry and put it in the hands of their competitor Jerry Falwell. Due to a dogged job of reporting from North Carolina journalist Charles Shepard, years of deception on Bakker's part were finally brought to light. The revelations concerning the running of Praise the Lord (PTL) network and Bakker's private life leaked out for months afterwards. The Bakkers resigned from their daily show and their expansive empire when it was discovered that Jim Bakker had sex with Long Island church secretary Jessica Hahn, then paid her $250,000 to keep quiet. The situation continued to worsen with rumors of Bakker's homosexual encounters with several men, and his wife's treatment at the Betty Ford Center for drug dependency. However, the revelations that were the most serious concerned their massive abuse of donor money.

Jim and Tammy Faye's love affair with the good life had only increased when they left CBN in 1974. In the fifteen years that they ran PTL, Bakker controlled the board and the ministry with an iron fist. Using this power the Bakkers granted themselves huge homes, cars, and raises until their annual income rose above $1 million per year (Robertson in contrast made a little more than $200,000 a year from the significantly larger CBN in 1986). Bakker also used PTL money to give his board members perks and cash gifts; those who balked were quickly removed. Bakker's Christian amusement park, Heritage USA, began construction with money dedicated to ministry projects. He then oversold the timeshares to pay for the rest of the park. Bakker also gave thousands of dollars to several men to whom he had been rumored to be romantically linked. Bakker and the staff of PTL had tried to keep a lid on the ministry's many problems until they realized that Shepard was going to break the story. They decided to beat him to the punch. On March 19, Jim and Tammy

Faye Bakker resigned; the story of their wild lives was published in the *Charlotte Observer* the next day.[41] The sensational scandal was easily the most popular news story of 1987.[42]

Just as the Bakker story was hitting the airwaves, Oklahoma televangelist Oral Roberts made what must be considered one of the oddest proclamations in the history of religious broadcasting. In early February 1987 Roberts announced that God had spoken to him and unless his ministry received $8 million by the end of March 1987, God was going to "call him home." This ongoing hostage–death threat saga made Roberts and all televangelists the focus of media ridicule. As the deadline approached Roberts went to the top of the prayer tower on his university's campus to await his fate. The drama ended when a dog track owner, neither a follower of Roberts nor an evangelical Christian, donated the money, and suggested that Roberts see a psychologist.[43]

All of this boded ill for Robertson, who was never a stereotypical televangelist as were Bakker and Roberts.[44] Robertson responded on the *Larry King Live* show and other places that the scandals were God-ordained. Robertson said, "Judgment starts with the house of God, and then it works out to the unrighteous sinners."[45] He saw the events as the start of revival, and therefore the church was being cleaned up for the event. However much that answer may have appeased his followers, it did not stop his detractors in the media. He had to distance himself from a great number of issues if he wanted to be a viable candidate, and the scandals made this all but impossible. When asked about the scandals after their initial disclosure, Robertson shifted and gave fewer spiritual answers. He then went on the offensive and commented that one crooked TV ministry did not mean they were all corrupt. As a *New York Times* writer commented about Robertson's change of opinion, "one approach came from the preacher, the other from the politician, for he is both."[46]

If he was to win the election, or at least receive a serious hearing for his views, Robertson needed to change his message and make it appeal to those who did not share his religious beliefs. That proved to be the one thing that he could not do. His faith was so intertwined with his political beliefs that he could often not explain his ideas without resorting to religious language. The televangelist scandals, coming so early in the campaign, crippled Robertson's efforts to gain support both in and outside of churches. A confidential AFR memo from May 4, 1987, reveals that "several petition packets had been returned with notes saying that due to the PTL controversy they could no longer help Americans For Robertson (AFR)."[47] These pastors were also not using the survey cards that the campaign had mailed out to thousands of evangelical churches across the nation.

The Korean War combat duty scandal reared its ugly head again in April 1987 when Robertson traveled to Washington, D.C., for four days of pretrial testimony in his $35 million libel suit against McCloskey. Court transcripts revealed

Robertson's anger at the charges that he used his father's influence to escape combat duty. Most damaging were Senator Robertson's letters, which showed that he had often interceded on his son's behalf. While the respondent, Pete McCloskey, was forced to admit that there was "no direct smoking gun," he held to his assertion about what Robertson had told him concerning his father's efforts. Other Marines who served with McCloskey and Robertson were brought in by both sides, but most of their recollections were hazy at best.[48] The days of testimony received just enough media attention to keep the embarrassing story in the limelight. To make matters worse, Robertson's own actions related to the suit were ethically questionable. Shortly before Robertson filed suit, he had a journalist who had occasionally worked for CBN interview McCloskey without mentioning his CBN connection. The meeting was never broadcast; instead it was used by Robertson to check for inconsistencies in McCloskey's story. McCloskey was never told the real intention of the interview.[49] The worst effect of the trial was that it kept Robertson from being able to totally distance himself from his disgraced televangelist brethren.

Yet another blow to Robertson came on May 1, 1987, when the very popular cohost of *The 700 Club*, Danuta Soderman, left CBN to return to California. Soderman had been a TV host on secular stations before coming to *The 700 Club*, and while she enjoyed being on the show, by 1987 her opinion had changed. Years later she reflected that "the entire complexion of *The 700 Club* changed, and I felt it was becoming more and more political. The politics we were to espouse were Pat's politics and not mine, and I felt uncomfortable about that."[50]

It appeared that the combination of scandals and Robertson's increasingly strident political posturing were harming CBN. A week after Soderman resigned it was announced that donations to CBN were down and that deep cuts were going to have to be made to keep the network afloat. The combination of scandals by other evangelists and Robertson's own absence from *The 700 Club* was costing millions. The show was now hosted by Robertson's eldest son Tim and the popular Ben Kinchlow. CBN's own estimate was that donations were off at least $10 million for the year 1987. Pat appeared occasionally on *The 700 Club*, mostly to ask viewers to send in donations. Approximately 74 percent of CBN's income came from donations, and the Bakker scandal was hurting all other television ministries.[51] There were still several people who blamed the loss of income at CBN on Robertson's campaign. The chief spokesman of the National Association of Evangelicals claimed that "his whole presidential thing has thrown a cog into the machinery of money at CBN."[52] For example, the January 1987 telethon saw CBN raise 55 percent less than it had the year before. Robertson was not there to tend to the day-to-day running of CBN, and the network continued to hemorrhage until he retook control in mid-1988.

Robertson wanted to do something to distance himself from other televangelists, something that showed that he was ethical. In 1987 it was announced that Robertson would start to pay CBNU $2,000 a month toward rent on his mansion. AFR campaign staff also announced that Robertson was going to move out of the home for the length of the campaign, to avoid any conflict of interest. However, he never fulfilled either promise.

The biggest problem for Robertson was what to do with CBN and *The 700 Club* while he was campaigning. Most outside observers thought that his presidential campaign would kill the network, but Robertson had made sure that it would remain stable in his absence. His oldest son, Tim, had matured from his wild years to become heavily involved in the television business. Tim, just thirty years old, had held many posts at CBN, from camera operator to producer, and at one time ran CBN's Boston station. He returned to Virginia Beach in 1982 when the station was sold so CBN could focus its energy on the growing cable industry.[53]

On January 1, 1987, Tim Robertson replaced his father as the president of CBN, which was in the midst of a series of tremendous changes that were unrelated to the scandals that were engulfing his father's colleagues. Early that same year the CBN cable network was officially renamed the CBN-Family Channel. After Robertson's presidential campaign, the name was shortened to the Family Channel. Aside from the duties of running the network, Tim Robertson also began to regularly host *The 700 Club*. All of the other major televangelist shows were personality driven, and its founder's absence was to be the first test of *The 700 Club's* survivability in a post–Pat Robertson era. While many others, like Jimmy Swaggart, had offspring who occasionally played minor roles, it was always the fathers who were in command. While it was true that Tim was not as charismatic as his father, any potential loss in viewers would be offset by the fact that any campaign scandal that hit Pat Robertson would be less likely to hurt CBN.

The scandals among the televangelists had a commonality: the men and women all believed that they were above reproach so they could act as they willed. They were still used to the time when the only ones who took note of them were their loyal viewers, but thanks to the rise of the Christian Right and Robertson's candidacy, those days were over. Bakker and Roberts dismissed their actions by pointing to all of the good things that he had done in God's name. It was as if they were owed a special grace since they were special people. Some of their defenders claimed that they were similar to Israel's King David who sinned famously yet was still described as a man after God's own heart. Unfortunately for them, the argument was not accepted either within or without the evangelical community.

Robertson's problem was not wine, women, and song, at least not since his conversion, yet he held the same philosophy as his fallen television compatriots.

He felt that he had done great things for the kingdom of God, and with that sense of power came arrogance. Among all of the televangelists, Robertson had run perhaps the cleanest ship when it came to his business dealings. He did not spend money on prostitutes, or lavish mansions, or try to build a religious theme park. However, when it came to the 1988 presidential campaign, Robertson was the worst offender in terms of the misuse of money and election laws. His abuse of Freedom Council funds and those of several other organizations, including CBN, were immense. Like his comrades that were caught in more salacious scandals, Robertson misused millions of dollars donated to his ministry. While it made better headlines to write about the Bakker's air-conditioned doghouse and Christian amusement park, Robertson's offenses were just as serious, if not legally criminal. His ministry had given more than $10 million to further his personal political ambitions. This money was given by donors who thought that their money was going to CBN, not to pay for AFR ads in Iowa or New Hampshire. The news of abuse of funds by Robertson and CBN was handled well by AFR staff and did not become a major scandal. The overall effect was negligible because Americans are more intrigued by sex scandals than money laundering schemes. Since Robertson did not spend the money on grand living, the abuses were largely ignored by the public.

This abuse of money and power did not stop with his run for the presidency. After his campaign faded away, his attitude remained. Money meant power and no questions asked. Although he did not seem to realize it, Robertson's campaign for the presidency changed him in a number of ways. His ministry, politics, and character would never be the same.

Notes

1. Pat Robertson, interview by author, tape recording, Virginia Beach, Va., May 25, 2000.

2. Paul Weyrich, interview by author, tape recording, Washington, D.C., August 16, 2000.

3. Jack Germond and Jules Whitcover, *Whose Broad Stripes and Bright Stars?* (New York: Warner, 1989), 83.

4. "Meese Aid Resigns to Join Robertson," *UPI*, October 16, 1986.

5. *Conservative Digest* reprinted the article in its August 1985 issue along with an interview of Robertson.

6. Paul Kirk, campaign letter, undated, circa early 1986. Americans for Robertson Archives (AFRA).

7. April Witt, "CBN Gave $3 Million to Group Backing Robertson," *Virginian-Pilot*, September 14, 1986.

8. Michael McManus, "CBN Contributions to Robertson Unethical," *Jacksonville Journal* [Fla.], October 24, 1987.

9. Thomas Edsall, "Pledge Made to IRS to Avoid Campaign," *Washington Post*, June 21, 1986.

10. William Martin, *With God on Our Side: The Rise of the Religious Right in America* (New York: Broadway Books, 1996), 261.

11. Paul Taylor, "Churches Were the Way to Robertson Recruits," *Washington Post*, May 29, 1986

12. Thomas Edsall, "Fund Raising Methods of Pat Robertson Council Questioned," *Washington Post*, June 6, 1986.

13. April Witt, "Robertson Campaign Used CBN Donor List, Letter Shows," *Virginian-Pilot*, October 17, 1987.

14. April Witt, "CBN Farm Aid Donation Focus on 1st Caucus State," *Virginian-Pilot*, October 12, 1986.

15. J. Gordon Melton, Phillip C. Lucas, and Jon Stone, *Prime-Time Religion: An Encyclopedia of Religious Broadcasting* (Phoenix, Ariz.: Oryx Press, 1997), 177.

16. AFR press release, May 4, 1987. AFRA.

17. Former California governor Jerry Brown's 1992 presidential effort was perhaps the last attempt at a truly grassroots campaign.

18. *Larry King Live*, April 23, 1987, CNN.

19. *Larry King Live*, April 23, 1987.

20. Interview with Pat Robertson, July 8, 1987. The Trinity Broadcasting Network. Regent University Special Collections (RUA).

21. Martin, *With God on Our Side*, 264.

22. For example, Louisiana moved its caucus before Iowa's in 1996, and large states like California have moved their primaries from June to March in order to have more influence in the nomination process.

23. Germond and Whitcover, *Whose Broad Stripes and Bright Stars?* 81.

24. Germond and Whitcover, *Whose Broad Stripes and Bright Stars?* 92.

25. April Witt, "Council Described as Front for Robertson Will Close," *Virginian-Pilot*, September 27, 1986.

26. Mel White, interview by author, tape recording, Laguna Woods, Calif., September 29, 1999.

27. Mel White interview.

28. Mel White, *Stranger at the Gate: To Be Gay and Christian in America* (New York: Simon & Schuster, 1994), 205.

29. Mel White interview.

30. White, *Stranger at the Gate*, 206.

31. Pat Robertson interview.

32. In his 1987 biography of Robertson, D. E. Harrell claims that *America's Dates with Destiny* is a useful book for understanding the mind of Pat Robertson because it so clearly showed his thinking. He is right, but not for the reasons that he thinks. The fact that the book's supposed author spent so little time on it tells us just as much about Robertson's attitude and priorities at the time.

33. Straub, Gerard Thomas, *Salvation for Sale: An Insider's View of Pat Robertson* (Buffalo, N.Y.: Prometheus Books, 1988).

34. Ben Kaufman, "Holier than Thou: Straub's Salvation Sheds Little Light on Inner Circle," *Cincinnati Enquirer* [Ohio], October 12, 1986.

35. Hubert Morken, *Pat Robertson: Where He Stands* (Grand Rapids, Mich.: Revell Co., 1988).

36. April Witt, "Robertson Aid Ok's Cuts, Ex-aid Says," *Virginian-Pilot*, January 1, 1988.

37. Robertson used similar rhetoric to explain the September 11, 2001, terrorist attacks in New York and Washington, D.C.

38. Pat Robertson speech, September 17, 1986. AFRA.

39. Pat Robertson speech.

40. Associated Press, "Robertson's Father Wrote to General," circa early 1987.

41. For the full story of the Bakker scandal see Charles Shepard, *Forgiven: The Rise and Fall of Jim Bakker and the PTL Ministry* (New York: Atlantic Monthly Press, 1989).

42. In 1989 when Jim Bakker was sentenced to forty-five years in prison Robertson was not kind. Robertson said that Bakker "has been flawed since childhood" and said that Jim and Tammy Faye "lived in a fantasy world like two little children." Robertson predicted that people would soon stop paying attention to them altogether.

43. Martin, *With God on Our Side*, 275.

44. For a fascinating analysis of Robertson's television ministry see Janice Peck, *The Gods of Televangelism* (Cresskill, N.J.: Hampton Press, 1993).

45. *Larry King Live!* April 23, 1987. CNN.

46. Wayne King, "Robertson Shifts Political Tack in Bid to Steer Clear of Evangelist Battle," *New York Times*, March 29, 1987.

47. Memo to AFR staff, May 4, 1987. AFRA.

48. April Witt, "Robertson Fighting for Honor," *Virginian-Pilot*, April 12, 1987.

49. Witt, "Robertson Fighting for Honor."

50. Jane Harper, "Whatever Happened to Danuta Soderman of The 700 Club?" *Virginian-Pilot*, August 18, 1997.

51. April Witt, "Scandals Hurt CBN Donations Cutbacks Likely," *Virginian-Pilot*, May 12, 1987.

52. April Witt, "Robertson Campaign Taking a Toll on CBN," *Virginian-Pilot*, May 16, 1987.

53. Mark Robichaux, "Conflicting Values: Tim Robertson Turns TV's Family Channel into a Major Business," *Wall Street Journal*, August 29, 1996.

CHAPTER 11

INTO THE RING

I N early February 1987 Americans for Robertson (AFR) was officially formed and could now take over the work that the Freedom Council had been doing. However, by the summer of 1987 money was tight at the AFR campaign, partially due to the fact that Robertson had the largest campaign staff of any of the Republican candidates. Bush had around forty to Robertson's seventy-five, who were spread around the states that held the first caucuses and primaries. Robertson feared that expenses were spiraling out of control and something had to be done. In his typical off-the-cuff fashion, he unleashed an angry memo to the AFR staff in early May 1987. His first concern was that people who had volunteered to work for the campaign were now expecting paychecks. After explaining the hiring procedure, Robertson wrote, "[M]erely because some nice soul decides to volunteer at the state office does not entitle him or her to a paycheck." He no longer wanted to receive "messages telling me that their morale is bad because they haven't been paid, when there had been no obligation to pay them to begin with." Finally, Robertson tried to get his campaign staff to take care of problems on a local level and not bring all of their complaints to him. "I also look somewhat disfavorably [sic] about a continuous flood of negative memos. People are supposed to be problem solvers, not problem reporters."[1] Things were becoming unruly in the campaign, and Robertson's anger at his workers was just one sign. By late in the year, the number of paid AFR employees grew to 107. Volunteers were given a newsletter called *In House*, which focused on the candidate's activities and the Herculean efforts of selected AFR workers. The volunteers were offered special benefits for their labors. The newsletter listed people who had reached significant volunteer milestones. Any worker who surpassed 250 hours in a certain amount of time was invited to attend a special luncheon and meet Robertson.

There is a political theory that has been used in the Republican Party since the days of Richard Nixon and as recently as in 2000 by George W. Bush. It is thought that a Republican candidate should appeal to the Right during the primaries and then seek out the Center for the general election. In 1988, Robertson appeared to have a solid base among voters on the farthest right wing, but he realized that he would have a harder time swinging to the center.

During the early stages of his campaign Robertson had spent considerable time distancing himself from his compatriots in the world of televised ministries. His early speeches were also replete with his defense of the separation of church and state. While Democrat Jesse Jackson wished to be known as a minister, Robertson went to great lengths to be known as a religious broadcaster and a successful businessman. Since he seriously wanted to be considered for the highest office in the land, he wanted to make clear that he was "running for chief executive of the United States, not chief pastor."[2] Questions concerning church and state in a Robertson presidency were never fully put to rest, even after he resigned his ordination in the Southern Baptist Church immediately before declaring his candidacy. Robertson claimed that "anybody who is a conservative religious person, if he is also a conservative person politically, they just incur the wrath of the media, whereas Jesse Jackson got a free ride."[3]

It is a fascinating side note to the 1988 campaign that Robertson and Jackson, both ministers, were treated in a totally different fashion by the national media. "The media never gave him [Jackson] the scrutiny they gave me," Robertson said. While they were attacking some of Robertson's more peculiar ideas, they ignored nearly all of Jackson's. According to Robertson, "[w]hen he went to Cuba, and said, 'long live the revolution,' well to the conservatives it was anathema, but to the media it was just wonderful. . . . They wrote glowing reports about him."[4] Yet for all of these problems with the media Robertson was a very experienced communicator and knew how to handle an audience. What he discovered is that his grassroots campaign could achieve an incredible momentum, but it was never enough to convince the news media that he could really be considered a viable candidate.

The Pat Robertson who appeared on the campaign trail could be very different from the man his followers saw each day on *The 700 Club*. On the show, he was seated on a couch or an easy chair where he discussed political and theological issues in a gentle Virginia accent that gave him the air of an educated gentleman. He smiled broadly, chatted amiably, and always had an air of confidence and sincerity that made him one of the most popular of the many religious television personalities. In his campaign speeches, however, he appeared to be a different man. On live call-in shows such as *Larry King Live* or *C-SPAN*, he was quick and amiable, but on the stump he was fired up. Often he appeared angry, especially when discussing the Soviet Union. A vicious streak could also appear when mentioning the Trilateral Commission, the American Civil Liberties Union (ACLU), or communists. He spoke with such disdain that it became difficult to believe that he was the same gentle-spoken man.

There was a difference, noted by several journalists, between how Robertson acted in front of secular crowds and in front of his evangelical base. Perhaps the largest difference was that Robertson tackled controversial topics like AIDS and school prayer in front of religious audiences and tried to avoid those topics elsewhere. This worked well in most places, like Iowa, Michigan, and the South, but in New Hampshire he had a harder time. When there were no friendly audiences to be had he tended to do some of the attention-getting actions that Paul Weyrich had recommended.

Since Robertson was a political outsider, he wanted to bring in some heavyweights from Washington, D.C., but he had to look elsewhere for help. Since it was doubtful that any other well-known consultants would work for his dark horse campaign, Robertson looked to the world of marketing to sell himself as a presidential candidate. The New York advertising firm of Young & Rubicam had handled marketing for the Christian Broadcasting Network (CBN) as it metamorphosed into the Family Channel. The woman given the task of promoting the newly renamed network was a young Christian from Virginia named Constance (Connie) Snapp. Robertson quickly realized that this was the person he needed to help get his message to the voters. Snapp joined the campaign in January 1987 as director of communications and immediately began using her Madison Avenue advertising skills to sell Robertson as a viable candidate.[5]

From the very beginning it was clear that the Robertson campaign was going to resemble neither a standard political campaign nor a church revival; Robertson was a product to be advertised and sold. The obstacles that this particular product had in reaching the marketplace were considerable. An early poll taken by the *Atlanta Journal Constitution* warned of looming disaster for the campaign. Seventy-two percent of people had a negative view of Robertson, and only 2 percent of those polled thought favorably of him. Another problem was that while 85 percent of people polled recognized him, the mix of high recognition and high negatives proved to be considerable.

The Robertson campaign was run by political novices because, as Connie Snapp said, "[N]obody wanted to risk their career." Given her advertising background it was no surprise that the first thing Snapp did was form focus groups to determine why Robertson was so unpopular and what the campaign could do about it. The next step was to determine their "target market," which included people who were unaware of Robertson. The initial tests were done in South Carolina, a state thought to be predisposed to Robertson. These groups were shown a set of four different commercials, each advertising different points of Robertson's life and ideas. The most successful commercial, which received a response as high as 30 percent more than the others, was a commercial in which he said the following.

> In 1980 they called Ronald Reagan an actor and said he couldn't win. But he did win because he offered a strong patriotic leadership. Well in this presidential race our campaign is just beginning to fill that same need for traditional values and strong conservative government. Right now I'm not asking for your vote, I'm asking you to listen.

While many in the campaign, including Snapp, originally disliked the ad, they could not escape the fact that it was popular with their focus group. Their hope rested on merely trying to open people's minds to Robertson. It was decided that this commercial would be the first one of the campaign.[6]

Although Robertson had hoped to broaden his appeal beyond his *700 Club* viewership, the initial flood of mail that came into the offices of both CBN and AFR showed how difficult this move was going to be. The majority of the mail was explicitly religious in tone. Many letters had originally been sent to CBN and had been rerouted to AFR. In addition to letters addressed to "Brother Pat" and "Reverend Robertson" were letters with resumes from people looking for full-time work with the campaign. It was the personal letters, however, that showed the makeup of Robertson's supporters, who were called "the invisible army."[7]

Coming from all across the country, the letters showed an intimate connection with CBN. In September 1987 *The 700 Club* ran a special series of programs called "Seven Days Ablaze" on the need for prayer. Many of the letters that came to AFR via CBN were written on CBN response cards mailed out during the rally. Some letters came on fancy letterhead stationery, while many were simple handwritten notes. A man from Columbia, South Carolina, wrote, "[T]he point of this letter is to offer help to a Christian brother who's entering a battle that I would love to participate in. . . . I've never done this kind of thing before." A legal secretary from Georgia offered her support: "I work part time, however, I do have one day off a week that I would be glad to devote to the Robertson campaign in any way which could be of assistance." Others offered more spiritual help. A woman from Seattle, Washington, stated, "I am praying daily for you and, as the campaign progresses, I will be available to pray for special needs and crisis as they arise. You may phone me during working hours or at my home." She also gave $100 to the AFR campaign. A teacher at a Christian school in Missouri offered the support of his church and school, clearly offering to violate the church's nonpartisan status. He wrote, "[W]e would, as a church, like to get actively involved in supporting Pat for president." He then listed other political campaigns the church had assisted. This letter got noticed. A handwritten note on the letter said, "[T]his needs special attention."[8]

The link between Robertson and CBN was demonstrated in a letter from a couple from San Jose, California. They were "full of eager anticipation to see a man of faith and prayer get the Republican nomination. . . . P.S. it occurs to us that Danuta Soderman would be a terrific compliment to the Robertson for President ticket, as Vice President!?!" Robertson's political heritage was recalled by one woman from Virginia. "I would vote for you and I'm a diehard Democrat. I've never voted for a Republican in my life. I can remember when my Grandparents were always campaigning for your father." Most of the letters had small checks attached, and even more offered help.[9]

In addition to letters, odd pieces of mail continually came into the office. Many people sent in tapes with proposed campaign theme songs. Most sounded like church worship music, and they left much to be desired. One song entitled "Hooray for Robertson" was based on the song "I'm Proud to be an American (where at least I know I'm free)." Robertson eventually chose to use the theme "Gonna Fly Now" from the *Rocky* movies for advertisements and in rallies. The campaign asked for and was refused permission to use the song, but used it anyway. According to memos, AFR staff members began to evade calls from SBK Catalogue Partnership, which owned the rights to the song. The staff sent a memo promising not to use the song anymore, but then continued to do so. This all came to an abrupt halt in October 1987 when a letter from SBK's law firm threatened a lawsuit and demanded that damages be paid.[10]

There were also letters from a wide variety of religious fanatics. One lady sent a series of campaign slogans and crudely drawn logos, which she claimed were divinely inspired and would guarantee Robertson's victory. Another woman sent a ten-page single-spaced typed letter with Robertson's name written over Jimmy Swaggart's, which had been crossed out. Still another person sent a twenty-page handwritten letter claiming special knowledge from God that Robertson needed to win. This letter came complete with a curse on anyone who did not deliver the letter to Robertson immediately.

More than any other candidate except perhaps Jesse Jackson, Robertson relied on support from grassroots organizations, especially churches, to help move his campaign forward. The pastors of evangelical churches of any size were approached by the campaign, and many church leaders, both laypeople and clergy, volunteered their help. The initial mailing lists were mostly comprised of church membership and *The 700 Club* rolls. Many state AFR leaders, like those in South Carolina, were pastors. Eventually churches became a battleground. Early in 1988 the Republican campaigns looked for "Bush churches" or "Robertson churches."[11] The churches had been natural targets for most of American history, although they had never been mined to the extent that they were in 1988. One unexpected problem that Robertson's campaign had was that Jesse Jackson was pulling support from black churches that Robertson had counted on. The water was made even murkier by the touchy issue of church and state separation. While Robertson was ready to give up his ordination to settle this issue as it related to him, AFR's use of churches as a political base raised some troubling issues. A memo written to Robertson from a Washington, D.C., law firm tried to draw an exact line that the campaign could not cross. The letter listed the activities that a pastor and church could do, including handing out voter guides and selling their mailing lists. The only two things that were expressly forbidden were churches' endorsing candidates or donating money to a campaign.[12] What was missing was any discussion of how a church organization, in this case a television ministry, could donate its time and mailing list to its own pastor. Such an oversight cost Robertson dearly, but not until the campaign was over.

Pat Robertson had already spent several years working in the evangelical Christian community, through both CBN and Operation Blessing. He had already developed a large following, and he thought that his organization was already more powerful than the Moral Majority had ever been.[13] While Jerry Falwell was only able to advise the president occasionally, Robertson hoped to actually become the president. According to a Gallup poll conducted on behalf of CBN in 1983, 35 percent of Americans based their political opinions on their religious beliefs. There were other findings that gave Robertson reason to be optimistic. The report stated that "Americans, by a 2 to 1 ratio, say they are more likely than five years ago [1978] to say that religion can answer the problems of the world."[14] This was more than the three million that he was looking for to win his party's nomination.

There was, however, significant division in the conservative Christian ranks about who to support in 1988. Jerry Falwell had thrown his support behind George Bush. Religious Roundtable founder Ed McAteer also threw his support behind the vice president, which many considered a major coup, although Robertson was not fazed since McAteer was little known outside of political circles. Phyllis Schlafly supported Robertson and blamed the media for his poor showing, claiming that they held Robertson to a standard that was never applied to Jesse Jackson.[15] Ben Armstrong, the longtime leader of the National Religious Broadcasters (NRB), was swamped with requests by the Republican challengers. Each candidate wanted to speak to this important constituency at its annual meeting. In his own words, Armstrong decided to "let the bird talk, we gave them equal billing." Gone were the days when Ronald Reagan could claim that he endorsed the NRB; now it was a bevy of politicians who were waiting to pay homage. Armstrong had a long relationship with Robertson and found it tough to not publicly support his friend.[16] The reaction of the rest of the television ministry community was more hostile than expected. A combination of anger and envy was propelled by Robertson's repeated claims that he was a television executive and not a televangelist. Several well-known Pentecostal leaders, including Jimmy Swaggart and Oral Roberts, both of whom had previously steered clear of politics, changed their minds and supported Robertson for president. Unfortunately their ministries were soon rocked with scandal and their support proved damaging to Robertson's campaign.[17]

The 1988 campaign was, like that of 1976, charged because it demonstrated the power and popularity of evangelical Protestantism in America. For the first time in American history two ministers, Pat Robertson and Jesse Jackson, were both running for president. Both men were Baptists who had been speaking out on political matters for decades. In an interesting irony Jesse Jackson, who had not resigned his ordination, had consistently been treated as a serious candidate, even though he did about as well with the Democrats as Robertson did with the Republicans. Like Robertson, Jackson did very well in caucus states, even winning large states like Michigan.[18] Gary Wills notes that the press treated these men very differently. Wills writes that had reporters "not shown a determination to keep Robertson boxed into his religious past, and an obliviousness to Jackson's religious rhetoric, the similarities between the two men would have been more frequently noted."[19] The two men's campaigns are also a fascinating study in interest groups. African Americans had been a solid part of the Democratic Party for fifty years, and Jackson's campaign was, in a sense, a test of how well blacks and their agenda were accepted by party leaders. Robertson represented much the same thing to Republicans. Evangelicals had become so powerful since 1976 that this candidacy was also seen as a test of their power and the Republican Party's willingness to align itself with the Christian Right. Both groups were destined to experience the highs and lows of the campaign, then move on to seeking power by other means.

Robertson had spent most of his life as a broadcaster who had made it his goal to go outside a media establishment that he thought was hostile to both Christianity and conservative political values. For years he had used *The 700 Club* as a bully pulpit from which to attack people like Dan Rather of CBS News, who Robertson vaguely hinted was part of an understanding not to give him or Christianity a fair say in the media. Now he was confronted by these men and institutions. When Tom Brokaw of NBC News introduced Robertson as a "former television evangelist" Robertson accused him of "religious bigotry."[20]

The essence of primary politics is getting the media's attention, which in turn brings out financial support and votes. In Robertson's case the problem was that he received boisterous responses from the public in places like Iowa, but the media was so busy focusing on the Bush–Dole race that everything else was considered a mere sideshow. In response, Robertson's campaign tactics were designed to constantly upstage both men and do things that would distance him from his televangelist label. The media bias that Robertson complained about was real to an extent. He knew that he had to act decisively lest the media anoint a winner before the first few primaries were over. Another example of how his standing as a minister influenced his campaign was when the Great Midwestern Ice Cream Company named flavors after all the presidential candidates. The AFR staff wrote a letter to the company protesting the name they had chosen for their candidate: "Robertson's Born Again Chocolate." They suggested "Peppermint PAT-y" instead. The company wrote back that AFR's idea wasn't clever enough.[21] If they couldn't change the mind of a small ice cream company, how could they change the nation's?

Meanwhile, in early 1987, the work continued in getting the last of the three million signatures. The campaign was spending millions of dollars each month on the effort, and it was hoped that this list would help bring in more money. Banners and placards reading "Run Pat Run" and "Robertson for President" had been printed up, and he was busy making the rounds as his staff sought out enough people to fill the petitions. He had made it known in April 1987 that he intended to run if he got the signatures. He spoke in Iowa, New Hampshire, the South, and even in California. Still, during all of this he rarely missed a taping of *The 700 Club* no matter where he was speaking at night. He was flown back to Virginia Beach in time to tape his show for broadcast the next morning.[22] His segments on *The 700 Club* entitled "Pat Robertson's Perspective" became more overtly political as the days progressed.[23]

One of the more memorable events early in the campaign took place as Robertson spoke at the Iowa straw poll convention in September 1988. *Love Boat* actor turned congressman Fred Grandy was introducing the Republican candidates to the delegates. When he announced Pat Robertson the crowd roared so loudly that Grandy could not complete his introduction. After several failed attempts to quiet the crowd, he became visibly frustrated. In the midst of all of the commotion, out walked Robertson, who put his hand on Grandy's shoulder as the crowd went wild. Once Robertson had completed his speech he made his way off the platform and into the adoring crowd. Out came Grandy again who, for the next five minutes, tried to get the crowd to calm down so that he could introduce the next candidate.[24]

The crowd was so filled with Robertson supporters that the entire event had become little more than a showcase of his ability to organize. However, Robertson's performance began to worry the heir apparent. One reporter stated that what frightened Bush's staff the most was not their own candidate's passionless performance at the Ames, Iowa, convention; it was Robertson's people. Bush campaign advisor Mary Matalin recalls, "[Y]ou walked into the gym where the straw poll was being held and you could feel disaster." She described the moment when Robertson appeared as "his own personal revival meeting."[25] They were people having a "foot stomping hand clapping, praise the lordly intensity." That fervor proved to Bush's campaign chief Lee Atwater that "the invisible army was real—real enough anyway to stack a meeting or swamp a precinct caucus."[26] Robertson won handily with 1,293 votes to Dole's 958 and Bush's 846.[27] Matalin later wrote that Atwater looked liked he had been kicked in the face after the straw poll. He fired Matalin over the loss, but soon changed his mind and brought her back.[28] The straw poll had little significance, as delegates had to pay $25 to get in and vote, but if nothing else it was a tremendous demonstration of the devotion of Robertson's supporters and his campaign's ability to organize a meeting.

Days after this victory, Robertson sent out a fund-raising letter that used a combination of political and televangelist ploys. After recounting the Iowa straw poll victory and the fact that it had propelled Jimmy Carter's candidacy in 1976, Robertson asked for money. By mid-September 1987 the three million signatures were in and the bills were mounting. While most campaigns ask for contributions in standard amounts ($100, $1,000), there were a number of ways for people to contribute to AFR. First, people were invited to become part of the "1988 TEAM" by sending in $19.88 a month. The other option was to join the '88 BRIGADE and send in $88 a month. From this and other AFR documents it is clear that Robertson infused his campaign with techniques that had made *The 700 Club* so successful. Without support from political action committees (PACs) and large corporations, he had to rely on small contributions from average citizens.

Despite the Iowa victory, Robertson remained concerned with the hostile press regarding his status as a minister.[29] The media consistently questioned his commitment to church–state separation. In response, Robertson wrote to the church that had ordained him, the Freemason Street Baptist Church in Norfolk, Virginia, and resigned his ordination. This was a controversial move among many evangelical Christians. The church's pastor, Donald Dunlap, said that it would probably not make "any difference with the voters."[30] For his part, Robertson still defends the action. "I had mine surrendered because I think it is inappropriate for an ordained clergyman to hold the highest office. Secondly I did it out of respect for the classical meaning of the separation of church and state."[31] It was his role as a television evangelist and ordained minister, more than anything else, that struck fear into the hearts of his liberal adversaries. "The major perception," Robertson said, "was that people thought that if they were me, they would impose their religious values on other people. . . . [People] had their minds made up and it was very hard to change it."[32] He was trying to distance himself from his past, but it was already too late.

On September 15, 1987, Robertson held a huge rally in Virginia Beach surrounded by the three million signatures, on petitions, postcards, and letters. He announced that he was going to formally announce his intention to run for president. The crowd cheered as Robertson recalled the victories that the campaign had already racked up in Michigan and the Iowa straw poll. The *New York Times* commented, "Robertson was considered a fringe candidate until his stunning victory in the Republican straw poll in Iowa."[33] While the picture may have appeared bright, there were some significant problems. For one, it took millions of dollars to obtain the three million signatures, and the list itself was no guarantee that these people would donate money. Secondly, this lack of money meant the campaign was very front loaded; if it did not do extremely well in Michigan, Iowa, and New Hampshire, it would grind to a halt for lack of cash. Robertson had already spent the $10 million that he had raised, more than any candidate from either party. During the rally, Robertson announced that his campaign would attempt to get a total of seven million signatures.[34] This comment was related to what he had told Paul Crouch of TBN; he planned on using these names to win the Republican nomination on the first ballot. However, his optimism was misplaced, the campaign was actually in debt, and there appeared to be no relief in sight.

These fears seemed to be the last thing on his mind when Robertson formally announced his candidacy on October 1, 1987. The day began with Robertson making his last appearance on *The 700 Club* for the duration of the campaign. Robertson and his cohost Ben Kinchlow talked about resigning his ordination and what his campaign plans were. Before the show ended, his son Tim, who was taking over the show, presented his father with a plaque with several hundred signatures of CBN staff, CBN University faculty, and students who had promised to pray daily for his campaign.

A few hours later Robertson, his wife, and their children and grandchildren stood in front of the apartment house in the Bedford-Stuyvesant neighborhood in New York City where they had briefly lived for three months in 1959. This time, however, instead of using the slums to fulfill a spiritual mission, this trip was his formal announcement of his candidacy for president. The idea had been to show Robertson as a man of the people, someone who had risen up from poverty. Unfortunately, it was not accurate, and it did not work. Instead of choosing an easily controlled environment as most candidates did, Robertson wanted to make a bold statement. However, many of the groups that were most hostile to him were based in New York City; it was as if he was showing up in their own backyard—they were ready for him.

On a truck platform outside the apartment Robertson stood with his family and supporters surrounded by approximately five hundred people and one hundred hostile demonstrators. He was introduced by football star Rosey Greer, who mistakenly called him "Robinson." Robertson had prepared a carefully worded speech, but departed from it to heckle the protesters three times. He eventually abandoned most of his speech and spoke about how the protesters represented an America that "respects hopelessness."[35] Robertson attempted to calm fears of his religious convictions and present himself as a Republican populist. "This will not be a campaign of a small, well-organized minority. It will be a campaign to capture the hearts of the American people." He hit a familiar theme about the challenges to the American family. "With divorce comes poverty," he proclaimed, and in response he looked to tax breaks for families with dependants.[36] Most of the other ideas in his speech were left out or drowned out by the protestors. Afterwards, Robertson flew to New Hampshire where he called the protesters "a well-organized gay-lesbian group" that wanted to destroy him.[37]

Actually, the protesters represented several groups, including the National Organization for Women, ACT UP, and the Moral Resistance, a group made up of members of Fundamentalists Anonymous. They held signs that said "Robertson be gone," and "God isn't a bigot, why are you?"[38] In their press release, Moral Resistance, led by James Luce, claimed that "of all the people running for president, Pat Robertson has the least moral credibility." ACT UP, a strident AIDS activist group, accused Robertson of using AIDS as an excuse to round up HIV positive people with "Hitlerian proposals of tattooing" the infected.[39]

The Robertson campaign was angered and surprised by the hostility that it had encountered. In a confidential memo passed around the AFR offices, the problems that the campaign had in New York were dissected. While the staff had arranged for twelve buses to bring in supporters, only four buses actually showed up. So while AFR had expected 685 people, only 230 had actually been bused in. Campaign worker Dick Thomas explained the reasons. "The crowd no shows was a direct result of FEAR and the expectation of violence at the site." He also claimed that racial tensions in the poverty-stricken neighborhood were to blame for the poor turnout. Explaining why only forty of two hundred expected members of a Chinese church attended the rally, he wrote, "[T]he Chinese feared the Black community in general." According to the memo, the time and place of the rally was supposed to be a surprise. Members of the AFR staff contacted fifty local churches, and one of them had evidently leaked the location to the protestors. Thomas's message to the campaign staff was clear. "Control the environment and crowd at all costs! We shall not have another Bed-Stuy during the campaign trail."[40] The raucous rally was only the first bump on a long road.

Every political campaign has its scandals, and the 1988 cycle had them in abundance. In the Democratic camp, the extramarital affair of Gary Hart and the plagiarism of Joseph Biden were headline news and campaign killers. The Republicans were more fortunate; their scandals were smaller in number and stature. Unfortunately for Robertson, most of these small scandals were his alone. Just days after the debacle in New York City, the *Wall Street Journal* reported the story about Tim Robertson being conceived out of wedlock. The story was quickly picked up by every major newspaper in the country. To make matters worse, Robertson had told reporters that he and Dede had been married in

March 1954, not August, which was the real date. Robertson protested that he had done this to keep his family from being embarrassed. After the news was out, he no longer denied it; he merely chalked it up to his wild pre-Christian days.[41] Dede made a rare appearance on *The 700 Club* to admit to the truth. She then prayed for forgiveness for her sins.[42] While the national media gave significant publicity to the scandal, it was not a problem in the evangelical community. When the couple met, they were not devout Christians, and so their supporters did not hold them responsible for their actions before conversion. The secular media regularly ignored this important point. The Robertson shotgun marriage story was only one of many minor scandals to hit the campaign as it began its long march. The Pete McCloskey allegations were still being talked about, as were supposed exaggerations on Robertson's resume. In particular, journalists questioned whether he had ever actually studied at the University of London (he had taken one summer class) or whether he was serving on the board of the United Virginia Bank (he was on their community relations board). The AFR staff released a memo clearing up facts, including letters from bank officers, in an attempt to quell the growing controversies.[43]

On the heel of these scandals came the news about the deleted section of Robertson's autobiography, *Shout It from the Housetops*. Robertson had removed the section dealing with Senator Robertson's election defeat, which also contained an attack on Christian involvement in politics. When this story came to light Robertson denied any knowledge of the memo or the change. However his defense ran hollow when the *Virginian-Pilot* ran a story with a former CBN writer who claimed that Robertson meticulously read everything that came before him.[44] The truth was that Robertson had indeed approved the changes, but did not consider the news a scandal.

Robertson tried to use these scandals to his advantage. As soon as they hit, he mailed out a letter to AFR supporters. The three-page letter attacked those who dared to challenge him by using his family, military record, or his resume. According to Robertson, these attacks were being led by "those who deny the greatness of this nation." He warned his supporters that since AFR was required by FCC regulators to include their names and addresses in a public report of donations, they could expect a flood of anti-Robertson hate mail. He ended the letter by comparing himself to the Old Testament prophet Nehemiah, who rebuilt the walls of Jerusalem.[45] Although Robertson made claims that his campaign was reaching far beyond the evangelical constituency, it is hard to imagine any other politician using such biblical imagery in a political fund-raising letter. Robertson realized that he needed to start piling up victories, and the upcoming presidential debates proved to be the perfect vehicle.

On October 28, 1987, the six Republican presidential candidates had their first debate, featuring Vice President George Bush, retired general Alexander

Haig, former Delaware governor Pete du Pont, Senator Bob Dole, New York representative Jack Kemp, and Robertson. The entire field consisted of politically experienced men, except for Robertson. Their meeting in Houston turned out to be a plus for Robertson, who had little to lose since he was either totally unknown or completely disliked by the majority of Americans. Hosted by conservative writer William F. Buckley Jr., the debate started out with a videotaped introduction from each candidate, and then Buckley began to ask questions. Most of the debate featured the five other candidates taking turns attacking Vice President Bush. Robertson made a backhanded compliment to Bush when he claimed that he had been the greatest vice president in American history, and then offered him the number two spot in a Robertson administration.[46]

Aside from the job offer, Robertson avoided attacking the vice president directly. His most interesting comments were in relation to the Soviet Union. While most of the other Republican hopefuls attacked the Reagan–Bush attempts at nuclear arms control, Robertson attacked the Soviets. "I don't think they really want peace, I think they want their own advantage." Robertson had the benefit of being lightly regarded by his opponents in the debate, which allowed him to appear successful just by not failing.

Robertson's massive airtime experience, mixed with low expectations, gave him a boost in the postdebate polls. While 34 percent of viewers thought that Bush had won the debate, Robertson came in a surprise although distant second with 15 percent, beating both Dole and Kemp. Thirty-one percent of respondents thought that he had done better than expected. He also was ranked highest (35 percent) for his explanation of social issues. Despite those positive numbers, his handling of foreign policy was not well received. He came in second to last with 4 percent of those polled thinking he had done a good job. Despite the positive numbers, the overall boost was limited for the Robertson campaign. He jumped 4 percent in likely voter polls, but that jump only pushed him to 16 percent. Political scientist Thomas Morris commented that "if Robertson's goal was to be taken seriously as a candidate, he clearly achieved that." However, Larry Sabato from the University of Virginia thought that Robertson still looked and acted too much like a preacher. "You can take the preacher label off of Pat Robertson, but you can't take the preacher out of Robertson," Sabato concluded.[47] Still, the positive performance led to crowing in the Robertson camp. In a press release issued the day after the debate, Connie Snapp claimed, "I believe the debate last night clearly establishes him as one of the top three candidates and illustrates a broad base of appeal."[48]

Not everyone was impressed with Robertson's performance. The *Washington Post's* Tom Shales wrote that the debate was so odd that it "would be hard to satirize." He claimed that Bush and Dole had won the debate and gave Robertson merely one short paragraph in the lengthy article. The lone mention of

Robertson focused on the only religious comment he made during the debate. His statement that he thought America was a "God fearing nation" led Shales to compare Robertson to Jim Bakker and write "maybe we should be a Pat-fearing nation. Just in the interest of self-preservation."[49] Clearly Robertson was seen as merely a novelty to this veteran Washington, D.C., reporter.

Every modern presidential campaign spends a significant amount of time and effort trying to raise millions of dollars and not just shaking hands and kissing babies. Due to the massive expense related to obtaining Robertson's demanded three million signatures, cash was in short supply and federal money was too sweet a plum to pass by. On October 16, 1987, it was reported that Robertson had raised $11 million, more than any other presidential candidate of either party, except George Bush, who raised $12.6 million. AFR was bringing in more than $1.4 million a month, but it was spending cash faster than it was coming in. Most contributors gave less than $100, and no political action committees helped out. The October report noted that although AFR had only $263,221 in cash on hand, it owed more than $637,141.[50] This desperation for cash led to more ethical trouble. In September 1987, AFR sold its main computer system to a company from Denver for $100,000 more than it had cost to purchase in January. A *Washington Post* reporter discovered that the Denver company's only listed official was Colorado lawyer and AFR area campaign manager Clarence Decker. The system was then leased back to AFR at a significant discount. The *Post* reported that it was unusual for a campaign to go to the expense of buying a large computer system, but AFR had done so to settle some debts that the Freedom Council had racked up with a Norfolk computer company.[51] Robertson had sought out twenty people to pay $50,000 to lease the computer system to AFR. It was supposed to bring in $1 million, but not enough donors could be found.

All of the various campaign ploys to raise money quickly started to backfire. In October the Internal Revenue Service (IRS) announced that it planed to audit both CBN and the Freedom Council for alleged misuse of tax-exempt funds. The IRS asked for the two groups to hand over all pertinent documents by January 12, 1988. Robertson's lawyers fought the order, mostly to keep it from making news in the middle of the primaries. The IRS eventually took CBN to court to force turnover of the documents, and Robertson's lawyers battled the government at every step.[52] The IRS did not make its audit of Robertson's empire public until early in April 1988, when Robertson's campaign was all but finished.

Thanks to successful fund-raising, the campaign could look to receive more than seven million dollars in federal matching funds in early January 1988, but Robertson had other ideas. On New Years Eve 1987, AFR produced an unusual press release. In it were details of how the Robertson campaign was asking the

Federal Election Commission (FEC) to withhold the matching funds until needed, so that the government could receive the interest on the funds and save the taxpayers money.[53] While this was a noble gesture done for public relations purposes, it hid the fact that the Robertson camp was in desperate need of money. The real reason for not immediately taking the funds was that Robertson wanted to see if his staff was able to determine if it was better to pay for the election on his own.[54] Robertson had a sizeable fortune, and he could avoid the federally mandated spending limit if he refused the matching funds. In what must be considered a clear sign of Robertson's own opinion of his odds of winning, he chose to keep his bank account intact. Thus the man who became a multimillionaire thanks to the charity of loyal CBN viewers campaigned around the country, helped with taxpayer dollars, on a platform based on ending wasteful government spending.

This hesitation about taking federal funds could not have come at a worse time. An October 1987 memo from Connie Snapp to campaign manager Marc Nuttle complained about the money problems the campaign was having. "Obviously, I don't have to tell you about our money problems," she began. Snapp was worried about past-due bills and the effect they could have on Robertson's image. She attached a letter from a printer who had not been paid in two months and was complaining that his phone calls were not being returned. He had received a 50 percent down payment and was waiting for the final 50 percent, which totaled thousands of dollars. Perhaps the most striking fact was that the letter was personally hostile to Robertson. The printer was an evangelical Christian who had given the campaign a cut rate, and was now regretting doing so. Snapp's assertive letter to Nuttle was one of several of the campaign that dealt with AFR's inability to pay its bills.[55]

In mid-January 1988 AFR sent out a letter to all previous campaign contributors asking for more help. In the letter Robertson described the impact that a newspaper insert was having on his campaign. "It will cost just $47 to put this material in the newspapers of 1,000 potential voters. $25 will put the brochure in 500 homes."[56] The plea for an odd amount like $47 sounded familiar to regular supporters of CBN. This was a tried-and-true televangelist formula being applied to politics.

Despite these financial problems Robertson made stump speeches all around the country, focusing on Iowa, Michigan, and South Carolina, where he figured that he would do well. As 1988 began the press started to warm up, every so slightly, to Robertson. What remained a total mystery to his rival candidates was the true depth of his popularity. Since many of the people he had attracted were political neophytes, the polls were missing them. Mary Matalin believed that her campaign never had accurate numbers on Robertson's support, and she learned the hard way to not always trust the polls.[57] One political reporter summed up these fears perfectly when she said that Robertson's rivals were "certain that he can't win and almost as certain that he can cause trouble: they also want his followers."[58] With that constituency in mind the two leading contenders for the Republican nomination, George Bush and Bob Dole, treated Robertson kindly in public. The theologically liberal *Christian Century* named Pat Robertson as its religious newsmaker of the year, even though it said that he "first amused, then intrigued and frightened the public."[59] Not surprisingly, the editorial spent more time attacking his faith than his politics. In 1988 *Newsweek* magazine ran an article entitled "Is It Time to Take Pat Seriously?" in which it predicted (accurately) that he would do better than expected in Iowa, and that his support was deep and committed.[60]

Robertson had a group of campaign advisors who assembled every other week to discuss strategy. Paul Weyrich, Chuck Colson, and other leading Christian conservatives united to support the Robertson campaign. Although the men shared ideology, their ideas on how to run a campaign were very different. Weyrich thought that Robertson was so low in the polls that he had to take some radical actions to get noticed. One idea he had was to announce the names of people whom Robertson planned to appoint to various offices if he was elected. Colson was strongly opposed to this idea, fearing that any baggage the appointees had would drag the campaign down. Weyrich responded that "this was a terrible missed opportunity." Sadly for Robertson, even this group could not get along. "Colson and I clashed every week," Weyrich remembers. "Colson was so cautious, and never wanted to take risks. When you are as far down as Robertson, and you have as far to go as he does, you have to take risks, roll the dice, you can't act like you are the front runner."[61]

In one speech in New Hampshire, Robertson did mention people he wanted to see in his administration. The most notable was the then little-known Ross Perot, who Robertson thought would be the man to run the Department of Defense. Another time Robertson took Weyrich's advice was when he made controversial statements that he hoped would get him noticed. In a speech given on October 17, 1987, at Puget Sound in Washington State, Robertson lashed out at Ronald Reagan and his administration after a thinly veiled attack on Nancy Reagan for pushing her husband to appease the USSR in order to win the Nobel Peace Prize. He also lashed out at the Reagan cabinet, accusing them of being a part of the "Eastern liberal establishment." Not everyone was held in contempt: Robertson suggested that Reagan's secretary of the interior, Donald Hodel, would be a better man to be chief of staff or secretary of state.[62] Robertson said that he wanted to select people who "stand up for America instead of somebody who would try to move the nation toward a one-world socialist government."[63] Perhaps only Pat Robertson or Norman Podhertz was capable of accusing the Reagan administration of collusion with the Soviets. This attack had the desired effect; most reporters at the event gave Robertson more lines in their stories than Bush, Dole, and Kemp put together.

The further along his campaign went, the less cordial the relations between Robertson and the White House became. In July 1987, Robertson's name came up during the Iran-Contra hearings. Robertson reported that he had run into Oliver North in September 1985 while he was in Washington, D.C., to interview Ronald Reagan. Robertson claimed that North told him that he was about to fly to Iran to negotiate the release of American hostages. When asked about the encounter, North denied ever meeting Robertson, who still insisted that it had occurred. North testified that he had not made plans to visit Iran until February 1986. To back up his claim, Robertson released transcripts of *The 700 Club* interview where Reagan didn't deny Robertson's comments about secret trips to Iran in order to release American hostages.[64] The issue was significant because it taught Robertson the wrong lesson. For decades on CBN when he made accusations, he was used to being believed. He was not used to being challenged, not used to investigative journalism and the rough world of presidential politics. His campaign collapse was hastened when he again made wild accusations, and again tried to use his connections to prove his point.

Robertson had spent considerable time and energy creating an "invisible army" as many liked to call it. He clearly had a motivated group and was attempting to raise money, and he hoped that those two things would counter political connections and media bias against him. Perhaps he was influenced by Jimmy Carter and Ronald Reagan—both came out of the thin air to win their parties' nominations. Each of them was discounted by the politically connected, yet they still managed to win. Most importantly, since many politicians had discounted his campaign, Robertson was able to organize without interference.

Notes

1. Pat Robertson memo to campaign staff, May 6, 1987. Americans for Robertson Archives (AFRA).

2. "Populist Pat's Outreach Program," *Newsweek*, February 29, 1988, 18.

3. Pat Robertson, interview by author, tape recording, Virginia Beach, Va., May 25, 2000.

4. Pat Robertson interview.

5. William Martin, *With God on Our Side: The Rise of the Religious Right in America* (New York: Broadway Books, 1996), 273.

6. Connie Snapp, "Media Case Study: Pat Robertson," American University Campaign Management Institute, video, January 8, 1990. American University Library (AUL).

7. Collected letters to Pat Robertson. AFRA.

8. Campaign letters. AFRA.

9. Collected letters to Pat Robertson. AFRA.

10. Collected letters to Pat Robertson. AFRA.

11. Allen D. Hertzke, *Echoes of Discontent: Jesse Jackson, Pat Robertson and the Resurgence of Populism* (Washington, D.C.: Congressional Quarterly Press, 1993), 147.

12. Marion Edwyn Harrison to Pat Robertson, May 1987. AFRA.

13. David Edwin Harrell Jr., *Pat Robertson: A Personal, Religious, and Political Portrait* (New York: Harper & Row, 1987), 135.

14. Gallup Organization, *The Spiritual Climate in America Today* (Princeton, N.J.: Gallup, 1983), 27.

15. "Schlafly Says Media behind Robertson Ills," *Rocky Mountain News* [Denver, Colo.], March 13, 1988.

16. Interview with Ben Armstrong, June 16, 1989. Billy Graham Center (BGC).

17. Robert Booth Fowler, *Unconventional Partners: Religion and Liberal Culture in the United States* (Grand Rapids, Mich.: Eerdmans, 1989), 126.

18. For more on this topic see Hertzke, *Echoes of Discontent*.

19. Gary Wills, *Under God: Religion and American Politics* (New York: Simon & Schuster, 1990), 63.

20. Elizabeth Drew, *Election Journal* (New York: Morrow, 1989), 115.

21. Collected Letters to Pat Robertson. AFRA.

22. Robertson's appearances became less frequent, and his final broadcast on *The 700 Club* was in October 1987.

23. Robert Abelman and Stewart M. Hoover, *Religious Television* (Greenwich, Conn.: Ablex Publishing, 1990), 104.

24. Americans for Robertson, *Iowa Straw Poll Victory*, September 22, 1987, videocassette. AFRA.

25. Mary Matalin and James Carville, *All's Fair: Love, War, and Running for President* (New York: Random House, 1994), 48.

26. Peter Goldman et al., *The Quest for the Presidency, the 1988 Campaign* (New York: Simon & Schuster, 1989), 230.

27. Goldman et al., *The Quest for the Presidency*, 231.

28. Matalin and Carville, *All's Fair*, 47.

29. An example of this media hostility is the *Doonesbury* cartoon that was pulled from several Iowa papers the week of September 15, 1987. That week's cartoons featured a less than subtle attack on Robertson's religious views.

30. Martin, *With God on Our Side*, 280.

31. Pat Robertson interview. Robertson was reordained in January 2000.

32. Pat Robertson interview.

33. Wayne King, "Robertson, Displaying Mail, Says He Will Join '88 Race," *New York Times*, September 16, 1987.

34. King, "Robertson, Displaying Mail, Says He Will Join '88 Race."

35. Cathleen Decker, "Returns to Where Ministry Began; Robertson Opens '88 Bid amid Jeering Protestors," *Los Angeles Times*, October 2, 1987.

36. Pat Robertson, "Formal Declaration of Candidacy" speech, October 1, 1987. AFRA.

37. Robertson, "Formal Declaration of Candidacy" speech.

38. Martin, *With God on Our Side*, 323.

39. Moral Resistance and ACT UP press releases, October 1, 1987. AFRA.

40. Memo, Dick Thomas to Connie Snapp, no date. AFRA.

41. April Witt, "Robertson Fights Credibility Gap," *Virginian-Pilot*, October 6, 1987.

42. April Witt, "Robertson's Wife Makes TV Confession," *Virginian-Pilot*, October 10, 1987.

43. Collected Letters to Pat Robertson. AFRA.

44. Witt, "Robertson's Wife Makes TV Confession."

45. Pat Robertson, fund-raising letter, October 8, 1987. AFRA.

46. E. J. Dionne Jr., "Bush Draws Foes' Fire in First Debate," *New York Times*, October 29, 1987.

47. April Witt, "Robertson Held His Own in Debate, Observers Say," *Virginian-Pilot*, October 29, 1987.

48. AFR press release, October 29, 1987. AFRA.

49. Tom Shales, "The Debate: Some Sparks, but No Fire; 'Firing Line's' GOP Face Off," *Washington Post*, October 29, 1987.

50. April Witt, "Robertson No. 2 in Campaign Fund Raising," *Virginian-Pilot*, October 16, 1987.

51. Charles Babcock, "Computer Sold to Firm above Cost, Complex Transaction Raises Legal Questions," *Washington Post*, October 22, 1987.

52. Charles Babcock, "Robertson Campaign Yields Records for IRS Inquiry," *Washington Post*, April 12, 1988.

53. AFR press release, December 31, 1987. AFRA.

54. Collected letters to Pat Robertson. AFRA.

55. Connie Snapp to Marc Nuttle, October 1987. AFRA.

56. AFR campaign fund-raising letter, January 15, 1988. AFRA.

57. Matalin and Carville, *All's Fair*, 437.

58. Drew, *Election Journal*, 40.

59. James Wall, "Robertson as 1987's Religious Newsmaker," *Christian Century*, January, 6–13, 1988, 3.

60. Tamar Jacoby et al., "Is It Time to Take Pat Seriously?" *Newsweek*, January 4, 1988, 21.

61. Paul Weyrich, interview by author, tape recording, Washington, D.C., August 16, 2000.

62. Hodel eventually became president of the Christian Coalition.

63. Robert Shogan, "Robertson Rips Reagan in Bid for Support on the Right," *Los Angeles Times*, October 18, 1987.

64. Jess Bravin and Daniel Weintraub, "Robertson Insists North Did Tell Him about Iran Trip in 1985," *Los Angeles Times*, July 15, 1987.

CHAPTER 12

Iowa Corn and
Cuban Missiles

ALMOST a full year before Iowans went to the polls, the Robertson campaign launched its attempt to get people just to listen. A key element was a newspaper insert sent out in March 1987. It was a detailed story of Robertson's history and qualifications. Some in the campaign disliked the idea of an ad that was mixed among the coupons and thus easily ignored. Many, including Robertson himself, wanted to focus on TV ads and direct mailing from the outset.[1] Snapp, however, was able to convince the rest of the AFR staff that voters would not ignore these ads, and that they needed to take the time to reach people willing to listen. Her opinion, based on her advertising experience, eventually won out.

The ads were sent to small papers, mostly weeklies that reached a limited rural Iowa audience and were usually no longer than twelve pages. The campaign was able to buy what is called the outer-wrap position on many of these papers, which meant it was the first thing that the reader saw. All of the coupons and advertisements that came with the Sunday paper were wrapped inside the Robertson ad. While others worried about people throwing the ad away without looking at it, Snapp was confident. "Lets face it, those people don't have as much to read as someone who gets the *New York Times*," she said.[2] A later telephone poll found that 25 percent of the people who received the insert read it from cover to cover. Snapp reported that "I had never seen a statistic like that on anything I have tried to sell and I had worked with AT&T, IBM, and Ford. . . . It may have looked like small readership, but [one that] you can penetrate deeply."[3] The insert featured a response card for people to write about their concerns and mail it back to the campaign; from this the AFR database was made even larger. This campaign that was designed to fly below the radar made it hard for the other camps to gauge Robertson's strength, hence the nickname Robertson's "invisible army."

Another unconventional idea was the use of half-hour TV shows and a toll-free number. The campaign produced four specials entitled "Perspectives 88," featuring Robertson talking about foreign policy, the economy, education, and domestic issues. It was hoped that the viewers would watch him talk about these issues in depth, again to demonstrate his qualifications for the Oval Office. These shows were broadcast across Iowa in the evenings, replacing such popular programs as *Jeopardy* and *Wheel of Fortune*. At the end of the programs, a toll-free number was displayed, the use of which was another Robertson campaign anomaly. The conventional campaign wisdom was that toll-free numbers were a bad idea since competitors would use auto-dialing machines to block the number from being used by actual callers. As Snapp put it, "[F]or about three days before AT&T can catch up with you, you've tied up the network and run up a tremendous bill that the candidate is liable for."[4] The consensus among the Robertson campaign staff was that since they were being ignored by the other Republican candidates they could get away with it, and they were right. After the first show aired, the response was so great that it overloaded a local toll-free number and a new centralized one for the entire state of Iowa had to be set up. These were not crank calls, but people serious about Robertson and his campaign. The callers were also put into the database that was created with the respondents to the newspaper preprint. The campaign leaders realized that they needed thirty thousand votes to win in Iowa, and they were fairly sure that Robertson could count on getting at least twenty thousand; they were closing the gap, slowly but surely.

Two weeks before the election the second phase of the Robertson Iowa campaign began. When people called the campaign's toll-free number, they were sent a video entitled *Pat Robertson: Who Is This Man?* The thirty-minute tape showed the candidate in various humanitarian efforts and tried to explain his vision for America. The campaign encouraged locals to have video viewing parties. If the callers did not know enough people, the campaign supplied a list of interested people who lived nearby. These "Robertson video parties" ranged in size from five to two hundred, and were mostly attended by political novices.[5]

The campaign also hit the airwaves with a series of radio ads featuring Robertson asking Iowans to help "make common sense, common practice in Washington." Christian stations were sent a pack of ads that dealt with issues like the threat of secular humanism and world communism while secular stations received ads on foreign policy and government spending. There was never one central message sent out during the Robertson campaign. He spent considerable time proving to evangelicals that he was still with them, while showing the rest of the electorate that he was not just a candidate for evangelical

Christians. While this duality in advertising worked in Iowa, it faired less well in New Hampshire and in the Super Tuesday elections.

During the third week of January the campaign sent out its first direct mail, a small brochure with a cassette tape of Robertson's most popular speech, "What I would do as President." It was Robertson's attempt to propose solutions and address specific problems. The accompanying brochure was tailored by using the database so that each recipient received one that addressed his concerns on the front page. This was no simple task. It was the fruit of eleven months of effort in Iowa. This very direct approach finally had the desired effect. The local Iowa media began to take an interest in the Robertson campaign. While the campaign was gaining steam, it was still considered a sideshow by his competitors, especially Vice President Bush and his team, who still believed Michigan was not a warning, but an anomaly.

Bush had less interest in evangelicals than even Ronald Reagan, so it should come as no surprise that he was unaware of Robertson's increasing momentum. Bush felt that he had extinguished that flickering flame back in Michigan with some deception and political maneuvering. After the Iowa straw poll debacle, Mary Matalin was sent to the political wilderness of Michigan. The battle had been raging in that state for over a year. Robertson was able to form an alliance with Jack Kemp to keep Bush from victory. While this union appeared logical, Bush still held the trump card of being the heir apparent to a very popular president.

The Bush team was able to put pressure on the Kemp staff, and Matalin worked hard to destroy the alliance. According to many sources, the Bush team made it clear that they were going to win, and that Kemp could either help or suffer the consequences. Robertson and his supporters were considered outside the Republican mainstream, and Kemp was a party loyalist. The biggest internal threat to the Robertson–Kemp coalition was the nature of the Robertson supporters. Not only were they political neophytes, they were more interested in pushing a Christian agenda than in the Republican platform. Kemp regulars also began to fear that Robertson would renege on his deal to give Kemp some delegates. The final strain came in September 1987. Robertson was making a speech to the Republican Party faithful on Mackinac Island, where he announced his intentions to remove the Republican leadership of Michigan and claimed that Kemp had asked to be Robertson's vice president.[6] The Bush camp was more than eager to help divide the uneasy alliance. As Matalin recalls, "[I]t was old time political dealing, and not everyone could deal with it." Matalin and others in the Bush staff "had a top-of-the-lungs screaming match . . . about whether or not to make it [the deal]."[7] She was able to persuade the vice president to make an offer to Kemp. Soon the Bush camp offered the same deal to Kemp that Robertson had, a secure second-place finish in Michigan if they promised to support Bush. Kemp's team took the deal. Jack Kemp was reportedly personally angry at the switch. He had publicly given his word to Robertson, but most of Kemp's delegates had sworn to work with the vice president. In the end just enough delegates stayed with the original coalition to keep Bush from controlling the state committee and therefore delegate selection. The delegates in turn would control the 1988 primary. While the exact number of delegates that each man got was in dispute, one fact was not. All of Bush's hopes for a knockout victory early in the campaign season were ruined by Robertson. The party regulars were able to squeeze out the insurgents, and the huge delegate pool that Robertson had counted on was drained away.

When the Michigan caucus was held January 28 and 29, 1988, it was clear the struggles of 1986 were far from over. The sections that were still controlled by Robertson made it difficult for Bush supporters to vote and vice versa. One observer likened the scene to how whites prevented blacks from voting in the pre–civil rights era South. Robertson–Kemp workers kept Bush delegates waiting in the freezing night while their credentials were checked and counterchecked by "several agents who could have played linebacker for the Detroit Lions." Among those kept out in the cold was Bush's own son Marvin. Bush campaign vans kept their engines running to keep their delegates warm while they waited; many decided not to, which was the entire point.[8]

Of the state's 124 districts, thirty-three were rump (or protest) conventions; of those, twenty-eight were held by Robertson and five by Bush.[9] Unsurprisingly, it was the well-oiled Atwater machine that was able to convince the media that the vice president had won. The Bush camp claimed it had won more than 50 percent of the delegates, with Robertson at 22 percent and Kemp at 17 percent. Robertson claimed to have won 47 percent to Bush's 25 percent. However, the truth was not so simple. The Robertson–Kemp coalition had split, and Kemp's delegates went to Bush. Years later, Robertson was still incredulous about this stab in the back. "I won Michigan," Robertson proclaimed. "It was really really dirty . . . but they [Bush] had the spin doctors going and everyone believed them."[10] Bush regulars were also the main office holders and controlled the party operations, and they were determined to notch Michigan firmly in the win column for Bush. "If we had my guy in there [as party chairman] we would have won Michigan," Robertson believes. Still, Bush loyalists did control the state, and the press happily reported the vice president's point of view. Even though Bush was able to win in a caucus that was murky at best, when he didn't control the leadership, things were more problematic.

In the midst of the battle in Michigan, longtime *700 Club* cohost Ben Kinchlow announced that he was leaving the Christian Broadcasting Network (CBN) effective January 1988. He had been a popular and complimentary sidekick to Robertson since 1975. The *Virginian-Pilot* predicted that this could very well prove to be a "crippling blow" to the ministry. While that prediction did not come true, Kinchlow's departure came just as the Robertson campaign was hitting rough seas. The stated reason for Kinchlow's departure was his desire to focus on more hands-on ministry. Another reason for the timing of his departure could have been to take some heat off of Robertson's campaign. In 1985 Kinchlow became the executive vice president for ministry and development at CBN. This new job put Kinchlow in charge of Operation Blessing just months before the organization began to funnel money to Robertson's presidential campaign. Perhaps his retirement from CBN was designed to help Robertson's campaign, as was the sudden closing of the Freedom Council. No matter what the reason, it was a shock to many loyal viewers. In less than eight months the three people who had helped make *The 700 Club* into the largest television ministry were suddenly gone from the show. Tim Robertson still struggled on, but his discernable lack of on-camera charisma and his resemblance to his father only emphasized the network's loss.

Back in Iowa Robertson was attracting the support of Reagan Democrats who were not being reached by the polls of the other campaigns, according to Connie Snapp. As she put it, "[T]hey were unable to take the pulse, because they didn't know who to call."[11] The other campaigns got a heads-up when the CBS evening news did a feature on Robertson a week before Iowa. In the piece, seasoned campaign reporter Bob Schieffer warned that the other campaigns were thinking that Robertson was little more than a country preacher. Schieffer predicted that Robertson would do better than anyone expected. While Robertson was happy to hear the kindly report, his staff wished it was aired after Iowa; as Snapp said, "[A]t that point, we got all the votes we were going to get, so all it did was alert the competition."[12]

The day before the caucus Robertson ran an ad in the *Des Moines Register* that featured two large photos. Under the first photo, which was of a smiling John F. Kennedy, a caption read, "In 1960, the opposition said this candidate wasn't fit to be president. Why? Because of his religion." Under the second photo was the caption "In 1988, the opposition is saying the same thing about this man." That photograph was of Pat Robertson. He had occasionally tried to compare himself to Kennedy, but this ad went beyond pointing out the similarities in their smiles. Robertson, ever the careful user of history, was seeking to show evangelical Christians that he was not running from his faith, while proving to others that his faith was nothing to be feared. Iowa's Catholic and Democratic population admired Kennedy, and Robertson was hoping this ad would provide a boost.

Robertson felt that he was on a roll, for he boasted just before the Iowa caucus that great things were in store for him. He told his supporters, "If I win on Monday, I promise you I'll be the next president of the United States. . . . Just give me the pleasure of seeing Dan Rather's face when he has to announce it."[13]

Robertson did not win first place; that honor went to midwestern hero Bob Dole. But Robertson did come in a close second, with Bush third.[14] Robertson's successful finish was enough to "humble George Bush, and bury Jack Kemp and Pete du Pont, his principal rivals on the right."[15] More than that, it made Robertson look like a real contender for the party's nomination. Unfortunately for Robertson, this was the high point of his campaign, because George H. W. Bush had finally awakened and got his campaign staff into high gear after the humiliating defeat in Iowa.

While Robertson raced off to New Hampshire to prepare for the state's primary, his campaign was involved in several successful caucuses, which were essentially political beauty contests. Robertson came in first or second in Alaska, Hawaii, Arkansas, and Nevada. These victories were both a blessing and a curse; they brought publicity and money, but they led Robertson and his staff to believe that the campaign was going better than it actually was. It is one thing to bring the zealous into an election they have to pay to participate in; it is much more difficult to win a general election. Everything that the Robertson campaign had learned in Iowa and Michigan was going to be useless in the cold climate of New Hampshire.

February 16, 1988, was the New Hampshire primary. The state had few evangelicals, so Robertson played the Reaganite cold warrior to the hilt. A poll by University of New Hampshire political scientist David Moore showed that Robertson was the least popular candidate in any election in the state in fifteen years. According to the poll his unfavorable rating stood at 56 percent.[16] The campaign staff had expended so much time and energy in Michigan and Iowa that their preparations for New Hampshire were limited and, even worse, late. Robertson was not outwardly bothered by these problems. Buoyed by his surprise performance in Iowa, he was in the mood to boast. Upon his arrival in New Hampshire he proclaimed, "I am the only conservative who is able to win the presidency." He even made an appearance in the town of Dixville Notch, voting population thirty-four, to make his case.[17] Former New Hampshire governor Meldren Thompson supported Robertson and was featured in radio ads that attacked Bush, who, according to the ad, "cannot tell a missile from a warhead."[18] The spots also called Bush a liberal. The radio ads were different in that Robertson did not appear in them, and family issues and religious rhetoric were nonexistent.

Robertson was constantly telling his staff that he wanted more campaign commercials on television, but money problems, which had been severe for months, were getting worse. On February 5, the campaign put a freeze on all purchases and hiring. The campaign was more than $1.3 million in debt, and it could not make the kind of media buys that were required to do well in New Hampshire. Meanwhile Robertson's twenty-car caravan of reporters and secret service agents traveled the Granite State, hoping that one more good showing would open the floodgates of support and money.

February 14, Valentine's Day, featured another Republican debate. This time Robertson did not make headlines with his wit and mastery of the topics, but with an odd remark. Robertson claimed that there were still Soviet missiles in Cuba, left from the Cuban missile crisis of 1962. He stated that an aide to North Carolina senator Jesse Helms told him that Cuban refugees had seen Soviet SS-4 and SS-5 nuclear missiles hidden in caves around the island. This comment became bigger news the next day when Robertson refused to back down in the face of White House and Pentagon statements that refuted his claims. Bush accused Robertson of trying to frighten people into voting for him.[19] This kind of odd accusation would be trouble to any politician, but for Robertson, who was always fighting for credibility, it was a mortal error.[20] Pete McCloskey was in the audience for the debate, and he spoke with any reporter who would listen about his libel suit against Robertson. Robertson was angered by McCloskey's appearance and claimed that his lawsuit and visit to New Hampshire were being funded by one of his rivals, possibly George Bush.

When cracks in the Robertson campaign appeared, the attacks from the other Republican candidates started. Robertson recalled the eleventh commandment that Ronald Reagan had given to all the Republican candidates in 1988: do not speak ill of your fellow Republicans.[21] Since obvious attacks were out of the question, the other campaigns, especially the Bush camp, played a series of dirty tricks against Robertson. One morning AFR staffers arrived to find that the phone lines in their New Hampshire office had been cut. Other times Robertson, his wife, and their staff arrived at hotels to find that their reservations had been canceled by a caller claiming to be from AFR. Worse yet were the press conferences. Robertson arrived in a small New Hampshire town for a press conference and the room was empty. Someone had called and moved the meeting up two hours. In time, the campaign learned to use a password system in order to tell which messages were genuine. Robertson claimed that Lee Atwater later admitted his guilt in these pranks, although he denied responsibility for the hotel cancellations.[22]

Other problems included cancellation of lunches with Robertson supporters, sometimes by phone call and other times by people claiming to be with AFR. Robertson explains, "[T]hey did these things to goad you into doing foolish things [to] get a candidate to blow up."[23] All of these tricks are not surprising considering that the 1988 campaign was one of the dirtiest in American history. The mudslinging peaked with the infamous race-baiting Willie Horton ad and George H. W. Bush's vitriolic attacks on Democratic nominee Michael Dukakis. Horton, who was black, was a convicted rapist from Massachusetts who brutally beat and raped a white Maryland woman while he was on a weekend furlough from prison. While Dukakis had not instituted the program, Bush was successful in linking the governor to Horton's crime. As Lee Atwater said, he made it seem like Horton was Dukakis's running mate.[24]

Robertson's campaign was spinning out of control, and things were only going to get worse. When campaign worker Marlene Elwell arrived from Iowa, she was amazed that so little work had been done in New Hampshire. She recalls, "[I]t didn't take long for me to realize that we were in trouble. They didn't have the organization that we were able to put together in Michigan and Iowa, and by the time I got there, it was too late."[25] Everything about Robertson's campaign in New Hampshire seemed tentative; even *The 700 Club* didn't talk about the primary, or the election results. This was in response to Federal Election Commission (FEC) and Internal Revenue Service (IRS) inquires into CBN's support of Robertson's campaign, and the news blackout certainly hurt his chances in the south.[26] When the nation's first primary was over, the campaign's worst fears had been realized. Robertson did poorly, finishing fifth out of five.[27]

Things were getting worse for the campaign. On February 19, a memo from the public relations firm Goldberg/Marchesano and Associates, which had produced the campaign commercials, expressed concern about the failure in New Hampshire and the multitude of problems looming ahead. The ad executives placed the blame squarely on the AFR managers. "All of the other candidates bought [TV ads] before us and got the best prime. We got the leftovers." This was due to "AFR's late authorization to place spots on television."[28] While the TV ads in Iowa had been well placed, the ones shown in New Hampshire were placed randomly, with no strategic planning. The memo went on for another two pages, begging for money to help pay for airtime in South Carolina and Super Tuesday states. The advertising agency had budgeted for $4 to $5 million, then revised it downward to $2.5 million; AFR informed the advertising office that the most it could spend on TV ads was $750,000. The memo warns in uppercase, "THIS SMALL AMOUNT CANNOT DO THE JOB." The memo ends with a request for money to buy airtime in South Carolina, no matter what the amount was. Money was just about the last thing that the campaign could provide; by the beginning of February AFR was $1.3 million in debt, and costs were still mounting.

Matters took a turn for the worse that same day when a new televangelist sex scandal, this time featuring Jimmy Swaggart, made headlines. Robertson, shaken by the collapse of his campaign, accused Bush of helping to engineer the televangelist's downfall. He could offer no proof, and the comment, along with his unsupported accusations about Soviet missiles in Cuba, hurt his credibility. George Bush made one of his few public references to Robertson when he demanded an apology over his Swaggart allegations. The vice president challenged Robertson to "stand up like a Southern gentleman, show a little evidence, or else apologize." When he denied making the accusation, the Bush camp provided a videotape to the media, which made Robertson look like a liar and a crackpot.[29] Swaggart, who had been so instrumental in the downfall of Jim

Bakker, had been seeing a prostitute on a regular basis for years. This was brought to light when the reverend Marvin Gorman, whom Swaggart had outed in another sex scandal, staked out the hotel and had Swaggart photographed.

While there were never the claims of massive fiscal wrongdoing, as had been the case with Bakker, the Swaggart case proved to be embarrassing to Robertson on a number of points. The Louisiana preacher was one of the only televangelists to publicly support Robertson for president. Furthermore, like the Bakker fiasco of a year earlier, the Swaggart scandal kept growing. Weeks after Swaggart made his famous "I have sinned" speech, and tearfully repented, he was again caught with a prostitute. Swaggart seemed incapable of controlling himself.[30] This newest scandal was daily fodder for the news media and late-night talk shows. The scandal was given new life when Swaggart's denomination, the Assemblies of God, ordered him to step down from the ministry for one year. The evangelist refused, claiming that God had told him to keep preaching and not obey the commands of men. This caused David Letterman to quip, "If he was really talking to God, don't you think God would have told him to lay off the hookers?" This almost daily attack on televangelists crippled Robertson's campaign. He was never able to separate himself from his past, and the effect of these scandals merely reinforced the connection in the most negative way.

The Swaggart debacle also illustrated the rift in the televangelist world. While Robertson was hostile to Bakker as his scandal played itself out, he made several supportive statements about Swaggart. When Bakker fell, Robertson told CNN that it was God clearing house in preparation for revival. The day after Swaggart repented, *The 700 Club* replayed the entire sermon, with Robertson's eldest son Tim explaining the importance of repentance and forgiveness. Robertson also publicly supported Swaggart while campaigning in Louisiana. However, he had stayed clear of the struggle between Falwell and Bakker for control of the remnants of the PTL ministry.

The overall effect of the scandals in the world of televangelism could not have been worse for Robertson. They hurt his already struggling presidential campaign and crippled his own television ministry. Robertson's campaign could certainly have done better without the scandals taking up precious media time. What is certain is that the scandals hurt him far more than Lee Atwater's pranks ever could have. A *Los Angeles Times* poll surveyed the depth of the damage. According to the poll, the number of people saying that they would never vote for Robertson jumped to 70 percent after the Bakker scandal hit. Compared to other televangelists his negative rating rose from 20 percent to 30 percent by late March 1987 even as his recognition rating only rose 8 percent.[31] Even though it appeared as if Bush would probably win the nomination, Robertson was determined to fight on. He believed that if he could win in South Carolina, he just might surprise Bush as he had in Iowa.

The next elections, a caucus in Minnesota and the South Dakota primary, gave Dole victories and Robertson close seconds in those states, and then the roof fell in. In critical pre–Super Tuesday primaries Bush began to pull ahead of the pack. Robertson had counted on doing well in Michigan and Iowa (which he had) and then finishing by taking most of the South during Super Tuesday. He firmly believed that he was the only Republican who could win the South.

Robertson had pinned his last hopes on the South Carolina primary. It was a hotbed of religious conservatism and the place where he had tested his campaign ideas in focus groups. In several earlier presidential elections, this state had been the breaking point of many campaigns. Robertson had an intense organization in South Carolina and he had spent considerable time and money there. Still, events did not go smoothly. After his defeat in New Hampshire, he boldly predicted that he would win in South Carolina, and reporters noticed that his campaign manager cringed.

The campaign had spent considerable time and energy in South Carolina, hoping it would be a springboard into Super Tuesday. As in Michigan, Robertson had been in a long battle with Republican regulars over the manner and substance of the state's primary. In late spring 1987 Robertson and his Carolina Conservative Coalition tried unsuccessfully to unseat the state party chairman, who was also running Bush's campaign in the state. Robertson had a number of delegates to the state convention who were being challenged by the Bush camp and feared the chairman would side with his candidate. In the end, it was much ado about nothing as both sets of delegates were allowed to be seated in the convention.

Despite the battle with the state Republican Party, Robertson had every reason to believe that he would do well, and possibly win, in South Carolina. A May 1987 AFR campaign memo about the state was, in retrospect, far too rosy. While the staff feared the popularity of South Carolina native Lee Atwater, they realized that Senator Bob Dole was almost a nonentity in the state, making it a two-man race. After listing all of the difficulties that the campaign was overcoming the memo ended with this prediction: "Pat is well-positioned for a strong showing."[32] By the time the primary rolled around about ten months later, the campaign was in a position that they could not have dreamed of.

Robertson's South Carolina campaign was run by pastor Ray Moore and future Christian Coalition director Roberta Combs. Moore was responsible for the battle over the chairmanship of the state Republican Party, while Combs worked to build a statewide support base. They did the same things that had worked in Michigan and Iowa, hitting large and small churches and drumming up support for Robertson. However, this time Bush was playing the game as well.

Douglas Wead had successfully shown the Bush campaign that Robertson was a real threat, and it was up to Atwater to find out how to destroy it. The Bush camp realized that much of Robertson's strength was found in conservative evangelical churches. Wead, the "token evangelical" in the Bush campaign, came up with an idea. The Bush team found 160 large evangelical churches in South Carolina, churches that had budgets in the millions. These churches were the hotbed of Robertson campaign organizing. Members of the Bush campaign would find one wealthy, pro-Bush board member in each of these churches and ask them to talk to their pastors about organizing for the vice president. As Wead recalls, "[M]ost pastors would shut it down right there [and say] we can't do it for everybody so we're not going to do it for anybody. And that would shut it down."[33] Wead claimed that it was one of the campaign's most successful projects. They stopped the invisible army by appealing to the rich and well connected.

The worst problem facing the Robertson campaign was still a lack of money. Television advertisements in South Carolina had to be canceled, and accusations flew as the campaign collapsed. When word of the canceled TV ads hit the press, Robertson's already weakened campaign looked anemic. Connie Snapp lashed out at her advertising staff, whom she assumed had leaked the news. This in turn was answered by a hostile letter from Carole Marchesano, who sought to explain where the problems were coming from. "Why are you slaying your soldiers?" the memo began. "When no funds were released last week, we were forced to cancel AFR schedules on every major radio and television station in the state. . . . Their news departments are under the same roofs! It doesn't take a brain surgeon to figure out that AFR must be out of money." She then claimed that her agency was owed more than $50,000 by AFR and feared reprisal by the FEC due to their cut-rate help to the Robertson campaign. The ad agency also had AFR employees on its payroll, to help Robertson even more. Marchesano then concluded with "so what do you want from us Connie? Our resignation? If these things had happened with any other account we would have resigned."[34] The Robertson campaign was drowning in debt and taking other people with it.

When all the votes were counted in the March 5th South Carolina primary, Robertson garnered only 19 percent, in a state that he repeatedly claimed was a must win. Bush won 48 percent and all of the states' delegates, Dole won 21 percent, and Kemp 11. The primary had an unusually high turnout, and this also helped to swamp Robertson's army and dilute the power of its votes.[35] More than New Hampshire, the South Carolina primary was the real test of Robertson's strength and his death knell. He had done well in caucus states, and many feared that New Hampshire was a fluke and that in the south he would again be strong. Those fears, based on the inability of pollsters to gauge Robertson's numbers, dissipated when the votes were announced in South Carolina.

On Super Tuesday, March 8, 1988, Bush swept sixteen of seventeen states, losing only to Robertson in the Washington state caucus. After the disaster that was Super Tuesday, Robertson fought on, although his bravado was gone. When he arrived in Chicago three days later, he laughed about his campaigns troubles. "We've got a stripped down operation that's living off the land." Gone was the large jet; Robertson rode in a small plane with room for him, his bodyguards, and practically no one else. He held out hope that Bush could still be stopped if someone else won the Illinois primary, but oddly enough, he wished Dole well in his effort.[36] Later on, Robertson predicted that he would surprise the nation with a strong showing in the June 5 California primary, but his campaign did not last that long.

On March 28, Kemp dropped out, followed by Dole the day after. The convention was months away and only Bush and Robertson were left. Robertson had no chance at this point, but he stayed in the race. The AFR staff, which had been cut in half after South Carolina, was cut even more. In late March, Connie Snapp was let go and even more support staff members were laid off. On April 3 Robertson was still holding on to his campaign ideas, even though he had officially endorsed Bush. While in Denver, he told a church of about three thousand people about his plans. "Out of what seems to be defeat, we are laying the foundation for a great victory for this nation. It may not be 1988 . . . but I am not going to quit." Robertson even hinted that he might run again in 1992.[37]

By April 26, 1988, Bush had won enough delegates to win the nomination, yet Robertson claimed that he would fight on. Robertson later said that Bush "had spent four years organizing in the South and when we got down there we thought I had some natural support. But we couldn't touch what he had, they really had a fire wall. Bush was viewed as the heir to Reagan and the public wanted Ronald Reagan's heir, it was as simple as that."[38] It was perhaps the South more than anything else that mystified Robertson as his support seemingly evaporated overnight. It appears that while many conservative Christians were willing to support his TV ministry, they did not believe he was a realistic choice, and they voted for Bush.

On May 11, 1988, Robertson formally announced that he would suspend his campaign and endorse George Bush. Later that night President Reagan endorsed Bush, now that the nomination had all but been decided.[39] Robertson did have the unwelcome distinction of being labeled the "Loser of the week" by CNN's *Inside Politics*, for his late withdrawal and his comments about Cuban missiles. There were several pressing problems for Robertson by the time the campaign ended: the massive debt that his campaign had accumulated and the anger at CBN over the campaign from viewers and employees.

In a confidential memo written two weeks before Robertson officially suspended his campaign, the AFR staff tried to decide the best way to handle his inevitable concession. "Our first concern is with our supporters. . . . Pat needs to convince his supporters that he is not compromising himself or his ideals and that they should not feel cheated." Another concern was the response by the media. "We can anticipate that the press will be scrambling to contact all kinds of people that we don't want them talking to." The memo then listed people who should be asked to keep a low profile.[40] The majority of those listed were obscure AFR staff members, not any of the team's major players. Finally another memo dealt with Robertson's return to CBN. Campaign worker Barbara Gattullo wrote, "[A]re you aware of the animosity that exists over at CBN toward Pat and the campaign? I'm not quite sure that Pat knows the honest extent of it." She also warned of future problems with "land mines" from the campaign, especially the Freedom Council and Pete McCloskey scandals.[41]

Still Robertson was not deterred. He returned to the helm of CBN and *The 700 Club*, which had suffered huge losses of revenue and viewership during his absence. In early August it was announced that Robertson would have a chance to speak during prime time to the GOP convention during the second night of the convention. *Newsweek* reported that "the Bush campaign is now treating the evangelist and constituents like long lost political allies."[42] And indeed he was, because the Religious Right was quickly becoming for the Republicans what African Americans had been for the Democrats—a small but solid constituency that they dared not alienate.

Robertson never campaigned for Bush, who wanted the Religious Right vote without Robertson's agenda attached. The ideas that he had fought for were mostly ignored for the remainder of the campaign. Bush was interviewed by Robertson on *The 700 Club* the week before the convention. Still, some of the political capital that Robertson had expended was about to bear fruit. The nation was caught up with the Bush–Dukakis presidential race, and Robertson was not widely mentioned until he was invited to speak at the Republican National Convention. Whereas Jesse Jackson had made huge waves at the Democratic convention, hurting Michael Dukakis in the process, Robertson was more of a party man. Unlike Jackson, he never tried to become vice president or force his agenda onto the party platform. He spoke on the second night of the convention, in what must be considered one of the most partisan speeches he had ever delivered.

Robertson had an interesting theme for his speech. It was based on the keynote address given at the 1984 Democratic National Convention, and reiterated by Jesse Jackson at the 1988 DNC meeting in Atlanta. Jackson claimed in his speech that the conservative policies of President Ronald Reagan had made America into a *Tale of Two Cities*, one rich and one poor. In response, Robertson took the analogy in a different direction: he went from merely using the title of Charles Dickens's book, to looking at what Dickens had written. Robertson said that the *Tale of Two Cities* showed just where the Democrats had gone wrong.

The Robertson family home in Lexington, Virginia. Even today it is one of the largest homes in the neighborhood. (Photo courtesy of the author.)

Robertson in his Marine uniform. (Photo courtesy of the Christian Broadcasting Network.)

During the early years of CBN, Robertson had to master every aspect of television production. Here he runs the camera at CBN in the early 1960s. (Photo courtesy of the Christian Broadcasting Network.)

Robertson in the CBN studios in the early 1970s. (Photo courtesy of the Christian Broadcasting Network.)

Robertson and CBNU administrators checking on the progress of construction on CBN University. (Photo courtesy of the Christian Broadcasting Network.)

The lobby of Regent University's library, featuring the school's motto, "Christian leadership to change the world." The phrase sums up Robertson's goal for the school. (Photo courtesy of the author.)

A statue of the four horsemen of the apocalypse, a physical manifestation of the pre-millennial attitude at Regent University and in evangelicalism in general. The statue, mounted on a wall of black lava rocks, was moved in 2002 to make room for a walkway to the new performing arts building. (Photo courtesy of the author.)

Robertson announces his candidacy for president in New York City in October 1987. (Photo courtesy of the Christian Broadcasting Network.)

Debate night for the contenders for the GOP's presidential nomination in 1988. From left to right: Vice president George H. W. Bush, Robertson, Representative Jack Kemp, Governor Pete du Pont, and Senator Bob Dole (AP images/Jim Cole).

Robertson and Ralph Reed: The men behind the Christian Coalition and the 1994 Republican revolution (AP images/John Bazemore).

The most recent line up of *700 Club* hosts: Gordon Robertson, Terry Meeuwsen, and Robertson. (Photo courtesy of the Christian Broadcasting Network.)

Nobody had better on-set rapport with Robertson than Ben Kinchlow, here on the set of *The 700 Club* in the early 1980s. (Photo courtesy of the Christian Broadcasting Network.)

Robertson and cohost Lisa Ryan greet the studio audience before a taping of *The 700 Club* in 1999. (Photo courtesy of the Christian Broadcasting Network.)

Pat and Gordon Robertson during an Operation Blessing trip to India. (Photo courtesy of the Christian Broadcasting Network.)

The facade of CBN headquarters. Notice the eternal flame in the foreground. (Photo courtesy of the author.)

The first city, Paris, was liberal, and analogous to the Democratic Party. Robertson claimed that the people of this city "demanded that the new government buy them happiness."[43] Instead, according to Robertson's accounting of the tale, the people got "liberal divorce laws, breakup of families, anarchy, looting, ruinous inflation, financial chaos." Then it ended with the worst event of all, a reign of terror that put all of the city's citizens in danger of losing their lives.

The second city, London, was a model of the Robertson ideal for the Republican Party. The city did not follow the destructive road of liberalism, but "kept its faith in God." The people's property and incomes were protected, and as a result England had "a strong, stable conservative government that survived with prosperity for a hundred years."

To these attacks he added that the Democrats had gone to great lengths to avoid saying the "G word," God, and that they were even afraid to tell the American people that they were liberal (the "L word") or that they would raise taxes (the "T word"). In a fit of hyperbolic excess, Robertson called Democrat Michael Dukakis "the most liberal candidate ever put forward for the presidency by any major party in American History." Throughout the speech, Robertson made the implicit and explicit claim that God was on the side of the Republican Party and that the election of the Democrat Dukakis would surely be the end of democracy for God-fearing Americans. The welfare state would endlessly increase and threaten all. Robertson ended the speech by releasing all of his delegates to vote for George H. W. Bush. So ended Robertson's presidential campaign.

Robertson remained sidelined during the rest of the campaign, which became one of the ugliest in recent American history. The dirty tricks of Lee Atwater were turned on Dukakis with the same devastating effect that they had on Robertson's campaign. Evangelicals voted for Bush, following the voting pattern that was established in 1964 with Barry Goldwater. However, since this new wave of evangelicals were attempting to get power in its own right, they were no longer willing to sit and wait for the fruits of victory, as they had done during the Reagan era. Instead of blind obedience, evangelicals wanted Bush to act or face the consequences. While it was highly unlikely that the group would vote for a Democrat in 1992, they might just stay away from the polls, which could have the same result.

Pat Robertson ran for office because he genuinely thought he could win. He believed in the power of his constituency more than he should have, but he was always willing to take risks. Because of his candidacy, his empire suffered and he was vilified almost daily by the media, most of whom had refused to take him seriously. Still, for all of the slings and arrows he faced, he came away a stronger man. Robertson went from being a political blip to the leader of a serious constituency. While he chose not to run again, Robertson became the self-appointed spokesman for millions of politically conservative evangelicals.

In some later interviews Robertson denied that he really wanted to win. Instead, he claimed that his candidacy was part of a continuation in a long line of political involvement. In 1999 he told Cal Thomas that he never wanted to be president. "It wasn't an ego thing for me per se. It was something, I thought, to enunciate the ideals that many of the evangelicals felt deeply in their hearts."[44] However much he denied it, Robertson desperately wanted to be president and honestly believed that he could have won. The millions that he spent and his willingness to risk his empire demonstrated his real intention. Robertson was not always consistent in his denials about his campaign. A year after the Thomas interview, Robertson eagerly defended his campaign and talked at length about what he thought his term in office would have been like.[45]

The concerns that he voiced lived beyond his campaign. Most of his foreign policy positions were held by others, like Jack Kemp, or they were made moot by the collapse of the Soviet empire soon after Bush's election in 1988. It is in the area of domestic policy that Robertson has had the most impact. The family values issue that lived on years after the 1988 election is a testimony to this. While not his invention, it was impossible for a candidate seeking a major office not to address the issue, and it was even more daunting for a Republican candidate to alienate the bloc of voters that Robertson had mobilized. During the 1990s, conservative politicians lined up to appear at Christian Coalition meetings and ask for their support.

What would a Robertson presidential administration have looked like? Robertson was brutally honest. "Without a Congress sympathetic to my point of view I would have been slaughtered. The media and the Democratic Congress would have killed me. It would have been absolutely horrible. So the Lord was good in not letting me get elected."[46] Robertson thought that if Ronald Reagan, the Great Communicator, could not make Congress act, his own chances of success were limited. "It is tough for anybody to come up against the bureaucracy which is entrenched in power with huge budgets, and of course the media." Still, despite all of the trials of campaign life, Robertson was able to look at the events with a sense of humor. "You have to be a little off base to want to run for president. You have to be a little strange. It is just so hard, a terrible battlefield, the abuse and strain are horrible."[47]

For Robertson, the toughest aspect of the campaign was the hostility of the media. He recalls, "[T]hey just didn't want substance. I would give a substantive speech and it wouldn't get covered. And I would say something that they thought was a little nutty and they would laugh at it. . . . Whatever I said that they felt was outrageous they would print."[48] Some of the policies that Robertson was calling for, the year of jubilee, a flat tax, the privatization of Social Security, were very controversial, yet they were lost in the tidal wave of televangelist scandals and talk of missiles in Cuba. Paul Weyrich, the veteran of many campaign battles, nicely summarizes the trouble with Robertson's campaign. "It was technically competent . . . but it was front loaded in Michigan and Iowa, so when they did well in Iowa it could not translate into New Hampshire. I think it did a lot better than a lot of people thought it would."[49] If Robertson had spent less time and money getting the three million signatures, and more time campaigning in New Hampshire and the South, he could have done much better.

More than anything else, it was Robertson's insistence that he needed three million signatures that doomed his campaign from the start. The amount of time and effort that were expended on the petitions did not produce the desired results. Robertson, who was often able to manage business so well, refused to pay heed to his staff's recommendation to forget about the signatures and spend money on radio and television ads. This is particularly striking when we consider that Robertson got more federal matching funds that any candidate in history up to that point. His tally of $10.1 million beat the previous record set by Ronald Reagan, who received $9.75 million in 1984.[50] Robertson also received more money than either Democratic nominee Michael Dukakis, at $9 million, or George Bush, at $8.3 million, did for their entire campaigns. In 1992 Bush barely beat Robertson's record by getting $10.6 million.[51] Some of this money came after the campaign was all but over. The bulk was delivered from January to March 1988. While Robertson certainly would not have won the election, he would have done much better had the campaign been able to better control spending. Robertson's indecision over his acceptance of the federal matching funds was another reason that he raised so much money but was still cash poor.

Still, Robertson was able to leave the campaign battlefield a winner. He was now more politically powerful than Jerry Falwell or Billy Graham had ever been, and this power was only going to grow in the years to come. As Robertson was preparing to return to the helm of CBN and *The 700 Club*, he received a phone call from Billy McCormack, the former state director for AFR from Louisiana and Freedom Council leader. McCormack wanted to form a national organization using the campaign mailing list as a base. Robertson recalls the director saying, "[W]e gotta keep these people mobilized. . . . They do not want to feel like their sacrifice was in vain."[52] The Robertsons then went on vacation while Pat thought about what kind of organization he should create.

Notes

1. Pat Robertson, interview by author, tape recording, Virginia Beach, Va., May 25, 2000.
2. Connie Snapp, "Media Case Study." American University Library (AUL).
3. Snapp, "Media Case Study."
4. Snapp, "Media Case Study."

5. Collected Letters to Pat Robertson. Americans for Robertson Archives (AFRA).

6. Jack Germond and Jules Whitcover, *Whose Broad Stripes and Bright Stars?* (New York: Warner, 1989), 95.

7. Mary Matalin and James Carville, *All's Fair: Love, War, and Running for President* (New York: Random House, 1994), 48.

8. Germond and Whitcover, *Whose Broad Stripes and Bright Stars?* 99.

9. Germond and Whitcover, *Whose Broad Stripes and Bright Stars?* 97.

10. Pat Robertson interview.

11. Snapp, "Media Case Study."

12. Snapp, "Media Case Study."

13. Peter Goldman et al., *The Quest for the Presidency, the 1988 Campaign* (New York: Simon & Schuster, 1989), 249.

14. Germond and Whitcover, *Whose Broad Stripes and Bright Stars?* 101.

15. Goldman, *The Quest for the Presidency*, 249.

16. Cathleen Decker, "Robertson Least Liked Hopeful, N.H. Poll Finds," *Los Angeles Times*, November 7, 1987.

17. Dixville Notch is historically the first New Hampshire town to vote in the primary, and more often than not, it chooses the eventual winner.

18. Robertson radio advertisement. AFRA.

19. Douglas Jehl, "Robertson Retains 'Strong Suspicions' about Missiles," *Los Angeles Times*, February 16, 1988.

20. On March 1, 1988, AFR sent out a press release entitled "Eyewitness to the Soviet Missiles in Cuba." The notice gave details about loopholes in the INF treaty. But by the time the notice was sent out, the damage had been done.

21. Pat Robertson interview.

22. Pat Robertson interview.

23. Pat Robertson interview.

24. Michael Duffy and Dan Goodgame, *Marching in Place: The Status Quo Presidency of George Bush* (New York: Simon & Schuster, 1992), 26.

25. William Martin, *With God on Our Side: The Rise of the Religious Right in America* (New York: Broadway Books, 1996), 288.

26. New York Times News Service, "CBN Says It Won't Cover New Hampshire Primary," February 15, 1988.

27. Germond and Whitcover, *Whose Broad Stripes and Bright Stars?* 145.

28. Carole Marchesano to Pat Robertson, February 18, 1988. AFRA.

29. James Gerstenzang, "Bush Demands Robertson Apology over Allegations," *Los Angeles Times*, February 25, 1988.

30. For an excellent biography of the evangelist see Ann Rowe Seaman, *Swaggart: The Unauthorized Biography of an American Evangelist* (New York: Continuum Publishing, 1999).

31. Russell Chandler, "Bakker Scandal Damages Standing of TV Preachers," *Los Angeles Times*, March 31, 1987.

32. South Carolina background memo, May 29 and 30, 1987. AFRA.

33. Martin, *With God on Our Side*, 289.

34. Carole Marchesano to Connie Snapp, March 2, 1988. AFRA.

35. Germond and Whitcover, *Whose Broad Stripes and Bright Stars?* 153.

36. John Balzar, "Robertson, at Spending Limit, All but Gives Up," *Los Angeles Times*, March 11, 1988.

37. Associated Press, "Robertson Not Quitting," April 4, 1988.

38. Pat Robertson interview.

39. Germond and Whitcover, *Whose Broad Stripes and Bright Stars?* 156.

40. AFR memo, May 3, 1988. AFRA.

41. AFR memo, May 3, 1988.

42. George Hackett and Ginny Carroll, "Where Have You Been Mr. Robertson?" *Newsweek*, August 8, 1988, 29.

43. Pat Robertson, RNC speech, August 16, 1988. AFRA. All quotes are from this source.

44. Cal Thomas and Ed Dobson, *Blinded by Might: Can the Religious Right Save America?* (Grand Rapids, Mich.: Zondervan, 1999), 251.

45. Pat Robertson interview.

46. Pat Robertson interview.

47. Pat Robertson interview.

48. Pat Robertson interview.

49. Paul Weyrich, interview by author, tape recording, Washington, D.C., August 16, 2000.

50. "Robertson Matching Funds Set Record," *Los Angeles Times*, March 10, 1989.

51. Federal Election Commission, data on 1988 campaign.

52. Pat Robertson interview.

CHAPTER 13

ROBERTSON'S RHETORIC

A LTHOUGH Robertson's presidential campaign suffered from many flaws, one of the more important ones was the disregard with which he was treated by the media. He was correct in his complaint that the newspapers and television networks largely ignored his substantive ideas and focused only on his more sensational comments. Similar to Howard Dean after his famous scream during a speech in 2004, Robertson was fatally boxed into a corner fairly early in the campaign. Indeed, this has been a problem for Robertson for his entire career. This media blind spot had affected Jimmy Carter in the 1970s, and very little had changed since.

Robertson's rhetoric in the campaign is a story all on its own. Some of the ideas that he espoused, like the flat tax and the privatization of Social Security, later became popular. Other, more radical ideas like the year of jubilee, for which he was ridiculed in 1988, were so popular by the year 2000 that some members of Congress, Pope John Paul II, and Bono, the lead signer of U2, supported it. While Robertson did have some ideas that became widely influential, he was very much a man stuck in the Cold War mindset. His attacks on the Soviet Union were so aggressive and pervasive that they brought him to support an invasion of Nicaragua and the racist white regime in South Africa.

A study of his beliefs at this point is critical because it helps explain why he started the Christian Coalition and why he has made so many controversial statements throughout his career. In many ways his political thinking crystallized during his campaign because he was expected to have a well-reasoned answer to even relatively minor issues. Robertson's campaign rhetoric was a springboard to the several books that he published in the 1990s. By studying them both it is easier to understand the many different directions that his career took after his 1988 campaign.

One constant focus of Robertson's campaign rhetoric was foreign policy. While he is usually thought of as a domestic policy person, Robertson spent more time talking about the Soviet Union than family values. He made many speeches that demonstrated how far he had come since the days when he was warning of an imminent nuclear holocaust.

For Pat Robertson, the beginning and end of foreign policy rested with the Soviet Union, which he saw involved in every conflict across the globe. By the time Robertson began his run for office, Soviet leader Mikhail Gorbachev had begun glasnost and perestroika and was in the process of de-escalating the Cold War. Indeed his country, as he knew it, ceased to exist in just three years time. All of the peaceful rhetoric coming from the Kremlin was not enough to convince many, including Robertson. As far as he was concerned the Cold War was the ultimate struggle between good and evil, God and Satan, in a quite literal way. Reagan may have used such rhetoric, but Robertson believed it.

Many evangelicals believed that the USSR was the biblical land of Magog and Gog, which the Old Testament prophet Ezekiel predicted would herald the end of the world with a mighty attack on Israel in the valley of Meggido, or Armageddon.[1] Robertson has often professed a belief in this battle after which, according to the Bible, it will take Israel seven months to bury all the dead invaders.[2] With that in mind, Robertson's Cold War rhetoric takes on an entirely different tone, one which is not obvious to one who does not understand his eschatology. His views were based on a pessimistic outlook that told him that the final world conflict would be brought about by the USSR and that anything that made it easier for the Soviets in their planned attack on the nation of Israel would be judged harshly by God.

In one of his most impressive speeches, given in Concord, New Hampshire, in November 1987 Robertson spoke extensively about foreign policy. He dedicated it mostly to world communism and specifically to what he would do about it if he was elected president. For Robertson, the key difference between Americans and the Soviets was that "they are chess players and we are poker players."[3] That was why, according to Robertson, American political rhetoric uses poker terms like the *New Deal* and *Fair Deal*. He said that Americans "talk about deals because we think quick, we want to have a deal and if it isn't a deal then give us another set of cards." The Soviets, however, were chess players. "They look strategically, in the global scene they have specific targets." According to Robertson, these targets included control of Middle East oil wealth, South African mineral riches, and the world's naval choke points. He called for the "decolonization of the Soviet empire" and promised he would use "all of the political muscle of the presidency" to achieve that goal. He specifically mentioned that the Soviets should withdraw from Afghanistan, tear down the Berlin Wall, release their political prisoners, and let Russian Jews emigrate to Israel.[4]

What was fascinating about Robertson was his apparent willingness to go beyond conventional means of ending the Cold War in America's favor. He believed that communism was the enemy of God and of freedom, therefore it was acceptable to launch a modern-day crusade against these infidels. The lengths to which Robertson was willing to go, at least rhetorically, reflected his open confrontational style. In a climax to his New Hampshire speech he said, "I favor sending arms and supplies to the brave men and women who fight for freedom in such places as Angola, Mozambique, Afghanistan, and particularly Nicaragua." There were other places where his rhetoric bordered on the dangerously confrontational. Speaking in San Jose, California, the summer before he declared his candidacy, Robertson declared that the policy of containment was not enough to beat the Soviets. He went on to say, "We should stand for the ultimate overthrow or elimination of Communist tyranny from the face of the Earth including one day the Soviet Union itself."[5] This was hardly the talk of détente, or even the second administration of Reagan. Robertson demanded that any treaty with the Soviets be preceded by their withdrawal from Afghanistan; in short, there needed to be linkage. In reference to dealing with the Soviets he said, "If a man had stolen my wallet, I want him to give my wallet back before I sit down and negotiate a loan with him."[6] There was no room for forgiveness for a nation that had proved openly hostile, as he saw it, to the will of God and the independence of the free world.

Robertson's hatred of the Soviet Union meant that he was willing to support nearly any regime that claimed to be a bastion against the communist threat. One such country was South Africa. In the 1980s the worldwide outcry against South Africa suggested that the system of apartheid might soon crumble. Many of that nation's most respected religious leaders, such as Nobel Prize winner Bishop Desmond Tutu, had called for economic sanctions against South Africa. The African National Congress (ANC), whose leader Nelson Mandela had been imprisoned for decades, was also calling for sanctions. Ronald Reagan turned away from Carter's tack when he took office in 1981. Reagan called for "constructive engagement" that he hoped would gently bring South Africa into the modern world.

CBN television network broadcast reports for *The 700 Club* viewers were followed by a commentary by Robertson contrasting sharply with these opinions. One report claimed that if the United States put sanctions on South Africa, that nation would respond with its own sanctions and would make America dependent on the USSR for strategic minerals.[7] The report left many questions unanswered, such as when the reporter Bruce Page asked, "[S]hould our moral judgment of human rights violations outweigh our industrial and military needs?"[8] Robertson offered no answer. In his follow-up segment, he talked about the conditions in South Africa and what America's response should be. After explaining that the ANC was led by communists and was hostile to Israel he made a most amazing comment. "The ultimate issue facing the United States is not one view of morality versus another one, the thing that we must concern ourselves with is the long range strategic interests of this country."[9] The man who called for a "year of jubilee" to relieve the burden on the poor had no trouble keeping them chained in order to stop communism.

His campaign literature made similar claims for the need to support the white government. His statements reflected his desire to engage in "assertive engagement," and he claimed that sanctions "create the climate for revolution." He called for an end to apartheid, but stated that the ANC was far too radical an element ever to work with.[10] Robertson then wondered aloud why people were decrying the abuses in South Africa and yet were doing nothing about the starvation and massacres that were taking place over the rest of the continent. He then ended with two interesting comments: "I know that not being able to vote is bad, but not having food to eat, and being slowly starved to death is much worse." He tried to answer those who saw the events in South Africa as analogous to the American civil rights movement. He warned his listeners not to "transpose the struggle for American racial freedom into the African context to the exclusion of other abuses that are taking place over there that we should address as well."[11]

During his presidential campaign Robertson was involved in a public debate with Joseph Lowery of the Southern Christian Leadership Conference. Robertson's comments on South Africa had become well known, and Lowery publicly took him to task for his statements and his condescending attitude to African Americans. Robertson complained that "if you want support among American blacks for American political office you have to bash South Africa. I think that's bad."[12] Lowery fired back that blacks in America have the same feelings about Africans as most whites do about Europeans. It is their homeland, and there will always be a connection, no matter how far removed people are from their original culture.

Besides his tough talk against the Soviets, there was another focus of Robertson's foreign policy: Israel. The Jewish nation had been a serious concern of Robertson's for decades. As a part of *The 700 Club*, he had interviewed prime ministers and other significant Israeli political personalities. Robertson had also interviewed Yasser Arafat of the Palestine Liberation Organization while the group was still the avowed enemy of Zionism. His record on Israel was so clear that when Robertson appeared on a live call-in show on C-SPAN, a caller from the Zionist Organization of America phoned just to praise Robertson for his strong support of the Jewish nation.[13]

In a book published just before he declared his candidacy, Robertson deals at length with what the Bible has to say about the end of the world. Here, more than anywhere else, it is clear how his religious beliefs influence his politics. It is nearly impossible to imagine a president or major American official making the claims that Robertson did about Israel. "At the climax of history," Robertson wrote, "the Israelis will turn to God and the nation will once again become a center of God's revelation to all mankind."[14] A man who held such beliefs would undoubtedly be an ardent supporter of the Jewish state, seeing his role as a protector of God's chosen people. As in the Crusades or an Islamic jihad, the military could become part of an instrument of those who felt they are doing the Lord's will. This was the biggest fear of many of Robertson's opponents, that he would willingly blur the line between the Constitution and his religious beliefs. While Robertson tried to maintain at least the semblance of separation of church and state during his campaign, such writings contradicted his speeches.

Later in the same book, Robertson looked to the capture of Jerusalem by the Israeli army in June of 1967 as a fulfillment of one of Jesus's prophecies. In fact, he called that event the signal of "the approaching end of gentile world power." He went even further by claiming that "the regathering of Jews to Israel is a clear sign . . . that our age is just about over."[15] While this was standard dispensational theology, he avoided such language on the campaign trail; he rarely mentioned Israel, and only in reference to its vulnerable position against Soviet aggression. He kept his feelings about Israel to himself and let his writings be investigated by those who cared enough to wade through them. Had he won in 1988 he might have been the most ardent supporter of Israel in American history. A premium had been placed on the nation of Israel, and even in the face of the worsening Intifada revolt that began in the summer of 1988, Robertson avoided criticizing the Jewish state too harshly.[16]

In all of these issues rested the freedom of America and the ability that it should have to defend itself militarily. The Reagan era had seen a huge increase in defense expenditures, and the central questions about the end of his era was whether it would continue, and what the modern defense department would look like. Here Robertson had answers that showed his nongovernmental thinking in a clear manner. His businesses and ministries were all kept on a tight budget. He often boasted that his Operation Blessing operated on a budget that saw 99.5 percent go directly to help those in need and not to bureaucracies.[17] This was to spill over to his ideas on how to run the government: first tame the Defense Department and then deal with the domestic programs that he had successfully outperformed in the private sector. On the campaign trail, Robertson often spoke about the need to rein in the defense industry. "The question is," Robertson said, "do we get a defense establishment that is appropriate for the job at hand to defend the nation."[18] Robertson spoke of the need for reforms in the military, but he never mentioned specific issues that he would handle differently. While he wanted to be known as a foreign policy expert, this was the toughest thing for him to prove to the voters.

Robertson's domestic concerns were varied and dealt with many issues that other Republican candidates had never considered. Robertson's earlier training and self-study in economics led him to champion the standard conservative ideas, yet his biblically based ideas sometimes appeared off track to those who did not understand his views. The domestic policies that he most often spoke about were the economy and family values. The latter issue is the one for which he was best known.

While appearing as a guest on the *Larry King Live* show, Robertson decried the waste in domestic spending; King replied that this was also the case in the defense industry and asked Robertson why he favored guns over butter. Robertson replied, "I favor getting work to the people as efficiently as you can." His Operation Blessing had given out $125 million to the poor during the previous ten years (1978–1988). He claimed that government programs spent as much as 70 percent on overhead, whereas his operation operated with a .5 percent overhead.[19] He offered no proof for his figures, and he is notoriously secretive about his giving.

Robertson had formed a group to combat poverty through such activities as teaching people to read and write, but he never envisioned a new set of Great Society programs. He stated that the "problems of poverty, inequality, and injustice are problems of the human spirit. And federal spending, even within limits, will never create a fully great society."[20] He also called for a presidential line-item veto, and promised to cut $100 million from the budget by fiscal year 1990. Moreover, he called for a constitutional amendment to balance the federal budget.[21] While those were all standard conservative political fare—many of those ideas he had inherited from his father—there were other elements that were even more radical. In the book *Answers to 200 of Life's Most Probing Questions*, he called for a "year of jubilee." The concept of the year of jubilee is a biblical admonition that every fifty years all debts are canceled, all land goes back to its original owner, and all slaves are set free.[22] Robertson wrote that the capitalist system was corrected periodically by depressions and recessions and thought that having a year of jubilee would be the natural balance that would be less harsh to the economy. He also believed that this would help to alleviate the debt that was crushing many third-world nations. It is doubtful that even liberals like Martin Luther King Jr. would have thought that it was an appropriate policy, but Robertson's conservative theology told him that the year of jubilee was a God-ordained process. Therefore it would work.

Robertson has made the biggest mark on modern American politics under the large banner of family values. The issues, though not original with him, have lived on as themes that the Republican Party used more frequently after 1988.

This is the area where Robertson's Christian beliefs come most heavily into play and where they continued to have an impact years after he left electoral politics.

In what may be one of the most interesting ironies, it was Robertson, the archconservative, who promoted women's issues more than any other Republican presidential candidate in 1988. Not only was Dede Robertson instrumental in the early success of CBN, she helped her husband run for the White House. Unlike other famous wives of televangelists like Tammy Faye Bakker or Jan Crouch, Dede did not wear obscene amounts of makeup, and she was not called "dragon lady" behind her back as was Jimmy Swaggart's wife Frances. She was not her husband's crying cohost or a power behind the scenes; she had a life and career in her own right. This independence allowed her to be a helpful element of the campaign. When Robertson was in the process of making campaign commercials, the film crew and political handlers were amazed at his insistence that his wife make a comment. He was the only candidate to let his wife take such a role.[23] It is easy to view this act as an attempt to help win votes among women, but taken as a whole, the Robertsons' marriage has been one of mutual support.

The family, Robertson believes, is the foundation of the society, and therefore he, as a candidate, must have necessarily been against anything that is seen as a threat to the traditional family unit. On that basis he swung his rhetorical ax wide in attacking gay rights, the Equal Rights Amendment, the feminization of poverty, and the breakup of the family.[24] The traditional (two-parent) family received almost daily mention on *The 700 Club*, and it was the cornerstone of Robertson's domestic agenda. There were limits to what the government could realistically do to address the needs of the family. Robertson realized that the federal government could take some of the economic pressure off families so that they had one less problem to worry about. He stated that women should have the right to work any job they chose and that they should receive equal pay for equal work. Robertson declared that poverty in America had become "feminized," by which he meant that single mothers were a disproportionately large segment of the nation's poor. He believed that divorce laws allowed men to keep most of the wealth while women kept most of the responsibility for raising children. That was something that the government could regulate, and he intended to go further. "I believe," Robertson said, "that if we can afford to give tax deductions for childcare support to working women, we can also afford to give tax deductions to women who want to stay home and look after their children."[25] Beyond mere economic issues of whether a woman should stay home or not, Robertson had detailed ideas on the family and made statements that other Republican presidential candidates did not.

Among the more commonly mentioned ideas that are associated not just with Robertson, but with the Religious Right in general, is the issue of prayer in school. In March 1988, Robertson appeared on *Meet the Press*. When he was questioned at length about his plans to reinstate prayer in school, he avoided the question several times. Robertson claimed that the nation was producing "not just functional illiterates but cultural and moral illiterates as well. What I want is a return to moral values—right and wrong . . . that isn't being taught." When he finally was cornered on what he believed a prayer in school should sound like, he offered faint Judeo-Christian themes of praying to "our father, God almighty."[26] The newsmen let that answer stand without comment when it appeared that he was willing to accept a prayer having no specific mention of Christian beliefs.

In the years following his run for office, Robertson published a series of books dealing with religious and political topics. Thanks to the campaign he had become a national political figure, and this status brought with it a pronounced increase in the amount of attention that his political enemies paid to him. While Robertson had attained notoriety among his political opponents, he did not expect them to take much notice of his nonpolitical activities. While his campaign experience should have led him to different conclusions, he still acted as if only the Robertson faithful were interested in what he had to say in his books. He was wrong.

Part of the problem with the statements in Robertson's books is that no one is certain if he actually wrote them. Several of his earlier books had been coauthored, and it has been proven that *America's Dates with Destiny* was totally ghost-written. Therefore, it stands to reason that at least portions of the books that he published in the 1990s were written by others. When Harvard theologian Harvey Cox visited the Regent University campus, he was told by several faculty members that someone else had written Robertson's books.[27] These books were published in quick succession, about one a year, an impossibly rapid pace for someone as busy as Robertson. Whatever the truth of the authorship of these works, the fact remains that they were published under Robertson's name and they often echoed his daily comments on *The 700 Club* and his newsletter, *Pat Robertson's Perspective*. These books reveal Robertson's political agenda and show how his religious views continued to change as time progressed.

The biggest problem that he had to face upon the conclusion of his campaign was a theological one. The Charismatic world believed that God spoke to believers, so if Robertson was wrong about God wanting him to be president, it called everything else he said into question. A simple explanation on *The 700 Club* was not going to suffice. Robertson had to mend fences with his viewers if he hoped to avoid the fate of his fellow televangelists. In early 1989 he published *The Plan*, which attempts to answer the question, if God told him to run, why didn't he win?[28] One advantage of the Charismatic movement is that it allows believers to make radical claims about God's will, then give a different interpretation if things do not work out as planned. This ability is not limited to Charismatics; the histories of Mormonism, Christian Science, and many other religious groups are filled with stories of leaders who made bold claims, then had to eat their words.

Like any savvy religious leader, Robertson did not try to deny saying that God wanted him to run for president. In a chapter titled "Did I Miss It?" he writes, "I knew absolutely that I had received clearer, stronger guidance to run ... than I received when I was unmistakably directed by the Lord to go to Virginia in 1959 and start a television ministry."[29] He then spends the majority of the book explaining "the eight keys to receiving God's direction in your life." The keys include the importance of knowing scripture, surrendering to God's will, and believing that God will guide you. The last key deals with removing sin from your life and was the chapter where Robertson mentions the scandals that destroyed other televangelists. As he had said on the campaign trail, those scandals were the result of God cleaning house in preparation for a massive revival that Robertson predicted would hit in the 1990s. In each chapter about the keys, Robertson tells stories from either his days at CBN or on the campaign trail that show how God had led him and it always worked out. He uses the chapter on believing in God to explain to his followers why he seemed to avoid his religious beliefs while on the campaign trail. On *The 700 Club* he often claims that prayer and the saving power of Jesus were all that a person, or a country, needs to better their condition. While his faith was obvious and ominous to many, some evangelicals felt that he tried to hide it when he made statements that did not have explicitly religious themes. Robertson explained that the media wanted to portray him as "a wild-eyed fanatic who heard voices."[30] He quoted Jesus, who warned his disciples not to cast their pearls before swine and claimed that "I soon learned to avoid religious language and idioms during the campaign because they only invited the slashing tusks of the press."[31]

The book concludes in typical Robertson fashion; he points his followers toward the next goal. God told him to run, but perhaps, he says, the point was to get Christians involved in politics so that they can make a long-term impact on America. He predicts that if Christians become more involved in politics "we all will know whether their presence in American public life was God's reason for leading me to enter the race."[32] These ideas dovetailed nicely with his simmering plans for the Christian Coalition. If his readers joined this new organization, it would be the fulfillment of God's call to Robertson. In this short book, he is able to take the burden of his campaign off his shoulders and onto his supporters. Robertson did his part for God's kingdom and now it was their turn.

Robertson's first book of the 1990s was *The New Millennium*.[33] The book is a study of ten trends that Robertson thought would be important as the world approached the year 2000. Among the trends that he foresees is the growth of the Christian Gospel around the world due to the collapse of communism. Other trends include the fall of political liberalism and secularism, which resulted from the fall of the Soviet Union. There are also threats to America and Christianity that Robertson predicts will provide a serious challenge in the years ahead. At home, he predicts a continued "assault on the family," which comes from militant feminism and a federal tax system that punishes mothers who stayed home to raise their children. He also blames the government's welfare system for promoting single-parent families, which in turn raises maladjusted kids who are more likely to use drugs. Such arguments were standard conservative fare. In the chapter "The Undermining of America" Robertson claims that there are a wide variety of sources that worked in concert to destroy the nation: groups such as radical Marxist university professors, liberal bias in the media, and the very concept of liberalism itself. Their goal, Robertson writes, "has not just been to supplant Christian values with humanism, but to weaken American sovereignty and supplant it with a one world socialist government."[34] Apparently communism had been rejected nearly everywhere except among Western civilization's elite. An external threat to America that is important enough to warrant its own chapter is the rising power of Asian nations, especially Japan, whose economy in the early 1990s was growing while America's remained stagnant.

The final group of trends focuses on the growth of technology, the globalization of economics, and a rise in anti-Semitism as the world nears the end times. Robertson predicts that the federal government's debt will eventually crush the economy and that economic collapse is more than likely. Related to this is Robertson's complaint that the ever increasing Social Security withholding tax is crippling families and will continue to create "a growing underclass." While it is significant that Robertson blames the government for these failings, he says the source of the problems is the welfare state, not Presidents Reagan or Bush. The most fascinating section of the entire book is his study of a trend that he calls "The Rise of Anti-Semitism." Robertson writes that the 1990 Gulf War pitted "all of the nations of the earth" against Iraq, which controls the ancient city of Babylon. It is this city that has always stood opposed to Jerusalem and is "the spiritual symbol of those who refuse God's grace."[35] For Robertson, anti-Semitism takes the form of opposition to the state of Israel. The real threat to Israel's security comes from the U.S. government, which pressures Israel to make peace with its Arab neighbors. In turn these Muslim nations, and the Palestinians in and around Israel, might decide to attack. For Robertson this was made even more likely by both the collapse of the Soviet Union and lingering European anti-Semitism. This chapter is especially important because Robertson has been, from time to time, accused of anti-Semitism, especially after his next book, *The New World Order,* was published in 1991.

On a more sinister note, Robertson predicts that the European economic union is a sign that the Antichrist is alive and the end of the world is near. In the last chapter, "Looking Ahead," Robertson quotes Patrick Buchanan about his fears of massive immigration from the Middle East, Africa, and Latin America.[36] Finally, Robertson ends with a warning about the coming creation of a one-world government as a sign that Christians should soon expect the end of the world. He also reverts to his old form of predicting the approaching return of Jesus, claiming that April 29, 2007, is the most likely date. This date was arrived at by adding forty years, the span of a generation, to the date of the Jewish reconquest of Jerusalem in 1967. According to Robertson, the capture of Jerusalem is a fulfillment of Jesus's prophecy about collapse of the gentile powers.[37] He ends with this prediction since it serves to highlight his main point, that Western powers are in decline.

In 1991 Robertson published the most controversial book of his career, entitled *The New World Order*.[38] The book reads more like a graduate student's dissertation than something Robertson actually wrote. The thesis of the book is that secretive powers are conspiring to create a one-world government. The process has been underway for over a hundred years, and a small group of wealthy elites is ready to take over. What got Robertson into hot water is the book's attempt to figure out exactly who is behind the new one-world government. In the introduction he lists several possible suspects, including New Age religions, secret fraternal orders, and even the anti-Semitic myth of the Bavarian Illuminati. The Illuminati, he claims, are "clearly occultic and satanic. The carnage that they have brought about is also understandable, given its ultimate source."[39]

He claims that there is a link between "Marxist communism and the occult Illuminati" to control the world through their control of the international banking system. In the United States, this one-world government is being promoted by the Council on Foreign Relations (CFR), whose members include every secretary of state and defense secretary since 1940. Robertson also claims that the council controls the Central Intelligence Agency, among other U.S. government agencies. Among the more outlandish claims in the book is that Richard Nixon's diplomatic recognition of China and desire for nuclear weapons treaties were part of the CFR's plan. Robertson claims that Nixon's strong record of anti-communism is proof that he was forced to make these concessions to communists in order to win the approval of the CFR.[40] At one point Robertson recalls his father's achievements in the U.S. Senate and how closely tied he was to the power brokers of the world. Since he was well connected, "some readers might wish to say to me . . . why don't you just keep your mouth shut, go along, and take the wealth and privilege that is there to enjoy?" He responds to his own question by stating, "I believe in Jesus Christ and I do not think that a man-made new world order is His will for mankind."[41]

The book's labyrinth of conspiracies is so complex that it is difficult to believe that every millionaire and government official is not somehow involved.

Besides his favorite target, the Eastern establishment led by the Rockefeller family, Robertson links the United Nations, wealthy European and American families, the Federal Reserve System, and a host of other groups together in the plot. One of the most interesting passages of the book refers to the elites' desire to create a utopia, which has already led to a long list of horrors. Robertson claims that Margaret Sanger, the founder of Planned Parenthood, promoted "unrestrained licentiousness so that she could bring on involuntary sterilization." This is why, according to Robertson, the Rockefellers supported her.[42] The elites want anarchy to sweep the world so that they might be seen as heroes for bringing peace.

What is disturbing to most critics is the hint of anti-Semitism in *The New World Order*. William Martin calls the book a "perhaps naive resurrection of several classic anti-Semitic themes."[43] While Robertson is not hostile to Jews, his book's less than careful use of Enlightenment-era fables is a cause for concern. Robertson, or his ghostwriter, borrows several ideas from Gerald Winrod, an evangelist popular during the 1930s who started an antimodernism group called "Defenders of the Faith," which eventually became a semi-fascist organization.[44] Some discovered that the author borrows more than that. Parts of *The New World Order* are apparently plagiarized from British anti-Semite Nesta Webster.[45] Among the borrowed ideas is the claim that Jews created the Illuminati from Masonry and that Karl Marx was influenced by the Illuminati.

The book was popular in the evangelical community and even made the *New York Times* bestseller list. The American Civil Liberties Union (ACLU) and Americans United repeatedly used some of the book's more outrageous quotes as campaign fodder, and even conservative William F. Buckley took Robertson to task for his ideas.[46] Some commentators who were hostile to Robertson claimed that he was anti-Semitic. However, this idea does not stand up to Robertson's previous book, *The New Millennium*, in which he warns against anti-Semitism and claims that it is a sign of the end of the world. In *The New World Order* every time Jews are mentioned it is as a special group who are "God's chosen people." Although his conspiracy theories mention several prominent Jews by name, this does not make him anti-Semitic. Determining if Robertson is anti-Semitic depends on how you define the term. He is consistently pro-Israel, but sees the conversion of the Jews to Christianity as a part of the end times scenario predicted in the New Testament. His support of Israel is based on the belief that the Jews will one day accept Jesus as the Messiah. In the most common use of the word, Robertson is not anti-Semitic on any level. He supports religious liberty for Jews around the world and Israel's right to defend herself against her hostile neighbors, and has never really spoken of Jewish conspiracies besides the passages in the *New World Order*. It is important to note that those who claim Robertson is anti-Semitic are also those who would benefit the most if he fell from power.

Considering the negative publicity he received on his previous book, Robertson decided to strike a more standard conservative political note with his 1993 book *The Turning Tide: The Fall of Liberalism and the Return of Common Sense.*[47] Although he keeps to political issues and tries to avoid blaming everything on vague conspiracies he does strike a very hostile, partisan tone. In the book, liberalism is characterized by a "vitriolic repression of historic Judeo-Christian religious values."[48] He labels the Clinton administration "the enemy," and refers to it as "the regime." He even claims that atheist Madalyn Murray O'Hair's body had been "ravaged" due to her war against God.

Despite the less than loving tone, Robertson accurately claims that Clinton's 1992 victory has energized conservatives more than any event since Reagan took office. The most remarkable part of the book is Robertson's seemingly accurate prediction that Clinton's success in 1992 would be the final victory of liberalism and that a conservative backlash would result. Since America was by then the world's only remaining superpower, it was essential that Christians take an active role to bring "moral leaders" into power and thus delay the onset of the socialist one-world government that he had been predicting for more than a decade.

Robertson begins this book by dissecting an article by conservative writer Irving Kristol that claims that liberalism is "at the end of its intellectual tether." To this end, *The Turning Tide* examines the many elements of liberalism that are at war with evangelical Christianity. This time his enemies-of-God list includes President Clinton, homosexuals, the judicial system, the liberal media (again), public sex education, and public education in general. He holds special contempt for the Democratic-controlled Congress, which he refers to as "The Cookie Monster" due to its insatiable appetite. He writes that public schools are controlled by "ideological extremists who are so fixated with their illogical educational theories that they have lost touch with reality."[49] The rising rates of teenage pregnancy and the spread of AIDS are, according to Robertson, due to a public education system that refuses to take moral stands on issues. A liberal judiciary is responsible for many horrors, but the most surprising is its supposed link to America's defeat in the Vietnam War. Robertson incorrectly claims that our involvement in the conflict started the same year that prayer was banned from public schools in 1962. *The Turning Tide* also brings up many of the same issues as *The New Millennium*. These ideas were, in turn, discussed almost daily on *The 700 Club*.

In the chapter "The Tide of Freedom" Robertson writes about the collapse of communism (again) and how people are rejecting political liberalism. In one section that he now might consider embarrassing in a post–9/11 world, he uses the Soviet Union's failed war in Afghanistan as an example of how "a determined band of resolute and deeply religious" fighters stopped the tide of communism.[50] While he does not urge the use of violence, he does use the Afghanistan war as a metaphor for the power of religious belief to resist the powers of liberalism and secularism.

The book ends with a discussion of America's two destinies: "The Destiny of the Cursed and the Destiny of the Blessed."[51] According to Robertson America has been blessed by God because it founded itself on biblical principles. All of that prosperity is now at risk due to liberalism's hostility to God. The judgment of God is going to destroy the nation unless it turns back the tide of liberalism. "Even though the danger is very real, America has not yet passed the point of no return."[52] A flicker of hope still remains to save America from God's wrath; that hope is the Republican Party. If in 1994 and 1996 Americans would only elect a "responsible, conservative" Congress and president, the nation could get back on the right track. For Robertson the consequences are serious: "Either we decide to serve God and obey his commandments . . . or we can witness the imminent collapse of our culture."[53] With the publication of *The Turning Tide* the circle was complete. Robertson was no longer willing to write about shadowy figures whose power over the world seemed total. He was openly and aggressively partisan and was by 1993 trying once again to get his readers to follow him down this path.

Increasingly after his run for president he began to see the importance of making his group appear to be willing to work in the political system, and not openly claim to dominate it as the Moral Majority and Reconstructionists had. Robertson used the memory of the civil rights movement as an example of how the Christian Right could achieve their goals. In *The Turning Tide* he promotes the use of the two main weapons that were employed by African Americans in the 1950s and 1960s: civil disobedience and legal action.[54] In several instances he urges his readers to participate in religious acts of nonviolent civil disobedience. Robertson encourages public school children to meet at their schools' flagpoles to pray. He also writes at length about the work of his legal organization the American Center for Law and Justice (ACLJ), which he calls God's hammer of justice.[55] On *The 700 Club*, Robertson has compared evangelicals to civil rights movement members several times. Comparing themselves with blacks who were forced to stay at the back of the bus, he claimed "that is what is happening now. Christians can go into a tiny, little corner."[56] He took this idea one step further in April 1991 when he claimed that America had been a Christian nation, but "we've come to the point where Christians are being hunted, a persecuted minority in the nation that we founded." He also claimed that secularists were in charge of both the nation and the media, and that evangelicals were in "submission."[57]

Robertson's writings during the 1990s were a sideshow to his main goal of obtaining political power and financial success. There were few people who were willing to challenge Robertson in a direct manner. Most conservative politicians were reluctant to attack him for fear of alienating his constituency and being buried in mail from his supporters. Those who did attack him were more likely to be allies of the ACLU, who used him as a fund-raising tool. His status as the leader of the Christian Right that the Left loved to hate is a clear sign of the power that he held after 1988.

During the late 1980s and early 1990s Robertson became wealthier and more politically powerful than he could have ever dreamed. He was better known and had more political power than his father had ever enjoyed after decades in Congress. During the 1990s the growth of his business ventures and the Christian Coalition consumed most of his time. What had been the story of a man who ran a Christian television network was significantly more complicated after 1988. The simple story line of Robertson's life had splintered into multiple subplots of political bargains, overseas corporations, and a media empire. This complexity made it increasingly difficult to trace his activities. Some scholars focus on his religious beliefs or his political acumen, but Robertson's life has touched many areas, and his influence has been much more widespread than most people realize.

Notes

1. Ezekiel 38, 39.
2. Ezekiel 39:12.
3. Pat Robertson, speech in Concord, New Hampshire, November 20, 1987. All quotes from the speech are from this source. Americans for Robertson Archives (AFRA).
4. Robertson, Concord, New Hampshire speech.
5. Pat Robertson in San Jose, California, Rotary Club speech, July 17, 1987. AFRA.
6. Robertson, Concord, New Hampshire speech.
7. *The 700 Club*, CBN, circa early 1987. Regent University Special Collections (RUA).
8. *The 700 Club*, CBN, circa early 1987.
9. *The 700 Club*, CBN, circa early 1987.
10. *Robertson '88* Americans for Robertson, 1988. AFRA.
11. *The 700 Club*, CBN network, circa early 1987.
12. Lewis Baldwin, *Toward the Beloved Community: Martin Luther King, Jr., and South Africa* (Cleveland, Ohio: Pilgrim Press, 1995), 132.
13. C-SPAN Call In, April, 27, 1987. RUA.
14. Pat Robertson, *Answers to 200 of Life's Most Probing Questions* (New York: Thomas Nelson Publishing, 1984), 147.
15. Robertson, *Answers to 200 of Life's Most Probing Questions*, 152.
16. During his presidential campaign Robertson was accused of anti-Semitism by people who saw his support of Israel as based upon a desire to Christianize the nation. While he did foresee them turning to see Jesus as the Messiah, he was not against Judaism or Israel. He was thinking through the lens of his eschatology.
17. John B. Donovan, *Pat Robertson: The Authorized Biography* (New York: Macmillan, 1988), 166.
18. Robertson, Concord, New Hampshire speech.
19. *Larry King Live!* CNN, April 23, 1987.
20. Donovan, *Pat Robertson*, 140.
21. Robertson, Concord, New Hampshire speech.

22. See Robertson, *Answers to 200 of Life's Most Probing Questions*, 168, and Leviticus 25: 8–55.

23. Roger Simon, *Road Show* (New York: Farrar, Straus & Giroux, 1990), 101.

24. David Edwin Harrell Jr., *Pat Robertson: A Personal, Religious, and Political Portrait* (New York: Harper & Row, 1987), 205.

25. Pat Robertson, Concord, New Hampshire, November 20, 1987. AFRA.

26. *Meet the Press*, March 6, 1988 (Washington, D.C.: Kelly Press Inc., 1988), volume 88.

27. Harvey Cox, "Warring Visions of the Religious Right," *Atlantic Monthly*, November 1995, 61.

28. Pat Robertson, *The Plan* (Nashville, Tenn.: Thomas Nelson Publishing, 1989).

29. Robertson, *The Plan*, 24.

30. Robertson, *The Plan*, 43.

31. Robertson, *The Plan*, 44.

32. Robertson, *The Plan*, 178.

33. Pat Robertson, *The New Millennium* (Dallas, Tex.: Word Publishing, 1990).

34. Robertson, *The New Millennium*, 163.

35. Robertson, *The New Millennium*, 265.

36. The great irony of the book is that Robertson warns of immigrants from Africa while running a diamond mine there at the same time.

37. Robertson, *The New Millennium*, 312.

38. Pat Robertson, *The New World Order* (Dallas, Tex.: Word Publishing, 1991). Robertson's authorship of the book has been questioned, but no ghostwriter has been discovered.

39. Robertson, *The New World Order*, 115.

40. Robertson, *The New World Order*, 101.

41. Robertson, *The New World Order*, 126.

42. Robertson, *The New World Order*, 221.

43. William Martin, *With God on Our Side: The Rise of the Religious Right in America* (New York: Broadway Books, 1996), 333.

44. Leo Ribuffo, *The Old Christian Right* (Philadelphia: Temple University Press, 1983), 80.

45. Anthony Lewis, "Abroad at Home: The Crackpot Factor," *New York Times*, April 14, 1995.

46. William F. Buckley, "Christian Coalition Isn't Harming GOP," *The Record*, February 17, 1995.

47. Pat Robertson, *The Turning Tide: The Fall of Liberalism and the Return of Common Sense* (Dallas, Tex.: Word Publishing, 1993).

48. Robertson, *The Turning Tide*, 32.

49. Robertson, *The Turning Tide*, 215.

50. Robertson, *The Turning Tide*, 34.

51. Robertson, *The Turning Tide*, 291.

52. Robertson, *The Turning Tide*, 301.

53. Robertson, *The Turning Tide*, 303.

54. See, Robertson, *The Turning Tide*.

55. Robertson, *The Turning Tide*, 125.

56. *The 700 Club*, CBN, September 29, 1993.

57. *The 700 Club*, CBN, April, 1991.

CHAPTER 14

PAT ROBERTSON, INC.

HERE have been times in American history when it was difficult to tell the evangelists from the salesmen. George Whitefield, the first famous traveling evangelist in America, visited all of the thirteen colonies raising money for an orphanage. Founding father and religious skeptic Benjamin Franklin once heard the preacher speak and, although he vowed to resist the preacher's call for donations, found that he could not help himself. "He finished so admirably," Franklin recalled, "that I emptied my pocket wholly into the collector's dish, gold and all."[1] Later evangelists blurred the line between religion and commerce. In recent decades, evangelists have sold prayer cloths, recordings of their sermons, nearly anything that can be imagined. The purpose of these business ventures was usually to support the ministry and its endeavors. There have been men like Jim Bakker who used their ministry to create business empires with selfish goals, although few took it to the extremes that he had. Robertson has followed in these same footsteps, but with a distinctive twist. For most of his adult life Robertson has remained focused largely on his television empire; however, after 1988 his business activities split in a variety of directions. Like a firework shot into the sky, the explosion of his popularity in 1988 led Robertson to spread his interests out in every direction. This also meant that his life no longer flowed in a simple narrative; instead it spread out in increasingly thin strands as time wore on.

In 1990 Robertson declared that the 1990s were going to be "a decade of opportunity," and for him it certainly was. Robertson returned to the Christian Broadcasting Network (CBN) a significantly different man than the one who had left only two years earlier. Many reporters eagerly declared his 1988 campaign a disaster and predicted that the years afterward would witness his decline into obscurity. However, quite the opposite was true. His life was his work, not just his politics; to understand him, one needs to understand how he poured himself into his business dealings. These deals became an end in themselves, as Robertson moved from one to the other, whether it was in politics or business. Robertson was intent on making his empire larger.

As George H. W. Bush battled his way past Michael Dukakis in one of the ugliest presidential campaigns in American history, Robertson returned to his unsteady empire. Several prominent television ministries had vanished since he had left Virginia Beach to run for president two years earlier. The two most popular televangelist shows besides *The 700 Club*, those of Jim and Tammy Faye Bakker and Jimmy Swaggart, had been forced off the air. Other TV preachers, like Oral Roberts and Jerry Falwell, had been badly shaken by the televangelist scandals. Many smaller televangelists had sunk in the wake of the scandals, even though they were innocent of any wrongdoing.

Due to all of this bad news many media organizations, especially the Norfolk area paper the *Virginian-Pilot*, were eagerly predicting CBN's demise. In 1985, the year before Robertson started his presidential campaign, the network took in more than $75 million through their telethons. This amount dropped to $33 million in 1987 as Robertson became more politically involved. The next year the network laid off forty-two employees and sold television stations. In June of 1987 CBN laid off five hundred more workers and another 145 more people that fall while budgets were slashed by the millions.[2] However, like the many earlier reports of the network's death, this one was premature.

The situation at CBN was bad but repairable, especially when Robertson returned to the helm of the network and *The 700 Club* in May 1988. Tim Robertson was happy to return to his work behind the camera and continue his work with the Family Channel.[3] One of his father's actions upon returning was to order another round of layoffs. Many workers at CBN, while supportive of Robertson's run for office, had been worried that if he failed it would hurt the low-wage CBN workers before it hit Robertson or the network's officers. Their fears proved to be well founded. Before the presidential campaign CBN had more than two thousand employees; two years later there were less than twelve hundred. Soon, several vice presidents were laid off and even groundskeepers were let go. Many of the workers who stayed found salaries reduced and benefits canceled. One Americans for Robertson (AFR) memo regarding the end of the campaign expressed displeasure with comments that some reporters had made as they stood on the grounds of Robertson's house. The memo said that the grass needed to be mowed and weeds were overgrowing the formerly well-manicured lawn. In early 1989 CBN's toll-free number was canceled, which saved the network an estimated $4 to $5 million per year.

Robertson resumed his hosting duties on *The 700 Club* on May 17, 1988, the day after he suspended his campaign. His first day back on the job was an exercise in damage control. Robertson took questions from his son, the studio audience, and callers on the more controversial aspects of his presidential campaign. The bulk of that first broadcast was spent on the allegations of Pete McCloskey. Robertson showed selected parts of the pretrial depositions that made McCloskey appear to contradict himself. A few minutes of the show were also spent defending the Freedom Council. Robertson took great pains to show that the council had nothing to do with his presidential campaign. In the weeks following his reappearance on *The 700 Club*, Robertson rarely mentioned his campaign or the election in general. He used his book *The Plan* as a way to deal with lingering questions. Robertson was never one to look backward; he marched on toward his next objective.

Besides clearing the record he also had to find a new cohost for *The 700 Club*, which proved more difficult than he thought. The departure of popular cohosts Ben Kinchlow and Danuta Soderman had left a huge gap in the show. The first new cohost seemed to be a coup for CBN. In July 1987 well-known Emmy- and Golden Globe-nominated actress Susan Howard joined *The 700 Club*. Howard had appeared on the hugely successful drama *Dallas* for nine seasons until she was let go after years of struggling to keep her character from behaving in ways that violated her faith.[4] She had become popular with audiences and used her fame to speak out for religious causes and for politically conservative ones as well. She appeared on *The 700 Club* while Ben Kinchlow was still the cohost, and at the time she said, "I feel I have a place. After *Dallas* I asked God, 'where do I fit' and he showed me."[5] Her tenure did not last long; she left CBN in November 1987. After leaving *The 700 Club* she remained supportive of Robertson's politics, unlike Soderman, and even attended Christian Coalition rallies and later became a board member of the National Rifle Association.[6] In 1988 Sheila Walsh was chosen as Robertson's new cohost. Walsh, a successful contemporary Christian music performer from Scotland, was ready for the task. She previously had her own talk show in Great Britain and was popular among American evangelicals. While there was some concern that her accent might bother some of *The 700 Club*'s southern viewers, it quickly proved to be a nonissue. Walsh stayed with the show until a serious bout of emotional problems prompted her sudden resignation in September 1992.

A consistent female cohost was finally found when Terry Meeuwsen joined the set in June 1993. Meeuwsen was crowned Miss America in 1973 and prior to that had a singing career with the folk group the New Christy Minstrels. She had been appearing irregularly on CBN since the early 1980s, but her full-time job at a TV station in Milwaukee and a young family kept her busy. She had been part of a short-lived CBN version of NBC's *Today* show and made a favorable impression with Robertson.[7] Her arrival at *The 700 Club* coincided with Ben Kinchlow's return in April 1992. After spending four years running another TV ministry, he returned to CBN. However, this second coming of the Robertson–Kinchlow partnership lasted until the latter again left CBN in July 1997. In 1999 Pat's younger son Gordon Robertson joined the set of *The 700 Club*. Gordon had graduated from Yale and went to Washington and Lee's law school. He had spent several years in the Philippines, where he created CBN Asia, which broadcast *The 700 Club Asia* in numerous Asian languages.[8] Gordon is similar in appearance to his father, and his hosting duties have continually increased since he joined CBN. This revolving door of cohosts hurt donations to CBN, but by 1992 the situation had settled down.

One thing was certain, no matter who Robertson's cohosts were, CBN had to be put on a firm financial foundation if it was going to survive this crisis. Robertson decided that CBN should use some of its revenue to create for-profit businesses that could support the ministry during lean times. If donations dropped and resulted in massive layoffs while he ran for president, what would happen when Robertson finally left CBN? Longtime Robertson associate Harold Bredesen said, "[I]t was an eye-opener of how dependant we are on Pat and the money he raises."[9] From a business perspective it was a practical decision, but there were complications. The use of ministry money could be explained away by Robertson's "Law of Use," which he details in his book *The Secret Kingdom*. He could claim that he was being a good steward of God's money, but what about those who donated to CBN thinking that their money was being used to support a ministry? For the most part, Robertson tried to keep the business side of CBN a secret, and he was careful to cover his bases. An example is a 1994 CBN fund-raising letter that asked for donations in order to help spread the Gospel. The letter, however, contained fine print that contained a mix of legalese and Christian-speak. "All funds are used for designated projects and for the world-wide ministry of CBN in accordance with Ezra 7:17–18."[10] The Old Testament scripture is an admonition to spend money to serve God, but ends by saying "you and your brother Jews may then do whatever seems best with the rest of the silver and gold, in accordance with the will of your God." With this passage, Robertson was telling his followers that he was free to spend donations in any manner that he saw fit, as long as he thought it was what God wanted. Such letters were only one of many rationalizations that Robertson made as he tried to build a business empire.

One of the first places that Robertson tried to build profitable businesses was on CBN's Virginia Beach property, since it was already receiving visitors from around the nation. The CBN studios had long been a place of pilgrimage for Robertson's fans. Since *The 700 Club* was taped five days a week, it was easy for almost anyone to get a ticket and see Robertson in person. Some families planned their annual summer vacations around a trip to Virginia Beach and CBN. The city's convention and visitor department featured the CBN campus on its maps and advertised the free studio tour in its promotional brochures.[11]

An early idea was a retirement community, which made sense because most of *The 700 Club's* viewers are elderly. The original plan for the community, which was rejected by the city council, called for the seven hundred-unit facility to be built on the main CBN campus, and thereby be tax exempt. The community was designed for wealthy seniors who could afford to pay as much as $490,000 for a spot.[12] After being rebuffed Robertson did what he had done when Norfolk had questioned his nonprofit, tax-free ventures; he moved to another city. This time it was neighboring Chesapeake. This new city was quick to approve the project, with the caveat that he build something that would generate tax revenue on the remaining two hundred acres that CBN owned in the city. This project, which Robertson advertised on *The 700 Club*, was canceled in early 1999 when only 119 people had made deposits ranging from $9,000 to $20,000. The project required that at least 210 deposits be in hand before construction could begin. The project had already cost CBN a reported $3 million. According to reports, Robertson assumed that supporters of his ministry would want to retire near the CBN campus, but he had obviously overestimated his popularity.[13]

In 1991 CBN spent $35.5 million to create Founders Inn, a 249-room four-star hotel and conference center also located on the CBN campus. Dede Robertson helped with the interior decoration and donated some of their collection of Persian rugs as well. The hotel is alcohol free and is mostly staffed by evangelical Christians, but it still had selling points for non-Christians as well. The hotel is only ten miles from the beach, and is able to utilize CBN's massive satellite network so that conferences can link up to virtually any place in the world.[14] The hotel hosted guests of *The 700 Club* and dignitaries such as President George H. W. Bush and Vice President Dan Quayle. After losing money for several years, the hotel slowly began to turn a profit. In 2001 it was sold to Regent University for $21 million. The school continues to operate the hotel. Related to the hotel was the creation of CBN Travel, a short-lived travel agency that set up package tours to Israel. CBN Travel was closed in 1995 as Robertson began to rethink the wisdom of the ministry running for-profit activities.

Before his presidential run, Robertson had kept most of his business dealings to television-related concerns. After 1988, he started to branch out his corporate empire in many directions. The catalyst for this was a federal government investigation into Robertson's campaign finances, which led to penalties and orders to divest of some of his business holdings. However, what the government intended as a punishment was turned into a financial windfall for Robertson.

While Robertson attempted to keep CBN afloat, the federal government finished its preliminary study of his campaign violations. In December 1988 the Federal Election Commission (FEC) levied a fine of $25,000 against Pat Robertson and AFR. The fine was based on Robertson's September 1986 rally in Washington, D.C., where he all but announced his candidacy. The FEC claimed that

Robertson was a candidate a full year before his October 1987 official declaration of candidacy. While the report made Robertson look unethical, the amount of the fine was paltry, and he turned it into another fund-raiser.[15] In early 1989 CBN sent out letters to supporters, signed by Dede Robertson, which claimed that the government was persecuting them and asked loyal viewers to send in donations.[16] Like many Christian Right groups, Robertson and CBN were able to lobby the government and claim that they were being oppressed by it at the same time. AFR claimed that the charges were baseless but refused to challenge the ruling. That was not the last conflict over the 1988 campaign between Robertson and the federal government.

In April 1988 AFR turned over all of its fund-raising materials from 1986 to the Internal Revenue Service. During the next ten years, CBN, AFR, and the Internal Revenue Service (IRS) battled over the rest of the campaign's documents. In 1998 the IRS announced that CBN was having its tax-exempt status retroactively lost for 1986 and 1987. The IRS also announced that CBN had to pay a "significant" penalty, which was later rumored to be several million dollars.[17] Before making this decision, the IRS told Robertson that the relationship between CBN and the Family Channel had long ago ceased to be nonprofit so they had to be separated. CBN was created as a ministry and was a nonprofit organization and *The 700 Club* was asking for tax-deductible donations from its viewers. Meanwhile, the Family Channel was bringing in millions of dollars a year in advertising revenue, also tax free. It was this type of nonprofit status abuse that led to Jim Bakker's trouble with the IRS, and for a time it appeared as if CBN, which was still struggling, was going to be crippled if not killed outright.

CBN may have been in hot water, but its offspring, the Family Channel, was quickly becoming a cable TV powerhouse. In 1991 the network made $20 million, after subtracting costs of $114 million. The network reached fifty million viewers by 1992, and was more popular than MTV. It was the tenth largest cable network by the early 1990s, and was still listed as a not-for-profit company.[18] Tim Robertson had done such a good job of making the Family Channel marketable to advertisers that it brought the attention of the IRS. The cash-strapped ministry that had started in a dilapidated building in the early 1960s was now an immense and mostly secular network worth several hundred million dollars. While trouble with the IRS had landed Jim Bakker in jail and other televangelists in financial ruin, it made Robertson wealthier. He realized that he needed to take the channel public if the IRS was going to allow CBN to remain a tax-exempt organization. Robertson had been looking to sell the channel since his run for the presidency, but no potential buyer would meet his demands for control over broadcast content. While the network was still remarkably profitable, competition from other cable networks had led to thinner profit margins.

In November 1989 Robertson created a new company, International Family Entertainment (IFE) with his son Tim as president. The sole purpose of IFE was to facilitate Robertson's purchase of the Family Channel from CBN. In January 1990 Robertson made a deal with Denver cable TV magnate John Malone to help the Family Channel separate itself from CBN as the IRS was probably going to demand. Malone owned Tele-Communications Inc. (TCI), the nation's largest cable company, and was a controversial figure. Malone's most famous critic was Senator Al Gore, who once compared him to Darth Vader and said he was the head of the "cable Cosa Nostra."[19] Robertson approached Malone because they share similar politics and CBN was carried on cable systems owned by TCI. Two appraisal firms were hired by CBN to prepare a valuation of the Family Channel. At the time of the appraisals the network appeared to owe as much as it was worth. The higher of the two appraisals was $250 million, which became the sale price to IFE. In order for IFE to make the purchase of the Family Channel it had to borrow the necessary funds from CBN at 6 percent interest.[20] Robertson, who sat on the board of both organizations, reportedly excused himself from CBN's discussions about the deal.[21]

Two years later, Robertson decided to make IFE a publicly traded company. In order to maintain their control over the network, Pat and Tim Robertson were allowed to buy "super shares" of Family Channel stock. Unlike most publicly traded companies, CBN had two types of common stock. Class A common stock gave the shareholder ten votes per share, and Class B common stock gave one vote per share. The two Robertson men bought more than 4.5 million shares of class A stock, which gave them 100 percent control of that class. In addition, they purchased another 1.5 million of Class B common stock. In all, they spent $183,000 on their six million shares of IFE stock, or slightly more than three cents a share.[22]

The firm of Donaldson Lufkin & Jenrette was selected to head the underwriting syndicate. The plan was to offer ten million shares of Class B common at $15 per share. IFE sold 3,333,333 of the shares offered, and CBN sold 6,666,666, which was a part of their IFE holdings. Federal law forbade Robertson from discussing the impending sale, but it was mentioned on *The 700 Club* nonetheless. The show had a news feature on investing during which investment adviser Joe Gandalfo said that he planned to buy IFE stock when it went public. According to the underwriters their offices were "flooded with calls" after the segment aired.[23] The stock opened on the New York Stock Exchange in March 1992 at $15 per share and did better than most had hoped, closing slightly higher than the opening price. The initial investment by Pat and Tim Robertson of $183,000 in IFE stock had grown to $93 million at the end of the first day of trading.[24] IFE received approximately $50 million, and CBN received $100 million from the sale of its shares in IFE. Some Wall Street companies predicted that the stock would rise significantly from its initial offering price but the shareholders were happy with the smaller results.

IFE was flush with cash, and Robertson began to purchase other entertainment operations that he felt would help the Family Channel grow. In 1993 the Family Channel bought MTM Productions. The company, started by Mary Tyler Moore, had a large catalog of family friendly shows including *The Mary Tyler Moore Show, The Bob Newhart Show,* and *Hill Street Blues.* In all, the Family Channel added two thousand hours worth of TV programs with the purchase of MTM.[25] Robertson paid nearly $90 million for MTM, which was a good deal considering it had been sold to a British company five years earlier for more than $300 million.[26] In 1994 the Family Channel bought the Ice Capades, an ice show that had toured America for decades. The show was sold a few months later for a small profit, and after that experience Robertson and the Family Channel kept to television-related entertainment venues.

By the late 1990s, the Family Channel had grown as much as it could under the guidance of Pat and Tim Robertson. They began to seek out a partner to take the Family Channel to the next level. While there were many corporations, including CBS, that were interested in buying the network, they all balked at Robertson's insistence that *The 700 Club* be aired twice a day. One man who didn't mind was Rupert Murdoch, the head of the Fox Network. By 1997 Murdock and Robertson agreed to a $1.9 billion purchase price and buyout of all IFE shareholders. The network changed its name again, to the Fox Family Channel. Murdock and Robertson served as cochairmen of the network, and *The 700 Club* was guaranteed a daytime and prime-time slot. Although Robertson's and Murdoch's politics were similar, the deal with Murdoch was unusual. The Fox network had a reputation as the raciest of the four major broadcast networks and seemed to promote the types of values that Robertson complained about daily on *The 700 Club.* While the sale caused the Fox network offices in Los Angeles to be briefly picketed by gay rights advocates, by and large, American viewers never knew or seemed to be concerned about Robertson's involvement.

In 2001 the Fox Family Channel was sold to Disney for almost two billion dollars. In the press release, Walt Disney chairman Michael Eisner announced that he was happy to be working with Pat Robertson.[27] *The 700 Club* was still a centerpiece of the newly renamed ABC Family Channel. Disney had offered to buy the Family Channel in 1997 but had refused to air *The 700 Club.* However, just a few years later Eisner changed his mind and agreed to air Robertson's show. The pairing of Robertson and Disney was even more ironic than his deal with the sometimes raunchy Fox network. In 1988 Robertson warned that God's wrath would hit Orlando because Disney had given benefits to gay workers and allowed "gay days" at the Florida resort. Robertson warned that "terrorist bombs, earthquakes, tornadoes and possibly a meteor" could hit the park as a result.[28]

He also supported the Southern Baptist Convention's boycott of Disney, for awhile at least.

Robertson had come a long way—from seventy dollars to his millions in forty years. Most of the hard work and years of struggle were financed by small donors, who thought they were supporting a ministry. This fact was not reported in the mainstream media, which usually failed to mention that the Family Channel had formerly been a nonprofit Christian television ministry. This is the biggest scandal in the story of Pat Robertson. Whatever one thinks of his religious or political views, the fact remains that he raised millions of dollars from his viewers, most of whom were elderly, and then took their money to create a business that was sold for almost $2 billion. What is most surprising about this scandal is that nobody cared. The evangelical world did not seem to notice, and the federal government was only concerned with legal actions, even if they were morally questionable. Democratic congressman Pete Stark said that the sale of the Family Channel was an example of "transactions in which individuals have enriched themselves at the public's expense while nonprofit organizations have been looted."[29] CBN spokesman Gene Kapp tried to give this scandal a positive spin when he told *Newsweek* that the sale of the network was actually a blessing to the ministry of *The 700 Club* since it received over $600 million and a guarantee that it would continue to be on the air.[30] He also accused people who questioned Robertson's business dealings of practicing "religious bigotry."[31] Robertson had dodged a bullet fired by the IRS, taking a bad situation and making nearly one hundred million dollars in the process.

The shareholders of IFE were not the only ones that benefited from the sale of the Family Channel; CBN suddenly found itself with more money than it knew what to do with. About a third of the company's income came in the form of donations from viewers; the rest was from several for-profit operations that it owned. After the sale of the Family Channel to IFE Robertson used CBN's money to invest in a wide array of operations. Some of them made money; some lost millions. Some of CBN's money was loaned to Robertson for his own business opportunities. The types of companies that Robertson and CBN became involved with literally spanned the globe.

Since he made his fortune as a broadcaster, it makes sense that this remained the most successful part of his new empire. In the early 1990s Robertson created, with CBN's money, the United States Media Corp., which was a holding company for other entertainment ventures. The company lost a reported $10.9 million in its first two years, and in 1994 Robertson fired the company's president, Mark A. Barth. As was to become the case in many of his business deals, lawsuits quickly began to be traded between Robertson and fired employees. In this case, Barth filed suit for $3 million, first claiming that he was fired for expressing concern over Robertson's business ethics. According to court documents, $9 million worth of "production assets" were given to IFE without compensation. True to form, Robertson sued back, claiming that Barth was inept, knowingly prepared false financial statements, and cost the company a $10 million deal. In his suit he sought $12 million in damages.[32] Both suits were eventually settled out of court. One of Robertson's attorneys said no money was involved in the settlement; "everyone just walked away."[33]

After a rough beginning, the company eventually became profitable. Among its many ventures was the creation of Northstar Studios in Nashville, Tennessee. The studio leased space to many other networks including Fox, CNN, NFL, ESPN, the Home Shopping Network, and a host of smaller companies. CBN producer and *The 700 Club* cohost Lisa Ryan kept an office at the facility, and it was estimated that the studio brought in $3–$4 million per year.[34] Another profitable enterprise was Porchlight Productions, which was a Los Angeles-based animation studio. Among its projects was a TV series based on William Bennett's popular work *The Book of Virtues*. Robertson was not content with broadcasting and CBN-centered companies; he wanted to expand his empire even further, but money continued to be a problem.

During the years prior to his presidential campaign he had used CBN's ministry Operation Blessing to funnel money to farmers in Iowa. As a consequence he had to pay a minor penalty for using the ministry for political purposes. Most men would have been wary of using a tax-exempt ministry for personal gain, especially if they had already been caught red-handed, but Pat Robertson is not like most men. In 1996 he once again used Operation Blessing for his own personal gain. The great wealth he had acquired by the early 1990s allowed him to pursue business interests beyond the reach of U.S. law.

In 1992 Robertson created the Africa Development Corporation in Bermuda with himself as the company's only officer. The next year, the Clinton administration placed an embargo on the nation of Zaire and the government of longtime dictator Mobutu Sese Seko. Robertson had given money to rebel groups in Africa that had fought communism, and Mobutu's fierce anti-communism appealed to him. In early 1993 Robertson began to lobby the American government, and especially his friends in Congress, to ease the sanctions. Herman Cohen, the assistant secretary of state for Africa at the time, claimed that Robertson was not taken seriously by the administration because Mobutu had a history of scamming Americans.[35] In 1994 the Mobutu government gave Robertson the rights to mine diamonds in a river near its border with Angola.[36] Robertson had been working with right-leaning governments since his work in Latin America in the early 1980s, and in those cases Operation Blessing was also his chosen vehicle for pushing his political agenda. While the nonprofit ministry was usually under close scrutiny in the United States, offshore operations allowed him to operate with more freedom.

In 1994 Operation Blessing bought three Vietnam War–era cargo planes and some spare parts for them for $1 million. The aircraft had the ministry's logo painted on the side and were sent to Zaire supposedly for ministry work. *The 700 Club* raised money for the poor in Africa while only two of the planes were registered with the Federal Aviation Administration under Operation Blessing's name. The third plane was registered with Robertson's African Development corps.[37]

The three planes spent the next two years hauling mining equipment from Zaire's capital of Kinshasa to the remote mining site that Robertson had been awarded. One of the men hired to fly the plane, Robert Hinkle, reported that of the forty flights he made in Zaire during the six months he worked for Operation Blessing, only one was a humanitarian flight. The rest of them were for Robertson's diamond mine operation.[38] After flying the planes for three months, Hinkle had the Operation Blessing sign removed from the plane. Hinkle recalls, "[I]t was embarrassing to be flying around these places doing diamond mining operations and not humanitarian stuff."[39]

The rule of President Mobutu was in peril as a rebel movement began to spread westward toward the capital. Operation Blessing moved its operations out of the country as the war accelerated. The mining company, which never found any valuable diamonds and had lost millions of dollars, was put on a hiatus while revolution swept through Zaire. By the spring of 1997 President Mobutu's regime was toppled and rebel leader Laurent Kabila took the reins of power. In anticipation of this, Robertson had been making diplomatic moves toward Kabila months before the latter came to control the entire nation. In April 1997 a lawyer representing Robertson handed a personal letter to Kabila inviting him to visit the United States as his guest.[40] Robertson hoped to get further diamond mining concessions from Kabila, whom he rightly assumed would eventually take over Zaire. Even with the new government's help, Robertson's company continued to lose millions before he eventually pulled the plug.

Robertson later admitted that his mining company had used the planes, but reported that he had reimbursed Operation Blessing for their use. However, records made available by the IRS do not show that the ministry was reimbursed for any outside work by its aircraft the entire time they were owned by Operation Blessing. In early 2002 *Fortune* magazine ran an article covering many of the same charges that both *GQ* and the *Virginian-Pilot* had made years earlier, but this time Robertson fought back.

In June 2002, Robertson wrote an angry letter to *Fortune* claiming that most of the accusations in the article were false. While a section of the letter defended his purchase of an oil refinery in Los Angeles, part of it was a defense of his business ventures in Africa. The most important piece of the letter was Robertson's statement that "None of the contributions from charitable donations were in any way invested in businesses owned by my trust."[41] He also denied losing millions in the venture, although business records showed otherwise.[42]

Zaire was not the only African nation that had Robertson's attention in the 1990s. Soon after his move into Zaire, Robertson began to donate large amounts of money to the nation of Liberia and its dictator president Charles Taylor. The regime had been labeled a "kleptocracy" where human rights abuses were common. Taylor had been part of a coup that took control of Liberia in 1980. A few years later Taylor was arrested in the United States after he fled his country with $900,000 in stolen money. He escaped from a Massachusetts jail and made his way to Libya, where he organized a rebel army with the help of dictator Moammar Gadhafi. Taylor took control of Liberia in 1989 and made the nation his personal kingdom.[43] Taylor ruled his nation using child soldiers, officially sanctioned rape, and massive corruption to maintain control. He even exported violence to neighboring Sierra Leone, allowing his nation to be a conduit for smuggled diamonds to help fund that country's civil war. By 2001 both the United Nations and United States had slapped embargoes on Liberia and pressured Taylor to step down. He did eventually abdicate as part of a United Nations–brokered deal to end a civil war. While all of this turmoil was going on, no one in the United States supported Taylor more frequently than Pat Robertson.

In 1998 Robertson, American investor Ken Ross, and two representatives of Taylor's government met in Virginia Beach to talk about mining for gold. Liberia was especially rich in alluvial gold, which is relatively inexpensive to mine. By the end of 1998 Robertson set up Freedom Gold Limited in the Cayman Islands and began to take over the gold operation that had belonged to Ross, which was potentially worth as much as $1.5 billion. During the negotiation process Robertson donated a reported $15 million to the nation.[44] Robertson received bad press for his actions in Africa. One article showed three photos together. On the left was Robertson, all smiles, in the center was Liberian president Taylor, and on the right was a severed head resting on a table, a victim of Taylor's violence.[45]

In 1999 Freedom Gold signed an agreement with Liberia for mining rights. The contract stated the Liberian citizens would be allowed to buy stock (totaling up to 10 percent) in the company after five years, although it was assumed by most people that this 10 percent would be owned by Taylor himself. So while war raged in Liberia and Sierra Leone, and Amnesty International, the UN, and the U.S. State Department compiled a list of Taylor's crimes, Robertson both defended Taylor and attacked the U.S. government.

During the fall of 2001 Robertson came under intense scrutiny over his relationship with Taylor. Joseph Mathews, who essentially ran Freedom Gold from his Virginia Beach office, claimed that the Robertson–Taylor relationship was analogous to any foreign company's ties with President Bush.[46] That is to say, it was a casual business relationship. The facts, however, do not add up. Besides the millions that were given to Taylor and the Freedom Gold contract that promised more, Robertson publicly supported the dictator. CBN financially supported a series of revival meetings in Liberia in 2002, highlights of which were broadcast on *The 700 Club*. At one of the rallies, Taylor appeared, prostrated himself on the stage, and then told the audience, "I am not your president. Jesus is."[47]

As news of Taylor's crimes was revealed, Robertson claimed that he was involved because his "focus is the welfare of the Liberian people." His staff even denied that his work there had anything to do with the gold mine.[48] Officials from Freedom Gold called their company a "responsible corporate citizen" in Liberia and claimed to have built wells and set up sites with safe drinking water. In a moment of bravado they claimed that "Freedom Gold has done more for the people in this region in the past two years than any other company over the last thirty years."[49] While war raged across West Africa, and the human rights abuses mounted, Freedom Gold continued to search for its prize.

By the summer of 2003 Robertson was again dealing with Liberia, this time by attacking the U.S. government. Both the UN and the United States had put embargoes against Liberia, and a UN international war crimes committee indicted Taylor. He was losing friends and there were reports that he had been using stolen diamonds to help finance Al Qaeda terrorists. Freedom Gold had still not found anything, yet Robertson hoped they would, and he defended Taylor to the last. Robertson used the politics of the post–9/11 world to put the Liberian situation in a new light. Now instead of defending his company, Robertson portrayed the civil war against Taylor as a war between Christians and Muslim extremists. He accused the George W. Bush administration of helping Muslim Fundamentalism by "undermining a Christian, Baptist president to bring in Muslim rebels to take over the country." He claimed that Taylor was democratically elected and that Bush should be ashamed to ask him to step down.[50] Robertson stepped up his attacks on the Bush administration after National Security Advisor Condoleezza Rice called Taylor "a menace to his own people." During one episode of *The 700 Club* Robertson said, "Liberia is a predominantly Christian country and the United States State Department is paving the way for the Muslims to take over."[51] Robertson never mentioned Freedom Gold on *The 700 Club*, or where the money to start the company had come from.

In an effort to be a good Republican, he did what the GOP had been doing since 1992: when in doubt, blame Bill Clinton. He hoped to mend fences with the George W. Bush administration by blaming the Liberian situation on the former president, who had been out of office for two and a half years. While appearing on Fox News, Robertson said that while Bush said Taylor had to step down, it was not his idea, but the State Department's. According to Robertson, the Clinton State Department pressured the UN to put sanctions on Liberia, which "deliberately brought them into a state of poverty." He was upset that Clinton's policies were still being enforced while Bush was in office. Since he was being interviewed on conservative Fox News, he was not asked about why Bush supported these policies. He was allowed to shift the blame to Clinton, without any proof, and was never asked a single question about Freedom Gold.

Taylor went into exile in Nigeria in August 2003 as part of a UN–sponsored peace treaty, and Robertson said nothing. In an interview for the *Washington Post*, he said, "[M]aybe once the dust has cleared on this thing . . . if I could find some people to sell it to. I'd be more than delighted." He even claimed to have "written off the $8 million" that he had invested in the company, Liberia, and Taylor.[52] In May 2005 the UN accused Taylor of taking money from Al Qaeda for purpose of destabilizing west African nations. While Taylor stood accused of war crimes and crimes against humanity, Nigeria refused to turn him over, claiming that they had granted him political asylum.[53] Robertson's actions in Africa were another example of how the presidential campaign had changed him. He had moved beyond using his tax-exempt ministries for political gain. Robertson set up his work in Africa in Caribbean islands, to avoid paying taxes. He used Operation Blessing's name to mine for diamonds, and publicly and privately supported a ruthless dictator in order to increase his own considerable wealth. All of Robertson's ventures were supposed to be hidden from the American media and most importantly from *The 700 Club* supporters. When the news of his venture in Africa was made public, detractors gloated and some of his supporters blamed the liberal media for tarnishing Robertson.

Robertson was using his business power to do more than support third-world dictators; during the 1990s he became involved in a wide array of business deals. In late 1998 he purchased an oil refinery in Santa Fe Springs, California, using $20 million from a charitable trust to form a company, Cenco, of which he was the president and only board member. As he did with many of his other business dealings, Robertson claimed that the company was going to use its profits to support charitable causes. After he bought the refinery, he made headlines by claiming that big oil companies were pressuring local banks not to lend to Cenco, so that they could have a monopoly on the refining process. It was the protests of people living near the refinery, however, that sealed the fate of the plant. In November 2001 a judge used the Clean Air Act to keep the plant shut down.[54] Robertson continued to fight to open the plant, eventually spending $75 million from his charitable trust in a losing effort. He was later sued by lawyers for unpaid legal bills, the state of California levied fines and penalties, and he eventually sold the refinery off, piece by piece, for a loss.[55]

Despite Robertson's obvious business acumen, as the 1990s progressed, he discovered that his political positions began to cause him trouble in even minor business dealings. Robertson's other less-known ventures included his six-month tenure on the board of directors at clothier Laura Ashley. "I am on all kinds of boards of directors so one more board to me means absolutely nothing; it is just another pain in the neck. Listening to these boring discussions and reading business statements. I was just doing a friend of mine a favor," Robertson said.[56] He was reportedly brought on board so he could share his "experience in the North American market," according to the company.[57] When news came out that Robertson was on the board of Laura Ashley, some groups, especially in Europe, threatened to boycott the stores. Robertson offered to resign soon after the protests began and was given a $2 million severance for his services. "They protest and I ended up making more money," Robertson laughed.[58]

History repeated itself when the Bank of Scotland announced it had made a deal with Robertson to create an Internet bank. While in Scotland to meet with bank officials about raising money for a nursing home that he hoped to build in Virginia Beach, Robertson became interested in setting up a business venture with them. The bank made a deal with the televangelist partly in order to save itself from being taken over by other European banks, and because they realized that Robertson could help them tap into the American market. The deal made Robertson the chairman of the Internet bank, and gave him a 25 percent stake in the company. The deal also called for him to film commercials and help promote the bank in the United States.[59] Within hours of the announcement, protests began in Scotland, where Robertson's brand of evangelicalism is both rare and poorly understood. More than one hundred protesters marched into the bank's Edinburgh offices and were literally dragged away by police. The Episcopal bishop of the city recommended that people close their accounts at the bank. The Edinburgh City Council did the same thing, while Scottish newspapers attacked him mercilessly. One article called him a demagogue, and characterized his religious views as "cheap, addled, and populist."[60] Even the American media jumped in. *Money* magazine reported that in his book *The New World Order*, Robertson attacked international bankers for all sorts of evils and now he was trying to become one of them.[61] Robertson complained that compared to Scottish journalists, the American media were "choirboys."[62] Officials at the bank were surprised at the hostile reaction and hired a public relations firm to make it clear that Robertson's politics had nothing to do with this business venture, but to no avail. Meanwhile, Robertson only made things worse when he criticized the protestors and said that Scotland was a "dark land" in the grip of fanatics and militant homosexuals.[63] Eventually the Scottish Parliament threatened to withdraw their funds from the bank if the deal was not terminated, and this time the bank folded. As was the case with Laura Ashley, Robertson made millions of dollars due to protestors.

There were companies that were run in the United States that ended up being just as controversial as Robertson's deals in the United Kingdom had been.

In 1990 Robertson took $2.8 million from CBN in addition to his own invest-
ment of $2.5 million and created a company that was to sell home Bible study
courses. Two years later he changed business tactics and turned the company
into a multilevel marketing company, similar to Amway or Mary Kay Cosmetics. A multilevel is the legal version of a pyramid scam where people buy into a
company and reap profits by both selling products and bringing others into the
company's sales team. This new company, named American Sales Corporation,
sold the American Benefits Plus passport, which was a coupon book. For $139
the book promised savings on everything from breakfast cereal to airfare, hotels,
jewelry, and a host of other items.[64] Prospective buyers were told that their profits could be immense. Robertson himself said, "[W]ith God there is no cap. In
the multilevel business, the sky is the limit." In its first year, over twenty thousand people joined the company.[65] However, less than a year later, Robertson
had one of his famous seemingly spur of the moment decisions and changed
the company's focus to selling vitamins.

The company was renamed Kalo-Vita (good life) and for a time continued
to sell both the coupon books and the vitamins. Robertson toured the country to
drum up support, and the company sent out promotional videos in which Robertson claimed that Kalo-Vita "is much more than a business, it's a cause." It has been
alleged that Kalo-Vita's mailing list was taken from both CBN and the Christian
Coalition and that CBN funded the new company without being repaid.[66] Conservative operative Scott Lively appeared on the tape claiming to have always been
a lousy business man, but now having something to believe in. In a public appearance he said, "[A]fter my salvation and my family, this is the most exciting thing
I have encountered in my life."[67] Lively compared the opportunity to work with
Robertson to getting "into a time machine and [going] back to buy IBM stock at
the beginning of the company." Dan Hamilton quit his job at a Christian radio
station in order to sell Kalo-Vita products full time based solely on Robertson's
leadership in the company. The company even recruited during the Christian
Coalition's annual "Road to Victory" meetings. Robertson promised that a large
portion of the company's profits would go to Christian charities, and Lively said
that selling the products was almost like donating to a ministry.[68]

Unfortunately this euphoria did not last for long. It was decided that Kalo-
Vita should focus only on vitamins and health products. As a result, it stopped
supporting the coupon books and eventually refused to take them back or offer
refunds after it paid back $1.5 million. This left some people with losses over
$10,000. One seventy-six-year-old grandmother from Indiana lost $7,000 on
the coupon books. One Robertson follower was angry and commented, "I didn't
think a company backed by Pat Robertson would do that."[69] Kerry Young,
another investor in Kalo-Vita, gave a spiritual slant to the situation. "I know of
people who came to know the Lord through getting involved in the business.

When things happened in this business, they started to question God. It damaged their Christian walk."[70] In late 1992 both the Florida and Pennsylvania Attorney Generals' offices announced that they were investigating the claims made by Kalo-Vita and Robertson. The company had been making claims of potential income and lured people into buying a spot in Kalo-Vita by "taking advantage of the greed factor."[71] The Florida investigation was based on documents supplied to them by ABC. Among the items was a sample $15,000 check inside a promotional letter that said "can you imagine what you could be earning?" This letter had no disclaimer that the amount was not guaranteed.[72] The IRS also launched an investigation due to the company's ties to CBN. No charges were ever filed, but the company's legal problems had just begun.

After only two years of operation, Kalo-Vita had lost $2 million. In an attempt to right the ship, Robertson fired the president of Kalo-Vita, Mark Peterson, three days before Christmas. Peterson's wife was nine months pregnant when he was fired, but they did not initially take it personally. It was a business decision and the Petersons, whom Robertson had helped to reconcile and remarry after getting divorced, still thought kindly of their former boss. Then things got ugly. Robertson's chief of security allegedly threatened Peterson during a phone call, and when the *Virginian-Pilot* published an article on the problems at Kalo-Vita, CBN released a statement that blamed Peterson for the company's troubles.[73] Robertson laid the blame for the company's woes at Peterson's feet and claimed that he mismanaged the company and that any investor who lost money did so due to Peterson's actions. Peterson and his wife were stunned by what they felt was a stab in the back.

In November 1994 Robertson sold Kalo-Vita to Dallas-based cosmetics company Royal Body Care for an undisclosed sum. Besides the stock on hand, the company moved several employees to Dallas and continued to run the large warehouse and distribution center. The company's Virginia Beach headquarters was closed and its office equipment was auctioned off. A three-year employee of the company was anything but bitter about her experiences. "Everyone that worked there was like a family," she said. "When we got the negative publicity, we worked even harder to make it a go."[74]

Two years after he was fired, Mark Peterson gave scathing interviews to the ABC news program *Primetime Live* and to *Newsweek* magazine. In the interviews he claimed that Robertson was deceptive and selling products at too high a markup. Peterson said the company was "buying it [the vitamins] for $7 to $8 a bottle and selling it for $49.95." He also said that Robertson was "very cold, manipulative and calculating," and that he didn't care about the many complaint letters that arrived at the Kalo-Vita offices regularly.[75] Robertson denied all of Peterson's allegations on *The 700 Club* the day after the ABC show aired. He stated that "the distorted conclusions drawn by *Primetime Live* cannot be substantiated by fact." Robertson ended his comments by saying that although his lawyers had told him that he had a good case against ABC and *Newsweek*, the Lord wanted him to pray for his enemies instead of going to court.[76]

Evidently the Lord's message did not include a command to completely turn the other cheek. In September 1994 Robertson had called Peterson's home looking for Mark in an attempt to keep him from talking to the media. He was not there, but his sister Pam Johnson was. During their conversation Pam compared her brother to a wild stallion running free. Robertson allegedly told her to pass the message along to Peterson that "wild horses that kick and destroy things without a bit in their mouth have to be put down. They have to be shot. You tell him that."[77] In an attempt to calm the situation Andrea Peterson called Robertson and asked him to explain his threatening statement. In a phone call that was called "long and emotional" Robertson explained his comments. "This is a horse analogy. I meant nothing about Mark, but, wild stallions can hurt themselves. They can run over cliffs." Unknown to Robertson, Andrea Peterson had recorded the phone call. In May 1995 Peterson sued Robertson from their new home in North Carolina, for $70,000, accusing him of slander and intimidation.[78] That October Robertson announced that he was suing Peterson for libel, and asking for $1.3 million in damages.

The case took an odd turn in 1997 when Mark Peterson dropped his suit due to his "religious convictions." He told the judge that Robertson didn't offer him anything to end the legal action. However, after the case was dropped Robertson made a donation to the church the Petersons attended with the proviso that it be spent to send Mark to Bible school. Other money was sent to pay the Petersons' legal expenses. Andrea Peterson, meanwhile, was not as ready to give up her lawsuit. The matter dragged on for years and Robertson's name was removed from Peterson's lawsuit after the court decided that since he called her from Virginia, North Carolina had no jurisdiction.[79]

Robertson's interest in vitamins and health products was not merely based on the desire to make a profit. He was often chided by his *700 Club* cohosts for the handfuls of vitamins that he took each day. As Robertson aged, he began to take a keener interest in health and fitness and this interest began to be featured on *The 700 Club*. After the Kalo-Vita turmoil was behind him, he began to market products that he called "Age Defying." The first two of these products were health shakes heavy with antioxidants. In 2003 he introduced an "age defying protein pancake mix," and even cooked some up on his show. All of these products were marketed via the CBN website and within forty-eight hours of introducing the pancake mix, thirty-eight thousand people had called for the recipe or downloaded it.[80] His 2003 book *Bring It On* had an appendix with the recipe and suggested variations. The shake's ingredients included fruit juice, apple cider vinegar, flaxseed oil, various forms of soy products, glutamine, and fresh fruit. Robertson also suggested adding vitamins, creatine, and yogurt. He also encouraged the regular use of antioxidants in order to keep the human body producing essential hormones and chemicals.[81] *The 700 Club* occasionally featured people who had used the shake. In July 2005 Phil Busch appeared on the show and claimed that he had lost 198 pounds using the shake in combination with a serious exercise regimen. Few people outside of the regular viewership of *The 700 Club* realized that Robertson was so intense about his health. Robertson's role as a health guru and faith healer took a hit in December 2002 when he announced that he had prostate cancer. He was given a clean bill of health after undergoing surgery in early 2003 and he soon returned to *The 700 Club*. In 2006 he was widely mocked for claims that he had lifted two thousand pounds on a leg press. What the media focused on was his age and not his history of athleticism.

Perhaps in an attempt to keep the entire Kalo-Vita fiasco from repeating itself, Robertson signed a distribution deal with the General Nutrition Corporation, which operates the GNC chain of health food stores. Instead of dealing with local sales people, Robertson's new health product was available at stores across the nation. Phil Busch, who had appeared on *The 700 Club* to promote the shakes, had evidently left the CBN studios thinking that he was going to be the new spokesman for the shake. Busch complained to a reporter when Robertson used a GNC-affiliated bodybuilder instead. He told the paper, "I felt like an idiot. I felt used. All I was trying to do was inspire people. I did it for the viewers, not to help Pat Robertson make money."[82] GNC pulled the product from their stores after six months. While there was no reason given for the move there was speculation that Robertson's controversial comments played a role.

Like any businessman of his statue, there were a number of projects that never got off the drawing board. In 1992 Robertson tried to purchase United Press International (UPI), through his company United States Media, for $6 million. UPI had been losing money for nearly thirty years and had creditors waiting for the $60 million that they were owed. After pouring more than $300,000 into the company while his staff studied UPI's financial books, Robertson withdrew his bid.[83] In the wake of that experience he attempted to start his own news service. Standard News was founded in 1993 and provided news radio broadcasts to more than six hundred stations. This venture lost $2.9 million before it was sold in early 1995. Robertson also created ZapNews, which sent a daily newsletter via fax. It also lost money and was quickly sold.[84] Other random news-related business ventures started by Robertson include an attempt to buy several newspapers, including the *Houston Post*.

As the empire expanded, Robertson became involved in an ever widening array of companies. In 2000, Robertson joined forced with the Internet company that produces Christianity.com, a website that contains information, spiritual guidance, and sells products marketed to a Christian audience. Considering that Christians spend over $25 million a year on religious items, the Internet was a relatively untapped marketplace for Christian products.[85] A year later the $12 million investment of CBN's money was lost, and Robertson pulled the plug.[86] Robertson also owns International Jet Charters (IJC), which operates two Learjets out of Norfolk airport. This company remained little known until one of the planes crashed while attempting to land in Connecticut on June 2, 2006. The Associated Press reported that the planes were owned by a company called Robertson Asset Management and leased to IJC, although it did not mention that Robertson owned both companies.[87]

While most of the empire was strictly business, Robertson also invested in one of his favorite activities: horses. A stable of several horses was kept next to his home in Virginia Beach. In 2001 it was reported that Robertson had purchased a race horse, which he named Mr. Pat.[88] This is especially ironic since on *The 700 Club* and at Christian Coalition rallies, Robertson has denounced gambling. He must have meant Las Vegas–style gambling and not horse racing, the sport of kings. After the media broke the story, Robertson issued an apology, which, if anything, revealed how economically and socially removed he was from most of his followers. After recounting a short history of man's use of horses for athletic games, he recounted his childhood where he challenged his friends to race their horses in the countryside. Robertson claimed to not know why people were upset. "Very frankly," he wrote, "none of this brought any sense of embarrassment to me because I felt then, and felt now, there is absolutely nothing wrong with tests of skill, either between human athletes or equine athletes." He then apologized for any offense his "fondness for the performance of equine athletes" may have caused, and promised to sell all of his racing stock.[89] The letter reads like that of a patrician who is peeved at having to explain to commoners that horse racing is an acceptable practice for his class of well-born men. He never once mentioned gambling.

Pat Robertson owes his immense personal wealth to tens of thousands of people who regularly donated to CBN for years in the belief that they were supporting the preaching of the Christian message. His fenced-in homes, limousines, and security guards make it clear that he desires little or no contact with the people who paid for his lifestyle. Yet, he could still be remarkably generous. For example, he put all of his Class A shares in IFE in a trust that will go to CBN when he passes away. However, in the meantime Robertson can still take the trust's annual income payout.[90] Several local Virginia Beach area charities have also received donations from Robertson over the years. These gifts were special because Robertson asked that his generosity not be publicized.

By the turn of the century it was clear that the multiple business plans had not worked out as hoped, and CBN began to sell off the for-profit companies.

While Robertson was able to make millions off of these projects, CBN seemed to be hurt by the decade-long spending spree. In 1998 the network had $128 million in cash, but that amount plummeted to $7.4 million by 2002. According to CBN's filings with the IRS by 2004 it had $13 million in cash in hand. Part of this loss is accounted for in the failed businesses, but millions were used to expand the ministry and support local charities around the world.[91] What was most troubling for CBN's long-term health was its increased reliance on donations. In 1997 viewer donations accounted for a third of CBN's revenue, yet by 2001 that percentage had risen to two-thirds.[92] This means that if Robertson is involved in any scandal or health crisis the entire network could collapse. A sudden end to CBN is highly unlikely since it still has considerable assets at its disposal, including hundreds of acres along the 64 Freeway in the Virginia Beach region.

Quentin Schultze, who has studied televangelists for years, comments that when Robertson told people during his presidential campaign that he was a businessman, they laughed. "But in retrospect, it was truthful," Schultze says.[93] Still, his deals came at a cost. The sometimes over optimistic business world can quickly sour and hurt feelings turn into ugly lawsuits. It was in these business ventures that Robertson's ugly side came out. He is kind on *The 700 Club*, or stern and determined at Christian Coalition meetings, but he is always portrayed as a decent person. The scandal in Africa and court documents showed the world a side of Robertson that was less pleasing. Besides his shady deals, people were surprised at the lengths that Robertson would go to in an attempt to control his image. It is easy to explain how some lawsuits or questionable deals were misunderstood or the result of poor planning, but what is one to make of intimidation and threats that he has been accused of? In 1999 a British journalist was given extraordinary access to CBN leadership and financial records. At the end of his meetings, he sat through "an hour-long diatribe" by one of Robertson's executives who promised legal action if they were not happy with his article. "As in the days when the Inquisition required recalcitrants to view instruments of torture, I was made to understand in detail the devastation that would befall me if this paper did not report what was 'expected' of us."[94] Such stories gave credence to rumors that Robertson was perhaps not as pleasant a fellow as he wanted people to think. Still, his activities in Africa, his increasing wealth, and the unpleasant court battles were all overshadowed by his most famous creation, the Christian Coalition.

Notes

1. Harry S. Stout, *The Divine Dramatist: George Whitefield and the Rise of Modern Evangelicalism* (Grand Rapids, Mich.: Eerdmans, 1991), 107.

2. April Witt, "Robertson Returns to Ailing CBN," *Virginian-Pilot*, May 17, 1987.

3. April Witt, "Robertson to Air His Side of Campaign 'Funny Facts,'" *Virginian-Pilot*, May 18, 1988.

4. Holy G. Miller, "Life after Dallas," *The Saturday Evening Post*, October 1987.

5. Miller, "Life after Dallas."

6. Katy Kelly, "Political Heaven, a Rally 'Round God, Country," *USA Today*, August 18, 1992.

7. J. Gordon Melton, Phillip C. Lucas, and Jon Stone, *Prime-Time Religion: An Encyclopedia of Religious Broadcasting* (Phoenix, Ariz.: Oryx Press, 1997), 226.

8. Steven G. Vegh, "When Robertson Retires," *Virginian-Pilot*, April 22, 2005.

9. Mark O'Keefe, "Pat Robertson's Ever-Growing Business Kingdom," *Virginian-Pilot*, June 19, 1994.

10. O'Keefe, "Pat Robertson's Ever-Growing Business Kingdom."

11. Steven Vegh, "Pilgrims Wend toward The 700 Club," *Roanoke Times* [Va.], August 26, 2001.

12. Esther Diskin and Jeff Hooten, "Chesapeake Considers CBN Facility," *Virginian-Pilot*, June 1994.

13. Mike Abrams, "Beach Retirement Village Canceled," *Virginian-Pilot*, February 25, 1999.

14. Donald Baker, "A Virginia Beach Inn with a Message," *Washington Post*, May 6, 1993.

15. "FEC Levies $25,000 Fine on Robertson," *Virginian-Pilot*, December 23, 1988.

16. This tactic was successful and often repeated. In 2000 CBN sued the IRS, claiming discrimination against religious conservatives.

17. David Stout, "Christian Broadcasting Network to Pay Fine for Its Political Efforts in 1988," *New York Times*, March 21, 1998.

18. Anthony Ramirez, "From Evangelical TV Roots to a Stock Offering's Riches," *New York Times*, April 18, 1992.

19. Bill Menezes, "Gore Praises, Cautions Cable TV," *Rocky Mountain News* [Denver, Colo.], April 30, 1996.

20. Alec Foege, *The Empire That God Built: Inside Pat Robertson's Media Machine* (New York: Wiley, 1996), 45.

21. Benjamin Weiser, "An Empire on Exemptions?" *Washington Post*, February 13, 1994.

22. Anthony Ramirez, "From Evangelical TV Roots to a Stock Offering's Riches," *New York Times*, April 18, 1992.

23. Donna Rosato, "Robertson Offers Stock amid His Forecast of Doom," *USA Today*, March 30, 1992.

24. Benjamin Weiser, "Robertson, Ex-Aide Trade Accusations," *Washington Post*, January 12, 1995.

25. Foege, *The Empire That God Built*, 47.

26. UPI, "MTM Chief to Leave When Robertson Takes Over," March 3, 1993.

27. Jim Hill, "Disney Gets Religion," *Orlando Weekly*, August 8, 2001.

28. *The 700 Club*, CBN, June 8, 1998.

29. Weiser, "An Empire on Exemptions?"

30. Michael Isikoff and Mark Hosenball, "With God There's No Cap," *Newsweek*, October 3, 1994.

31. Weiser, "An Empire on Exemptions?"

32. Weiser, "Robertson, Ex-Aide Trade Accusations."

33. Marc Davis, "Pat Robertson Settles Defamation Suits before Trial Starts," *Virginian-Pilot*, April 29, 1998.

34. Amanda Wardle, "Former Qwest Studio Becomes Northstar," *The City Paper*, August 9, 2002, and M .B. Owens, "Northstar Brings TV to Tennessee," *The City Paper*, December 29, 2004.

35. Lynne Duke, "Preaching with a Vengeance," *Washington Post*, October 15, 2005.

36. Robert Block, "Will a Zairian Rebel Visit U.S. as a Guest of Pat Robertson?" *Wall Street Journal*, April 30, 1997.

37. Bill Sizemore, "Operation Blessing Planes Were Used Mostly for Diamond Mining," *Virginian-Pilot*, April 27, 1997.

38. Sizemore, "Operation Blessing Planes Were Used Mostly for Diamond Mining."

39. Sizemore, "Operation Blessing Planes Were Used Mostly for Diamond Mining."

40. Sizemore, "Operation Blessing Planes Were Used Mostly for Diamond Mining."

41. Pat Robertson, letter to the editor, *Fortune*, June 5, 2002.

42. Sizemore, "Operation Blessing Planes Were Used Mostly for Diamond Mining."

43. Colbert King, "Pat Robertson and His Business Dealings," *Washington Post*, November 10, 2001.

44. Bob Drury and Aram Roston, "Pat Robertson's Gold Fever," *GQ*, December 2001.

45. Drury and Roston, "Pat Robertson's Gold Fever."

46. King, "Pat Robertson and His Business Dealings."

47. Alan Cooperman, "Robertson Defends Liberia's President," *Washington Post*, July 10, 2003.

48. Corky Siemaszko, "Pat's Bloody Pal," *Daily News*, July 11, 2003.

49. Colbert King, "Pat Robertson's Gold," *Washington Post*, September 22, 2001.

50. Cooperman, "Robertson Defends Liberia's President."

51. Joseph Loconte, "Taylor's Christian Virtues Apparent Only to Robertson," *Milwaukee Journal Sentinel* [Wisc.], August 4, 2003.

52. Cooperman, "Robertson Defends Liberia's President."

53. Edith Lederer, "Prosecutors Say Charles Taylor Trying to Destabilize West Africa with al-Qaida Support," *Associated Press*, May 24, 2005.

54. Greg Winter, "Court Blocks Evangelist's Effort to Reopen a Refinery," *New York Times*, November 9, 2001.

55. Greg Winter, "Grand Plan Haunts Pat Robertson," *New York Times*, February 2, 2002.

56. Pat Robertson, interview by author, tape recording, Virginia Beach, Va., May 25, 2000.

57. Julia Finsh, "Ashley's Road to Robertson," *The Guardian* [London], January 22, 1999.

58. Finsh, "Ashley's Road to Robertson."

59. Jefferey Hiday, "Pat Robertson as a Banker?" *Wall Street Journal*, April 8, 1999.

60. John Macleod, "Righteous Are in the Wrong," *The Herald* [Glasgow], June 8, 1999.

61. Pat Regnier, "Pat Robertson, E-Banker," *Money*, May 1999.

62. Hiday, "Pat Robertson as a Banker?"

63. Liz Szabo, "Bank of Scotland Cancels Robertson Deal," *Virginian-Pilot*, June 7, 1999.

64. Steve Duin, "OCA's Lively Looks to Share His Blessings," *The Oregonian*, June 24, 1993.

65. Isikoff and Hosenball, "With God There's No Cap."

66. Gregory Palast, "Business: Inside Corporate America: I Don't Have to Be Nice to the Spirit of the Antichrist," *The Observer*, May 23, 1999.

67. Duin, "OCA's Lively Looks to Share His Blessings."

68. Duin, "OCA's Lively Looks to Share His Blessings."

69. Isikoff and Hosenball, "With God There's No Cap."

70. Esther Diskin, "Sold: Kalovita Disappears, Piece by Piece," *Virginian-Pilot*, November 18, 1994.

71. Isikoff and Hosenball, "With God There's No Cap."

72. Esther Diskin, "Robertson Rebuts ABC Report on Kalovita," *Virginian-Pilot*, October 29, 1994.

73. Marc Davis, "6 Years after Alleged Threat," *Virginian-Pilot*, August 27, 2000.

74. Diskin, "Sold: Kalovita Disappears, Piece by Piece."

75. Marc Davis, "Pat Robertson Sues Executive He Fired," *Virginian-Pilot*, October 11, 1995.

76. Diskin, "Robertson Rebuts ABC Report on Kalovita."

77. Davis, "6 Years after Alleged Threat."

78. Davis, "6 Years after Alleged Threat."

79. The Associated Press, "N.C. Appeals Court Cuts Evangelist Out of Suit," October 20, 2000.

80. Steven Vegh, "Pat Robertson Redeems Pancakes from Sugary Sins," *Virginian-Pilot*, January 26, 2003.

81. Pat Robertson, *Bring It On: Tough Questions. Candid Answers* (Nashville, Tenn.: W Publishing Group, 2003), 313.

82. Bill Sizemore, "Is Anything Wrong with Pat Robertson Making a Killing?" *Washington Post*, August 26, 2005.

83. Victor Zonana, "Robertson Cancels Plan to Purchase Ailing UPI," *Los Angeles Times*, June 11, 1992.

84. Gary Cohen, "On God's Green Earth," *U.S. News & World Report*, April 24, 1995.

85. Beth Healy, "Web Site Thinks There's Money to Be Made on Christianity," *Boston Globe*, February 12, 2001.

86. Steven G. Vegh, "CBN Donors Are Growing as Fiscal Core of Network," *Virginian-Pilot*, March 5, 2005.

87. The Associated Press, "Learjet Registered to Pat Robertson Crashes," June 2, 2006.

88. Cragg Hines, "What Would Secretariat Do?" *Houston Chronicle*, December 15, 2001.

89. Pat Robertson, "Pat Robertson to Disband Commercial Stable," CBN Press Release, May 10, 2002.

90. Foege, *The Empire That God Built*, 47.

91. Vegh, "CBN Donors Are Growing as Fiscal Core of Network."

92. Steven G. Vegh, "When Robertson Retires," *Virginian-Pilot*, April 22, 2005.

93. O'Keefe, "Pat Robertson's Ever-Growing Business Kingdom."

94. Palast, "Business: Inside Corporate America: I Don't Have to Be Nice to the Spirit of the Antichrist."

CHAPTER 15

THE CHRISTIAN COALITION TRIUMPHANT

W HILE many evangelicals were disappointed with the presidency of George H. W. Bush and horrified by Bill Clinton, the 1990s were a time of consolidation of power for Pat Robertson. By 1994 the Christian Right, led by the Christian Coalition, appeared to have considerable power in both houses of Congress and had a Democrat president on the run. Yet only two years later those heady days were just a memory. In 1996 Clinton was reelected, and the Christian Coalition slowly began to decline. Although the coalition fought on, it was clear by the 2000 election that it was a shell of its former self. Despite the coalition's eventual eclipse, the period from 1990 to 1996 was a time of unprecedented power for American evangelicals, and Pat Robertson was the leader of this latest wave of the modern Christian Right. However, following the collapse of his campaign for president, few could have imagined that his greatest political achievements were yet to come.

To many outsiders Robertson appeared to be a broken man in 1988. Sociologist Steve Bruce's 1988 work *The Rise and Fall of the New Christian Right* predicted that the movement was in its final death throes.[1] Like many others who studied the movement in the late 1980s, Bruce claims that its lack of success during the Reagan era proved that the movement was small and getting smaller. While he is correct in noting their political failures, he is wrong about their death. According to Bruce, Falwell's decision to close down the Moral Majority in 1987 was a sign that the movement had run its course. He predicted that a combination of their small numbers and a backlash from liberal groups would prevent religious conservatives from wielding political power in the future. Scores of journalists and academics predicted much the same thing.

There were few people outside of the leadership of the Christian Right who saw a future in the movement. One person who knew that the Religious Right was far from dead was Robert Boston, of Americans United for the Separation of Church and State. He warned, "[A]ny social-political movement has its peaks and valleys, and I have seen the obituary of the Religious Right written more than once. I know better than to believe it."[2] Boston realized that the Christian Right had a long-term outlook. They did not merely focus on the next election, but decades ahead. Some journalists noted that while Falwell had left politics, Robertson had not. However, most still doubted that his involvement would amount to anything, and the Christian Coalition was not taken seriously for a number of years.

Although it took a couple of years, Robertson was determined to make the Christian Coalition more successful than any of its predecessors. He also had no desire to waste the sacrifices that he had made or alienate his campaign supporters. This new group was not an entirely new organization. Its family tree included the Freedom Council and Operation Blessing, in addition to Robertson's presidential campaign. The coalition benefited from the mistakes and successes of these groups, and became a powerful political force. Although Pat Robertson created many political, business, and religious organizations during his lifetime, the Christian Coalition is the most famous. It was the political power broker that the Moral Majority never was. The coalition was larger and wealthier, and able to make actual changes in government. It was the first religiously based organization since Martin Luther King Jr.'s Southern Christian Leadership Conference that was able to make a large impact on American politics and on a political party.

The man Robertson chose to lead the Christian Coalition was Ralph Reed. Reed was born in Portsmouth, Virginia, in 1961, just months before the Christian Broadcasting Network's (CBN) first broadcast. He did not live in Virginia for long because his father's career in the navy meant that he was raised in several cities across the nation.[3] Raised in a conservative Republican home, Reed became the president of the National College Republicans while an undergraduate at the University of Georgia. Reed later attended Emory University and received a PhD in history. Among his early political accomplishments was his work on the reelection campaign of North Carolina senator Jesse Helms and the creation of Students for America (SFA). SFA was formed after Reed's conversion to evangelical Christianity, and was designed to be a religious version of the College Republicans. Although he supported Jack Kemp in the 1988 election, Reed studied Robertson's campaign and gave Robertson his brutally honest critique during their first face-to-face meeting at George H. W. Bush's inaugural dinner in January 1989.[4] At Robertson's request, Reed prepared a memo outlining where he thought Robertson's campaign had erred and how an evangelical Christian political organization might be run in the future. Reed wrote that theologically conservative Christians had both removed themselves and been removed from politics. "[W]e have now had two full generations of Bible-believing Christians . . . with virtually no hands on experience in the political decision making process."[5] Reed sent the report, and heard nothing for months. Then in September 1989, Robertson invited him to a meeting in Atlanta to talk about the formation of a new religious political organization. At the end of the meeting Robertson announced that Reed was the head of the new organization, called the Christian Coalition. Reed was stunned; it was the first he had heard of the offer. Robertson then said, "Congratulations, you have no office, no money, and no staff, welcome aboard."[6] He had once again plucked someone from obscurity and given them considerable power.

Reed moved to Virginia Beach and set up shop in the former offices of Americans for Robertson (AFR). The Christian Coalition had $100 to its name, and the office phones were only turned on after Reed put the deposit on his personal credit card. Besides the $100, Robertson donated the funds needed to mail the first fund-raising letter to the 134,325 people who had financially supported his presidential campaign.[7] The coalition was set up with the Internal Revenue Service (IRS) as a tax-exempt "social welfare organization." Its incorporation documents claim that the group's goal is to "encourage active citizenship among people professing the Christian faith." It proposes to do this through educating voters, distributing literature, "citizenship mobilization, the advocacy of public policy, and representation before public bodies."[8] The Christian Coalition claimed to be neutral while its first significant donor was the Republican Senatorial Committee, which gave $67,000. By November 1989 the coalition had $82,000 in the bank and two thousand members; by June 1990 that number swelled to twenty-five thousand. In January 1992 the coalition had 150,000 members, and a total of 250,000 by the time of the 1992 Republican Party convention.[9]

The Christian Coalition was designed to be different from the very beginning. Early Christian Right groups like the Moral Majority had mostly been direct mail organizations. They sent out letters to Congress and the president and tried to get their views heard. They were organizations that were run from the top down. Falwell and the Moral Majority leadership would issue marching orders to the state chapters and try to help encourage people to vote. One of the reasons that that group lacked staying power was that it presented itself as a majority when it clearly wasn't. This meant that their adversaries could portray themselves as underdogs while the GOP could afford to keep them in the shadows. The coalition was set up with the Moral Majority's flaws in mind. The name was more friendly. This was not a majority trying to impose its will; now evangelicals were a constituency looking for their place at the table. The very term *coalition* conjures up an image of people of various beliefs working together for the common good. Reed said that the coalition's focus was "niche marketing, finding and targeting your audience. Not broadcasting, but narrowcasting."[10] The great strength of Robertson's new group was its intention to be a grassroots organization. To that end they kept their offices out of Washington, D.C., until the late 1990s and focused on local elections across the country. Instead of pressuring politicians, the coalition would bring out voters to elect the right candidates. They would also teach people how to run for office. Reed often told Christian Coalition members that having an ally in the White House was not enough—Christians needed to control the government at every level. This was a mature Christian Right, one that thought long term.

The immediate concern of the Christian Coalition was the new Bush administration. While the president was supported by many evangelicals, he did not have the easy rapport with religious conservatives that Reagan had enjoyed. In 1989 Robertson once again started to publish his newsletter *Pat Robertson's Perspective* and the March issue warned Bush to be careful not to alienate evangelicals. Robertson wrote that Bush was a member of the Eastern establishment and his administration would be a battle between his social status and his religious beliefs.[11]

In September Robertson struck a familiar cord when he wrote that "evangelical Christians have virtually been excluded from any meaningful position in the government."[12] He again claimed that the president owed his election to evangelicals and warned him to be more supportive of their causes. Robertson shared with his readers a lesson that he had learned on the campaign trail: "Political power resides only with those who hold offices and appointees." To this end, Robertson wrote that Christians must do two things in order to change society. First they had to make sure that they were preaching the Gospel "with boldness throughout the land." Secondly, they had to "join with like minded people to insure that evangelicals are elected" to both local and national offices.[13]

An example of the growing rift between Robertson and Bush occurred in November 1989 when Bush invited evangelical leaders to the White House. As had been the case with Carter and Reagan, evangelical leaders were upset that Bush had appointed so few conservative Christians to his administration. White House director of personnel Chase Untermeyer stated that it was illegal to count people according to their religion. Robertson, who attended the meeting with Reed, said, "[Y]ou have no difficulty identifying evangelicals and their allies during the campaign, but you cannot find them after the election." Reed reported that the room exploded with laughter.[14] Bush's trouble with evangelicals only worsened as his administration progressed.

During the summer of 1990 Robertson wrote that since Bush was so popular with the American public, he felt that he could afford to slight religious conservatives. "They believe that neither the conservatives nor the evangelicals have any other place to go politically."[15] According to Robertson, since Bush felt the political right wing was trapped, he could "cater to the demands of the traditionally Democratic constituencies within the homosexual and black communities." Robertson then went on at length about the Trilateral Commission's control of Jimmy Carter and other famous politicians, including George H. W. Bush. He wrote that the power elite, whom he never defined, might replace Bush with a conservative Democratic southern governor, preferably Chuck Robb of Virginia, who was then a senator. "Absent some explosion in 1992, I believe that the plan of the world's power elite would be to insure the reelection of Bush and Quayle in 1992. Then bring Chuck Robb forward in 1996."[16] A year later, Robertson changed his mind. In the book *The New World Order* Robertson writes that although the elite had chosen Robb, a scandal had ruined his chances, so now they were going to put Senator John Rockefeller III in the White House. He claimed that the Eastern establishment realized that "a surrogate is not necessary when they can have the real thing." Robertson also claimed that "Rockefeller has been tapped by the elite to bring us that much closer to world government in 1996."[17] Robertson's first prediction about 1996 was closer to what actually happened.

During the Bush administration, the Christian Coalition was able to string together a series of small victories across the nation. The first part of the nation to form an effective local Christian Coalition chapter was Southern California. Conservative bastion Orange County, which had one of the nation's largest chapters of the John Birch Society, was the first county to start a local chapter. It was in San Diego, however, where the coalition achieved victories that brought it national attention. In 1990 the coalition supported candidates who won places on the city's school board and a number of other positions. These candidates made news because they didn't run traditional campaigns. Instead of holding rallies and participating in debates, the coalition taught them how to energize the conservative Christian base in their communities. They registered voters at churches, used church directories to contact voters, and distributed flyers at church parking lots. The result is that the incumbents were taken by surprise on election day. The tactics worked so well that religious conservatives took sixty of the eighty-eight offices. A San Diego school board member who had lost her seat complained that she never even saw her opponent until she was sworn in.[18] The media labeled these tactics stealth campaigns and portrayed the Christian Coalition as an ominous, secretive group that used tactics that were somewhat immoral. However, these candidates were using Reed's idea of narrowcasting—hitting your core audience. For evangelical candidates at the local level, this was fairly easy. In most cities across America the evangelical churches are the largest so they are natural places to reach a constituency that is likely to agree with the coalition's views. There are also Christian bookstores, rock concerts, and universities where candidates can reach people who are generally much more likely to vote for a conservative. These tactics proved to be so successful that they spread across the nation. By the end of 1990 chapters began to spring up around the nation, especially in states like South Carolina, where Robertson had established a base of support in 1988.

The use of stealth tactics led to some stunning successes, but it did not last for long. One Christian Coalition leader appeared to dismiss the democratic process when he claimed that "we don't have to worry about convincing a majority of Americans to agree with us. . . . They're not involved, they're not voting, so who cares?"[19] The most famous of all comments about the coalition's tactics in San Diego came from Reed himself. In a now infamous speech Reed said, "I do guerrilla warfare, I paint my face and travel at night. You don't know it's over until you're in a body bag. You don't know it's over until election night."[20] The coalition had to quickly back away from such comments, but their original desire for a low profile led many to believe that they had a secret agenda as well as secret candidates. Years later some still claimed that the coalition had ulterior motives. One accusation was that Robertson had purposefully taken a back seat to Reed in public so that Americans would not notice as Robertson "consolidates his hold on the Republican party."[21] These stealth tactics were based on Robertson's successful campaign in Iowa. The invisible army could be found all across the country.

On the national level the Christian Coalition had its first success with the 1990 reelection campaign of Republican senator Jesse Helms of North Carolina. The coalition handed out 750,000 voter guides, and was credited with helping Helms keep his seat. The voter guide was a powerful tool of the Christian Coalition. While other New Christian Right and liberal political groups had used them, the coalition made more effective use of the guides than any organization had before. The voter guides were the focus of controversy for the entire history of the organization.

The guides were designed to be simple aids for conservative Christians to take to the voting booth, but their simple design allowed for easy manipulation. If politicians refused to answer the questionnaires, the coalition would answer for them on the basis of the candidates' voting records and their interpretation of the candidates' beliefs. The guides never had a standard set of questions, instead they changed to reflect local political issues and the views of the candidate that the coalition was leaning toward. Across the country politicians, usually Democrats, complained that their views were being misrepresented. The coalition's staff was thorough at researching and would base some candidates' answers on votes taken a decade earlier or more. This was done to make sure there was a contrast between the two candidates, but this desire to show differences led to questionable practices. During a Road to Victory rally, coalition members were told to wait until the Sunday before an election to distribute the guides. The fear was that if a candidate became upset about how they are characterized, "you're going to have a real skittish pastor that is just going to pull them."[22] Holding the guides until the last minute limited the effectiveness of these complaints.

The most egregious story of the abuse of Christian Coalition voter guides happened in Robertson's home state of Virginia. In 1994 Robertson had supported Iran-Contra scandal figure Oliver North in his campaign for the Senate. North won the Republican nomination, but lost the general election. There were several factors at play in the loss, but what apparently bothered Robertson and the Christian Coalition was that Virginia's only Republican senator, John Warner, had refused to support North's campaign. Two years later Warner faced reelection, and the coalition went on the attack. The coalition voter guide for the 1996 Republican primary showed that James Miller III was perfectly aligned with the coalition's core values, while Warner only scored 20 percent. This was a shock to the senator, since he had enjoyed a 100 percent rating in the coalition's Congressional Scorecard, published just a few months earlier.[23] During a rally for the Miller campaign, Reed, with Robertson and North in attendance, explained that the primary was "a test of the ideological direction of the party."[24] Robertson and his wife donated $1,000 each to Miller, who still lost the primary. For the general election, Warner's rating went back up to 100 percent. The ratings drop that Warner experienced happened to others who opposed Robertson and the Christian Coalition.

The first in-depth analysis of the coalition's voter guides shows just how biased they actually were. Political scientist Larry Sabato and journalist Glenn Simpson studied hundreds of voter guides that were handed out for local, state, and federal elections. In nearly 75 percent of the guides dealing with House and Senate races, the Republicans and Democrats did not agree on a single point. When there was agreement, it was usually only on one of the ten questions. What was most damning about the guides was their use (or nonuse) of the abortion issue. The Christian Right's commitment to the pro-life cause is at the core of their values, but what did the coalition do when it encountered pro-life Democrats? In their study of 219 voter guides, abortion was only used sixty-two times since it was easier to find Democrats who did not agree with the coalition's conservative economic agenda.[25] In addition to finding that the voter guides were manipulated, Sabato and Simpson discovered that the coalition targeted races in critical swing districts. It is evident that the coalition was partisan from the very beginning, and was willing to bend election laws in order to promote its political agenda.

Besides the work with elections the Christian Coalition also spent its energies fighting government agencies that they thought were hostile to religious conservatives. One government program that most conservatives, including the

Christian Right, love to attack is the National Endowment for the Arts (NEA). The agency provides grants for artists in various fields in order to support their work. The NEA has been a target because most of the artists are politically and socially liberal, and an inordinate amount of the agency's funding goes to artists, galleries, and museums in New York City. Robertson often criticized the NEA on *The 700 Club*, and his rhetoric against it actually increased during Bush's term. The drumbeat against the NEA became so constant that the head of the agency, John Frohnmayer, asked to appear on Robertson's program so that he could defend the agency. On April 23, 1990, he was interviewed by Robertson and reminded the televangelist about the ninth commandment, which forbids lying. During their interview Robertson listed a host of accusations against the NEA and claimed that it supported a radical agenda that included among other things anti-Christian bigotry, homosexuality, and pornography. Frohnmayer vigorously defended the NEA and claimed that "none of that was done since George Bush has been president." He even claimed that his agency supported good Christian art including exhibits of Renaissance paintings, gospel music programs, and the first Black American Sacred Music Convention.[26] Robertson was unconvinced. As the 1990 midterm election neared, Robertson and the Christian Coalition attacked the Democrat-controlled Congress with their NEA straw man.

In June 1990 the Christian Coalition took out a full-page advertisement in the *Washington Post* and other papers. The ad was an open letter to Congress and focused on Democrats' support for the NEA. After mentioning controversial artists like Robert Mapplethorpe and listing specific NEA–funded projects that he found objectionable, Robertson ended with this threat.

> There may be more homosexuals and pedophiles in your district than there are Roman Catholics and Baptists. You may find that the working stiffs in your district want you to use their money to teach their sons how to sodomize one another. You may find that the Roman Catholics in your district want their money spent on pictures of the Pope soaked in urine.
>
> There is one way to find out.
> Vote for the NEA appropriation just like Pat Williams,
> John Frohnmayer, and the gay and lesbian task force want.
> And make my day.[27]

Frohnmayer remained at the NEA until he was fired in early 1992 when the agency became a factor in Bush's fight for the Republican nomination against challenger Patrick Buchanan.

To keep their state leaders and concerned followers informed the coalition began to hold yearly Road to Victory meetings starting in 1991. The first year the convention was held on the CBN compound in Virginia Beach, and from 1993 to 1996 the coalition met in Washington, D.C. The two-day event usually featured a series of brief speeches by prominent Republican and evangelical leaders. Concurrent with the main speeches was a series of meetings for states and others focused on specific political issues. Finally there was usually a large vendor section selling books, advertising political candidates, and representing all manner of Christian Right organizations, from Phyllis Schlafly's Eagle Forum to small political groups.

The Christian Coalition was designed to be the political and legislative arm of a new political revolution. Robertson wanted a legal way for conservative Christians to take control of the government. He hoped that this two-pronged approach would leave a permanent mark on American politics. Robertson had tried to create a legal counter to the American Civil Liberties Union (ACLU) in the 1980s, but with limited success. In 1990 Robertson founded the American Center for Law and Justice (ACLJ). The center had offices in Kentucky and Washington, D.C., but was based on the CBN campus. This allowed students from Regent University's law school to work as interns. The center specialized in religious freedom cases and was remarkably successful in a series of cases across the country and before the Supreme Court.

The primary reason for the success of the ACLJ was Jay Sekulow, the group's lead attorney. Sekulow was raised in what he called a "culturally observant" Jewish family and converted to Christianity while a teen. Sekulow had made a name for himself working as counsel for Paul Crouch and the Trinity Broadcasting Network. He came to Robertson's attention in 1987 when he argued and won his first case before the Supreme Court. The case, *Board of Airport Commissioners v. Jews for Jesus,* won religious groups the right to distribute leaflets and solicit donations at airports.[28]

During the first year of the ACLJ's life, Sekulow won what is considered the group's most significant victory, the Supreme Court case *Westside Community Board of Education v. Mergens.* In that case Sekulow worked in concert with Kenneth Starr, who at the time was the solicitor general for the Department of Justice.[29] The case, which was won by an eight to one decision of the Supreme Court, allowed student-run Bible study and other religious clubs to meet on public school campuses during school hours. In the following years he won cases dealing with protestor rights at abortion clinics and religious speech as a first amendment right. The ACLJ is one of the most successful and least known of Robertson's projects.

One of the most interesting things about Sekulow was his attitude toward Christian Right political rhetoric. While the ACLJ spent the majority of its time fighting for religious liberty, Sekulow rejected the notion that Christians are an oppressed minority. "We don't have the vaguest clue in this country what real persecution is. We do have a victim oriented culture these days and we have to be careful."[30] His courtroom demeanor was anything but tainted by victimhood. The main chamber of the Supreme Court is meant to be intimidating, but Seku-low was confident when he appeared there. The court allows both sides to make a half-hour presentation, which quickly devolves into a series of questions launched rapid-fire at the main lawyer by the justices. In his appearances, it was usual for Sekulow to ask questions of the justices, argue with them, and some-times talk over them. "The Supreme Court was used to Christian lawyers being meek and mild and manageable. I am a reasonable fanatic."[31] Sekulow's tougher than usual attitude served him well in the courtroom, and his forceful person-ality was the prime reason that the ACLJ had been so successful. On first appear-ance Sekulow does not seem to fit in with Robertson's worldview. He was against the death penalty, for gun control, voted for Jimmy Carter twice, and called him-self a "Jewish liberal."[32] The reason that Robertson and Sekulow got along so well was that they agreed on an important point: American politics was hostile to anyone with religious ideals and someone had to stand up for their rights. While they disagreed on the idea of the victimhood of the evangelical world, they agreed that something had to be done to protect its rights.

Despite its work the Christian Coalition was still not taken seriously dur-ing the Bush administration. Many journalists and political commentators believed that the coalition was the modern version of the Freedom Council, a front for Robertson's next campaign for president. However much he denied it, many people assumed that Robertson was going to run again. When asked about what it would take to make him run again, Robertson's answer was so clear that it left him little wiggle room had he changed his mind. "I think an angel com-ing down and standing in front of me, and then three of four other signs. . . . It's too big an ordeal and the price is too great."[33] Robertson was probably thinking that if CBN had barely survived his last campaign, another one would certainly kill it outright. Still, the rumors of another run persisted for a number of years. Part of the problem is that many of the people who had helped in his 1988 cam-paign now were members or leaders of the Christian Coalition. Some coalition members' comments also inadvertently made it tough on Robertson. During Bush's reelection campaign some GOP regulars were upset that evangelicals were taking control of the party in many states. It was thought that these new dele-gates would be focused, not on the Republican Party, but on getting their agenda advanced no matter the cost. One Louisianan involved in this debate, described only as "a born-again" by the *Washington Post*, claimed that it was alright to push their agenda because "God wants Pat Robertson to be president, anything we do to bring that about is God's will."[34]

If some Robertson supporters mistakenly thought he was positioning him-self to run again, the Bush administration was becoming increasingly concerned about the role that evangelicals were going to play in the 1992 election. Writing in the *New York Times* Ronald Smothers summed up the Christian Right's feelings about the president. "Mr. Bush is still favored among evangelicals, but with no shortage of exasperation."[35] There were a wide variety of reasons for their dislike of the president. For starters, Bush was a high-church Episcopalian who never seemed comfortable with religious conservatives. He was lukewarm to the Christian Right's agenda, and even invited gay couples to the White House for a bill-signing ceremony. The one thing that truly angered evangelicals and Americans in general was Bush's renouncing of his pledge to not raise taxes. To evangelicals this was a sign the president was not a man of his word and could not be trusted.

Despite Bush's enjoying the highest approval ratings of any president in history, by late 1991 his presidency was seen as so inept that he faced a challenge for the Republican Party nomination in 1992. Conservative political commentator Patrick Buchanan attempted to challenge Bush. Although he was popular among some conservative Christians, Robertson viewed the Catholic Buchanan as a threat to the party and the young Christian Coalition. Despite his lingering distaste for Bush, who according to *The New World Order* was controlled by Council on Foreign Relations, Robertson decided that it was better to have Bush in office than Buchanan or Clinton. During the Georgia primary the Bush campaign sent out a letter written by Pat Robertson, which encouraged evangelicals to vote for the president. The letter said that although many Christians had voted for Buchanan as a message to Bush that they were not happy, it was time to support the president or he would lose in November.[36] In April, when Buchanan's campaign was all but finished, Robertson predicted that the challenge to Bush would help him win, since the president now had to pay attention to his party's right wing.[37] He was wrong about the election but correct about getting Bush's attention.

Bush's 1988 campaign was successful because it had been vicious and petty, but he was never able to gain traction against his Democratic opponent, Bill Clinton. The Arkansas governor was young, energetic, and played the saxophone on late-night TV, while Bush berated a young female reporter during an interview on MTV. The American economy was in recession, and while the president criticized the morality of *The Simpsons* and rap music, Clinton continued to hammer away with his campaign's unofficial slogan, "It's the economy, stupid." The president was clearly in trouble, and Robertson made sure that his troops did what they could to help. Robertson supporters from 1988 were sprinkled throughout Bush's 1992 campaign team. The vice chair of Bush's campaign in Louisiana had run Robertson's efforts in that state four years earlier. By the spring of 1992 it appeared as if the president had suddenly realized that the Christian Right existed and his staff accepted their help wherever they could.

Under Robertson and Reed's leadership the Christian Coalition supported Bush's campaign, although it was still legally supposed to be nonpartisan. Political scientist Duane Oldfield writes that the Christian Coalition handed out forty million voter guides and 70 percent of white evangelicals voted for Bush, which was an "impressively high figure, given the low level of Bush's overall support in a three-way race."[38] In 1997 CNN released documents that showed how much the Christian Coalition did for the Bush campaign. In April 1992 Robertson asked for and got thirty-nine of his supporters put into positions of power in the campaign and the GOP organization. The coalition also sent the campaign the results of a poll it had conducted on the popularity of Ross Perot, who they predicted could get 40 percent of the evangelical vote. Reed wrote to Bush campaign chief Mary Matalin to tell her that the Christian Coalition was "ready and willing to help shore up this base." Soon afterward Bush was interviewed by Robertson on *The 700 Club*. Before the interview was conducted CBN sent a list of questions, along with suggested answers, to Bush's staff. The Christian Coalition then distributed pamphlets that had excerpts from the interview, which showed Bush's religious convictions.[39]

One document that CNN described as a potential "smoking gun" was an agenda for a meeting between Reed and Bush campaign officials. Among the many topics discussed was the coalition's most potent weapon, the voter guide. Handwritten notes on a copy of the agenda show that Reed estimated it would cost half a million dollars to print the guides, and that Bush would come to Virginia Beach for a fund-raiser to offset the printing cost. Reed denied that any such conversation had taken place. The Federal Election Commission (FEC) did not believe the Christian Coalition's arguments and by unanimous vote decided to launch an investigation.[40]

Bush attempted to pay for his sins against the Christian Right during the 1992 Republican convention. In order to compensate for his lack of attention to Robertson and his constituents, Bush gave prime-time speaking slots to both Robertson and Buchanan. Although the media spent the most time on Buchanan's "culture war" speech, Robertson's speech was just as strident. Speaking before the thousands of people packed into the Houston Astrodome and millions on TV, Robertson used more severe rhetoric than he had at the 1988 convention. Robertson gave the Republican Party credit for destroying communism and the threat of nuclear war. He then referred to the Democratic Party as the carriers of a plague that was just as evil as communism. It was the Democrats in Congress, Robertson alleged, who had raised taxes on the American family to the point that "our families now spend more to support wasteful government than the serfs paid in Europe in the middle ages." While he spent the majority of his speech on taxes and their impact on the family, he did eventually get to the standard Christian Right topics of abortion and homosexuality. Near the end of his speech he gave a definition of the year's hot button issue for conservatives: family values. "To me, and to most Republicans, traditional values start with faith in Almighty God." He claimed that Clinton was "running on a platform that calls for saving the spotted owl, but never once mentions the name of God." Finally, Robertson said that not only was Clinton the enemy of family values, but he planned to "destroy the traditional family and transfer many of its functions to the federal government."[41]

In September Bush became the first sitting president to address a Christian Coalition Road to Victory rally. His speech was interesting because he focused almost exclusively on economic issues, not the social concerns central to many evangelicals. In his speech he claimed that family values and his economic agenda were tied together. His campaign was clearly hoping that if he gave a moderate speech at the rally, it would lessen the criticism that he suffered after the Houston convention. In response to Bush's appearance at the rally a Clinton campaign spokesman said, "[T]he Republican party has now been taken hostage, and there's a gun to its head held by Pat Robertson."[42] The rhetoric became even more heated as election day neared. Randall Terry, the head of the radical pro-life group Operation Rescue said, "Christians beware, to vote for Bill Clinton is to sin against God." Robertson called Terry's statement "totally inappropriate" and said that a vote for Clinton was not sinful, just "stupid."[43]

As it turned out, the coalition's efforts were not enough. As was seen in their stealth campaign era, Christian Right candidates tended to win elections with low voter turnout, but this was not the case with the 1992 presidential election. Bill Clinton took 43 percent of the vote to Bush's 38. Third-party candidate Ross Perot took an impressive 19 percent of the vote. Clinton and Bush were in a statistical tie among white voters, but Bush took 53 percent of southern white Protestants.[44] The president's margin among religious conservatives was not impressive, especially when compared to what his son was able to accomplish in 2000 and 2004. Many media commentators blamed Bush's failure in 1992 on his close association with the Christian Right. However, scholars who reviewed the election data proved that it was the poor economy, not religious issues, that cost Bush the election.

Overall, Robertson was unimpressed with President Bush. While he wanted the president to be reelected, he was able to use Bush's defeat to take the Christian Coalition to an even higher level of power. Reed made it clear that his movement was here to stay no matter what the outcome. "If Bush wins, the evangelical vote will have made the difference. If George Bush loses, the evangelicals will step into the vacuum created by his defeat."[45] That is exactly what happened.

While the candidate at the top of the Republican ticket had met with failure, the Christian Coalition was able to achieve considerable success in local elections. This was what Robertson had designed the group to do, and it was a glimmer of things to come. People for the American Way claimed that Christian Coalition–supported candidates won six of twelve races in the Iowa state legislature and eleven of twenty-two in Kansas. Ralph Reed was ecstatic, and members of the coalition had taken control of many state Republican Party offices, including in large states such as Texas.[46]

The Christian Coalition received its biggest boost when Bill Clinton was elected president in 1992. Robertson realized that rather than appealing to a president who had several constituencies to balance, he could attempt to become the voice of conservative America. The Clinton era proved to be the high point of the Christian Coalition's power because they were able to turn their electoral loss into an eight-year-long fund-raising drive for the Christian Coalition.

While the Republican Party was in turmoil after the election of 1992, the Christian Coalition, with Ralph Reed at the helm, was hard at work. Clinton was able to give his enemies plenty of fodder. His first act as president was to try to integrate gays into the military. Instead of appeasing the groups that got him elected, the eventual compromise managed to enrage nearly everyone. Liberals were incensed at the "Don't ask, Don't tell" policy that failed to protect gays in the armed services, while conservatives and many of the nation's military leaders were angry at a policy that they saw as destructive to military cohesion.[47] Many leaders of the Christian Right viciously attacked Clinton. Some, like Jerry Falwell, even accused the new president of covering up murders that he had ordered while governor of Arkansas.

Meanwhile, Robertson decided to take a different course. He felt the time had come for the Christian Right to moderate itself, or it would be blamed for every electoral defeat. In the months following the 1992 election, prominent moderates within the GOP created the Coalition for a Republican Majority and described themselves as "A Coalition to Take Back Our Party." The leadership included Senators Arlen Specter, Nancy Kassebaum, and Warren Rudman, all of whom had run afoul of the Christian Coalition. While they claimed that they would work with the Christian Right, one of their goals was the deletion of the pro-life plank from the party platform. Reed attended their first new conference, to make sure that his coreligionists were welcomed and that they were not blamed for Bush's loss.[48]

In the November–December 1992 issue of *Pat Robertson's Perspective*, Robertson warned his readers that politics is the art of coalition building and patience, and that doctrinal purity is not a goal of a political organization. In a letter to coalition members, Reed had complained that the "pro-family movement" has become "ghettoized" in the Republican Party.[49] Robertson and Reed planned to add more than just white evangelical Protestants to the ranks of the Christian Coalition, and they decided to start with Catholics and African Americans. While both groups had been traditionally supportive of the Democratic

Party, many of their social concerns were conservative enough that Robertson and Reed thought a bridge to these groups might be built.

One of the tactics that allowed the Christian Right, with the Christian Coalition at the helm, to gain power was its deliberate decision to define itself as the descendant of Martin Luther King Jr. and the civil rights movement. While it seems astonishing that white middle-class Americans could claim to be oppressed, evangelical Christian theology is filled with such rhetoric (the *Left Behind* series of books is a good example). The Christian Right hoped to change its negative image by adopting the rhetoric and actions of the civil rights movement. Evangelicalism is a diverse religious movement that comprises many ethnic groups, although whites make up the vast majority of adherents. So while the leadership of some Christian Right organizations adopted this new rhetoric, it was not universally shared by religious conservatives.

When evangelicals reasserted themselves politically in the late 1970s, they were triumphant, and their rhetoric demonstrated their optimism. They used names like the Moral Majority, Christian Voice, and Religious Roundtable, names that were meant to project power and leadership. They hoped to promote the idea of evangelicals as a powerful conservative majority against a small group of liberal elites, as Richard Nixon had done with his "silent majority" speech. While triumphalism may make the movement's followers feel good, it also made it nearly impossible to influence outsiders who felt crushed by a mighty wave of people. In 1982 the Moral Majority claimed more than five million members. How a group that totaled less than 3 percent of the population could claim to be a majority proved to be the fatal, unanswerable question.

While many in the Christian Right used civil rights movement rhetoric, this shift was not complete. The human mind has tremendous capacity for holding contradictory views, and men like Robertson were no exception. Religious media networks allowed Christian Right leaders to live in a contradictory world. To the secular media they can claim minority status, then appear on a religious station like Trinity Broadcasting Network (TBN) or CBN and claim to be speaking for both God and the majority of the people. These different messages were rarely noticed by the secular media. In essence, the Christian Right wanted it both ways; leaders loved to rally the faithful with talk of God's will and the power of the ballot, then appear on secular TV and complain that they are an oppressed minority. Although there were obvious racial, economic, cultural, and political differences, some white conservative Christians looked to the civil rights movement as a model of what a group led by Christians could become.[50] So the move from majority to minority rhetoric was based on both tactical considerations and perceptions based on evangelical memory of their own history.

Reed explicitly claimed that the coalition was a descendant of the African American civil rights movement. While he did not agree with all of the political goals of the protest movements of the 1960s, he did learn from their methods. Originally Reed used majority rhetoric and even military metaphors in his Christian Coalition training sessions. In 1991 Reed was criticized in the media when he used violent imagery to explain his campaign strategy. As a result, in 1992 Reed wrote a memo to the Christian Coalition staff, telling them to change their rhetoric.[51] If the Christian Coalition was going to be a grassroots movement like most civil rights movement organizations, and not a top-down group like the Moral Majority, it had to adopt the words and tactics that went along with it. The change was made and by 1996 the *New York Times* reported that Reed's speeches now contained "quotations from liberal icons like the Rev. Dr. Martin Luther King, Jr., and Robert F. Kennedy."[52] More than any other conservative leader, Reed was able to realize the advantage in being considered a minority.

Reed did more than just tone down the violent rhetoric, he actively tried to use the memory of Martin Luther King Jr. to strengthen his own movement. In 1995 he introduced a pledge card for Christian Coalition activists to sign by which they promised to "refrain from violence of fist, tongue, or heart."[53] He claimed the card was based on the one that was passed out by King when he led the Southern Christian Leadership Conference (SCLC). In a speech to the coalition membership in 1995, Reed praised Dr. King and said that his peaceful actions and nonthreatening and inclusive language were keys to his success.[54]

In the two books written while he was the head of the Christian Coalition, Reed uses the minority idea and claims the mantle of the civil rights movement many times. Reed's 1994 *Politically Incorrect* emphasizes one aspect of the civil rights movement that he wanted evangelicals to co-opt. The idea is that a minority group can appeal to sympathy, while a majority always runs the risk of looking like a bully. Containing chapter titles like "To the Back of the Bus" and "The New Amos and Andy," Reed's book depicts conservative Christians as the moral equivalent of blacks in the civil rights movement. He claims both groups were oppressed, but by different groups with different agendas. He asserts that Christians are constantly "under attack whenever they enter the public arena."[55] While he does not believe, as Robertson does, that Christians are being systematically persecuted, Reed does claim that conservative Christians have been "viewed as less than full citizens."[56]

"To the Back of the Bus" presents a long list of ways in which religion (evangelical Christianity to be precise) has been marginalized by lawmakers and judges. The chapter not only compares evangelicals to blacks, but to women of an earlier era. "Like the separate spheres once assigned to women, religious people are now relegated to their churches and homes where their faith poses no threat to the social order."[57] One of the book's last chapters is an indictment of racism in the evangelical church. Reed makes clear his belief that the "pro-family movement" should be racially mixed, which would also make it more powerful.[58]

Reed's next book, *Active Faith: How Christians Are Changing the Soul of American Politics*, published in 1996, continues the Christian as minority idea and discusses the civil rights movement and Martin Luther King Jr. at length. A chapter entitled "All God's Children" is a history lesson on the Social Gospel movement and Martin Luther King Jr.'s life. Reed writes that a key component of King's success was his alliance with Democrats while not alienating liberal Republicans. By this Reed hopes to show his constituents that political success depends on building a coalition of like-minded people. This idea has been anathema to compromise-wary evangelicals, but Reed hopes to make it acceptable by an appeal to the memory of the civil rights movement.[59] In his first book and public statements, Reed attempted to identify the Christian Right with the marginalization of African Americans before the civil rights movement. However, *Active Faith* has a more nuanced approach; it is written less like a politician's book and more like an historian's. Though in his earlier book he links his movement to King's, in the second book he backs away from claiming that they are mirror images. "There is nothing like a crisp moral equivalence between the civil rights movement of the 1960s and the pro-life, pro-family movement of today," Reed admits.[60] This caveat shows that the use of the memory of the civil rights movement is selective. Although he tries to distance the Christian Right from 1960s liberalism, it is only after a lengthy section of comparisons. The memory that Reed uses is heroic and righteous, black and white, good and evil, and not the complete picture of the African American freedom struggle. The politics of the Christian Right had little room for nuance, which explains why only the most positive elements are mentioned.

The Christian Right was not the moral equivalent to the civil rights movement on a number of levels. While Robertson may have believed that evangelicals were an oppressed minority, the majority of Americans did not. Americans respond to minority rhetoric, but the words have to be backed up with near universal acceptance of a group's minority status in order to have a long-term impact. Not being able to pray silently in a public classroom is one thing; not being allowed to vote is another. So while King's rhetoric was appealing for conservative groups, it works best for those that have claims of victimization that the rest of the nation can clearly recognize.

While Reed wrote about the Christian Right as modern-day civil rights movement warriors for minority rights, he also attempted to get his group to act out his convictions. In this regard he differed from Robertson and most other Religious Right leaders in that he wanted to involve ethnic minorities in the largely white Christian Right movement. His efforts make for one of the most interesting what-ifs of recent conservative politics.

In the spring of 1993, the Archdiocese of New York City announced that it would distribute Christian Coalition voter guides to its 213 parishes in Manhattan, Staten Island, and the Bronx. The coalition had previously worked with the Catholic Church in Chicago and in Texas during the 1992 presidential election. The New York City voter guides were for a May 4 school board election, the kind of election that the coalition had been very successful in just a few months earlier in California. The coalition also made attempts to reach out to black churches, although it was up to local chapters to make outreach efforts.

In the year before the Christian Coalition reached its zenith in the 1994 election, Ralph Reed spent considerable time expanding the support of the group and moving ever so slightly to the center. Reed in particular was very nervous about being blamed for Bush's loss in 1992 and he hoped that by toeing the Republican Party line, he could meet with more success. Some smaller Christian Right groups, such as the Christian Action Network, attacked Robertson and Reed for moving away from their core beliefs. Even conservative stalwart North Carolina senator Jesse Helms warned against the Christian Coalition's movement toward the center.[61] The 1993 Road to Victory meeting was the first place where Reed announced his plan to mainstream the Christian Coalition. He feared that the coalition had limited itself by focusing strictly on issues such as abortion and homosexuality. He hoped that a broader range of issues (health care, taxes, crime) would bring Catholics and conservative Jews to the group.

Although 1994 was the high point of the Christian Coalition's power, the early part of that year showed no indication of just how successful Robertson's group was about to become. The coalition had reached the one million member mark, but there were some troublesome signs in early election results in his own state of Virginia. National news was made when five candidates supported by the Christian Coalition lost in their attempt to win seats in a school board race. What made this seemingly insignificant news so compelling was that the candidates were from Robertson's home of Virginia Beach. Even the *New York Times* took note and hinted that the Christian Right was in trouble. The paper also reported that Robertson had failed in his attempt to elect Michael Farris as lieutenant governor of Virginia.[62] Meanwhile, Robertson's support of Oliver North had helped North win the Republican nomination for senator, yet he still struggled in the polls against scandal-plagued incumbent Democrat Charles Robb.

Successes, however, could be seen elsewhere around the nation. In Texas the Christian Coalition achieved what must be considered its most significant low-level (or nonfederal) victory before the huge success of November 1994. Dallas lawyer Tom Pauken, a member of the Texas Christian Coalition, was named chairman of the state Republican Party despite facing an opponent who was supported by Republican senators Phil Gramm and Kay Bailey Hutchison. Their candidate, however, stood no chance in a meeting where an estimated 70 percent of the delegates were politically conservative evangelical Christians.[63] The *New York Times* reported that the Texas meeting had the feel of the 1992 Republican national convention.

The crowd even chanted "Bush, Bush," except this time they chanted for the former president's son, George W. Bush, who was running for governor.[64]

The final Road to Victory meeting before the Republicans took control of Congress was a sign of just how powerful Robertson and his Christian Coalition had become. The meeting, attended by three thousand people, featured future presidential hopefuls Phil Gramm, Lamar Alexander, former vice president Dan Quayle, Dick Cheney, and Bob Dole, as well as most of the major leaders of the Christian Right. During the first night of the conference Robertson predicted that the nation would see "the Christian Coalition rise to where God intends it to be in this nation, as one of the most powerful political forces that's ever been in the history of America."[65] He appealed for support from the Republican Party: "We have no intention of advocating bizarre positions which will lose elections."[66] Robertson then took credit for saving the career of Oliver North and the Supreme Court nomination of Clarence Thomas. The Christian Coalition with Robertson and Reed at the helm was moving full steam ahead.

The weekend before the 1994 November election the Christian Coalition handed out more than thirty-three million copies of its voter guides in precincts around the nation. In all, the coalition spent $5 million on the midterm election.[67] Robertson had made President Clinton and the Democrat-controlled Congress his great fund-raising tool, and it paid off in one of the most amazing returns in American history. During the months before the election *The 700 Club* featured almost daily attacks on Clinton and made repeated claims that a Republican-controlled Congress was the only hope for the nation. Many people realized that Clinton was in serious trouble, but few guessed how powerful the Christian Right had become.

During the run-up to the 1994 election the Christian Coalition became even more aligned with the Republican Party, and the infamous voter guides were used to great effect. One of the biggest campaign issues was the debate over having an amendment to the Constitution that required a balanced budget. The guides rated 143 Democrats as being opposed to the amendment and nineteen supporting it. Their figures showed that only 13 percent of Democrats had supported the popular measure, while the actual number that voted for it was 40 percent. The coalition distorted their votes by basing their ratings on a vote that was unrelated to the balanced budget amendment.[68] There was even deception in how the coalition distributed the voter guides. In Missouri a minister of a liberal Protestant denomination sent a request to the coalition's Virginia headquarters asking for one hundred voter guides. He was surprised when a staff member of a local Republican candidate showed up with the requested materials and a photocopy of the minister's letter. The coalition had forwarded the letter to the local GOP campaign office, in clear violation of FEC rules.[69] It was no surprise why the coalition wanted these guides released just before election day.

When the final votes were counted, it was clear that the Christian Right and the Republican Party had won a major victory. The Republican Party took control of the House of Representatives for the first time since 1954. The seventy-four freshman representatives were some of Congress's most conservative, some even more so than their leader, House Speaker Newt Gingrich. While the voter turnout was a low 38.7 percent, the number of Republican voters was sufficient not merely to return control to the GOP but even to defeat the Democrat speaker of the house, Tom Foley.[70] Dan Rostenkowski of Illinois, one of the Democrats' most powerful politicians, outspent his opponent twenty to one, yet could not overcome a financial scandal and misleading coalition voter guides. The congressman was portrayed as wanting to promote homosexuality to schoolchildren, although the vote that the coalition cited prohibited that very thing. The bill in question was not as antigay as a proposal that Congress had previously discussed but never voted on. Since Rostenkowski didn't support that earlier measure, he was labeled pro-gay by the Christian Coalition.[71] The *New York Times* reported that evangelical Christians amounted to a third of the Republican vote, the party's largest voting bloc.[72] President Clinton was so unpopular that at his next press conference he had to defend his role as still relevant, a shocking claim for a president to have to make.

Pat Robertson was ecstatic after the November 1994 election. He claimed "the Christian Coalition is probably responsible for the 40-year shift in the US Congress. I think we had a large role in that. I think the agenda that we enunciated has really come to be on top on terms of policy decisions."[73] Robertson also agreed with Gingrich that the Republicans had been given a mandate and they dared not waste it, as he believed Reagan had in done 1980. Paul Weyrich claimed that the election was the pinnacle of the Christian Right movement, high praise from a founder of the Moral Majority.[74] Weyrich was correct; never before in American history had a religious organization been able to take credit for electing so many members of Congress. What Robertson had been unable to accomplish as a candidate on his own, he was able to do through other means. Ralph Reed claimed that the election ended "once and for all the myth that we are a liability rather than an asset in the Republican party."[75] In fact, religious conservatives were becoming the heart of the party.

Thanks to the Christian Coalition, Robertson's hope of achieving his political goals finally seemed to be within reach. Besides Clinton-bashing, another reason that congressional Republicans were able to do well was that they had a clearly articulated plan of action. Before the November election, the congressional Republican leadership released *Contract with America*, which was a list of goals it promised to work on during their first one hundred days in office. The *Contract* contained most of the standard Republican goals from the past twenty years. The main items included a presidential line-item veto, a balanced budget amendment, congressional term limits, a variety of tax cuts, and an increase in defense spending.[76] Some of the items, such as welfare reform, were passed with the reluctant help of President Clinton and others like the line-item veto were passed and then later overturned by the Supreme Court. Most of the issues in the contract were secular in nature; they did not address the many social issues that brought evangelicals into politics. Still the Christian Coalition, and Pat Robertson in particular, supported it fully.

Yet by the spring of 1995 Robertson was sounding a familiar refrain when he complained that the new Republican Congress was "ignoring the concerns of Christian and pro-family voters."[77] He was concerned that evangelicals would be ignored as he believed they had been during the Carter and Reagan years. Robertson decided to apply immense political pressure on the new Republican-dominated Congress, and this complaint was his attempt at a running start. Two weeks after the letter went out, Reed announced the Christian Coalition's *Contract with the American Family*, which hoped to address the many social issues that were important to conservative Christians.

On May 16, 1995, the Christian Coalition officially unveiled its contract with a rally on Capitol Hill. Robertson and Reed had given the Republicans one hundred days to work on their contract, and now it was their turn to make political demands. Many legislators, including Phil Gramm, attended the event, although Senate majority leader Bob Dole did not. Newt Gingrich told the crowd, "I came by, as Speaker of the House, to say we are committed to scheduling the hearings, and we are committed to scheduling votes on the floor."[78]

The contract had ten major points, including abolishing the Department of Education, restricting abortion, giving tax credits to women who stay at home, and passing a constitutional amendment to allow public expressions of faith.[79] Other elements included the elimination of the National Endowments for the Arts and the Humanities as well as the Public Broadcasting Service, restrictions on pornography, and vouchers for parents to send their children to private schools.[80]

While it was obvious that liberal groups like the ACLU and People for the American Way disliked the contract, many Republicans were also less than pleased. Conservative Republican senator Rick Santorum claimed that the nation had other pressing issues. "What's confronting us today is the budget," said Santorum, who perhaps unknowingly echoed the Howard Baker proclamation of 1981. Fellow Christian Right leader Gary Bauer, who worked for James Dobson's Family Research Council, said, "[T]here's nothing really new there." Bauer also publicly doubted that the legislation would pass or be effective.[81]

Robertson was happy to take credit for the election of the Republican majority, but he was hesitant to discuss the fate of the Christian Coalition's contract.[82] Most of the main points of the contract died in House committees and very few were brought to the floor for a vote. The significance of the contract was that the issues that were central to many evangelicals and Robertson in particular remained in the forefront of American politics during the 1990s. They had finally been given the attention that Robertson had demanded for fifteen years.

By any measure the 1995 Christian Coalition Road to Victory meeting was the high point of Robertson's power and influence. The crowd had increased from the usual two to three thousand to more than four thousand. Furthermore, the meeting had become a mandatory stopping place for any serious contender for the 1996 Republican nomination for president. Suddenly men like Bob Dole, who had avoided Christian Coalition meetings, were there asking for votes. Dole even predicted, "[Y]ou're going to have a big, big say about what happens in '96."[83] The only Republican candidate for president not invited was Senator Arlen Specter, who was proabortion and regularly attacked the Christian Right.

On the heels of its greatest success Reed attempted to increase the size of the two million-member group. This move required two things: first, Reed had to increase minority representation, and secondly, he had to get the coalition to cover a wider range of topics. These goals, while initially supported by Pat Robertson, eventually moved the Christian Coalition to make some serious tactical errors which led to its downfall.

In the fall of 1995 the Christian Coalition announced that it was going to focus on a wider variety of issues.[84] Suddenly the group took stances on such topics as defense spending, the federal budget, foreign policy, and tax breaks for corporations. This move was a natural extension of Robertson's interest in all political issues, not just the "family values" that had been a core of the Christian Right since the 1970s. While this emphasis on a broader range of issues was a hallmark of the Christian Coalition since 1995, it was the other element of Reed's twofold plan, reaching out to minorities and Catholics, that was more problematic.

In December 1995 Reed announced the creation of the Catholic Alliance, which he referred to as a "wholly owned subsidy of the Christian Coalition." Before a crowd of four hundred Boston Catholics, and a smattering of politicians including Representative Henry Hyde, Reed asked his listeners to join with their evangelical brethren to promote a socially conservative political agenda.[85] The Christian Coalition claimed that 250,000 Catholics were members of the coalition when it was at its peak, but the Catholic Alliance was never able to become as powerful as Reed had hoped. Catholics were a difficult group for the Christian Coalition to court. While many Catholics were socially conservative, there remains a strain of anti-Catholicism in evangelicalism that has kept the two groups apart.

In the first few years of the Christian Coalition, Reed had accomplished an impressive string of minor victories. Yet he believed that while the Christian

Coalition may have been powerful, it needed to reach out beyond its evangelical base. In 1997 Reed announced the creation of the Samaritan Project, which was an outreach to traditionally Democratic African Americans.[86] Among the goals of the project were federal funds for low-income area schools and scholarships for disadvantaged youth. The Christian Coalition even pledged to raise $10 million to help low-income youth ministries. Blacks were a significant portion of *The 700 Club*'s viewership and Robertson's 1988 campaign had hoped to attract their votes, but Jesse Jackson's campaign had derailed that plan. On May 10, 1997, the Christian Coalition held a "congress on racial justice and reconciliation."[87] It was an attempt to build bridges between the Christian Coalition and blacks. While many blacks shared the socially conservative views of Robertson, they were generally opposed to his ideas on civil rights.

During an interview on the *Charlie Rose Show* on PBS, Reed denounced white evangelical hostility toward the freedom struggle of the 1960s. Reed claimed that the racist attitudes of evangelicals "came back to haunt us in our own trek for social justice." He also predicted that America would not accept the Christian Right movement until it "becomes a truly biracial or multiracial movement."[88] The Samaritan Project had lofty goals that remained viable only as long as Reed was a part of the Christian Coalition. Within months of Reed's departure in September 1997 the project was canceled. It had encountered resistance from the beginning, mostly from African American groups that did not trust the coalition's intentions. Despite Reed's efforts to convince Robertson and other Christian Right leaders to include blacks, the vast majority of members of the Christian Coalition were white.

After years of efforts and millions of dollars Pat Robertson was finally in the position that he had always dreamed of. By the end of 1995 he was more powerful than his father had ever been. He had been disappointed time and again by politicians who had made promises, then backed away from them once in office. He felt that in 1994 the Christian Right had given a clear mandate to Congress and they were expected to deliver. No one in those heady days could have foreseen the sudden collapse that the Christian Coalition experienced as the 1996 presidential campaign unfolded. The coalition's troubles were not caused by outsiders, but by the very leaders who had taken the group to the height of power. It took Robertson five years just to get the coalition going, but its decline happened much quicker.

Notes

1. Steve Bruce, *The Rise and Fall of the New Christian Right: Conservative Protestant Politics in America, 1978–1988* (Oxford: Oxford University Press, 1988).

2. Robert Boston, interview by author, tape recording, Washington, D.C., April 14, 1998.

3. Justin Watson, *The Christian Coalition: Dreams of Restoration, Demands for Recognition* (New York: St. Martin's Griffin, 1999), 42.

4. Watson, *The Christian Coalition*, 51.

5. Ralph Reed, *Politically Incorrect: The Emerging Faith Factor in American Politics* (Dallas, Tex.: Word Publishing, 1994), 3

6. Reed, *Politically Incorrect*, 3.

7. Reed, *Politically Incorrect*, 4.

8. Larry Sabato and Glenn Simpson, *Dirty Little Secrets: The Persistence of Corruption in American Politics* (New York: Random House, 1996), 111.

9. Duane Oldfield, *The Right and the Righteous: The Christian Right Confronts the Republican Party* (Lanham, Md.: Rowman & Littlefield, 1996), 189.

10. Watson, *The Christian Coalition*, 66.

11. Pat Robertson, *Pat Robertson's Perspective*, March 1989.

12. Robertson, *Pat Robertson's Perspective*, September 1989.

13. Robertson, *Pat Robertson's Perspective*, September 1989.

14. Ralph Reed, *Active Faith: How Christians Are Changing the Soul of American Politics* (New York: Free Press, 1996), 16.

15. Robertson, *Pat Robertson's Perspective*, July–August 1990.

16. Robertson, *Pat Robertson's Perspective*, July–August 1990.

17. Pat Robertson, *The New World Order* (Dallas, Tex.: Word Publishing, 1991), 129.

18. Seth Mydans, "Evangelicals Gain with Covert Candidates," *New York Times*, October 27, 1992.

19. Watson, *The Christian Coalition*, 64.

20. Clyde Wilcox, *Onward Christian Soldiers? The Religious Right in American Politics* (New York: Westview, 1996), 9.

21. Frank Rich, "Bait and Switch; Ralph Reed Becomes the Front Man for Pat Robertson," *Pittsburgh Post-Gazette* [Pa.], March 3, 1995.

22. John King, "Christian Coalition Guide Spurs Democratic Protests," Associated Press, November 3, 1994.

23. Mike Allen, "Senate Race Heats Up," *Richmond Times Dispatch* [Va.], June 6, 1996.

24. Associated Press, "Religious or Political Advocacy?" *Roanoke Times* [Va.], July 8, 1996.

25. Sabato and Simpson, *Dirty Little Secrets*, 134–35.

26. Randy Gragg, "Frohnmayer Defends NEA in Debate on 700 Club," *The Oregonian*, April 24, 1990.

27. "To the Congress of the United States," Christian Coalition advertisement, 1990.

28. 482 U.S. 569 (1987).

29. 496 U.S. 226, 110 L.Ed. 2d 191 (1990).

30. Marc Fisher, "Jay Sekulow, Messianic Jew of the Christian Right," *Washington Post*, October 21, 1997.

31. Fisher, "Jay Sekulow."

32. Fisher, "Jay Sekulow."

33. David Reed, "Robertson, Falwell Go Separate Ways on Religious Right," *The Oregonian*, July 14, 1990.

34. Jason Berry, "The Family Values Thing," *Washington Post*, August 16, 1992.

35. Ronald Smothers, "The 1992 Campaign: Conservatives," *New York Times*, March 10, 1992.

36. Smothers, "The 1992 Campaign: Conservatives."

37. Robertson, *Pat Robertson's Perspective*, April–May 1990.

38. Oldfield, *The Right and the Righteous*, 207–8.

39. Brooks Jackson, "The Christian Coalition and George Bush," *CNN.com*, August 19, 1997, www.cnn.com/ALLPOLITICS/1997/08/19/christian.coalition/ (accessed June 19, 2006).

40. Gregory Palast, "Business: Inside Corporate America: I Don't Have to Be Nice to the Spirit of the Antichrist," *The Observer*, May 23, 1999.

41. Pat Robertson, "Republican National Convention Remarks by: Reverend Pat Robertson," *Federal News Service*, August 19, 1992.

42. David Von Drejle and Michael Isikoff, "Bush Focuses on Economy in Talk to Fundamentalists," *Washington Post*, September 12, 1992.

43. Peter Applebome, "Religious Right Intensifies Campaign for Bush," *New York Times*, October 31, 1992.

44. Jack Germond and Jules Whitcover, *Mad as Hell: Revolt at the Ballot Box, 1992* (New York: Warner, 1993), 506.

45. Seth Mydans, "Christian Conservatives Counting Hundreds of Gains in Local Votes," *New York Times*, November 21, 1992.

46. Mydans, "Christian Conservatives Counting Hundreds of Gains in Local Votes."

47. William C. Berman, *From the Center to the Edge: The Politics and Policies of the Clinton Presidency* (Lanham, Md.: Rowman & Littlefield, 2001), 22.

48. Mary McGrory, "New GOP Coalition Seeks Middle Ground," *St. Louis Post-Dispatch* [Mo.], December 20, 1992.

49. Mark O'Keefe, "Robertson Group Seeks to Soften Its Approach," *St. Petersburg Times* [Fla.], December 12, 1992.

50. Randy Alcorn, *Is Rescuing Right? Breaking the Law to Save the Unborn* (Downers Grove, Ill.: InterVarsity Press, 1990), 118–32.

51. William Martin, *With God on Our Side: The Rise of the Religious Right in America* (New York: Broadway Books, 1996), 318.

52. Kevin Sack, "A Penitent Christian Coalition Offers Aid to Burned Churches," *New York Times*, June 19, 1996.

53. Watson, *The Christian Coalition*, 79.

54. Watson, *The Christian Coalition*, 79.

55. Reed, *Politically Incorrect*, 42.

56. Reed, *Politically Incorrect*, 53.

57. Reed, *Politically Incorrect*, 42.

58. Reed, *Politically Incorrect*, 241.

59. Reed, *Active Faith*, 63.

60. Reed, *Active Faith*, 64.

61. David Shribman, "A Time of Schism in Religious Right," *Boston Globe*, August 6, 1993.

62. "Evangelical Slate Loses in Televangelists City," *New York Times*, May 5, 1994.

63. Richard Berke, "Religious Conservatives Conquer G.O.P. in Texas," *New York Times*, June 12, 1994.

64. Berke, "Religious Conservatives Conquer G.O.P. in Texas."

65. "Religious Right Pledges All-Out War on Clinton," *The Record*, September 17, 1994.

66. "Christian Coalition Rails at Clinton, Moderates," *The Record*, September 18, 1994.

67. John King, "Christian Coalition Guide Spurs Democratic Protests," *The Record*, November 3, 1994.

68. Sabato and Simpson, *Dirty Little Secrets*, 136.

69. Sabato and Simpson, *Dirty Little Secrets*, 133.

70. Berman, *From the Center to the Edge*, 43.

71. Sabato and Simpson, *Dirty Little Secrets*, 138–39.

72. Gustav Niebuhr, "The Religious Right Readies Agenda for Second 100 Days," *New York Times*, May 16, 1995.

73. Pat Robertson, interview by author, tape recording, Virginia Beach, Va., May 25, 2000.

74. Paul Weyrich, interview by author, tape recording, Washington, D.C., August 16, 2000.

75. Michael Shanahan, "Religious Right Increases Influence in GOP Gains," *Plain Dealer*, November 10, 1994.

76. Edward Gillespie and Bob Schellhas, eds., *Contract with America: The Bold Plan by Representative Newt Gingrich and Representative Dick Armey and the House Republicans to Change the Nation* (New York: Times Books, 1994).

77. John King, "GOP Feeling the Heat of Robertson's Agenda," *The Record*, May 10, 1995.

78. Jill Zuckman, "Christian Right's Contract Is Embraced by Gingrich," *Boston Globe*, May 18, 1995.

79. Jill Zuckman, "Religious Right to Push Agenda on Capitol Hill," *Boston Globe*, May 17, 1995.

80. Zuckman, "Christian Right's Contract Is Embraced by Gingrich."

81. Zuckman, "Christian Right's Contract Is Embraced by Gingrich."

82. Pat Robertson interview.

83. Richard Berke, "Politicians Woo Christian Group," *New York Times*, September 9, 1995.

84. Jonathan Peterson, "Christian Coalition Adds National Budget to Its Agenda," *Los Angeles Times*, October 30, 1995.

85. Charles Sennott, "Christian Right Woos Catholics," *Boston Globe*, December 10, 1995.

86. Watson, *The Christian Coalition*, 68.

87. Watson, *The Christian Coalition*, 69.

88. Martin, *With God on Our Side*, 366.

CHAPTER 16

THE COLLAPSE OF THE CHRISTIAN COALITION

HANKS to his business and political deals, by 1995 Pat Robertson was wealthier and more powerful than he ever could have imagined. His Christian Coalition was the foremost power in Washington, D.C., and his hand-picked leader, Ralph Reed, was hailed as a political genius of the highest order. Yet within two years of the coalition's greatest victory it suffered a crippling defeat. After decades of waiting to take power it should have been easier for the Christian Right to enact its agenda. Politics, however, is rarely so simple. Instead of seizing the initiative, Robertson and the coalition sat back and let events unfold. As the decade wore on the group was beset with scandal, money problems, and internal power struggles.

Political power is the most ephemeral element in the universe. It is impossible to gauge, and vanishes as quickly as it arrives. While Robertson and the coalition were powerful, they were also cognizant of recent history that painted the Christian Right as the reason for the Republican Party's failures at the ballot box. This explains why Robertson allowed Reed to declare that the coalition would adopt a "wait and see" strategy for the 1996 presidential campaign. Although there were many conservative Christians who wanted to support former vice president Dan Quayle, Reed's idea prevailed. The coalition chose not to use its power to help nominate someone of its own choosing. Instead, it decided to wait until Bob Dole had all but accepted the nomination before the Christian Coalition began to support him. Perhaps the reluctance to choose a candidate was based on Reed's fear of having the Christian Right be labeled a loser in two presidential elections in a row. The media still regularly brought up the Houston 1992 convention as an example of the disaster that would follow if the Christian Coalition was put in charge.

This electoral strategy put Robertson in an odd position; instead of being a kingmaker, he and the Christian Coalition were reduced, by their own actions, to just another supplicant for the Republican nominee's attention. Dole had always been conservative, but disliked the Christian Right's emphasis on social and moral issues. Since he was not beholden to them, Dole felt free to move toward the center, and the Christian Coalition missed its best opportunity to be a true power broker.

The big news about the coalition's 1996 Road to Victory rally was Dole's refusal to address the group, even though he had done so in years past. Claiming schedule conflicts Dole shied away but sent vice presidential nominee and Christian Right favorite Jack Kemp to the meeting. During his annual address to the convention, Robertson was surprisingly critical of Dole. Citing his low poll numbers, Robertson said it would take "a miracle from Almighty God" for Dole to win. He claimed that religious conservatives were the margin of victory for Bush in 1988 and that Dole could not win without their support. The crowd was surprised an hour later when Dole took the stage to briefly address the crowd on the pretext of introducing Kemp, the night's featured speaker. According to reports, Reed had sent a personal letter to Dole asking him to make an appearance. The crowd of coalition activists was happy to see him, but one reporter noted that he "was not welcomed by the crowd with the same enthusiasm that greeted him at last year's gathering."[1] Robertson and Reed knew something critically important about most Christian Right voters. If they are not motivated to vote for someone, they won't vote for his opponent, they will just not vote at all.

What happened to the Christian Coalition and Pat Robertson's dreams of power in 1996 was nothing short of a disaster. President Clinton appeared so weak that House Speaker Gingrich was emboldened and "operated in a highly partisan manner and saw no need to compromise with either the White House or Democrats on Capitol Hill."[2] When the two men refused to make a deal on the federal budget, the Republican-controlled Congress shut down the government twice; once in November for six days and again in December for twenty-one days. What was intended as a power play by Gingrich backfired. The shutdowns damaged the Republican Party, and for the first time in over a year, Clinton's poll ratings began to rise. William Berman writes that the House Republicans had "over reached their mandate," and had moved the president "from near political death in early 1995 to a strong contending position for reelection in 1996."[3]

Clinton's rising poll numbers, based largely on the booming economy, and a lack of voter enthusiasm about Dole, allowed Clinton to stage an amazing political comeback. Although 1994 was the high point for the coalition, the 1996 election was their low point. Robertson blamed Dole for the loss, telling reporters, "[W]e were not consulted on this campaign. We were peripheral." He also promised that he would remain active in politics, saying, "[W]e're not going to sit by as good soldiers and take whatever is given us." Although that is exactly what they had just done. Paul Weyrich was amazed at the Christian Coalition's inability to stop Clinton so soon after their major victory. Weyrich recalls, "[H]e was so against their interests yet he won so clearly."[4] Not only did Clinton win reelection, but the Republican majority in the House decreased slightly.

One part of the fallout of the election was Ralph Reed's departure from the Christian Coalition, which he had led for eight years. He had become increasingly frustrated and wanted to start a political consulting firm where he could make more money and be in charge of his own political agenda. Reed had been incredibly successful in a few short years and politically there was little room to grow. He could either continue to run an increasingly shrinking organization, or leave while he still had mystique from the glory days.

Robertson was upset that Reed wanted to leave. For most of his life, Robertson was used to being the man in charge, someone who was rarely questioned. Earlier in his career Robertson and Jim Bakker had encountered serious trouble over who would control the Christian Broadcasting Network (CBN), but the Reed–Robertson relationship was different. Robertson respected Reed, and this allowed him to tell his boss when he was wrong. Some insiders in the coalition claimed that Reed was probably the only person who could confront Robertson on anything. Robertson even offered Reed the presidency of Regent University because he valued his opinions, but he declined.[5]

Reed did stay on long enough to help pick a successor. Unfortunately for the Christian Coalition Robertson decided to pick two men to take over Reed's job, and this proved to be a problem. In June 1997 Randy Tate was introduced as the new executive director of the Christian Coalition. Tate, who was first elected to office at age twenty-three, was a one-term congressman from Washington State. He had gone to Washington, D.C., as part of the Republican revolution of 1994 but had lost his seat in 1996.[6] Tate's conservative record and high approval rating by the Christian Coalition made him a target of labor unions, and he lost by a mere six thousand votes.[7] Two Republican congressmen who took office with Tate in 1994 opined that he was too partisan and would not be as able to expand the coalition's base as Reed had been attempting to do.[8] To most observers Robertson seemed to be replacing one young man with another.

The very next day, however, the Christian Coalition announced that Donald Hodel was its new president. Hodel had served in the Reagan administration as secretary of the interior and secretary of energy and had a long relationship with Robertson. It was hoped that Tate would appeal to young Republicans and Hodel would reach out to Reagan conservatives. Robertson called the two men "a double blessing," but the choice of two men led to divisions of labor and of emphasis.[9] Robertson claimed that the coalition had two million members, but they were mailing only several hundred thousand newsletters. Clearly its power was declining and continued to do so as the 1990s progressed.

The biggest change in the post-Reed era was that the Christian Coalition became more strident with Tate and Hodel at the helm. Gone was the attempt to mainstream, and the Catholic and minority outreaches were put on the back burner and eventually canceled in late 1997. They also laid off staff members, including twenty who were let go the day before Christmas without severance pay. In another cost-cutting move, they stopped publishing the glossy magazine and switched to a cheaper newsletter format. The new leadership decided to take their reorganization even further than just canceling programs. In order to put a halt to the Federal Election Commission (FEC) and Internal Revenue Service (IRS) investigations the coalition announced that it was considering creating a political action committee (PAC). The organization had taken in a record $26.5 million in donations in 1996, but that number had declined to $17 million in 1997.[10] The drop-off was partly due to the fact that 1996 was a presidential election year.

The attempt to reenergize the coalition was mortally wounded by a series of events in 1997 and 1998. Lawsuits from former employees, aggressive liberal groups, and actions by the IRS combined to bring the coalition to the verge of collapse. The problems began due to the actions of Judy Liebert, the coalition's chief financial advisor, who had been with the organization since its inception in 1989. The coalition was not yet three years old before she became concerned that donations to the group were being spent on activities expressly forbidden by the FEC. In 1991 a worried staff member told Liebert that the coalition had been mailing out letters for Virginia State Senate candidate Kenneth Stolle. The next day she discovered that the hard drive of her office computer had been removed and files relating to the activity were deleted. When Liebert confronted Ralph Reed about the mailings, he assured her that Stolle was paying a fair market price for them.[11]

One factor that helped Stolle win the election was a series of negative TV ads that were paid for by the Second District Republican Committee, and not Stolle's campaign. A week after the election, Liebert was told to send a check for $25,000 to the Second District Republican Committee, which was led by Gordon Robertson. The committee did not have to report who its contributors were, and in Liebert's eyes it was an illegal attempt to influence an election. By April 1996 Liebert claimed that she was so frustrated at Reed's questionable activities that she handed over pages of documents to the U.S. attorney's office in Norfolk, which immediately began an investigation. A month later Liebert was summoned to a Christian Coalition board meeting where she presented a ten-page memo that detailed her concerns about activities that violated federal laws. Two days after the meeting she was put on leave and was eventually fired for talking to the authorities before bringing her concerns to the board.[12] She was offered a year's pay as severance on the condition that she not publicly comment on the Christian Coalition or its leadership. Liebert refused. Although the coalition had her removed, the damage had been done and the FEC and IRS were both using the documents she supplied in their ongoing investigations.

The FEC filed suit against the coalition in 1996, charging that it had broken federal election laws by supporting Republican candidates during elections in 1990, 1992, and 1994.[13] The suit put the use of the very popular voter guides in question, and the coalition soon discovered that churches were hesitant to distribute them as long as the case was in court. In a demonstration of the power that both Robertson and the Christian Coalition enjoyed, the FEC itself came under attack soon after the lawsuit was filed. During an episode of ABC's news show *Nightline* that focused on the coalition's trouble with the federal government, host Cokie Roberts alleged that both the IRS and FEC were hesitant to pursue their cases due to the political power of the coalition and its leader.[14] Her claims were based on convincing, if circumstantial, evidence. A year after the FEC filed suit against the Christian Coalition, the Republican-controlled Congress tried to pass legislation that would have made it easier to remove FEC commissioners and attorneys. When that effort failed they forced the agency to pay $750,000 for an independent audit into allegations that it was unfairly targeting conservative political groups. In early 1999 the auditor, PricewaterhouseCoopers, concluded that while the FEC was significantly understaffed and underfunded, it operated "without partisan bias."[15] Such a conclusion seemed obvious because the FEC's commissioners are by law equally divided between Democrats and Republicans. Their investigation of the Christian Coalition was the result of a rare unanimous vote of the commissioners.

Due to the hostility of protesters in Washington, D.C., Robertson moved the 1997 Road to Victory meeting to Atlanta.[16] The meeting proved to be particularly difficult for several reasons. First, the media did not pay as close attention since the meeting was outside of the capital, and as a result the hoped for publicity did not materialize. Secondly, and more damaging, a person working for Americans United for the Separation of Church and State slipped a tape recorder into a secret strategy meeting. During the meeting Robertson made several off-the-cuff statements hostile to President Clinton and the Democratic Party in general, which were leaked to the press. While such comments were usual for Robertson, the fact that they were said in a "secret" meeting gave them a notoriety that they did not merit. They also helped keep alive the notion that

Robertson had a secret political agenda. He began the speech by stating that his comments were from his heart, not a prepared text. In the spirit of a "family" chat, Robertson said, "[I]f there's any press here, would you please shoot yourself. Leave. Do something."[17] The audience roared with laughter. Robertson quickly got to the matter at hand. "God has put a mandate on us, because this nation is in crisis." The spiritual rhetoric did not last long however, and soon he was discussing political strategy.

The first major section of Robertson's "secret" speech dealt with recent political history. Robertson took his leaders to task for their willingness to follow any politician who said what they wanted to hear. Robertson commented that at an earlier Road to Victory meeting one candidate made overly elaborate promises about his plans as president. The crowd responded enthusiastically, yet Robertson knew that the candidate could never deliver what he had just promised. "We've got to be knowledgeable. . . . We can't be swayed by just rhetoric."[18] He promised that the Christian Coalition would select the next president in the upcoming election because moderate Republicans could not win an election. This was a clear sign that he was determined to take the coalition on a different path from Ralph Reed's. In reference to the GOP's last two nominees Robertson said, "[W]e have had a couple of so called moderates. And moderates lose. You know, they lose. And we've had two major losers, and I don't want any more losers, I want a winner." The Christian Right had come a long way since 1980 and under his leadership the Christian Coalition "was not a bunch of ingénues anymore, we're a seasoned group of warriors."

The most controversial part of Robertson's speech were his favorable comments on the work of Tammany Hall, Richard Daly's Chicago machine, and Virginia's Byrd machine, which helped Robertson's father become senator. He made it clear that the Christian Coalition should emulate how these machines controlled the political process in order to win elections. According to Robertson these groups "had an identified core of people who had bought into the values whatever they were, and they worked the election and brought people out to vote. The other people were diffused and fragmented, and they lost and the people that had the core won. I mean, this isn't complicated, but this is what we've got to do." Once the coalition had this machine operating it would be able to control the government. It was only then that Robertson could tell the politicians, "[W]e just tell these guys, 'look we put you in power in 1994 and we want you to deliver. We're tired of temporizing. . . . This is your agenda. This is what you are going to do this year. And we are going to hold your feet to the fire while you do it.'"

Robertson was fed up after more than twenty years of political disappointments. First Carter, then Reagan, Bush, and the 104th Congress had all failed to act decisively on the Christian Right's agenda. He told the audience, "[Y]ou don't have to be modest and timid the way you talk. We're not going to be bomb throwers. We're not going to be crazies and make everybody mad. But we are going to say gentlemen, our time had come." He claimed that religious conservatives had been subservient team players too long and now "it's time for us to start leading the team." Robertson was widely criticized for this speech, and the IRS used it in their investigation of the Christian Coalition. The strategy that he laid out, however, was exactly what he ended up doing. The following year the Road to Victory meetings moved back to Washington, D.C. The release of transcripts of Robertson's speech was not the last problem that the coalition faced in the late 1990s.

The two men appointed to fill Reed's place had a difficult time trying to stop the coalition's slide toward oblivion. A lengthy *New York Times* article on Randy Tate detailed the problems that the group faced in Reed's absence. Claiming Tate was seen as "a little too nice—and not too effective" the article also featured some unintentionally less than complimentary quotes from Robertson. He said that Reed was very "analytical and cerebral in terms of political strategy. . . . He has a strategic mind that few have." Meanwhile he said that Tate was "an extremely dedicated person. . . . He's constantly up, always cheery, and it seemed like he could help mobilize the troops."[19] This was hardly a vote of confidence. It is not surprising that neither Hodel nor Tate lasted long.

The last few years of the Clinton administration were consumed in scandal, and Republicans tried to make the most of the situation. When the Republicans took control of Congress in 1994 they quickly launched investigations of the president's involvement in a land deal in his native Arkansas. These investigations ultimately led to the much more sensational accusations of the president's extramarital affairs, which he repeatedly denied. By the summer of 1998 Clinton appeared before a grand jury to deny the charge that he had sex with a White House intern. By December the House of Representatives had begun the procedure to impeach Clinton on the grounds that he had lied about his affair. In January 1999 the Senate began deliberations on Clinton's fate.

Many of the leaders of the Christian Right were highly critical of Clinton and eagerly awaiting his removal from office, yet Robertson held a more realistic view. While he was also consistently critical of the president, he realized that it was impossible to remove him from office. The day after Clinton gave a rousing State of the Union Address, Robertson told his viewers on *The 700 Club* that he could see the writing on the wall. "From a public relations standpoint, he's won," Robertson said of Clinton. "They might as well dismiss this impeachment hearing and get on with something else, because it's over as far as I'm concerned."[20] Robertson's comments angered some Republican congressmen, and it also bothered Don Hodel. In his capacity as president of the Christian Coalition, Hodel wrote Robertson a memo in which he complained that the coalition was losing members due to Robertson's comments on ending the impeachment hearings. He also suggested that Robertson resign as chairman of the Christian Coalition and become the chairman emeritus. In response Robertson sent a Hodel a "tersely worded letter" in which he accepted Hodel's resignation, even though Hodel had not offered to give up his position.[21] It was soon announced to the media that Hodel had retired, effective immediately. While Robertson only had very positive things to say about Hodel publicly, he clearly was not able to share his views as freely as Reed had been.

Instead of resigning from the Christian Coalition as Hodel had suggested, Robertson took over his job as president of the group. Other changes were on the horizon for the coalition as well. Six months after Hodel abruptly left, Randy Tate was demoted to executive vice president and his office was moved from the national headquarters in Chesapeake, Virginia, to a much smaller office in Washington, D.C. Officially it was announced that the coalition was not demoting Tate, but had merely eliminated the position of executive director as well as the job of the chief operating officer.[22] Tate continued to work for the coalition for a few months before leaving in late 1999. The new setup allowed Robertson to be in firm control of the coalition. He hoped that the organization could regain its focus and become a power in the upcoming 2000 presidential election. Before the group was able to move beyond the turmoil surrounding Ralph Reed's departure, it had to endure one more serious blow, this time from the IRS.

Since its inception in 1989 the Christian Coalition had operated as a 503 (c)(4) organization, which meant that while it was tax exempt, donations to the group were not. The group held this status provisionally for ten years while the IRS determined if the coalition was eligible for the status. It took an unusually long time for the IRS to make a determination in the case, and both Robertson and his opponents were constantly lobbying the government to reach a decision. For years Americans United and other liberal groups had been sending the IRS information on the political activities of the Christian Coalition, including Robertson's secret speech at the 1997 Road to Victory meeting.[23] Robertson would occasionally mention the ongoing investigation on *The 700 Club* and ask for support from his viewers to fight the government's "persecution."

Finally in 1999, a full ten years after the Christian Coalition first applied to the IRS, its petition for tax-exempt status was formally denied. The IRS came to the conclusion that the group was an actively partisan group and therefore ineligible in 1998, but kept their ruling a secret while the coalition appealed the decision. When they learned that the appeal had been denied they produced a press release that gave the event an interesting spin. "After 10 years of fruitless negotiations with the IRS, the Christian Coalition board of directors has decided to withdraw its application for tax-exempt status."[24] The coalition also announced that the group was splitting into two separate organizations with similar names. The Christian Coalition International (CCI) was formed as an openly political and non-tax exempt business. The other organization, named Christian Coalition of America (CCA), continued on as a tax-exempt "public education and issue advocacy" group. The CCA could do this because it was being formed from the Texas Christian Coalition, which had been granted 503 (c)(4) status by the IRS in 1992.[25] The CCI quickly faded into obscurity, even after Robertson promoted it during the 1999 Road to Victory conference. The CCA, however, continued to act as the partisan vehicle that Christian Coalition had been before. The average person could not notice a difference between the old and new coalitions, which was the entire point. Barry Lynn of Americans United called the action "a shell game in the sleaziest carnival."[26] Within months of the decision the Christian Coalition sued the IRS, claiming that it had been a victim of discrimination. The complaint alleged that the agency denied the coalition's application for tax-exempt status while it granted it to liberal organizations such as the Planned Parenthood Action Fund and the Democratic Leadership Council. In so doing the group alleged that the IRS penalized conservative and religious organizations because agency bureaucrats disliked the groups' political positions.[27] Randy Tate claimed that "the IRS in its attempt to stifle our activities, was engaged in arbitrary enforcement of the law."[28] Even *The 700 Club* got into the act. In a 2002 piece on the IRS the agency was accused of having "gagged churches seeking to provide spiritual guidance on political issues."[29]

Two months after the IRS's decision was made public the lawsuit that the FEC filed against the Christian Coalition in 1996 finally came to a conclusion. In her decision, U.S. District Judge Joyce Green threw out seven of the nine charges. In a move that surprised most observers, the judge ruled that the coalition's voter guides were not overly partisan. This decision meant that new voter guides could be distributed in time for the 2000 elections. Randy Tate, who was near the end of his tenure with the group, said that the judge had "cleared up what we had said all along; that the Coalition's voter guides were nonpartisan."[30] The two counts that went against the coalition were based on the allegations made by Judy Liebert. Judge Green found that the coalition had violated federal laws twice in 1994. The first incident was a flier distributed in support of Newt Gingrich's reelection campaign. The second finding was that the coalition illegally shared its mailing list with Oliver North's campaign for the Senate. Robertson called the ruling "an important victory for all citizen groups. It wasn't a victory just for conservative Christians. This was for citizen participation."[31] It wasn't just conservatives who supported the Christian Coalition in their lawsuit; they were also supported by the powerful labor union AFL-CIO and the liberal American Civil Liberties Union (ACLU). A Republican lawyer who specialized in election law told reporters, "[I]f they didn't find coordination [between the GOP and the coalition] in this case, they're not going to find it" with any supposedly nonpartisan group that gets involved in politics.[32]

Now that the most pressing legal issues had been resolved, Robertson was quick to act. He was determined not to repeat the mistakes of the 1996 campaign, so at his direction the Christian Coalition changed its tactics for the 2000 presidential election. Instead of a hands-off approach it decided to pick a candidate early. Robertson's first choice was Missouri senator John Ashcroft who was an elder in the Assemblies of God and a very conservative Republican. Robertson gave $10,000 to Ashcroft's campaign PAC, whose staff included Gretchen Purser, the former director of development for the Christian Coalition.[33] Besides Robertson, Phyllis Schlafly and Paul Weyrich also expressed their admiration for the senator. Despite this early interest in his candidacy, Ashcroft decided not to run after polls showed he was in danger of losing his seat in the Senate. In 2000 he lost to Missouri governor Mel Carnahan who had died three weeks before the election. As his interest in Ashcroft cooled, Robertson began to mention Texas governor George W. Bush on *The 700 Club* with increasing frequency.

Thanks to Robertson's decision to pick a candidate early in the campaign season the 1999 Christian Coalition Road to Victory meeting became a mandatory stop for Republican hopefuls. The meeting had over four thousand in attendance including every major Republican politician except the two who were making the most headlines. Perennial candidate Patrick Buchanan had announced his intention to leave the Republican Party and fight for the nomination of Ross Perot's Reform Party. He had planned to attend the convention but canceled soon after the Reform Party's most famous officeholder, Minnesota governor Jesse Ventura, referred to religious belief as a "sham and a crutch."[34] The other famous no-show was Senator John McCain, who was anathema to Robertson and was not invited; nor would he have been welcomed. His McCain–Feingold campaign finance bill would have crippled the Christian Coalition's ability to raise money for political campaigns.

Despite these two absences, the meeting featured presidential candidates Steven Forbes, Elizabeth Dole, Gary Bauer, and eventual winner George W. Bush. Other speakers included Senate Majority Leader Trent Lott; House Majority Leader Dick Armey; and coalition favorites African American representative J. C. Watts, preacher Bill Bright, and Dede Robertson. Perhaps the most significant thing about all the speakers was the one name that each of them mentioned: Ronald Reagan. Each politician claimed to be the heir to the former president, and each time the crowd roared in approval. Reagan was a ghost whose image and ideas permeated the entire weekend. Oddly enough, it was Reagan who had wanted to marginalize the Christian Right, and in the late 1990s the Christian Right had managed to marginalize itself. Reagan's name was repeatedly bandied about, even if most leaders of the Christian Right knew that the president had done little for them. Still, the 1999 rally was significant because it also contained two clear examples of the power that the coalition and Robertson enjoyed.

One of the more unusual people in attendance was presidential candidate Steve Forbes. In 1988 he had referred to Robertson as a "toothy flake" and had been totally dismissive of social conservatives when he ran for president in 1996. His antagonism of the Christian Right actually reached the point that coalition members picketed his campaign headquarters. Four years later, however, he was treating the Christian Right, and the Christian Coalition in particular, as a long-lost friend. At the 1999 meeting Forbes reserved a large room at the convention, which featured a catered buffet, non-alcoholic drinks, and copies of his book *A New Birth of Freedom* on every seat. He sat in the room for over an hour, shaking hands and signing autographs. Forbes's party drew a large crowd, including scores of journalists who attempted to figure out if evangelicals believed in his change of heart. On the whole, coalition members were more excited about the chance to meet Forbes than they were about his candidacy.

The other truly interesting person at the convention was Gary Bauer, who was a veteran of conservative politics and worked for the Family Research Council (FRC), a Christian Right political organization run by James Dobson. Bauer's campaign was an unacknowledged compliment to the success of Pat Robertson. If Robertson had the Christian Coalition to show for his work in 1988, Bauer and Dobson hoped to propel the FRC to the forefront of the Christian Right after 2000. He was the first person from the Christian Right to run for president since Robertson, but unlike the fiercely independent Robertson, Bauer seemed to be a puppet of James Dobson. Mel White called Bauer "James Dobson's man in Washington, D.C."[35] Dobson, the popular host of the radio program *Focus on the Family*, appeared to be trying to take over Robertson's place of leadership of the Christian Right. During the 2000 campaign Dobson made headlines when he threatened to leave the Republican Party if the leadership did not start to work on the issues that Christian conservatives had been advocating for more than twenty-five years.

Bauer's campaign made little impact on the election. At the time of the Road to Victory meeting Bauer was busy denying a rumor that he had been having an affair with a campaign worker. His wife, Carol, introduced him at the meeting and attacked those that were attempting to smear his name. While the audience was very receptive to Bauer, Robertson was not. He was the only candidate to attend the meeting that Robertson was openly critical of. Robertson criticized Bauer's judgment and said that his attempt to a build an army of religious conservative support had been crippled by his blunders.[36] The only notoriety that he was able to garner was when he ended his campaign and threw his support behind Arizona senator John McCain and not Dobson's choice, George W. Bush. McCain made a campaign stop in Virginia Beach and attacked the

Christian Right and several of Bauer's colleagues while Bauer sat on the dais behind him. Dobson fired Bauer from the FRC soon thereafter, and he faded from popular view only to reemerge a few years later with his own Christian Right lobbying organization, called American Values.

By the conclusion of the Road to Victory meeting it was clear that Robertson favored Texas governor George W. Bush. "I think he would be a very acceptable candidate," Robertson said. "We had lunch together and talked about issues. I think he's a solid guy. I think he'd make a good president." Robertson demonstrated how little the IRS actions against the coalition had changed his plans when he said that Bush was "worthy of the support of the Coalition were he the nominee of the party." He also hinted that Forbes, whom he had forgiven, would be an acceptable alternative if Bush were to fail.[37] He also advised Buchanan to return to the Republican Party and warned that the Democrats might win if he split the conservative vote.

The 1999 Road to Victory meeting had been a success, but it masked the serious problems that the coalition faced. The FEC and IRS had made their decisions, and while the group struggled on, it appeared to be mortally wounded. By the end of its first decade the coalition was $2.5 million in debt. While it claimed a membership of two million people, it was only mailing out half a million copies of its newsletter. In 1996 it boasted of active chapters in forty-eight states, but by 1999 only seven states, South Carolina, Georgia, Florida, Texas, Massachusetts, Oklahoma, and Washington, had legitimately functioning chapters. When journalists toured the coalition's Chesapeake, Virginia, headquarters temporary workers were brought in to make the office look busy, and even regular staff members "leapfrogged ahead of the reporters to fill empty offices and telephones."[38] Jerry Falwell shuttered the Moral Majority after it had sunk into political obscurity, but Robertson was not one to give up without a fight. In 1998 he donated $1 million of his own money to the organization. Instead of closing shop, he was determined to find someone who could make the Christian Coalition a force for the 2000 presidential election.

Although Robertson remained the president of the Christian Coalition he needed someone who could run the operation's day-to-day business. Instead of choosing someone like Reed, who had intense drive but no experience, or someone like Tate or Hodel, who had their own political careers to consider, Robertson went with a person who had proven to be a loyal lieutenant. Robertson wanted to be in control, but realized that he was too spread out to be effective, so he needed someone who could both follow orders and run a tight ship. Soon after the IRS and FEC settlements in 1999, Robertson announced that Roberta Combs was now more or less in charge of the coalition. Her title as executive vice president put her second only to Robertson. Combs had run Robertson's presidential campaign in South Carolina and later became the director of the state's Christian Coalition chapter. Under her leadership the South Carolina chapter became one of the most successful. At one point the chapter even tried to take over the leadership of the state GOP. With her promotion, Combs became one of the most powerful women in the Christian Right since Phyllis Schlafly defeated the Equal Rights Amendment in the 1980s.

One of her first actions was to lay off coalition staff members, many of whom had been appointed by Ralph Reed. Several longtime employees, including the director of grassroots communication and the national field director, quit or were fired. Robertson announced the action as "a whole new revitalization at the Coalition with new people and fresh blood." Combs had made enemies during her years in South Carolina, and it wasn't long before former coalition employees criticized her as well. One person who did support her was Ralph Reed. He said, "Roberta's getting a bum rap because she is taking the steps that Robertson wanted taken, and in some cases that involved asking people to leave. They blame Roberta when she's only loyally serving Pat."[39] The coalition was in free fall, and drastic measures had to be taken if the group was going to survive.

Soon after the 1999 Road to Victory rally ended, Combs, with Robertson's approval, closed the Chesapeake office and moved the headquarters and its thirty-five remaining employees to Washington, D.C. The move to Capitol Hill demonstrated that a significant change had taken place in the ideology of the Christian Coalition. Gone were the days when it tried to change the nation from the bottom up; now the group focused its political efforts almost exclusively in the nation's capital. Robertson revealed the change in the group's focus when he said, "[T]his is a case of simple logistics and the necessity of this organization to be near our elected leaders."[40] Grassroots organizations do not need to be a constant presence on Capitol Hill, but lobbying groups do. Paul Weyrich warned Robertson not to move the coalition to Washington, D.C. "I told him it was alright to have a branch here and to meet here from time to time but to be headquartered here meant that the major decisions would be made here and you'd get skewed. You would have the Newt Gingrich types dictating policies of the Christian Coalition. And I did not think that this was a good idea."[41] Weyrich's warning proved to be correct. For years the coalition had maintained a small office in the capital that only had six employees, all of whom had resigned by April 2000. The new offices were much larger, but problems still plagued the coalition. Many of the people that Combs had forced out caused problems for the group. Among them was former chief financial officer Kenneth Hill, who willingly gave helpful court testimony to a direct mail vendor that had sued the coalition for $400,000.[42]

One of Combs's ideas to revitalize the coalition was to use its most famous face as a way to raise money and support. Reed had taken the reins of the group to the point that some thought Robertson was purposefully hiding his influence. Combs, however, eagerly promoted her boss as a Christian Right celebrity at "God and Country galas," which were held around the nation starting in 1999. The galas cost $5,000 to $40,000 to put on, the cost fluctuating depending on the size of the audience and the price of flying Robertson to the event. Combs believed that the rallies would energize the local coalition chapters, but Reed was critical of the tactic. Reed recalls, "[I]t was a strategy that the Moral Majority followed. They raised a little money and got people excited, but there was nothing permanent."[43] Despite his initial criticism of the rallies, he eventually became a featured speaker at several of them during the 2004 presidential campaign. These galas fed Robertson's ego, and put the emphasis on his star power and not grassroots campaigning.

In addition to the galas Robertson realized that the coalition needed to raise money, and fast. In March 1999 he announced the "Victory 21 Campaign," in which the coalition would raise $21 million and register fifteen million conservative Christians to vote in time for the 2000 presidential election. "This isn't some radical extreme; it's straight down the middle of what the American people would like to see," Robertson said. "All we want to do is facilitate their knowledge of the issues and facilitate their citizenship involvement."[44] He hoped that this effort would allow the coalition to distribute seventy-five million voter guides. Robertson also claimed that it was "the most massive effort to mobilize the grass roots in our history." By the end of the year a former coalition official claimed that the drive had been a bust but nobody would admit it because, "nobody would look Pat in the eye and tell him the truth."[45] To all outward appearances, the coalition was struggling and could not be expected to have much of an impact in the upcoming election.

As the year 2000 dawned, it appeared as if Robertson and the Christian Coalition had become moribund. The Republican Party nomination had boiled down to a race between Bush and McCain. Despite the fact that McCain was opposed to a good deal of the Christian Right's agenda, the coalition had a hard time getting traction in the critical South Carolina primary. The Bush campaign even had trouble getting the state's conservative Christian leaders to attend a private meeting with their candidate. Apathy, their disappointment with Dole in 1996, and the strong economy all worked together to take the life out of the election. One South Carolina evangelical who supported McCain was happy that the coalition was so ineffective. "They have good minds and good hearts, but we will not be told by any organization who to vote for. We don't need a superstructure telling us to get in line."[46] The weakness in South Carolina was particularly troubling for the Christian Coalition since it was the home of Roberta Combs. If this state's chapter could not be energized, there was little chance that it would happen elsewhere.

The one event that brought Robertson into the Republican primary was a speech given by John McCain. While campaigning in Virginia Beach, McCain gave a speech that was critical of Robertson, Jerry Falwell, and the Christian Right in general. The senator accused them of distorting his positions, "because I don't pander to them. I don't ascribe to their failed philosophy that money is our message." He said that union bosses who "subordinate the interests of working families to their own ambitions, to their desire to preserve their own political power at all costs, are mirror images of Pat Robertson." He called Bush "a Pat Robertson Republican who will lose to Al Gore" and claimed that Robertson and Falwell were as bad for America as Al Sharpton and Louis Farrakhan.[47] The speech, the political equivalent of a Hail Mary pass, garnered a lot of attention. Bush said that McCain's speech was proof that the senator wanted to divide Americans.

If McCain, like most pundits in 2000, thought that the Christian Right was fading away, all it took was a speech like this to bring it roaring back to life. McCain's comments caught Robertson by surprise, since, in his eyes, McCain and the Republican Party owed Robertson their gratitude for his work in Virginia. Robertson said, "[H]e came into a town, where through really my efforts, some of my finances, we [the Republicans] had taken the delegation through the general assembly for the first time since the Civil War, the governorship, and the attorney generals office. First time in the history of the state, it had never happened before, in a non-military occupational context. And to come into a state that had such signal Republican victories and to attack one of the architects of that victory was just insane." He recalls, "[I]t violated every single tenant of an intelligent campaign. When it happened I knew that he had destroyed himself. So when your enemy is in the middle of destroying himself, you don't put a stop to it. So I just let it happen." Robertson also claims that McCain's speech doomed his campaign: "In any state where there was at least 15 percent or more evangelicals in the electorate, he lost. And Evangelicals voted against him 8 to 1."[48] His lingering anger at McCain led him to warn Bush not to nominate the senator to be his vice president. He told viewers on NBC's *Meet the Press* that he would be "very concerned" if Bush chose him.

During the 2000 Republican National Convention in Philadelphia, Robertson and the Christian Coalition held a "Faith and Freedom Celebration" as a demonstration of their continuing strength. This show was necessary because the leadership of the Christian Right had been excluded from the Republican convention. The memories of 1992 were still too fresh, and Bush was trying to steer a middle course with his rhetoric of "compassionate conservatism." Although he acted very differently once in office, as a candidate Bush tried to present himself as a moderate. The leadership of the Christian Right was worried; they had been burned by the Bush family before. During the convention an estimated eighteen hundred people attended the rally where Robertson vigorously defended the Christian Coalition. "I'm tired of reading stories saying the Christian Coalition is dead, we're just warming up folks," he said. Robertson was unhappy with the low status given religious conservatives and complained that the convention was "Democrat lite."[49] In contrast, Robertson was more than happy to engage in partisan rhetoric. In his speech he again called for the elimination of the Department of Education and the NEA, and an end to taxpayer funding for "dirty pictures or the operation of Planned Parenthood or other left-wing endeavors." Robertson voiced his disdain for the tone of the Republican convention when he stopped his attack because "this is a convention of sweetness and light. Nobody wants to rock the boat."[50]

A few days later, Robertson was more vocal in his disappointment with the Republican convention and even hesitant about the party's nominee. Referring to the convention as prepackaged, slick, homogenized, and pabulum, Robertson expressed his fears that the convention did not energize the party's base. He explained, "[Y]ou have to give people a reason why this party is different from the other party. What we're saying is we're the good Democrats and they're the bad Democrats." Robertson was upset that Bush's campaign strategist Karl Rove wanted to broadened his candidate's appeal and said that "people are more attracted today by a positive agenda than by wedge issues."[51]

Karl Rove's vision won out, and for the first time in twenty-five years, the Christian Right saw their key agenda items openly placed on the back burner. Causes like abortion, Supreme Court appointments, and homosexuality were largely ignored by the Bush campaign as it attempted to reach out to voters in the general election. Dick Anderson, the head of the Texas branch of the Christian Coalition, admitted that evangelicals were not sure what to make of their governor. "I can tell you from meeting with him that he is a directly religious man who isn't shy about expressing how important religion is to him," Anderson said.[52] Such comments were echoed by many others, including Phyllis Schlafly and Robertson, who expressed their misgivings, but were at least satisfied that Bush was a man of faith. The Bush team made moves to shore up its base in the Religious Right. Ralph Reed was hired as an advisor to the campaign and eventually oversaw most of its operations in the south.

Despite their fears over Bush's moderate positioning, Robertson and the Christian Coalition supported the candidate as much as they could. This was a matter of pride for Robertson as well as politics. He hated to see the coalition fade into obscurity. His desire was probably strengthened by comments made by people like Reed, who said that there was no longer a real need for groups like the Christian Coalition since evangelicals had found a place at the table with the GOP.[53]

Despite these obstacles the Christian Coalition went about business as usual. Although they did not raise the millions of dollars that Robertson had wanted, the group distributed millions of voter guides. Robertson made sure that *The 700 Club* regularly featured the campaign, and it always put Bush in the best possible light. During the 2000 campaign, Bush distanced himself from the Christian Coalition as well as a host of other conservative groups such as the National Rifle Association. While all of these groups worked quietly behind the scenes for Bush, Robertson eventually grew tired of being denied his place in the sun. He also no doubt remembered the difficult times he had with President George H. W. Bush. He sent out a Christian Coalition fund-raising letter in which he promised that the group would be the force in 2000 that it never managed to be in 1996.

When it came time for the 2000 Road to Victory meeting Robertson assumed that the Republican nominee would address the coalition, but Bush had other plans. Claiming a scheduling conflict, the Bush team announced that their candidate would not speak at the meeting that had welcomed him so warmly just one year earlier. Robertson had spent too many years in the political wilderness to tolerate this, and he made his displeasure known. The media was only too happy to report on Robertson's discontent with Bush. Robertson said that it was "very risky" of Bush to avoid the Christian Coalition meeting and that the Christian Right would have a hard time mobilizing for him if he did not show that he cared about its agenda. "They're very iffy. They've lost the commanding lead they had. Republicans have a marvelous facility for snatching defeat from the jaws of victory," Robertson said.[54] During the 2000 campaign he criticized Bush more often than any other leader of the Christian Right dared.

There was more at play in the Bush–Robertson struggle than the governor's desire to appear to be compassionate conservative. It is likely that the Bush campaign remembered the critical comments that Robertson had made about Dole at the 1996 meeting and wanted to avoid a repeat. Such a scenario was more than likely since Robertson had already been rather vocal with his criticisms of Bush. Still, they realized that they had to make at least a minimal attempt to appease the Religious Right, so Bush sent a videotaped message to the Road to Victory meeting. In do doing he became the first Republican candidate for president to not address the group in person since the coalition was founded in 1990. Bush's message met with wild applause as did a speech by Lynn Cheney, the wife of Republican nominee for vice president Dick Cheney.

Robertson continued to make his displeasure known regardless of the Bush campaign's sudden, if tepid, support. When asked if Bush's attempt to reach out to religious conservatives would be successful, a coy Robertson replied, "[W]e'll find out the first week in November."[55] Just days before the election, with the polls showing a virtual tie, Robertson still preferred to criticize rather than support Bush. Instead of predicting a great victory, he took the time to contemplate what would happen to the Christian Coalition if Bush lost. He said, "[S]ometimes it is more difficult to have a friendly administration than to have an administration with which you are fighting. Because people go to sleep when they have their friends in office."[56] Such a statement is quite revealing about Robertson's mindset. He was not concerned with his political agenda as much as he was with mobilizing his army and returning the Christian Coalition to its former glory.

When the votes had been cast, and the Supreme Court had made its ruling, George W. Bush was declared the victor of the 2000 presidential election. Some believed that the election showed just how weak the Christian Right was, but the movement was not weak, just uninspired by George W. Bush. Studies showed that four million evangelicals who voted in 1996 had stayed home in 2000.[57] However, despite the numerical drop in votes, evangelicals continued to be a larger percentage of the Republicans' base. They had accounted for 15 percent of votes that Reagan received, but 40 percent of George W. Bush's.[58]

Robertson finally had what he had wanted for more than twenty years, a politically conservative evangelical Christian in office. This meant that evangelicals would finally be in the president's circle of power. The election of 2000 proved two things about the Christian Right: first, the movement was anything but dead, and second, Pat Robertson was still the movement's most powerful leader. What he did not seem to know is that his days as the Christian Right's main power broker were about over. In part he was a victim of his own success.

Even though it now had a sympathetic president in the White House, the Christian Coalition continued its slide from a potential kingmaker to just another interest group in the Republican Party. At its height in 1996 the group pulled in $26 million, but in 2000 it received just $3 million, which failed to cover the organization's debts. In 1997 *Fortune* magazine had ranked them the seventh most powerful lobbying group in the nation; by 2001 it had fallen to sixty-fifth.[59] The group's most popular event, the Road to Victory meetings, which usually had attendance of up to four thousand people, had dwindled to fifteen hundred in 2000. The conference was canceled in 2001.

When Combs ran the offices in Chesapeake she received criticism when she used temporary workers to make the organization appear more active than it really was. In Washington, D.C., however, she was sued for allegedly trying to hide workers. In February 2001, the coalition was sued by ten female African American employees. In their complaint, they charged that they were forced to enter the building through the back door, but were not given keys for that entrance. Combs reportedly said that she did not want "important people" seeing these workers in the reception area of the office. They also alleged that they were segregated in the break room and made to feel uncomfortable at office prayer meetings. It would be difficult to imagine a scenario more damaging to the coalition than African American employees suing a group run by white southerners from Virginia and South Carolina. A few weeks later three more employees, two black and one white, also filed a discrimination suit. The white staffer, Trent Barton, claimed he was fired after refusing to spy on his black coworkers. He was also allegedly pressured by Tracy Ammons, Combs's son-in-law and coalition employee, to stay away from the lawsuit. The employees later filed an amended claim charging that the coalition was retaliating against them. The suits asked for a total $39 million in damages.[60] Four days after the first lawsuit was filed, Combs released a memo that denied the charges and ordered that all black employees be given keys to the coalition office's back door. The suits were settled in December for an undisclosed sum.

By the end of 2001 Pat Robertson apparently had enough and resigned as president and installed Combs in his place. In making his announcement he denied that he was leaving politics. "I'm just narrowing my concentration on things. I'm not abandoning anything. I will, of course, continue to comment sometimes on political affairs in my daily broadcast. I am 71 years old now, and my main focus in the active years of service left to me will be on religious broadcasting."[61] Many pundits predicted that his move spelled doom for the Christian Coalition, but the group struggled on.

Robertson's resignation came at a time when he was trying to refocus his life on the religious side of his empire. In March 2000 Robertson was reordained in the Southern Baptist Church in honor of his seventieth birthday. Robertson claimed that it was a "reaffirmation," and in keeping with his Charismatic theology, he had members of several denominations (Baptist, Assemblies of God, Presbyterian) perform sections of the ceremony.[62] The event was broadcast on *The 700 Club*, and it was, in part, an attempt to prove to his faithful viewers that he was more interested in religion than politics.

When Combs took over the day-to-day operations of the Christian Coalition in 1999, the group was $4 million in debt. She worked hard to eliminate the red ink, but it soon came back. According to IRS records the coalition owed $1.3 million in 2002, and its debt grew to $2.28 million by 2004. The organization was also repeatedly sued by creditors, including its former law firm, which sought nearly $70,000, and a moving company who helped pack up the Washington, D.C., office.[63] Insult was added to injury when Combs's daughter, who worked as the coalition's spokesperson, divorced her husband, Tracy Ammons, who subsequently talked to the media about his activities at the coalition. He sued his former employer, claiming that he was owed $130,000 in unpaid salary. The irony of the situation was not lost on him. Ammons said, "[L]ots of times we wouldn't pay until someone sued. I did it to others. Then [the Christian Coalition] did it to me."[64]

As debts mounted Combs began another round of cost cutting. In 2002 the coalition closed its Washington, D.C., office and moved to Combs's hometown, Charleston, South Carolina. The group, however, still had a Washington, D.C., area code, but calls to that number were automatically forwarded to Charleston. The coalition resurrected its Road to Victory meeting in 2004, but only a few hundred people attended. By 2005 it was reported that the group was having difficulty getting candidates at even the local level to fill out questionnaires for the voter guides.[65] The prospect of the coalition performing this service for them was no longer the threat it used to be.

Eventually the national office of the coalition lost its already tenuous control over some of its few remaining state chapters. In 2004 the Christian Coalition of Alabama and the national Christian Coalition took different positions on a controversial tax bill. Called Amendment One, the bill would have changed the state's tax code, which was the most regressive in the nation. The bill would have cut the taxes of half of the state's citizens and made up the difference by raising taxes on the wealthy and increasing taxes on cigarettes and some government services. Beyond making the tax code more just, the bill's sponsors planned to use the money to pay off the state's debt and fund education programs and help fight poverty. The bill was supported by its outspokenly Christian governor, conservative Republican Bob Riley. During a campaign stop for the bill he said, "According to our Christian ethics, we're supposed to love God, love each other and help take care of the poor. It is immoral to charge somebody making $5,000 an income tax."[66] In addition to the governor's support the bill was written by a lawyer who had attended an evangelical seminary and thought that the state's tax code should reflect Christian values. Although 93 percent of Alabamians called themselves Christians, the bill lost by a two to one margin.[67] The fact that two arms of the Christian Coalition were fighting each other on the matter did not help. The national office praised the bill as a model of Christian policy making, while the state chapter sided with wealthy business groups in opposing the measure as part of their blanket policy against any tax increases. In March 2006 its Iowa chapter announced it was renaming itself the Iowa Christian Alliance and totally disassociating itself from the national organization. They claimed that the coalition had lost any credibility it once had, especially in regards to its promises to pay bills when they were due.[68] The Ohio chapter of the coalition split off the same year. As a result of its weakened condition, the organization played virtually no role in the 2006 elections, which saw the Democrats take both the House and Senate back from the GOP. In fact, in that election the coalition even lost some staunch allies, such as Pennsylvania senator Rick Santorum, who had championed many of their issues.

In what must be considered the supreme irony of Robertson's political career, his greatest creation was eviscerated not by liberals, but by the presidency of George W. Bush. Things were going well for Robertson while Clinton and the Democrats were in power. However, all of that changed in 2000. Bush was the most explicitly religious president since Carter, and once in office Bush promised to make good on the Christian Right's agenda. In the process the president of the United States became the de facto leader of the Christian Right. Robertson could do little but sit on the sidelines and watch as his movement finally held the reins of power. This must have been very bittersweet for him. He had labored for the better part of thirty years just to see himself largely excluded from the halls of power.

During the 1990s Robertson created the three branches of government for the Christian Right. The ACLJ was the judicial branch, the Christian Coalition was the legislative, and Robertson definitely acted as the president with a daily broadcast from his bully pulpit. This three-pronged attack led to a surprising number of victories. Robertson can point to more political success than can Jerry Falwell, the Moral Majority, Paul Weyrich, James Dobson, and Gary Bauer combined. Despite all of these victories, he was not satisfied. Robertson knew that political victories are ephemeral; his experience in the 1994 and 1996 elections proved that clearly enough. What is important is long-term influence that will last for generations. For this reason, Robertson put great hope in Regent University. It has been his plan that generations of leaders would be taught at Regent, so that his goals and dreams would last generations, not just his lifetime. If he thought politics was a headache, academia would prove even more challenging.

Notes

1. Jerry Gray, "Politics: Christian Coalition Offers Dole Both Cheers and Sharp Prodding," *New York Times*, September 15, 1996.

2. William C. Berman, *From the Center to the Edge: The Politics and Policies of the Clinton Presidency* (Lanham, Md.: Rowman & Littlefield, 2001), 47.

3. Berman, *From the Center to the Edge*, 56.

4. Paul Weyrich, interview by author, tape recording, Washington, D.C., August 16, 2000.

5. Katharine Seelye, "Christian Coalition's Reed Quits for New Political Role," *New York Times*, April 24, 1997.

6. Richard Berke, "Christian Coalition Looking to Ex-Lawmaker as Leader," *New York Times*, June 11, 1997.

7. "GOP Victorious in Washington State Recount," *New York Times*, November 29, 1996.

8. "Randy Tate's New Job," *Seattle Times*, June 12, 1997.

9. Richard Berke, "From Cabinet to Leadership of Coalition," *New York Times*, June 12, 1997.

10. Associated Press, "New Leaders Explore Ways to Restructure Christian Coalition," *St. Louis Post-Dispatch* [Mo.], January 11, 1998.

11. Bill Sizemore, "Fired Official Is a Key Player in Christian Coalition Troubles," *Virginian-Pilot*, July 27, 1997.

12. Sizemore, "Fired Official Is a Key Player in Christian Coalition Troubles."

13. Liz Szabo, "Judge Oks Coalition Voter Guides," *Virginian-Pilot*, August 3, 1999.

14. *Nightline*, ABC, October 1, 1997.

15. Chris Carr, "Audit Finds FEC 'Without Partisan Bias,'" *Washington Post*, January 31, 1999.

16. Justin Watson, *The Christian Coalition: Dreams of Restoration, Demands for Recognition* (New York: St. Martin's Griffin, 1999), 56–57.

17. Pat Robertson, "1997 Christian Coalition 'Road to Victory' Speech," September 13, 1997. Tape recording, Americans United for the Separation of Church and State. All speech quotes are from this source.

18. Robertson, "1997 Christian Coalition 'Road to Victory' Speech."

19. Melinda Henneberger, "Ralph Reed Is His Cross to Bear," *New York Times*, August 9, 1998.

20. Ralph Z. Hallow, "Christian Coalition President Resigns," *Washington Times*, February 10, 1999.

21. Hallow, "Christian Coalition President Resigns."

22. Liz Szabo, "Christian Coalition Official Reassigned; Robertson's Own Leadership Increases," *Virginian-Pilot*, June 2, 1999.

23. Robert Boston, *Close Encounters with the Religious Right* (New York: Prometheus Books, 2000), 68.

24. Ron Fournier, "Christian Coalition Loses Tax Status," *Los Angeles Times*, June 10, 1999.

25. Jim Drinkard, "Christian Coalition Won't Get Tax-Exempt Status from the IRS," *USA Today*, June 10, 1999.

26. Thomas Edsall and Hanna Rosin, "IRS Denies Tax-Exempt Status, So Christian Coalition to Reorganize," *Washington Post*, June 11, 1999.

27. Associated Press, "Christian Coalition Suit Alleges IRS Discrimination," *Virginian-Pilot*, February 27, 2000.

28. Szabo, "Judge Oks Coalition Voter Guides."

29. Paul Serrell, "Setting Pastors Free from the IRS Speech Police," *The 700 Club*, June 10, 2002.

30. Szabo, "Judge Oks Coalition Voter Guides."

31. Bill Miller and Susan Glasser, "A Victory for Christian Coalition," *Washington Post*, August 3, 1999.

32. Miller and Glasser, "A Victory for Christian Coalition."

33. Thomas Edsall, "Christian Right Lifts Ashcroft," *Washington Post*, April 14, 1998.

34. Mark Barabak, "Buchanan Urged to Stay a Republican at Meeting," *Los Angeles Times*, October 2, 1999.

35. Mel White, interview by author, tape recording, Lake Forest, Calif., September 29, 1999.

36. Thomas Edsall and Terry Neal, "Christian Coalition Leader Praises Bush," *Washington Post*, October 2, 1999.

37. Edsall and Neal, "Christian Coalition Leader Praises Bush."

38. Laurie Goodstein, "Coalition's Woes Many Hinder Goals of Christian Right," *New York Times*, August 2, 1999.

39. Mary Jacoby, "What Has She Done to Christian Coalition?" *St. Petersburg Times* [Fla.], October 3, 1999.

40. Peter Hardin, "Christian Coalition Moving," *Richmond Times Dispatch*, November 15, 1999.

41. Paul Weyrich interview.

42. Liz Szabo, "Coalition's Last Lobbyist in Washington Steps Down," *Virginian-Pilot*, April 20, 2000.

43. Jacoby, "What Has She Done to Christian Coalition?"

44. Sonja Barisic, "Christian Coalition Seeks to Raise $21 for 2000 Elections," *Associated Press*, March 13, 1999.

45. Jacoby, "What Has She Done to Christian Coalition?"

46. Hanna Rosen, "Christian Right's Fervor Has Fizzled," *Washington Post*, February 16, 2000.

47. Bob Franken, Jonathan Karl, and Gary Tuchman, "McCain Assails Religious Right on Pat Robertson's Home Turf," *CNN.com*, February 28, 2000.

48. Pat Robertson, interview by author, tape recording, Virginia Beach, Va., May 25, 2000.

49. John Micklethwait and Adrian Woolridge, *The Right Nation: Conservative Power in America* (New York: Penguin, 2004), 132.

50. Tom Hamburger and Patricia Lopez, "Christian Coalition Raises Its Voice at Rally," *Star Tribune* [Minneapolis, Minn.], August 2, 2000.

51. Thomas Edsall, "Bush Abandons Southern Strategy," *Washington Post*, August 6, 2000.

52. Bruce Alpert, "Religious Right Wary of Squishy Bush," *Times-Picayune* [New Orleans, La.], June 20, 1999.

53. Tom Baxter, "Courting the Catholic Vote," *Atlanta Journal and Constitution*, May 6, 2000.

54. Richard Berke, "The 2000 Campaign: Conservative Organizations," *New York Times*, September 27, 2000.

55. James Dao, "The 2000 Campaign: The Christian Coalition," *New York Times*, September 30, 2000.

56. David Gibson, "Christian Coalition: Missing in Action?" *Star-Ledger* [Newark, N.J.], November 3, 2000.

57. Micklethwait and Woolridge, *The Right Nation*, 185.

58. Esther Kaplan, *With God on Their Side: George W. Bush and the Christian Right* (New York: New Press, 2005), 75.

59. Michael Schaffer, "Say a Prayer for the Christian Coalition," *U.S. News & World Report*, May 28, 2001.

60. Mary Jacoby, "Christian Coalition Bias Case Is Growing," *St. Petersburg Times* [Fla.], March 8, 2001.

61. B. Drummond Ayers Jr., "Robertson Resigns from Christian Coalition," *New York Times*, December 6, 2001.

62. Pat Robertson interview.

63. Alan Cooperman and Thomas Edsall, "Christian Coalition Shrinks as Debt Grows," *Washington Post*, April 10, 2006.

64. Cooperman and Edsall, "Christian Coalition Shrinks as Debt Grows."

65. Nora Koch, "Survey Touches Nerve with Candidates," *St. Petersburg Times* [Fla.], February 14, 2005.

66. Jim Tharpe, "Alabama Tax Plan Faces Uphill Battle," *Atlanta Journal-Constitution*, September 2, 2003.

67. Don Lattin, "Mostly Christian Alabama Defeated Tax Plan for Poor," *San Francisco Chronicle*, December 12, 2004.

68. Cooperman and Edsall, "Christian Coalition Shrinks as Debt Grows."

CHAPTER 17

TROUBLE AT REGENT UNIVERSITY

O
NE aspect of Robertson's empire that was not just alive but actually prospered after 1988 was Regent University. While the televangelist scandals of the late 1980s had hurt many of the universities that were tied to televangelists, Regent had managed to steer clear. Jimmy Swaggart's Bible college collapsed after he was found to be having an affair with a prostitute. Oral Roberts's odd behavior cost his university the right to have its graduates ordained as ministers in the United Methodist Church. Robertson's school was closely tied into the money that *The 700 Club* brought in, so he sought to separate them. His legacy had to be put on a solid foundation.

What Robertson wanted was a university that allowed diversity, as long as it was the right kind of diversity. Pentecostals, evangelicals, Charismatics, Fundamentalists, and mainline Protestants all have a core commonality, but their differences have caused the most trouble. The law school was a source of constant trouble for Robertson. This was mostly due to the narrow definition of Christianity that law school dean Herbert Titus and his hand-picked faculty members shared. Their adherence to Reconstructionist theology led to confrontations with other departments and the university's administration. Ultimately the school underwent a metamorphosis similar to what occurred at the creation of the Christian Coalition. Robertson unexpectedly tapped a young vibrant leader, this time Terry Lindvall, to broaden the school's appeal and made it a truly open university. However, as soon as this openness threatened other parts of Robertson's empire, heads began to roll. Robertson used people to make the university appear mainstream, then removed these same people once they were no longer needed.

In October 1989 the Christian Broadcasting Network University was officially renamed Regent University. The main reason for the name change was
that too many people thought the university was only a broadcasting school.
The name *Regent* was chosen because a regent is someone who rules in place of
a monarch while they are gone. The name change was another mixed signal to
the world about Robertson's adherence to Reconstructionist theology since it
taught that Christians were supposed to rule the Earth until Jesus returned. It
also had the effect of stabilizing the school's finances by distancing it from the
Christian Broadcasting Network (CBN), which was still on shaky ground.

Regent's road to financial security came, oddly enough, through an investigation of Robertson by the Internal Revenue Service (IRS). When the Family
Channel went public Robertson made tens of millions of dollars overnight, and
Regent benefited from this windfall. Robertson gave his school what was at the
time the largest gift in the history of higher education: a donation valued from
$100 to $115 million of stock in the newly created Family Channel. The university has since used some of the money for faculty raises and a new building
program.

By the late 1990s the school offered over twenty graduate programs, including masters degrees in business administration, education, theology, biblical
studies, government, journalism, public policy, and screenwriting.[1] Its doctoral
programs included communication, ministry, and psychology. Although it was
supposedly a school for evangelical Christians, there was no code of conduct to
sign, no mandatory chapel attendance required, and students needed only
to affirm seven basic Christian beliefs on their application.[2] The average age of
a Regent student is thirty-one, much older than most graduate students; of
these, about half are married. Regent had little trouble finding students. Indeed,
in the early 1990s, while enrollment dropped in every major university in Virginia, Regent's applications surged. In 1991 alone enrollment jumped 30 percent. As the law school's first dean Herbert Titus explained, "[P]eople recognize
that if they go to an ordinary school, they'll either have to park their Christian
faith outside the classroom or they will have to face a critical atmosphere."[3]

Despite the healthy enrollment figures, the rest of the university did not
always run smoothly. Theologian Harvey Cox writes that Regent University was
"not so much a boot camp for rightist cadres as a microcosm of the theological
and intellectual turbulence within what is often mistakenly seen as a monolithic
'religious right' in America."[4] In 1993 Regent University was the scene of a battle that reverberated for years. The school was divided into two warring theological camps—the mainline evangelicals against the Reconstructionists. At the
time Robertson was busy trying to broaden the appeal of the Christian Coalition, and having Reconstructionists on campus became a problem for him.
Robertson sought to put an end to the struggle and did so when the university's

president resigned in 1993. In his place came a president who was a radical departure from the past: Terry Lindvall, a film professor and founding faculty member. At age forty-five he was the second youngest college president in America and, more surprisingly, a registered Democrat. Lindvall's easygoing manner made him popular with both the students and the local media.

Lindvall had only met with Pat Robertson once in the fifteen years that he had been on campus, and that was during the first year of the university's existence. He was surprised to receive a call one day from Roberta Johnson, Robertson's personal secretary. "Pat wants to take you out to lunch today," she said. Lindvall politely declined because he was wearing shorts and an old shirt, but she persisted. While Robertson and his driver were on the way to the faculty building, Lindvall borrowed clothes from two other professors in order to assemble a suitable outfit. When he got into the car the first thing he told Robertson was "you need to pay your professors more, we can't even afford to buy one complete suit."[5] During their lunch meeting Lindvall told Robertson, rather bluntly, how the faculty felt about him and the university's progress. He figured that if it had taken fifteen years to get Robertson's ear, he might as well tell him everything.

Robertson must have been sufficiently pleased, because within two months, Lindvall was asked to repeat his comments to the university's board of directors as part of his interview for president of the university. Lindvall declined, since the meeting conflicted with a planned family vacation. Robertson convinced him to at least make a phone call to the board, which he did. Since he was a Democrat, non-Pentecostal, communications professor with no administrative experience, Lindvall figured that he stood little chance of getting the job and did not take the phone interview too seriously. A few nights after the interview, while on vacation in Pennsylvania, he received a call from the former president's secretary. "Congratulations on the job, the press release has just gone out." An hour later Robertson called Lindvall to congratulate him as well. As simple as that, he had the job.[6]

The few days between the time Lindvall accepted the offer and the day he moved into the office was the length of his honeymoon in his new job. As he carried boxes to his new offices, students were outside protesting both his appointment and the firing of Dean Titus, which both happened just days apart. It was hard to tell who was more surprised by Lindvall's appointment, his friends or his foes. One professor, who wished to remain anonymous, claimed that Lindvall was "the most liberal professor on campus." Titus claimed that Lindvall was chosen because Robertson liked to "hire people for jobs for which they were not adequately prepared in order to have more influence through them so that he can more effectively forward his personal agenda." Titus claimed that "when faculty and students heard that the board had appointed Lindvall as president, many people thought it was a joke."[7] Lindvall recalled that when he returned from his trip to Pennsylvania and the announcement had gone out, all of his friends were stunned. The tape of his answering machine was full, and every message was from his laughing friends and colleagues.[8]

It was an inauspicious beginning for the young Californian, but he quickly became the most dynamic and successful president that the university ever had. Lindvall invited controversial figures to the campus to debate and share their thoughts with the Regent campus. Among them were Harvard theologian Harvey Cox, Barry Lynn from Americans United for the Separation of Church and State, and the leaders of both the American Civil Liberties Union (ACLU) and the People for the American Way. Lindvall even brought a Catholic priest who openly supported gay rights.[9] He explained his philosophy of education as a battle to be balanced between two worlds, the Sadducees against the Pharisees. "Jesus told his disciples to beware of the leaven of the Pharisees and Sadducees. And the leaven was . . . . The danger of a Christian university is that you can drift toward the Sadducees, who were the secularists of their day. . . . The other danger is to become pharisitical, to see yourself as superior." He concluded by saying, "[S]o you have to walk down a very thin line of what it means to be a Christian, who doesn't move to the right or the left, but moves straight ahead."[10] This is clearly not the rhetoric of the Religious Right. Choosing Lindvall helped to improve the school's reputation, although some faculty members considered him to be an unorthodox Christian (in their narrow sense). Still, the young president saw himself as "a maverick with a sense of unpredictability."[11] Lindvall's hiring was the first shot in a battle to become mainstream and still hold true to an evangelical ideal.

If the university was designed to be a shield against liberalism, the law school was to be the sword. Robertson was determined to have a law school that could rival any in the nation, and this was the one aspect of the school that he did plan. Although the university opened its doors in 1977, the law school did not get underway until 1986. The first dean of the law school, Herbert Titus, seemed to be Robertson's kind of man, a mover and shaker, with a strong sense of his mission. He left the University of Oregon to teach at the newly opened Oral Roberts University Law school. After several years of trying and failing to become accredited by the American Bar Association (ABA) Roberts closed the school and sent the entire law school, professors, students, and even the library, to Regent.[12] The addition of these faculty members, and especially the library, gave Regent a serious chance to become accredited by the ABA.

A new $13 million building named Robertson Hall was put up to house both the law school and the Robertson School of Government. Eventually the school had a larger faculty, a large law library, and a dedicated student body. All seemed in line for receiving credentials, but Regent was repeatedly denied. Students with thousands of dollars invested in the school worried about getting a law degree from a nonaccredited institution. One student, himself a Harvard graduate, explained, "[I]n every job interview, I'm asked why I chose Regent. I chose it because it was a Christian school. That question will be tough to answer if the ABA doesn't accredit us."[13] While Regent attempted to reach the ABA's standards it was given provisional accreditation, which was renewed annually. There were two central concerns that the ABA claimed were holding up accreditation: Regent had no tenure policy, and, more important, the school was too religiously sectarian. For nearly eight years, the law school tried to become accredited, then as it appeared that they were close to being accepted, the roof fell in. The pressure had become too great, and Robertson thought that obstacles had to be removed; the main obstacle, as Robertson saw it, was Dean Titus.

A few days before Lindvall's appointment to the presidency, Titus was fired. Although Titus had been of a similar mind to Robertson, the dean lacked one trait that Robertson had gained while on the campaign trail: the need to adapt one's message for a mainstream audience. Titus was a Reconstructionist (Reconstructionism is also called Dominion theology). As noted earlier, Dominion theology is the belief that the laws that were in place for the Jews in the Old Testament are in place for Christians today. It also teaches that God's call in Genesis 1:28 to have dominion over the earth, and everything (and *everyone*) on it, is relevant today. Titus had many such controversial views, and this was the great threat to accreditation. Perhaps the most damaging thing to his position was a confidential memo written by then Regent University president David Geyrston. The president had asked the ABA accreditation team for a confidential answer as to why Regent was still being denied. The ABA staff reportedly told Geyrston that it feared that Titus was crushing academic freedom with his dictatorial management style.[14] Although the ABA may have had a liberal bent, its concern did have merit. The journal *American Lawyer* pointed out in 1987 that in the law school there was "a commonality of experience among the eight law professors that defies coincidence. . . . Each law professor is a charismatic Christian."[15] Each professor had been hand-picked by the dean, and they were the first to protest when he was let go.

Regent did not have formal tenure like most universities; instead, their rule of tenure consisted of three-year contracts that would be automatically renewed. They could be broken only for "insubordination, incompetence, immoral behavior contrary to biblical standards."[16] Titus was never accused of any of these violations; his contract was merely not renewed by the board of trustees. Titus saw his removal as an attempt to "get the university to go evangelical mainstream." He also claimed that he was removed because his views were hurting Robertson's chance of running for president in 1996, a charge that Robertson denied.[17] Other sources offered a very different version of events. According to Terry Lindvall, Titus had been offered the newly created John Marshall Chair of Constitutional

Law. His salary would have increased from $87,000 a year to $125,000, plus a budget of $175,000. All he was asked to do was to take a yearlong sabbatical and relinquish all power as dean of the law school. Titus claimed that the offer was never written down, and he refused to take it. It was after this incident that he was fired. This was only the beginning of the university's travails on this issue; Titus eventually sued the school for $70 million, and eight of the fourteen law school faculty members wrote a complaint to the ABA concerning their dean's dismissal.[18]

On February 22, 1994, Pat Robertson wrote an angry letter to the faculty of the law school, explaining the Titus situation thus: "Herb Titus left because he refused even for a few months to release his power lock on the Regent University Law School." Robertson called him "a rogue dean with a dominating spirit."[19] He went on to attack the faculty who jeopardized the school in order to support the fired dean. "I have never encountered a group of supposedly educated people, who were so myopic, so lacking in common sense, or so inept as lawyers." He claimed that "no rational professional person seeks to destroy the source of his own employment." Robertson went on to say that the faculty's complaint to the ABA only reinforced that group's belief that "Regent Law School was in the grip of extremist fanatics." He concluded this letter with this veiled threat: "If you are as smart as your letter says you are, I am sure you can guess who is going to win this little skirmish."[20] Far from finishing the battle, this attack only drew more blood. Lindvall called the conflict "a battle for the soul of the university."[21] Titus's side had lost the first round.

If the conflict was finished as far as Robertson was concerned, it was far from over for some of the law school faculty. Soon after Robertson wrote his letter, three of the dissenting faculty members were fired. The official causes were "a lack of scholarship" and poor "attitudes." The same day that the firings were announced, Regent hired five new law faculty members in order to bring a "broader scope of viewpoints."[22] Many students were angered that the administration waited until classes were over and students had vacated campus before the announcements were made. The student body president of the law school even went so far as to say that "academic freedom at Regent is a joke. There is none."[23] Although it appeared as if the tide had turned and the administration had just rid itself of four problem faculty members, the situation managed to get worse.

Three faculty members, two of whom had recently been fired, sued the school and Robertson claiming that his letter damaged their reputations. Their suit demanded $10 million in damages for each plaintiff. The three had sued the school before over tenure policies. In the weeks that followed, Titus sued over his dismissal.[24] The students were angry, the faculty was in "open rebellion" as Robertson termed it, and the local press was making the university's problems as public as possible. As the years passed and the dust settled, the angry students graduated, and the courts still had not resolved all of the lawsuits; yet the unexpected happened—the ABA accredited the law school in 1996. Robertson's gamble had worked, and he was pleased with the ABA. "We're sort of the poster child to show they really can be fair. They've been extremely gracious to us."[25] He was able to bring his university into the mainstream and win the accreditation that he so desperately desired.

Robertson brought in Titus but realized that a Reconstructionist could not take the law school all the way to accreditation. Thus a change had to be made. After a long drawn-out court battle, the university eventually triumphed, in that its theological position was not co-opted by Titus and his group. Despite his heavy-handed approach to the Titus issue, Robertson has actually acted as a moderating force in the Religious Right, in that he did not allow this radical theology to dominate his university. The school has become a center of thought and action for the Right, but it has taken many forms. More than removing Titus, the act that was meant to bring the school into the mainstream was the hiring of Lindvall. His presence, more than that of any other president, helped to shape the school. He was the voice of moderation that allowed the school to be a place where academic freedom could take root, even as it was being challenged in the law school.

While the struggle between Titus and Robertson had been portrayed in the press as a theological battle, it was also a contest of egos. Titus had repeatedly claimed that he was going to be the next president of Regent. When Lindvall was appointed instead, Titus was allegedly furious. While he later repeatedly denied that he wanted to become president, several current and former faculty and staff members at Regent University thought otherwise. Robertson recalls that Titus had "a really controlling attitude.... Titus had his fingers into it and he did not want to release it. So it was necessary to pry him loose."[26] Robertson admitted that he was fascinated by Titus's more interesting theories, but that those ideas, while amusing to discuss in an academic setting, caused trouble once he became a part of the administration.

As soon as peace began to return to Regent University, Lindvall sensed his time was up. He had repeatedly stated that he eventually wanted to return to teaching, and in 1997 he was happy to take a new endowed chair back in the Communications Department. In his place came retired army general Paul Cerjan, former president of the National Defense University and the Army War College.[27] Ralph Reed, who had left the Christian Coalition, was rumored as a replacement for Lindvall, but this was nothing more than rumor.

Ralph Reed and Terry Lindvall were in charge of Robertson's two most precious creations at the same time, and they had a lot in common. Both men were committed to moving evangelicalism toward the center of American life. It is one of the great ironies that during the 1990s, while Robertson's power was at its height, he spent considerable time trying to move toward the mainstream.

While he was regularly vilified in the media and by his political opponents, Robertson was actually moving from his conservative base. Although he was a strictly partisan Republican, Ralph Reed spent his tenure at the Christian Coalition trying to expand its base toward minorities and Catholics. Lindvall was brought in specifically to make Regent University less sectarian and more accepting of other Christian beliefs. They were both young and seemingly inexperienced, yet they were the most effective leaders for their respective organizations. Titus accused Robertson of choosing people specifically because they were inexperienced and easily controlled, but their freedom and their actions tell otherwise.[28] What these inexperienced men had in common was a willingness to speak their minds. However, it cannot be mere coincidence that both Reed and Lindvall left their jobs within months of each other. When Reed and Lindvall stepped down their successors had a difficult time. Robertson took hold of the reins of both Regent and the coalition. In both cases, the organizations had several top-level administrative jobs that were vacant, and they remained that way as Robertson studied each organization's needs. It appears that he would let mainstreaming go only so far. In the final analysis, both organizations were his, and he was going to run them the way he saw fit.

Only three years after taking the helm, Cerjan suddenly announced his retirement, effective immediately, in September 2000, just as the fall semester got underway. What was more unusual was that he announced his resignation from Florida, where he had been attending a conference. Cerjan also owned a home in the state. He claimed that he had only wanted to stay for three years and that his "tour of duty" was up.[29] His decision to quit, however, does not jibe with the timing of the announcement. It is normal practice for presidents to give notice so that a search can begin. It is also practically unheard of for a college president to leave at the start of a new school year.

The general was replaced by Robertson, who still holds the position. Although he was not one to hover over the campus, he was right next door taping his show at 8:00 AM every morning, so there was a tendency for his wishes to be enacted into law. Dede Robertson is chairwoman of the board of trustees and has also made her wishes known. After she expressed disappointment with the writing quality of some student papers, the school instituted a writing skills exam for all incoming students. Those who do not pass are required to take a remedial English class.[30]

In the years following its headline-making internal struggles Regent continued to grow and feed on the success that men like Lindvall brought. Additional buildings were erected on campus after the university was given construction bonds that were financed by the state of Virginia. The Americans United sued the state in an attempt to keep Regent from using the bonds in the early 1990s and again in 1999 when it applied for a different state-run bond program. A 2000 Virginia Supreme Court ruling held that while the school was "pervasively sectarian" it could still participate in the program because the money came from private investors and not the state.[31]

Thanks in part to the construction bonds, Regent underwent a massive building program. The school spent $35 million on a communications and performing arts center, complete with an eight hundred-seat theater. A student center was built at a cost of $5 million. The center featured a cafeteria, study, and recreational areas for students. Regent started a satellite campus in the Washington, D.C., area in 1998 and immediately made an impact. In 2000 Alexandria, Virginia, school superintendent Herbert Berg announced a deal that would have given discount tuition to Alexandria teachers who were seeking credentials in special education. The drawback was that Regent wanted to be the exclusive source for the credentials. The school board didn't approve the deal.[32]

One of the more lucrative venues in higher education is distance education, where students do most of their work online. These degree programs are cash cows since the facilities requirements are minimal and professors can teach more students. This is the reason that Regent, which was created to be a graduate school, entered this arena in 2000 and began to offer programs for undergraduates. By 2005 the program had an on-campus program for working adults. The program had 450 students; about 60 percent of undergraduates took classes on campus, and the rest were online.[33]

When he assumed control of Regent in 2000, Robertson said he would follow a policy of "benign neglect," and allow his deans to control the day-to-day operations. However, as was the case with the Christian Coalition after Ralph Reed left, Robertson took control and quickly exerted his influence. Thanks to the success of the Family Channel and the coalition Robertson was very well known, and any action that the university took could reflect poorly on its chairman. This in turn created negative publicity. As the faculty was quick to discover, any time Regent caused trouble for Robertson, he would return the favor fivefold. While the faculty rarely desired to cause trouble, it seemed that the Communications Department ended up causing the bulk of the problems.

Robertson was embarrassed in 1998 when it was discovered that students at Regent's film school had received a $1,000 grant from the National Endowment for the Arts (NEA). The agency had long been the target of Robertson and the Christian Coalition, who had both repeatedly pressured Congress to kill the program. An adjunct professor at Regent had helped her students apply for a grant from the Virginia Commission for the Arts, who received their money from the NEA. As might be expected when the grant became public knowledge Robertson's critics accused him of being a hypocrite. In reality, he knew nothing about the grant and "requested" that the university return the money, which it promptly did.[34]

Each spring the Communications Department held a student film festival in a rented movie theater in downtown Virginia Beach. The public was invited, and even Robertson regularly attended the event. According to one source, during the 2002 festival some of the movies were profane and Robertson stormed out of the theater. After the event he held a forum with the students, where he told them, "[W]e are supposed to represent the Lord. If we go into this black stuff . . . I don't think that exactly pleases the Lord." He also told the assembly that student films should not "glorify degradation."[35] The next year, students were given a list of artistic guidelines they were expected to follow if they hoped to receive university funding for their projects. This was the first time in the school's history that formal artistic limitations were placed on Regent's film students. This was not widely regarded as a scandal or breach of academic freedom, since even in Hollywood a movie's content can be controlled by the producers. In Regent's case, however, it was one more troubling sign that things were increasingly coming under Robertson's control. When he decided to reassert his power over the campus, it was the Communications Department that bore the brunt of his anger.

Robertson claimed that he only spent about 20 percent of his time dealing with Regent University. Due to his various business interests and *The 700 Club* his time was obviously going to be limited. As a result he had to bring someone on board who could run the campus and deal with the minutia of academia. The person that he chose reveals a lot about Robertson. In 2001 Barry Ryan was brought to the campus to serve as the vice president for academic affairs, a job second in power only to Robertson's. Virtually every department at the university had to answer to Ryan. In 2004 his control over Regent increased when he was also named the dean of the undergraduate program. Ryan had a PhD in history from the University of California, Santa Barbara, and a law degree from Berkeley. Before coming to Regent he had practiced law and taught at two evangelical schools in Southern California: Westmont College and Point Loma Nazarene University. After leaving Point Loma, he moved to Washington, D.C., to intern at the Supreme Court. Ryan appeared to be the perfect person to help run the university; however, critics saw his arrival as a sign that another purge was about to begin.

Although Robertson was by all accounts unaware, Ryan allegedly had a history of sexual misconduct that caused him to leave both Westmont and Point Loma. In addition, he reportedly had a reputation as someone who saw dissent as disloyalty and would remove anyone who challenged his authority. A university is not a great place for a person who dislikes dissent, but based on Robertson's choice, it was clear that he wanted to remove anyone whose actions on campus could threaten or even embarrass his greater empire. Professors at Regent had been a constant source of trouble for him, and he evidently had enough.

Ryan's arrival on campus caused a stir almost immediately. Several professors were openly critical of his selection and questioned his ethics. The first people to question him were also the first people he fired or forced out of the university. The Communications Department was the prime target of Ryan's attention. Out of all the departments on campus, they were the free thinkers, the artists. Although Robertson might be considered associated with communications he is not really one of them. He is a businessman and a politician, not an artist. He didn't want art; he wanted things that would promote his agenda. Taking grant money from the NEA and showing risqué films had not hurt the department, but it had made Robertson look bad in the secular media. He was not going to allow that to happen again. Soon after Ryan arrived several faculty members from the department did not have their contracts renewed and others were fired. The fact that Regent did not have formal tenure made it easier for this purge to take place.

The most surprising result of Ryan's activities was the departure of Terry Lindvall in 2004. While he refused to discuss the specifics of why he left, he made it clear that he was uncomfortable with the "changing vision" of the school. Among his concerns was that Regent's leadership was "going for numbers and quantity."[36] After considering offers from across the country, Lindvall decided to stay in the Virginia Beach area and teach at Virginia Wesleyan College. The school received an anonymous donation to create an endowed chair especially for the former Regent president. While there is no evidence, it is likely that Robertson was the donor. One source called the donation "hush money." What is clear is that Robertson used Lindvall to give Regent the appearance of a truly open, yet still evangelical, university. Lindvall improved the school's image, helped the law school win accreditation, and brought in donations. Robertson allowed his former president to be removed when it was clear that he would not remain silent. Ryan must have seen Lindvall as a threat, since as a former president, his opinions were sure to have an impact. Like so many others in Robertson's wake, when Lindvall had outlived his usefulness, he was brushed aside.

The Ryan purge continued in 2006 when the university's campus pastor, David Martin, was forced out. Martin had taken issue with Ryan's moral shortcomings and sent people to California to investigate the allegations and report back. By the time this occurred the allegations surrounding Ryan must have been known to Robertson as they were the talk of the campus, yet nothing happened. Instead Robertson ratcheted up the tension on campus when he praised David Horowitz, the author of *The Professors: The 101 Most Dangerous Academics in America*, on *The 700 Club*. During the March 2006 broadcast Robertson claimed that there were more than forty thousand radical professors in American universities. After referring to them as "termites," he claimed that these thousands of radical professors were "racists, murderers, sexual deviants, and supporters of

Al-Qaeda, and they could be teaching your kids." With comments like this one spewing from the president of Regent, it was clear that Ryan's purge was happening with his boss's approval.

In the wake of the purge of the school's Communications Department Regent was slow to replace faculty members, and many of the new professors did not have the same credentials as their predecessors. The current dean of the department only has a master's degree, and it is from Regent. The associate dean has a PhD, also from Regent, but it is in education, not communications. In fact several of the department's faculty members have graduate degrees from Regent. While it is not unusual to have a single professor teaching at the school where he or she got a PhD, it is rare to have a department with so many faculty members and administrators teaching at their alma mater. One graduate of Regent's Communications Department lamented the destruction of the school. "It was a top program, but Ryan killed it. I can't recommend it, and I tell my own students not to apply there."

One long-time associate of Ryan said that the dean was "self-destructive" and predicted that he would eventually have a falling out with Robertson. It is unclear exactly what happened between the two men, but on August 15, 2006, Robertson notified the Regent faculty and staff that the dean had tendered his resignation. In typical Robertson fashion, the email spent more time addressing the future than explaining why Ryan left. He only noted that Ryan had been a "valuable member of the Regent community for the past five years."[37] While he did not give a reason for Ryan's departure, Robertson was slow to realize the mistake that he had made in bringing such a divisive person to campus. A few days after the announcement, Robertson attended a student meeting at Regent Village, the university's campus apartments. According to students who attended the meeting, Robertson seemed surprised when the students thanked him for getting rid of Ryan. When he asked why they were happy, he seemed totally taken aback that there had been so much hostility toward the former dean. So whatever it was that got Ryan to leave, it apparently had little to do with his effect on the campus.

Why would Robertson allow his university to become so restrictive? He is not an academic, and does not enjoy the give-and-take of academic life. After decades of pontificating on *The 700 Club*, he is used to being the authority and was not about to be challenged by a bunch of PhDs. It is important to remember that although he founded a university, he did so because he held the educational system in such disdain. So a school founded by someone who disliked the U.S. Department of Education, public schools, teachers' unions, and most secular universities is never going to be comfortable with his own university. In the debate between academic freedom and maintaining control, Robertson chose to keep control.

What will happen to the university after Robertson is gone is anyone's guess. Some hope that Gordon Robertson will take over and allow a greater degree of academic freedom. Others fear that someone like Ryan will take over and make the school the sectarian hot spot that its critics long claimed it was. What is for certain is that for a time, Regent was a truly vibrant evangelical university that had the misfortune to have a founder whose interests lay beyond education.

Notes

1. Regent University Catalog 1998.

2. The beliefs that are confirmed include the second coming of Jesus, the inspiration of the Bible, the Trinity, the indwelling of the Holy Spirit, and Jesus as the only redeemer (Regent University Catalog 1994–1996).

3. Philip Walzer, "Outpacing Others in Va, Regent U. Lifts Enrollment 30%," *Virginian-Pilot*, October 22, 1991.

4. Harvey Cox, "Warring Visions of the Religious Right," *Atlantic Monthly*, November 1995, 61.

5. Terry Lindvall, interview by author, tape recording, Virginia Beach, Va., January 11, 2000.

6. Terry Lindvall interview, 2000.

7. Herb Titus, interview by author, written responses to mailed questions, June 19, 2000.

8. Terry Lindvall interview, 2000.

9. Terry Lindvall, interview by author, tape recording, Costa Mesa, Calif., February 22, 1996.

10. Terry Lindvall interview, 1996.

11. Roy Maynard, "Smoke but No Fire," *World*, January 22, 1994.

12. Francis Wilkinson, "Divine Instruction," *American Lawyer*, March 1987.

13. Roy Maynard, "On Pins and Needles," *World*, January 22, 1994.

14. Roy Maynard, "Titus Breaks His Silence," *World*, February 5, 1994.

15. Wilkinson, "Divine Instruction."

16. Maynard, "Titus Breaks His Silence."

17. Maynard, "Titus Breaks His Silence."

18. Maynard, "Titus Breaks His Silence."

19. Pat Robertson to James Duane, February 24, 1994. Regent University Special Collections (RUA).

20. Pat Robertson to James Duane, February 24, 1994.

21. Cox, "Warring Visions," 68.

22. Mark O'Keefe, "Regent Fires 3 Law Professors Who Had Backed Ex-Dean," *Virginian-Pilot*, May 24, 1994.

23. O'Keefe, "Regent Fires 3 Law Professors Who Had Backed Ex-Dean."

24. Esther Diskin, "3 Sue Regent, Robertson over His Statements about Them," *Virginian-Pilot*, October 8, 1994.

25. Philip Walzer, "Robertson Reflects on His Brainchild, Regent U., at 25," *Virginian-Pilot*, May 30, 2001.

26. Pat Robertson, interview by author, tape recording, Virginia Beach, Va., May 25, 2000.

27. Tony Warton, "Regent U. President Stepping Down, Replaced by Ex-Army General," *Virginian-Pilot*, September 6, 1997.

28. Herb Titus interview.

29. Paul Clancy, "President of Regent Steps Down," *Virginian-Pilot*, September 9, 2000.

30. Walzer, "Robertson Reflects on His Brainchild, Regent U., at 25."

31. Josh White, "Va. High Court Backs Robertson's Challenge," *Washington Post*, November 4, 2000.

32. Emily Wax, "Schools Chief Quits Post in Alexandria," *Washington Post*, March 13, 2000.

33. Philip Walzer, "Regent Plans Full Undergrad Program," *Virginian-Pilot*, April 25, 2005.

34. Jacqueline Trescott, "Two Robertson Causes Collide Head-On," *Washington Post*, July 17, 1988.

35. Steven Vegh, "Regent Film Students to Be Asked to Follow Artistic Guidelines," *Virginian-Pilot*, January 10, 2003.

36. Philip Walzer, "Former Regent President to Join Wesleyan Faculty," *Virginian-Pilot*, December 11, 2005.

37. Pat Robertson, "A Message from Dr. Robertson," email, August 15, 2006.

CHAPTER 18

ROBERTSON AND W

P AT Robertson started the 2000 presidential campaign season by announcing that the Christian Coalition would choose a candidate early and function as the kingmaker of the Republican Party. His boast proved hollow thanks to a poor performance by his favored candidate John Ashcroft and the sudden emergence of George W. Bush. Initially there was considerable resistance to Bush among evangelicals. They remembered his father all to well, and did not want a repeat performance. Once he took office, however, Bush proved to be more supportive of the Christian Right's agenda than any president before him. This was both a blessing and a curse for Robertson. It was a blessing because many of the issues that he had long championed would now be put into law. It was also bittersweet because the Bush administration was able to sideline the man from Virginia Beach.

To listen to Robertson's foes, it would be easy to assume that he held considerable sway over the new Bush White House. Such perceptions were far from reality. Karl Rove, Bush's political strategist, often referred to as "Bush's Brain," had managed to simultaneously secure the Christian Right vote and bypass the leaders who had made the movement what it was. As a result Robertson's life during the administration of George W. Bush has been one of constant frustration. While in office Bush has been able to sidestep men like Robertson by appealing directly to conservative Christians. The result was that Robertson was put in a difficult position. In order to maintain his popularity within evangelicalism, he had to support Bush, while at the same time the administration was actively undermining Robertson's power base. He was in a bind, and as was his nature, he struck out and continued to speak his mind on any issue that he cared to. As a consequence he was often attacked from all sides when he made comments similar to those that he had been making for decades. The difference now was that he could not count on the Republican president to support him. For this reason the relationship between Pat Robertson and George W. Bush is one of the more interesting tales in the history of the Christian Right.

Almost from the very beginning the relationship between the preacher and the future president was antagonistic. Robertson first noticed George W. Bush playing a role in the Christian Right when his father ran for president in 1988. George W. Bush had a midlife religious conversion in the 1980s and became an evangelical Christian. During the battle for the Republican nomination the elder Bush used his son to reach out to the evangelical community and thereby cut into Robertson's constituency. Christian Right leaders like Ft. Worth's James Robison were on friendly terms with the younger Bush, and connections such as these caused Robertson no end of frustration as his own presidential campaign progressed.

Robertson and George W. Bush also came into contact when the Christian Coalition became a powerful presence in Texas state politics. In 1994 Dallas lawyer Tom Pauken, a member of the Texas Christian Coalition, became the chairman of the state Republican Party. He became chairman even though Republican senators Phil Gramm and Kay Bailey Hutchison had publicly backed a rival.[1] Bush, who was running for governor, tried to remain above the fray and supported Pauken. This support lasted until 1997 when Pauken made the mistake of openly criticizing a tax plan proposed by the governor. In response the Bush team had their largest contributors move their donations from the Texas GOP to a private fund run by Bush and Rove. The governor also refused to back Pauken when he ran for Texas attorney general in 1999. Instead of supporting one of the leaders of the Christian Coalition, Bush supported John Cornyn, who was described as "an almost painfully country club Republican."[2] By the time Bush ran for president, Robertson had come to realize that Bush would be supportive of religious conservatives only so long as they were supportive of him in return.

The first time the two men publicly locked horns was over the fate of convicted murderer turned evangelical Christian Karla Faye Tucker. In 1983 Tucker and her then boyfriend, both reportedly high on drugs, killed two people during a robbery. Fourteen years later her death sentence was about to be carried out, but the convict had changed during her incarceration. While in prison, Tucker became an evangelical, led Bible studies, and appeared to be a truly changed woman. One person who believed she had changed was Robertson. In 1993, years before Bush became governor, Robertson began to champion her cause on *The 700 Club*, even though he was generally a supporter of the death penalty. When Bush took office, Robertson asked the new governor to show her mercy and commute her sentence to life in prison. The leader of the Texas Christian Coalition publicly disagreed with Robertson, as did Bush.[3] The governor was roundly criticized by Robertson and others when it was reported that he imitated and mocked Tucker's desperate final pleas for clemency.

Robertson continued to use his daily broadcast to criticize Bush on the issue. On *The 700 Club* the day after Tucker was put to death Robertson's cohost Terry Meeuwsen said, "I am so tired of politicians who put their careers ahead of principle and, in my opinion, ahead of mercy."[4] Her comments were significant because Robertson rarely allowed his cohosts to make substantial comments on such controversial issues. The Tucker issue is important because it illustrates the low-level dislike and general distrust between Bush and Robertson. As it turned out, Robertson did not choose to support Bush for president as much as he acquiesced to the inevitability of his candidacy. Journalist Molly Ivins reports that evangelicals had supported his run for governor because they could smell victory.[5] At the 1999 Christian Coalition Road to Victory meeting the evangelicals in attendance said the same thing. In 1994 they supported him in order to defeat Democrat Ann Richards, and in 2000 they choose him over Al Gore. In both cases the Bush team had been able to raise millions of dollars more than their opponents, and they did it before their competitors even had their campaigns organized. In today's world of money-rich campaigns, Bush had the overwhelming advantage.

Soon after George W. Bush took office his talk of compassionate conservatism vanished and was replaced with the most concerted effort to institutionalize a political ideology in American history. What is surprising was the lengths that the new president went to in order to mollify the Christian Right once he was in office. As is the case for every new administration, the months between election day and the inauguration were filled with rumors of who would be appointed to the president's cabinet. Despite his earlier criticism, Robertson told reporters that he trusted Bush to appoint true conservatives. He boasted, "I think conservatives will be very pleased with him. This is why I've given him an enormous amount of slack to play to the center so much and go after independent votes."[6]

Robertson's optimism was well placed. Several of Bush's key nominees to important government posts had religious backgrounds. Some were incidental, such as Condoleezza Rice, whose father was a minister, while others were more substantial. Karen Hughes, one of Bush's chief political strategists, was an elder in her church and once led an impromptu church service aboard *Air Force One*.[7] One of the administration's members who had close ties to Robertson and the Christian Right was Kay Coles James, who ran the Office of Personnel Management. James had served as the dean of the Robertson School of Government at Regent University until she left to work at the conservative think tank the Heritage Foundation. Her job in the new administration made her responsible for hiring employees for the entire federal government. Perhaps Robertson's decades-old dream of seeing evangelicals finally taking more jobs in the government was about to become reality.

The clearest sign that the Christian Right was actually being given a place at the table was the nomination of John Ashcroft for attorney general. Ashcroft had been a friend of Robertson's for a number of years and his credentials as a conservative and a member of the Pentecostal denomination Assemblies of God were impeccable. During his 1988 run for president, Robertson had mentioned Ashcroft as someone he would choose for attorney general. However, his nomination was the most hotly contested of any cabinet member, and Robertson made sure to support his friend. In January 2001 he appeared on ABC's *This Week* and debated California senator Barbara Boxer, who opposed Ashcroft's views on abortion and civil rights. Robertson's answers to the numerous charges were so well thought out that they seemed prepared in advance. He had facts and figures about Ashcroft's career that were designed to fight every charge that Boxer brought up. As the nomination battle continued, Robertson recorded a telephone message that the Christian Coalition used in its effort to marshal support. Despite a barrage of attacks Ashcroft was approved by the Senate just as Robertson had predicted. The friendship remained strong during his tenure in the Bush administration, and when he left office, Robertson had him come to Regent University to teach a few special seminar classes.

One of the programs that Bush promoted early in his presidency was faith-based initiatives, in which federal money would be given to private groups to do charitable works. This was popular in some conservative circles as a free-market approach to welfare. Since they viewed government agencies as too bureaucratic and bloated, they hoped that money given directly to charities, churches, and other groups would let the funds be spent more efficiently. This program was criticized by liberals who saw it as a dangerous breach of the wall between church and state. That critique was to be expected, but the Bush administration was surprised that it was also disliked by many Christian Right leaders, including Pat Robertson. Besides criticizing it on *The 700 Club*, Robertson wrote an editorial for *USA Today* in which he explained his position. Robertson made it clear that he liked the concept of taking money from the government and giving it to effective social welfare agencies. The examples he cited included Teen Challenge, an evangelical drug rehabilitation program, and Chuck Colson's evangelical prison ministry. One problem with Bush's proposal, Robertson believed, was that it was based on a "tortured definition of separation of church and state" that demanded that religious groups that participate in the program be forced to "give up their religious activities." Worse still was the prospect that if the program gave funds to the big three religious groups in America (Protestants, Catholics, and Jews), then it would have to give it to everybody else. This meant that religious organizations that some evangelicals thought were disreputable would also get money. It was inconceivable to Robertson that grants could go to groups like "the Hare Krishnas, the Church of Scientology or Sun Myung Moon's Unification Church—no matter that some may use brainwashing techniques or that the founder of one claims to be the messiah and another claims that he was Buddha reincarnated."[8] Robertson then claimed that the only remedy for the program was to establish a government office that would vet each religious group and keep the questionable ones out. If Bush's program was on shaky legal ground, Robertson's solution was certainly a serious infringement on religious liberty. Liberal groups such as the National Organization for Women (NOW), the American Civil Liberties Union (ACLU), and Americans United joined with liberal religious groups such as the Unitarian Church in their opposition to the faith-based initiative. A program that was able to unite NOW and Pat Robertson in opposition obviously needed damage control.

The general hostility toward faith-based initiatives was a cause for concern in the Bush White House, but they managed to make things worse. In March 2001 the head of the faith-based office, John Dilulio, spoke at a meeting of the National Association of Evangelicals and attempted to paint Robertson as an extremist on the issue. He explained that the bulk of the government grants would go to inner-city churches that had a history of helping the poor. Dilulio cast doubt on the ability of groups like Robertson's Operation Blessing to do any good. "Literally hundreds of millions of dollars raised and spent each year by national para-church organizations seems hardly to reach, and only weakly and episodically to benefit, the community serving urban churches that witness truth and action to the poor every blessed day," Dilulio said. He also claimed that "predominately white, exurban evangelical, and national para-church leaders should be careful not to presume to speak for any persons other than themselves."[9] By July the struggle between Dilulio and evangelicals had "burst into open warfare."

The White House hoped to put out a quickly growing fire by inviting several prominent evangelical leaders to Washington for a meeting. Most of those that attended quickly changed their tune and openly supported the faith-based initiatives. Jerry Falwell said that he had changed his mind and had decided to fully support the program. Other Christian Right groups such as the Eagle Forum and the Family Research Council also decided to support the program.[10] The hostility between evangelicals and Dilulio was resolved in August when revelations about a secret deal between the Salvation Army and Karl Rove made it clear that Dilulio was not in control of the program that he was supposedly in charge of.[11] That same month his office published a report on the first six months of the program called *Unlevel Playing Field*, which said that local groups were being ignored and that there existed a bias against religious organizations among the government agencies charged with distributing the money. He resigned his job the day the report was released.[12] After Dilulio left, it became clear that evangelical and Christian Right organizations were now going to be the main beneficiaries of the faith-based program.

The program, which Bush had promised would have $8 billion a year, was cut to $200 million a year, then further reduced to only $30 million by late 2001. Over three hundred groups applied for grants, and their applications were reviewed by a committee of their peers. The group in charge of vetting each grant application was dominated by evangelicals, who despite orders to remain nonpartisan and nonsectarian showed a bias described by an evangelical White House staffer as "transparent."[13] The committee rated each application on a scale of 1 to 100, and it was the politically connected evangelical groups that came out on top. For example, Robertson's Operation Blessing received a score of 95, and another organization started by a former Robertson employee got a 94. Meanwhile, more established organizations such as Big Brothers/Big Sisters of America received a score of 85.[14]

Despite his concerns over certain aspects of the program, Robertson's Operation Blessing was one of the first groups to receive federal funding. In October 2002 the group won a $500,000 grant that was renewable for three years.[15] Robertson never criticized the program after the money started rolling in. All twenty-one of the religious groups that received grants in the initial $30 million spent on the program were Christian, mostly evangelical, organizations.[16] Due to the controversy over its leadership and questions over who should get government funding, the project was eventually put on the back burner. Critics were increasingly vocal with their fears that Bush was an agent of the Christian Right and was too closely allied with men like Robertson. These critics were given additional ammunition in late 2006 when former special assistant to the president David Kuo, an evangelical, published a book that was very critical of the faith-based initiative program. Kuo had worked on the faith-based program for years, and his book makes it clear that the Bush administration was intent on using the program almost exclusively for political gain. When Karl Rove heard how many people, especially minorities, were showing up at conferences on the faith-based program, he ordered that they be held in every battleground state in anticipation of the 2004 election.[17] The most damning of Kuo's accusations was that most White House officials were regularly dismissive of evangelical Christians, whom they reportedly referred to as "the nuts," "ridiculous," and "goofy." Kuo claimed that Rove's Political Affairs office was the worst offender. His staff complained about nearly every event in which Christian Right leaders were involved, although these leaders seemed totally unaware.[18] To most outsiders, it appeared as if the Christian Right and Bush were joined at the hip, but the administration's discomfort with most Christian Right leaders was soon made crystal clear.

George W. Bush's generally aimless presidency found new purpose after Muslim terrorists attacked New York and Washington, D.C., on September 11,

2001. On the news and on the streets Americans said that the world had changed, and if it had, no one told Robertson. Two days after the attacks Robertson interviewed Jerry Falwell on *The 700 Club*, and the two men set off explosions of their own. Robertson asked Falwell what his response was to the attacks, and Falwell compared the events to Pearl Harbor and Hitler's campaign against Jews. As he often does when confronted with serious events, Robertson saw the attacks as the beginning of a religious revival in America. Falwell, however, saw the events as a sign that God had removed his protection from America due to its adherence to liberal social ideas. He said, "[T]he ACLU has to take a lot of blame for this," to which Robertson agreed. Robertson said he concurred with Falwell that pro-choice advocates, feminists, homosexuals, pagans, and those who tried to "secularize America" were directly responsible for the attacks. Robertson backed up his friend's comments by saying, "[T]he problem is that we have adopted that [liberal] agenda at the highest levels of our government." He then ended their conversation by predicting that God was going to start a massive revival.

The fallout from the interview was swift and severe. The nation was still reeling from the attacks, and no one knew if this was the start of a series of terrorist acts. In this context Falwell and Robertson's comments were insensitive and even cruel. They were not unique, however. Robertson had been threatening God's wrath for more than thirty years, so to him the attacks were something that fit into his worldview. He did not seem to realize that the public's reaction would be so angry. The day after *The 700 Club* show aired President Bush issued a statement calling their comments "inappropriate." Talk show hosts relentlessly mocked the televangelists, and their liberal opponents used their statements as campaign fodder. The hostile reaction may have given Robertson pause, but not for long. In 2006 he was interviewed by Disney CEO Michael Eisner, who asked about his opinion of Islam. Robertson replied that "Muhammad was a very violent person," and noted that the Christian Broadcasting Network (CBN) owned a TV station in Lebanon for eighteen years until it was damaged by a car bomb and taken over by militants.[19] What Robertson failed to mention was that the station was in Israeli-held territory in Lebanon, and was attacked after Israel pulled out.

The Bush administration's reaction to Pat Robertson demonstrated that a significant change had occurred in the historic relationship between the White House and Christian Right leaders. While Presidents Reagan and George H. W. Bush went to great lengths to meet with and appease specific leaders of the Religious Right, George W. Bush and his team were able to effectively circumvent these men and appeal directly to conservative evangelicals themselves. Whereas earlier presidents needed someone to act as a translator, Bush spoke the coded language of evangelicalism. This meant that he could speak for himself and did not have to rely on outsiders for help. The leadership of the Christian Right should have seen such an obvious problem coming a mile away, but it apparently blindsided most of them.

In early December 2001 Robertson resigned as president of the Christian Coalition, and journalists were quick to write about the declining power of the Christian Right. While this story had been repeated for nearly thirty years, this time the media focused on the loss of power among the Christian Right leadership and not of the movement itself. On Christmas Eve two different articles traced the Christian Right leadership's lack of influence on the White House. Lorraine Woellert, writing in *BusinessWeek*, made the insightful observation that since the Christian Right had transformed itself into a grassroots movement, its leaders had become less important. She also noted that Bush had become the "most prominent spokesman for Christian conservative causes."[20] Bush's emergence as the leader was accelerated by Falwell and Robertson's controversial statements after 9/11. *The Washington Post* declared, "[F]or the first time since religious conservatives became a modern political movement, the president of the United States has become the movement's de facto leader."[21] In the article Gary Bauer emphasized Robertson's irrelevance, saying, "I think Robertson stepped down because the position has already been filled." Ralph Reed even questioned the necessity of the Christian Coalition when he said that the Christian Right movement "no longer plays the institutional role it once did." He also added, "[Y]ou're no longer throwing rocks at the building; you're in the building." For the Christian Right movement in general, the lack of visible leaders could be a good thing. Michael Farris, the head of the Home School Legal Defense Association, said, "We're not going to be led by giants any longer. Instead, you will see a coalition. It's harder for the Left to attack you when there's a variety of leaders."[22]

Forcing men like Robertson to the sidelines was the result of more than Bush's rhetoric and grassroots workers; it was a deliberate political move. Karl Rove wanted to maintain the evangelical base that the GOP enjoyed without the baggage that came along with it. One journalist commented that "liberals see Robertson the way right-wing groups see Senators Edward Kennedy and Hillary Rodham Clinton, as tried and true boogeymen." In short, Robertson had become a liability to the Right and a fund-raising tool for the Left. The 2004 election was sure to bring up comparisons to the 1992 GOP convention, many still incorrectly blamed for George H. W. Bush's defeat. As a result, it was decided that Bush would infuse his speeches with religious rhetoric and reach out to Christian conservatives on his own. This process was aided by speechwriter and evangelical Michael Gerson, who crafted many of the president's speeches and the famous phrase "axis of evil." Thanks to Gerson, Bush's speeches became the most overtly religious of any president in American history. Not only did they mention religious themes more often, but the manner in which they were used changed. While presidents usually put themselves in a position as spokesmen to God on behalf of the people, Bush "positions himself as a prophet, issuing declarations of divine desires for the nation and world."[23] A senior White House advisor commented, "[I]n the old days, Republican presidential candidates went to religious conservative leaders to seek their imprimatur. George W. Bush was able to go directly to those who sat in the pews."[24] This strategy worked because his administration was filled with prominent evangelicals, especially Attorney General Ashcroft. Another method that helped them accomplish this was redefining what it meant to be a part of the Christian Right. Specifically, the Bush team wanted to reach out to conservative Catholics and religious conservatives from outside the South. Since southern evangelicals were likely to vote for Bush in 2004, it was important for the president to reach out to other groups, especially in the Catholic-heavy states of the Rust Belt.[25]

Robertson made it clear that he blamed Rove for the Christian Coalition's loss of power. In an interview with Patrick Buchanan he said, "I think they [Bush and Rove] pretty much were responsible for the demise of the Christian Coalition." When asked to clarify his accusation he said that Rove "wasn't too keen on keeping it going. I mean there was a studied indifference."[26] This explains why Bush would have nothing to do with the coalition's Road to Victory meetings and why Robertson, Falwell, and other Christian Right leaders were kept in the shadows during Bush's first term.

Robertson was clearly frustrated by his lack of power in Washington, D.C. The Christian Coalition had essentially ceased to function, and he no longer had the clout that he had once enjoyed. As a result Robertson felt free enough to be critical of Bush when it suited him, and it also meant that since he felt he had little to loose, he could speak his mind. During the George W. Bush administration Robertson took more heat for his controversial comments than he had in his entire career. This was in part due to his lack of power, which brought out attacks from the Left, but he was also criticized by the Right and the White House. He perhaps realized that since he was in his seventies, it was unlikely that he could become a power broker again, so he spoke from his heart, knowing that at the very least his constituents would respond positively.

One of the most consistent objects of Robertson's ire has been the U.S. Supreme Court. His displeasure with the Judicial branch did not begin with *Roe v. Wade*, but years later when he became fully involved in politics. Since that time he has held the court out for special contempt. The court and the judges therein have been a campaign issue for both liberal and conservative groups for decades. This meant that over the years Robertson's comments were used to energize both groups to action.

Robertson's hostility for the court came to a head during the George W. Bush's first term. During the summer of 2003 Robertson asked viewers of *The 700 Club* to join him in Operation Supreme Court Freedom, a twenty-one-day prayer vigil, the goal of which was to get three justices to retire. While part of the reason for this "prayer offensive" was Robertson's apparent fear that Bush was becoming another Reagan, it was primarily in response to a recent court decision. In June the Supreme Court struck down a Texas law that forbade sodomy. In a letter posted on CBN's website Robertson declared that the ruling "has opened the door to homosexual marriage, bigamy, legalized prostitution and even incest." He also pondered, "[W]ould it not be possible for God to put it in the minds of these three judges that the time has come to retire? With their retirement and the appointment of conservative judges, a massive change in federal jurisprudence can take place." In later interviews Robertson claimed that he was specifically thinking of John Paul Stevens, Ruth Bader Ginsburg, and Sandra Day O'Connor as the three who should leave.[27] As could be expected, he was roundly criticized for his actions, but he kept at them none the less. Even though he was attacked in the media, among many evangelicals his comments resonated.

In January 2004 Robertson published *The Ten Offenses*, which was a defense of the importance of the Ten Commandments in American history. In an interview on MSNBC Robertson said the book also focused on "activist judges, how the Supreme Court has turned the Constitution on its ear. And they've done things the framers never intended." He also claimed that the entire nation was being held hostage by five unelected judges and called upon his readers to "take back our government."[28] In the introduction of the book, Robertson states that liberal elites are waging war on the "nation's foundation and spiritual heritage," by which he means the forced removal of a statue of the Ten Commandments from the Alabama Supreme Court Building. This case led to Alabama chief justice Roy Moore's removal from the bench since he had refused to remove the statue from the courthouse. Moore became a martyr to the Christian Right cause, and he toured the country with the statue on a flatbed truck. In one interview Robertson compared Moore to Martin Luther King Jr., and wondered why King got a national holiday for disobeying evil laws and Moore lost his seat on the high court.[29]

He goes on to repeat the evangelical myth that America was founded by evangelical Christians for evangelical Christians. Each of the chapters that follow focuses on one of the Ten Commandments and their impact on the nation. For example, in the chapter on the fourth commandment, Sabbath rest, Robertson writes of a nation that had turned its back on God. He laments the fact that blue laws, which had kept businesses closed on Sunday, had mostly been repealed and now Sunday has become a busy shopping day. In his version of American history, every one of the Ten Commandments was part of the fabric of America, until they were torn out by the Supreme Court. In the conclusion Robertson repeats the comments that got him and Jerry Falwell into such trouble after 9/11. "Knowingly or unknowingly, the ACLU, Abortion Rights Action League, Planned Parenthood [and several other liberal groups] . . . are hastening the destruction of the United States of America."[30] He ends the book by telling his readers to get politically active and challenge Congress to take back the power it gave away to the Supreme Court.

Later that year Robertson followed up with another book about the Supreme Court. This book, titled *Courting Disaster*, has a picture of the justices on the cover and the phrase "the end of American Democracy" in large letters on the back. While his first book on the court focused on the Ten Commandments, *Courting Disaster* covers a broad range of court decisions that Robertson feels have hindered the exercise of Christianity. In a chapter entitled "Our Black Robed Masters" Robertson claims that America's democracy is being actively thwarted by liberal justices. While most of the book is critical of the court, he does hold out hope that things could eventually change. Robertson writes that he hopes Bush would be reelected so that he could "make conservatives the majority on the high court bench. The left is apoplectic at the prospect of losing their hold on government power. But this could happen, God willing."[31]

Robertson eventually got his wish in 2005 when Bush was able to nominate two new justices to the high court. The first nomination, for future chief justice John Roberts, went smoothly. As predicted, liberal groups challenged the nominee's Catholic faith and feared it would hamper his ability to follow the Constitution. The Bush team made it clear that questions about religious faith were unfair, while Christian Right leaders cried religious bigotry was behind the anti-Roberts campaign. What is interesting about Roberts's nomination was that a Catholic received such effusive praise from evangelicals. In 1960 presidential candidate John F. Kennedy had to defend his Catholic faith to evangelicals, but forty years later John Roberts had to defend his to political liberals. If the Christian Right's support of Roberts did not show their willingness to follow political conviction over religious principals, Bush's next nomination did.

Just a few months after Roberts was nominated to the court, Sandra Day O'Connor announced her resignation. Bush's first choice to replace her was longtime friend and evangelical Christian Harriet Miers. Surprisingly, her nomination was quickly challenged by conservatives, including many Christian Right leaders, who thought she would be too moderate in her views. The White House immediately changed tactics and began to use Miers's religion as her strongest selling point. This tactic was criticized as the blatantly hypocritical move that it was, and it even failed to win evangelicals to Miers's cause. "She sounds to me like another swing vote, which is the last thing conservatives want," Gary Bauer said on *Fox News Sunday*.[32] Robertson supported Miers, however, and in the midst of the battle, he went on *The 700 Club* and threatened retribution on any conservative senator who had supported Ginsburg in 1993 but voted against

Miers. "They're going to turn against a Christian who is a conservative picked by a conservative president and they're going to vote against her for confirmation?" Robertson asked. "Not on your sweet life, if they want to stay in office."[33] He continued to support her nomination until it was withdrawn and Samuel Alito, a Catholic, was announced as the new nominee. Robertson proclaimed that Alito's nomination was "a slam dunk," and would be widely supported by other evangelicals. Few people commented on the irony of the evangelical Christian Right attacking one of its own in order to put another Catholic on the Supreme Court. Politics truly had trumped religion. While it seemed that many of the Right's agenda items were about to be set in place, world events drew the attention of the president and the nation to matters beyond America's shores.

Even more than the 9/11 terrorist attacks, the defining story of George W. Bush's presidency will be the war in Iraq. The situation in the Persian Gulf had remained unchanged since 1990 when President George H. W. Bush pushed Iraq out of Kuwait, but stopped short of removing Iraq's dictator Saddam Hussein from power. During the 1990s the United States kept Iraq contained within its borders. However, when George W. Bush took office the rhetoric against Iraq was ratcheted up significantly, and it only increased after 9/11. In the months following the terrorist attacks Bush prepared the American people for a war with his father's old adversary Hussein. Although there was never any evidence to support his claim, Bush repeatedly told the world that there was a link between the secular Hussein in Iraq and the Fundamentalist Muslim Osama Bin Laden, who was hiding in Afghanistan. The fact that Bin Laden had also called for Hussein's removal from power was never widely reported.

During the first Gulf War Robertson wrote in *The New World Order* that the George H. W. Bush administration had essentially given a green light for Hussein to invade Kuwait. The reason for this, Robertson believed, was that Bush and his advisors wanted to create a new world order in which the entire planet was ruled by a single government.[34] While Bush said that Hussein was as dangerous as Adolf Hitler, Robertson saw him as a pawn of dark forces. Late in 1999 Robertson suggested that the U.S. government should stop trying to contain Hussein and just assassinate him. As usual his comments were part of his off-the-cuff remarks on *The 700 Club*. Robertson said, "[I]sn't it better to do something like that . . . to take out Saddam Hussein, rather than to spend billions of dollars on a war that harms innocent civilians and destroys the infrastructure of a country?"[35] What was truly unusual about his remark was that it may have been right, or at least a better alternative to invading Iraq. One of the other people that he mentioned should be assassinated before they could attack the United States was Osama Bin Laden, the head of the Al Qaeda terrorist network.

After the 9/11 attack and as war with Iraq seemed inevitable, Robertson said little about the situation except to criticize Islam. The Bush administration had gone to considerable lengths to quell the fears of Muslims in the United States and around the world concerning both the war on terror and Iraq. It was hoped that a clear distinction would be made between terrorists and Muslims. Many evangelicals were not willing to cooperate with the White House on this issue. Robertson continued to claim that Muslims wanted to kill every Jew in the world, and Falwell called Islam's prophet Mohammed a terrorist. Infamous televangelist Jimmy Swaggart briefly regained national attention when he called the Muslim prophet a sexual deviant.[36] Average evangelicals were also less than willing to portray Islam as a benefit to society. In the late 1990s a group of pastors in northern Virginia tried to block the construction of an Islamic school funded by Saudi Arabia to protest the lack of religious freedom in that country. In the months preceding the 9/11 attacks, the Fundamentalist Muslim Taliban regime in Afghanistan held two female American missionaries prisoner for sharing their Christian faith. These incidents, taken with their support of Israel, indicated that most evangelicals did not agree with the president. Nevertheless, the White House forged ahead in its attempt to attack Muslim terrorists but not demonize Islam. Secretary of State Colin Powell made a speech in which he specifically mentioned Robertson's anti-Islam comments and said, "[T]his kind of hatred must be rejected." His speech was part of a broad effort on the part of the administration to win public support for the coming Iraq war.

Even though his own foreign policy outlook was very aggressive, Robertson seemed to think that an invasion of Iraq would be a mistake. In the weeks leading up to the attack *The 700 Club* had Colorado mega-church pastor Ted Haggard as a guest. The purpose of his visit was to share a vision he had in which Saddam Hussein left office peacefully due to the prayers of millions of Christians across America. Haggard said, "[T]here's no reason for a soldier to die in this effort. There's no reason for there to be one widow in America because of this effort."[37] CBN and *The 700 Club* supported Haggard's vision, even though Robertson himself was not on hand for the interview.

When the invasion of Iraq commenced, Robertson, like most evangelicals, supported the troops and the president. However, Robertson was not one to keep his opinions to himself. In October 2004 Robertson was interviewed by Paula Zahn on CNN. During a discussion of Bush's errors while in office, Robertson recounted a conversation he had with the president before the invasion of Iraq. According to Robertson, during a meeting in Nashville, Bush was very confident and acted like he was "sitting on top of the world." He told the president that "I had deep misgivings about this war, deep misgivings. And I was trying to say, Mr. President, you better prepare the American people for casualties." Robertson said that the president replied, "Oh, no, we're not going to have any casualties." To which he said, "[W]ell, I said, it's the way it's going to be. And so, it was messy. The lord told me it was going to be, A, a disaster and, B, messy.

And before that, I had deep, in my spirit, I had deep misgivings about going into Iraq."[38] When Zahn pressed Robertson about why the Lord would tell him about the casualties and not the president, he blamed Bush's advisors, especially the neoconservatives, for giving him bad advice. By late 2005 Robertson was so supportive of the war that during a broadcast of *The 700 Club* he attacked Democrats who dared to question the president's handling of the war. "The president is the commander in chief of the armed forces," Robertson explained. "And attempts to undermine [him] during a time of war amounts to treason."

Many evangelical organizations were quick to send in help to the people of Iraq, but not without controversy. While no one begrudged them the right to help, the overtly religious nature of their mission troubled both liberals in the United States and Muslims in Iraq. Franklin Graham, son of famous evangelist Billy Graham, sent his organization Samaritan's Purse, even though he had characterized Islam as an evil religion. Since Robertson had consistently seen traumatic events as an opportunity for revival, or as in Liberia's case, a chance to make a fortune, it should not be surprising that he sent Operation Blessing volunteers, mostly doctors and nurses, as soon as the invasion was over. CBN also sent reporters to Iraq to cover the conflict.[39]

As the 2004 campaign approached it appeared that evangelicals and Robertson were more supportive of Bush than they had been four years earlier. The year began with Robertson on the set of *The 700 Club* boasting that Bush was going to win in November. "I really believe I'm hearing from the Lord it's going to be like a blowout election in 2004. It's shaping up that way." However, like many of Robertson's comments concerning Bush, it was a compliment mixed with a criticism. Robertson went on to say, "[T]he Lord has just blessed him. I mean he could make terrible mistakes and come out of it. It doesn't make any difference what he does, good or bad, God picks him up because he is a man of prayer and God's blessing him."[40] Despite the fact that he had been marginalized, Robertson tried to make it clear that he would not be a good soldier just to get back in the good graces of Bush and Rove.

When it was time for the GOP convention, the Christian Right found itself locked out, or more precisely, Christian Right leaders like Robertson were. Falwell, Robertson, and Franklin Graham were not invited to speak at the convention, which was held in New York City. Roberta Combs, the head of the Christian Coalition, unintentionally undermined the reason for her group's existence when she attempted to downplay the president's snub. "We have the president," Combs said, "he's a professed, born-again Christian," and that meant it was not necessary to have Robertson address the convention.[41] This sentiment was echoed by many who attended the coalition's Faith and Freedom Rally, held at a hotel near the convention. A coalition member from Oregon claimed that while the Christian Right was not on the main stage, it was everywhere else, especially in the state delegations. For example, he claimed, "I went to Texas, and almost all of them are born-again Christians. And they say, 'You can't get on this delegation without that.'"[42] Clearly, there was a sense at the convention that the Christian Right was present, even if its most recognizable leaders were not. Another reason that these men were left out was the memory of Bush's controversial victory in 2000 and the desperate need to expand his base. A study by the Pew Research Center showed that issues that were important to religious conservatives were not significant to the general population. Pursuing issues such as a ban on stem cell research, gay marriage, and abortion were likely to lose the president some much needed support.[43]

Despite being cast into the shadows for the campaign, Robertson did his best to keep his agenda in the limelight. In September 2004 he resurrected the Christian Coalition's Road to Victory meetings, and even Jerry Falwell attended the event. Besides the main convention held in a Washington, D.C., hotel, the coalition held a workshop in a U.S. Senate office building thanks to Kentucky senator Mitch McConnell, the majority whip. Senator Orrin Hatch, a Mormon from Utah, also spoke at the workshop along with Representative Walter Jones of North Carolina. The main meeting only had "several hundred" attendees, as compared with the thousands who had gone to them a decade earlier.[44] President Bush did not attend or send a video message to the 2004 meeting.

Robertson still managed to have an impact on the election. His coalition distributed millions of its voter guides, and his former protégé Ralph Reed took his grassroots tactics to the White House. In West Virginia, a traditionally Democrat state that Bush had won in 2000, Republican workers were actively recruiting churches to help with the campaign. This was the tactic that Robertson had used to great effect in 1988 and with the Christian Coalition in the 1990s. Reed had become a key political advisor to the Bush campaign, and he used strategies that had worked so well for him in 1994.[45] The GOP even sent Reed to the 2004 annual meeting of the Southern Baptist Convention. Bush addressed the group via video, as Jimmy Carter had done when he was in the White House. Reed was there to attend a "pastor's reception," which was sponsored by the Bush campaign. The purpose of the meeting was to encourage pastors to register their congregations to vote, and about one hundred of them signed a pledge promising to publicly support Bush's reelection.[46] The denomination even set up a voter registration drive and website called "I vote values." This change in attitude in Southern Baptists is significant because the denomination was founded by people who wanted the government and the church to be totally separate. It is a testimony to the influence of the Christian Right that this metamorphosis has come about. This irony has been lost on nearly everyone, except historian Randall Balmer, who devotes an entire chapter to the topic in his 2006 book *Thy Kingdom Come*.[47]

One of the more controversial actions of the 2004 campaign was a letter that the GOP sent out in West Virginia and Arkansas that claimed that, if Bush lost, liberals would attempt to ban the Bible and Christianity. CNN reporter Mark Shields wrote an op-ed piece in which he claimed that Bush and Rove "must be convinced that the churchgoing folks of West Virginia and Arkansas are so gullible and so ill-informed that this baseless charge could scare them into voting Republican."[48] It was a low blow on the part of the GOP, and the type of argument that had traditionally been promoted by Christian Right groups, not the White House or the Republican National Convention.

When the votes were counted it was clear that evangelical Christians remained the political power in the GOP. Journalists began to discuss the "religion gap" that separated the Republican and Democratic Parties and found that Bush had made some interesting gains in 2004. Evangelicals had given Bush 72 percent of their votes in 2000, but that number rose to 78 percent for 2004. Their support was essential because they made up 23 percent of the electorate, representing nearly twenty-six million votes.[49] Still, Bush's 50.7 percent of the total vote was the weakest for any incumbent president since Woodrow Wilson in 1916. In his book *American Theocracy*, Kevin Phillips suggests that it was clear that Bush's presidency "rested on an uncommonly narrow base." This base consisted of "the increasingly narrow even theocratic, sentiment among Republican voters."[50] In his estimation this led the Republican Party to become the nation's first religious party.

For Robertson the news must have been a bitter pill to swallow. The Christian Coalition had become operationally irrelevant, yet the Christian Right was still mobilized and helped Bush to victory. The Bush administration had succeeded in its attempt to marginalize the Christian Right's traditional leadership, and Robertson was not able to stop it. Journalist Dana Milbank wrote, "[F]or the first time, vast numbers of evangelical Christians showed their clout at the grassroots level without being organized by a national group."[51]

Although he had largely been marginalized, Robertson still mostly played the good soldier by using *The 700 Club* to attack liberals. Since he had little to lose after 2004, however, he was still more than willing to criticize the Bush administration when he felt the inclination. For the better part of forty years he had been commenting on the day's events and was still unwilling to change his ways. *The 700 Club* had been broadcast live since its inception, and Robertson refused repeated suggestions by the CBN staff to add a six-second delay. Those few seconds would be enough to edit out any questionable statements he might make. While such practices were common on most live TV shows, Robertson did not want anyone to have control over his comments; he was still in charge.

Besides his critique of Islam in the weeks following 9/11 Robertson took considerable heat for a series of statements on world leaders and on Bush's foreign policy. During an interview on MSNBC Robertson characterized the State Department as a bunch of wimps who "sell out on many issues." A few weeks later on *The 700 Club* he went even further when he interviewed Joel Mowbray, author of *Dangerous Diplomacy: How the State Department Endangers America's Security*. After repeatedly praising the book Robertson joked that it made him realize that the only way to fix the State Department was to "get a nuclear device inside Foggy Bottom. I think that's the answer." The federal government was quick to condemn his comments.[52]

Such criticism did not slow Robertson down one bit. In August 2005 *The 700 Club* did a feature on Hugo Chavez, the president of Venezuela. Chavez's left-wing politics and threats concerning oil shipments to the United States had made him a focus of concern in Washington, D.C. In his commentary after the news piece Robertson said, "[I]f he thinks we're going to try to assassinate him, I think that we really ought to go ahead and do it." As the secular media took hold of the story, Robertson denied saying that Chavez should be killed, but claimed to have wanted him just "taken out." He went on to explain "take him out can be a number of things, including kidnapping. There are a number of ways to take out a dictator from power besides killing him. I was misinterpreted." His disingenuous defense collapsed when the videotape of his comment was repeated on nearly every news program. If he wasn't going to accept a six-second delay he should have at least accepted responsibility for his statements. Robertson eventually issued a full apology, but the damage had been done. Politically liberal evangelical Jim Wallis suggested that Robertson's comments "put Venezuelan evangelicals in jeopardy" and called on Robertson to resign. TV commentator Chris Matthews spoke for many Americans when he wondered aloud if Robertson had lost his mind.[53]

Put into the context of recent American history, Robertson's assassination solution was not crazy, merely behind the times. Officially the Bush administration denounced Robertson's call for Chavez's death; however, there were members of the Bush White House who had also worked there in a time when political murders were not uncommon. When Richard Nixon was president, Salvador Allende, the democratically elected president of Chile, was assassinated by the CIA with Nixon's approval. Ronald Reagan ordered a raid on Libyan military bases and a U.S. Air Force pilot became "lost" and "accidentally" bombed the house of Libyan dictator Moammar Gadhafi in hopes of ending his reign. So when members of the Bush administration feigned horror at Robertson's words, they were ignoring their own history. As a Christian minister Robertson should not be calling for the death of anyone except perhaps the devil; however, as a politician he had a sense of realpolitik that should make Henry Kissinger proud.

In January 2006 Robertson's freewheeling statements finally seemed to give him pause. On January 3, Israeli prime minister Ariel Sharon suffered a severe stroke and was on the verge of death. Robertson had met with Sharon on several occasions, and while he was a vocal supporter of Israel, he had been critical of Sharon's plan to pull Israeli troops out of the Gaza Strip and give land to the Palestinians. The day after Sharon was hospitalized Robertson claimed that his stroke was the result of God's anger. "The prophet Joel makes it very clear that God has enmity against those who 'divide my land,'" Robertson said. "I would say: Woe unto any prime minister of Israel who takes a similar course to appease the E.U. [European Union], the United Nations or the United States of America." His comments ironically put him in agreement with Mahmoud Ahmadinejad, the president of Iran, who publicly hoped that Sharon would die as punishment for his sins.[54]

Even though he had been harshly criticized for his statements more times than he could count, his diatribe against Sharon cost him dearly. A week after his remark Israel's Department of Tourism announced that it was canceling Robertson's participation in a planned $50 million Christian heritage center near the Sea of Galilee, even though he had led the effort to have it built.[55] Robertson eventually issued a public apology and spoke with Sharon's son to express his regret as well. Back in the United States, even his fellow evangelicals tried to distance themselves. "He speaks for an ever-diminishing number of American evangelicals, and that process accelerates every time he makes a statement like this," said Richard Land, president of the Southern Baptist Convention's Ethics and Religious Liberty Commission.[56] It is interesting to note that the evangelicals who tend to be the most critical of Robertson, Land and Gary Bauer, for example, are the very ones who are trying to take his place as the head of the Christian Right.

A sign that despite everything Robertson still enjoyed some influence in the Bush administration came in the aftermath of Hurricane Katrina, which destroyed much of New Orleans in 2005. The Federal Emergency Management Agency (FEMA) was the much criticized agency that was supposed to handle the recovery of the city. In the scandal regarding FEMA's inaction its leader Michael Brown was forced to resign. Amidst the public outcry against the agency's failure to act, one of its actions went largely unnoticed. On FEMA's website was a listing of relief agencies that people could donate to. The Red Cross was predictably the first one, but Robertson's Operation Blessing was listed second. This was despite the fact that the IRS had reported that Operation Blessing had given almost half of its two-million-dollar budget to CBN.[57] Operation Blessing sent teams of volunteers from around the nation to help with the cleanup efforts. This was publicized by *The 700 Club* and CBN for over a year.

Six years into George W. Bush's term in office Robertson had been marginalized by his own actions and the actions of those in power. Lynne Duke, writing in the *Washington Post*, said that Robertson was either "an embarrassment to the conservative movement who has yet to realize his own irrelevance, or he is a valuable Christian leader of millions, a man still capable of marshaling votes and influencing politics." A staff member of a Republican senator claimed, "I don't know anybody on the Hill who's going to quake in their boots when Pat Robertson issues some sort of a threat or a decree."[58]

If Robertson had become irrelevant, signs of his power and success can still be seen everywhere. The people he supported were in office; he had friends in the administration who were enacting policies to his liking. More than anything else, Robertson helped make conservative politics virtually inseparable from evangelical Christianity. Even though Robertson was often critical of President Bush, the vast majority of the news on *The 700 Club* was still supportive of the administration. He managed to be critical, but still overwhelmingly partisan.

Notes

1. Richard Berke, "Religious Conservatives Conquer G.O.P. in Texas," *New York Times*, June 12, 1994.

2. Molly Ivins and Lou Dubose, *Shrub: The Short but Happy Political Life of George W. Bush* (New York: Random House, 2000), 83.

3. Sue Anne Pressley, "Pro-Death Penalty but Chivalrous Texans Debate Fate of Karla Faye Tucker," *Washington Post*, January 25, 1998.

4. Carol Guensburg, "Living with Conviction," *Milwaukee Journal Sentinel* [Wisc.], March 15, 1998.

5. Ivins and Dubose, *Shrub*, 75.

6. Robin Toner, "The 43rd President: Conservatives," *New York Times*, December 15, 2000.

7. John Micklethwait and Adrian Woolridge, *The Right Nation: Conservative Power in America* (New York: Penguin, 2004), 146.

8. Pat Robertson, "Bush Faith-Based Plan Requires an Overhaul," *USA Today*, March 5, 2001.

9. Esther Kaplan, *With God on Their Side: George W. Bush and the Christian Right* (New York: New Press, 2005), 50.

10. Kaplan, *With God on Their Side*, 51.

11. David Frum, *The Right Man: The Surprise Presidency of George W. Bush* (New York: Random House, 2003), 103.

12. David Kuo, *Tempting Faith: An Inside Story of Political Seduction* (New York: Free Press, 2006), 180.

13. Kuo, *Tempting Faith*, 214.

14. Kuo, *Tempting Faith*, 214.

15. Kaplan, *With God on Their Side*, 52.

16. Chris Mooney, "W's Christian Nation," *The American Prospect*, June 2003.

17. Kuo, *Tempting Faith*, 212.

18. Kuo, *Tempting Faith*, 230.

19. *Conversations with Michael Eisner*, CNBC, June 20, 2006.

20. Lorraine Woellert, "The Religious Right Isn't Weaker, It's Just Different," *BusinessWeek*, December 24, 2001.

21. Dana Milbank, "Religious Right Finds Its Center in Oval Office," *Washington Post*, December 24, 2001.

22. Woellert, "The Religious Right Isn't Weaker, It's Just Different."

23. David Domke and Kevin Coe, "How Bush's God Talk Is Different," in *Jesus Is Not a Republican: The Religious Right's War on America*, ed. Clint Willis and Nate Hardcastle (New York: Thunder's Mouth Press, 2005), 120.

24. Milbank, "Religious Right Finds Its Center in Oval Office."

25. Micklethwait and Woolridge, *The Right Nation*, 147.

26. *Buchanan & Press*, MSNBC, September 3, 2003.

27. *Seattle Times* news service, "Prayer Offensive Waged against Justices," *Seattle Times*, July 18, 2003.

28. Pat Robertson interview, *Scarborough Country*, MSNBC, January 28, 2004.

29. Pat Robertson interview, *Buchanan & Press*, MSNBC, September 3, 2003.

30. Pat Robertson, *The Ten Offensives: Reclaiming the Blessings of the Ten Commandments* (Nashville, Tenn.: Integrity Publishers, 2004), 204.

31. Pat Robertson, *Courting Disaster: How the Supreme Court Is Usurping the Power of Congress and the People* (Nashville, Tenn.: Integrity Publishers, 2004), 267.

32. Michael Maculiff, "Rev's Got Explaining to Do," *New York Daily News*, October 10, 2005.

33. Charlie Savage, "Bush, Promoting Miers, Invokes Her Faith," *Boston Globe*, October 13, 2005.

34. Pat Robertson, *The New World Order* (Dallas, Tex.: Word Publishing, 1991), 14.

35. Hanna Rosin, "Robertson Espouses Assassin Solution," *Washington Post*, August 10, 1999.

36. Oliver Burkeman, "Threat of War: Powell Attacks Christian Right," *The Guardian*, November 15, 2002.

37. Interview with Ted Haggard, *The 700 Club*, www.cbn.com/spirituallife/prayerand counseling/intercession/haggard0301.aspx. CBN (accessed August 24, 2006).

38. *Paula Zahn Now*, CNN, October 19, 2004.

39. Larry Bonko, "Hello, Goodbye: New Talent Arrives at WVEC as Old Hands Exit," *Virginian-Pilot*, June 29, 2003.

40. Associated Press, "Robertson: God Says It's Bush in a Blowout in November," *USA Today*, January 2, 2004.

41. Don Lattin, "Christian Right Not on GOP Speech List," *San Francisco Chronicle*, August 28, 2004.

42. Linda Wertheimer, "Importance of the Christian Right to the Republican Party," *All Things Considered*, National Public Radio, September 1, 2004.

43. Bruce Davison, "Progressives Refuse to Turn Other Cheek," *San Antonio Express-News* [Tex.], September 5, 2004.

44. Scott Shepard, "Election 2004: Evangelicals Claim to BE GOP'S BASE," *Atlanta Journal-Constitution*, September 25, 2004.

45. Rick Klein, "Candidates Are Targeting Evangelical Base in W.VA," *Boston Globe*, October 3, 2004.

46. David Kirkpatrick, "Bush's Allies Till Fertile Soil," *New York Times*, June 18, 2004.

47. Randall Balmer, *Thy Kingdom Come: How the Religious Right Distorts the Faith and Threatens America* (New York: Basic, 2006).

48. Mark Shields, "Bush Campaign's Contempt for People of Faith," *CNN.com*, October 4, 2004.

49. Dana Milbank, "For the President, a Vote of Full Faith and Credit," *Washington Post*, November 7, 2004.

50. Kevin Phillips, *American Theocracy: The Peril and Politics of Radical Religion, Oil, and Borrowed Money in the 21st Century* (New York: Viking, 2006), 195.

51. Milbank, "For the President, a Vote of Full Faith and Credit."

52. Associated Press, "State Dept. Condemns Robertson Comments," *San Diego Union Tribune* [Calif.], October 12, 2003.

53. *Hardball*, MSNBC, August 25, 2005.

54. Alan Cooperman, "Iranian Leader, Evangelist Call Prime Minister's Illness Deserved," *Washington Post*, January 6, 2006.

55. Avi Krawitz, "Israel Rejects Robertson Funding," *Jerusalem Post*, January 11, 2006.

56. Laurie Goodstein, "Even Pat Robertson's Friends Are Wondering," *New York Times*, January 8, 2006.

57. Lenore Skenazy, "Dems Must Expose GOP," *Daily News* [New York], September 14, 2005.

58. Lynne Duke, "Preaching with a Vengeance," *Washington Post*, October 15, 2005.

CHAPTER 19

THE EMPEROR IN TWILIGHT

CRUISING down the 81 Freeway in the Shenandoah Valley near Lexington, Virginia, drivers will see a sign for Lake Robertson. The man-made lake was named in honor of Senator A. Willis Robertson, but today his son's face is what is more likely to come to mind. Pat Robertson was raised in a world of power and prestige, and in light of that, his considerable accomplishments in politics are not surprising. What is interesting is the divergent path he took to power when he became a Charismatic-evangelical Christian and set off to serve the Lord and live a life of poverty. It seems as if it was his destiny to return to politics, and when he did he brought millions of evangelicals with him. Since he has spent most of his life in a flurry of activity, it is not surprising that his influence has been widespread. His life has affected America in three areas: evangelical religion, business, and politics.

When Robertson converted to Charismatic Christianity, it was considered by many to be either heretical or a fringe group of American Protestantism. Robertson's ecumenical outlook was similar to that of evangelist Billy Graham, whose interdenominational spirit was one of the hallmarks of twentieth-century American Christianity. Robertson did what no other television evangelist was able to do: he purposefully built bridges across denominations and led organizations that appealed to many groups. While he did not make any major contributions to theology, he helped his particular beliefs reach the mainstream. In that regard, Robertson was closer to evangelist Billy Sunday than his hero Charles Finney. Through *The 700 Club* he helped popularize his brand of Christianity and tried to bring it to a wider audience with innovations in television that now seem standard. Robertson's prominence allowed him to serve as a gatekeeper of acceptable evangelical theology. He popularized the work of theologian Francis Schaeffer and the apocalyptic writings of Hal Lindsey. Robertson's fame also brought him into contact with controversial theological ideas such as Reconstructionism, which he found fascinating yet flawed. His rejection of Reconstructionism, like his earlier denunciation of the Shepherding movement, helped keep them from reaching a wider audience. He was not a theological innovator like Jonathan Edwards; instead he was content to refine the presentation of his faith and make millions of dollars in the process.

He also impacted religion with his innovations in religious television, especially with the creation of an entire network dedicated to religious programming and the introduction of the talk show format. Before *The 700 Club* most religious shows were taped church services or conversations on cheap sets that looked like churches. Robertson borrowed from men like Johnny Carson to create a religious talk show, not just a vehicle for sermons. This new format was very successful and was imitated by several of his competitors. Today, nearly every religious broadcast features innovations that Robertson had introduced in the 1960s. In short, Robertson took the presentation of evangelical Christianity from the backwaters of broadcasting to the modern age. Today, religious broadcasters are expected to use computer graphics and flashy sets in order to attract an audience. Robertson raised the stakes and brought professionalism to a world that truly needed it. Through his innovations he has become both wealthy and famous.

The world of businesses is his least known and appreciated area of impact. His skill in the business world is apparent in his ability to turn a $70 company into a two-billion-dollar media powerhouse. No other televangelist, or megachurch leader for that matter, became a multimillionaire through nonchurch-related activities. While it is true that Robertson made millions with his religious programs, he made millions more in his other business ventures. His pioneering work in cable and satellite broadcasting were later copied by Disney, Nickelodeon, and a host of other networks.

The most fascinating aspect of his business activities is his ability to avoid being tainted by his sometimes questionable business practices. Most of the people who donated to *The 700 Club* to support Christian television had no idea that their donations also helped make Robertson a multimillionaire. For twenty-five years Robertson took donations and then used the empire that he built with tax-free money to create for-profit businesses. The main reason that he was never tainted by scandal was that he did not spend the money on himself, but to further his business interests. Robertson is not the kind of man to take long vacations in the south of France. For him, success is its own reward, and his dedication to the Protestant work ethic and free market Christianity has led many of his followers to actually admire him for his wealth. Besides television, Robertson's work in African diamond mines is an example of the activities of a man who is more interested in money than in the people that his businesses affect. Just as Robertson does not live lavishly, he never seems to consider what impacts his deals have on others. His willingness to use money gained from tax-exempt ministries for business use and vice versa is remarkable. While it is true that Robertson has used donated money for secular purposes, he has also frequently given money from his business back to his ministries. This is, perhaps, how he is able to rationalize the use of tax-exempt money to fund diamond mines and political campaigns. In the end he seems to have hoped that by giving the ministries more money than he has taken he would avoid ethical problems.

Pat Robertson is best known to most Americans for his political activities. He is not the originator of conservative politics, or even a new branch of politics, but as is the case with his contributions to religion, he is a refiner of ideas. Robertson's political ambitions arrived with the wave of evangelicals who hoped to move into the halls of power with Jimmy Carter in 1976. As the New Christian Right movement waned in the mid-1980s, Robertson was able to inject it with new life. Under his leadership the Christian Right actually gained power instead of sinking into obscurity as many scholars had predicted. When the Democrats controlled both the Congress and the White House, Robertson was able to make sure that the goals of the Reagan revolution were not forgotten. After the stunning election of 1994 it was clear that Robertson was a powerful political figure and someone who had to be taken seriously.

He is also responsible for helping to mainstream politically conservative evangelicals into the political world. Just as he helped bring Charismatics into wider acceptance theologically, he has helped conservative Christians claim their place in the sun. There are still many groups that continue to resist any person or organization who attempts to use religious dialogue in the political sphere, but since the mid-1980s religious groups have had a permanent place at the table. While many people played a role in this development, Robertson's success in politics has reached a level that contemporaries such as Jerry Falwell and Gary Bauer were unable to achieve.

Pat Robertson also represents the limits of Christians in government and politics. Modern politics may allow conservative Christians to share their views on political matters, but there is still resistance to their holding office. John Ashcroft encountered opposition in part due to his religious views, and Robertson's own campaign was limited by people's fears of his religious beliefs. Even if he had not been a "religious broadcaster," Robertson would have been kept from winning the presidency because of his lack of political experience. The fact that he had a religious background became just another reason, albeit the prime reason, that many people were hostile to his candidacy. The bias against him or anyone else based primarily on their religious beliefs is unfortunate, because American history is replete with examples of the mixture of religion and politics, although Robertson and the Christian Right in general are a break from the political stances that evangelicals have traditionally held.

One hundred years ago politician William Jennings Bryan was the most famous theologically conservative Christian in America. He was the Democratic Party's nominee for president three times, and his campaign speeches were fiery and filled with angry "us versus them" rhetoric. Like the Christian Right leaders of today he believed that the Bible was the inspired word of God and that God would bless America if the people were faithful to him. So on the surface it appears nothing has changed, but everything is different. If Bryan were alive today, he would be amazed at the political positions that his fellow religious conservatives have taken. While he would probably align himself with the pro-life elements of the Christian Right movement, most of its positions on other issues would horrify him—its neglect of the poor and the working class, the unquestioning support of militarism and war. These issues are not part of traditional evangelical politics but are by-products of the Christian Right's relationship with the GOP. Evangelicals hoped to get their social agenda items put in place if they supported secular Republicans in their free-market politics. As a result, many leaders of the Christian Right, including Robertson, made compromises that only increased as time passed. They forgot which positions were theirs and which violated their faith's historic beliefs. The end result has been the transformation of evangelicalism to include set political as well as religious beliefs. The Republican Party may be better off for the exchange, but evangelicalism has lost the ability to effectively spread its message to those opposed to the GOP's agenda. Robertson bears a good deal of responsibility for this change and for its consequences.

In the final analysis, Robertson's life is a metaphor for both evangelicals and the Christian Right. When Robertson became a Christian, he chose to live in poverty on the outskirts of society. He rejected his heritage in order to follow a religious calling. As time passed he used his ministry to help him lead a more comfortable life, similar to how evangelicalism embraced American culture and created a vibrant subculture. Like evangelicals, Robertson's first forays into politics were hesitant and largely ignored by the power brokers. It was when he attempted to get power on his own terms that he was finally given a modicum of respect. Unfortunately, the changes that Robertson and evangelicalism went through to gain power were steep.

Recently some scholars and political pundits have returned to predicting that the Christian Right is dead or dying. History shows us that they are most likely wrong, again, even if there are intriguing new signs of its collapse. The serious policy failures of George W. Bush's administration have called much of the Christian Right's agenda into question. However, this time many of the questions are coming from evangelicals themselves. The resistance to the Christian Coalition that Robertson encountered from many evangelicals after the 2000 election has spread. Once they began to reject a central political organization, it became easier for dissenting voices to be heard. America is a country that has always been welcoming of religious diversity, and now that its leaders have been taken down a notch, average believers are beginning to find their own way.

Over the past thirty years Robertson has had an impact on America that rivals that of any other religious leader and even most politicians. The big question is what will his legacy be? What will remain long after he is gone? Political victories are ephemeral and will be the first to vanish, even if evangelicals remain mobilized for decades. His religious influence will wane as new technologies are developed that make broadcast television less important. It seems that Regent University will be the main source of his legacy, which is why he has kept an increasingly tight rein on the campus. He spent his political career trying to get Christians into powerful government positions, and the university is his best chance to see that long-term goal accomplished. Whether that dream remains after Robertson is gone is anyone's guess. What is clear is that it is a goal that has always been close to his heart.

⁂ SELECTED BIBLIOGRAPHY

Abelman, Robert, and Stewart M. Hoover. *Religious Television*. Greenwich, Conn.: Ablex Publishing, 1990.

Ahlstrom, Sydney E. *A Religious History of the American People*. New Haven, Conn.: Yale University Press, 1972.

Alcorn, Randy. *Is Rescuing Right? Breaking the Law to Save the Unborn*. Downers Grove, Ill.: InterVarsity Press, 1990.

Allen, Steven, and Richard Viguerie. *Lip Service: George Bush's 30-Year Battle with Conservatives*. Chantilly, Va.: CP Books, 1992.

Anfuso, Joseph, and David Sczepanski. *Efrain Rios Montt, Servant or Dictator?* Ventura, Calif.: Vision House, 1984.

Averill, Lloyd J. *Religious Right, Religious Wrong: A Critique of the Fundamentalist Phenomenon*. New York: Pilgrim Press, 1989.

Badger, Anthony. *The New Deal: The Depression Years, 1933–1940*. New York: Noonday Press, 1989.

Bakker, Jim, and Ken Abraham. *I Was Wrong*. Nashville, Tenn.: Thomas Nelson Publishers, 1996.

Bakker, Jim, and Robert Paul Lamb. *Move That Mountain*. Plainfield, N.J.: Logos International, 1976.

Baldwin, Lewis. *Toward the Beloved Community: Martin Luther King, Jr., and South Africa*. Cleveland, Ohio: Pilgrim Press, 1995.

Balmer, Randall. *Thy Kingdom Come: How the Religious Right Distorts the Faith and Threatens America*. New York: Basic, 2006.

Barna, George. *The Barna Report*. Ventura, Calif.: Regal Books, 1991.

Barron, Bruce. *Heaven on Earth? The Social and Political Agendas of Dominion Theology*. Grand Rapids, Mich.: Zondervan, 1992.

Bellah, Robert N. *The Broken Covenant*. Chicago: University of Chicago Press, 1992.

Bennett, William J. *The Index of Leading Cultural Indicators*. New York: Simon & Schuster, 1994.

Berman, William C. *From the Center to the Edge: The Politics and Policies of the Clinton Presidency*. Lanham, Md.: Rowman & Littlefield, 2001.

Bloesch, Donald. *Essentials of Evangelical Theology*. New York: Harper & Row, 1978.

Boston, Robert. *Close Encounters with the Religious Right*. New York: Prometheus Books, 2000.

———. *The Most Dangerous Man in America? Pat Robertson and the Rise of the Christian Coalition*. New York: Prometheus Books, 1996.

Boyer, Paul. *When Time Shall Be No More*. Cambridge, Mass.: Harvard University Press, 1992.

Brown, Ruth Murray. *For a Christian America: A History of the Religious Right*. New York: Prometheus Books, 2002.

Bruce, Steve. *Pray TV: Televangelism in America*. London: Routledge, 1990.

———. *The Rise and Fall of the New Christian Right: Conservative Protestant Politics in America, 1978–1988*. Oxford: Oxford University Press, 1988.

Cannon, Lou. *President Reagan: The Role of a Lifetime*. New York: Simon & Schuster, 1991.

Carpenter, Joel. *Revive Us Again: The Reawakening of American Fundamentalism*. New York: Oxford University Press, 1997.

Carroll, Peter. *It Seemed Like Nothing Happened: America in the 1970s*. New Brunswick, N.J.: Rutgers University Press, 1990.

Carter, Jimmy. *Our Endangered Values: America's Moral Crisis*. New York: Simon & Schuster, 2005.

Carter, Stephen L. *Culture of Disbelief*. New York: Doubleday, 1994.

Christian Broadcasting Network. *The CBN Ministry Handbook: Biblical Solutions to Everyday Problems*. Wheaton, Ill.: Tyndale, 1985.

Conway, Flo, and Jim Siegelman. *Holy Terror: The Fundamentalist War on America's Freedoms in Religion, Politics, and Our Private Lives*. New York: Delta Publishing, 1984.

Cromartie, Michael, ed. *No Longer Exiles: The Religious New Right in American Politics*. Washington, D.C.: Ethics and Public Policy Center, 1993.

Crouch, Paul. *I Had No Father but God: A Personal Letter to My Two Sons*. Santa Ana, Calif.: Trinity Christian Center, 1993.

Dayton, Donald W. *Theological Roots of Pentecostalism*. Grand Rapids, Mich.: Francis Avery Press, 1987.

Diamond, Sara. *Not by Politics Alone: The Enduring Influence of the Christian Right*. New York: Guilford, 1998.

Diggins, John Patrick. *The Proud Decades*. New York: Norton, 1988.

Dionne, E. J. *Why Americans Hate Politics*. New York: Touchstone, 1991.

Donovan, John B. *Pat Robertson: The Authorized Biography*. New York: Macmillan, 1988.

Draper, Theodore. *A Very Thin Line: The Iran-Contra Affairs*. New York: Simon & Schuster, 1991.

Drew, Elizabeth. *Election Journal*. New York: Morrow, 1989.

Duffy, Michael, and Dan Goodgame. *Marching in Place: The Status Quo Presidency of George Bush*. New York: Simon & Schuster, 1992.

Durfey, Thomas, and James Ferrier. *Religious Broadcast Management Handbook*. Grand Rapids, Mich.: Zondervan, 1986.

Edwards, Janis. *Political Cartoons in the 1988 Presidential Campaign*. New York: Garland, 1997.

Ehrman, John. *The Eighties: America in the Age of Reagan*. New Haven, Conn.: Yale University Press, 2005.

Elwell, Walter A., ed. *Evangelical Dictionary of Theology*. Grand Rapids, Mich.: Baker Book House, 1984.

Eskridge, Larry, and Mark Noll, eds. *More Money, More Ministry: Money and Evangelicals in Recent North American History*. Grand Rapids, Mich.: Eerdmans, 2000.

Fackre, Gabriel. *The Religious Right and Christian Faith*. Grand Rapids, Mich.: Eerdmans, 1982.

Falwell, Jerry. *Strength for the Journey*. New York: Simon & Schuster, 1987.

Feldman, Glenn, ed. *Politics and Religion in the White South*. Lexington: University Press of Kentucky, 2005.

Feldman, Noah. *Divided by God: America's Church–State Problem and What We Should Do about It*. New York: Farrar, Straus & Giroux, 2005.

Felsenthal, Carol. *The Sweetheart of the Silent Majority: The Biography of Phyllis Schlafly*. New York: Doubleday, 1981.

FitzGerald, Frances. *Way Out There in the Blue: Reagan, Star Wars and the End of the Cold War*. New York: Simon & Schuster, 2000.

Foege, Alec. *The Empire That God Built: Inside Pat Robertson's Media Machine*. New York: Wiley, 1996.

Fowler, Robert Booth. *Unconventional Partners: Religion and Liberal Culture in the United States*. Grand Rapids, Mich.: Eerdmans, 1989.

Fraser, Steve, and Gary Gerstle, eds. *The Rise and Fall of the New Deal Order: 1930–1980*. Princeton, N.J.: Princeton University Press, 1989.

Frum, David. *The Right Man: The Surprise Presidency of George W. Bush*. New York: Random House, 2003.

———. *Dead Right*. New York: A New Republic Book/Basic, 1994.

Gallup Organization. *The Spiritual Climate in America Today*. Princeton, N.J.: Gallup, 1983.

Gaustad, Edwin, and Leigh Schmidt. *The Religious History of America*. San Francisco: Harper San Francisco, 2002.

Germond, Jack, and Jules Whitcover. *Mad as Hell: Revolt at the Ballot Box, 1992*. New York: Warner, 1993.

———. *Whose Broad Stripes and Bright Stars?* New York: Warner, 1989.

Gillespie, Edward, and Bob Schellhas, eds. *Contract with America: The Bold Plan by Representative Newt Gingrich and Representative Dick Armey and the House Republicans to Change the Nation*. New York: Times Books, 1994.

Goldman, Peter, et al. *The Quest for the Presidency, the 1988 Campaign*. New York: Simon & Schuster, 1989.

Gottfried, Paul, and Thomas Fleming. *The Conservative Movement*. Boston: Twayne Publishers, 1988.

Green, John, James Guth, Corwin Smidt, and Lyman Kellstedt. *Religion and the Culture Wars: Dispatches from the Front*. Lanham, Md.: Rowman & Littlefield, 1996.

Greene, John Robert. *The Presidency of George Bush*. Lawrence: University of Kansas Press, 2000.

Hadden, Jeffery, and Anson Shupe. *Televangelism: Power and Politics on God's Frontier*. New York: Henry Holt, 1988.

Hadden, Jeffery, and Charles Swann. *Prime Time Preachers: The Rising Power of Televangelism*. Boston: Addison Wesley, 1981.

Hambrick-Stowe, Charles. *Charles G. Finney and the Spirit of American Evangelism*. Grand Rapids, Mich.: Eerdmans, 1996.

Hamby, Alonzo. *Liberalism and Its Challengers: From FDR to Bush*. New York: Oxford University Press, 1992.

Harrell, David Edwin Jr. *Pat Robertson: A Personal, Religious, and Political Portrait.* New York: Harper & Row, 1987.

———. *Varieties of Southern Evangelicalism.* Macon, Ga.: Mercer University Press, 1981.

Hart, D. G. *That Old Time Religion in Modern America: Evangelical Protestantism in the Twentieth Century.* Chicago: Ivan R. Dee, 2002.

Hatch, Nathan O. *The Democratization of American Christianity.* New Haven, Conn.: Yale University Press, 1989.

Heinemann, Ronald. *Depression and New Deal in Virginia.* Charlottesville: University of Virginia Press, 1983.

Hertzke, Allen D. *Echoes of Discontent: Jesse Jackson, Pat Robertson and the Resurgence of Populism.* Washington, D.C.: Congressional Quarterly Press, 1993.

Hill, Samuel, ed. *The New Encyclopedia of Southern Culture, Vol. 1, Religion.* Chapel Hill: University of North Carolina Press, 2006.

Hixson, William B. *Search for the American Right Wing: An Analysis of the Social Science Record, 1955–1987.* Princeton, N.J.: Princeton University Press, 1992.

Hoover, Stewart M. *Mass Media Religion.* Newbury Park, Calif.: Sage, 1988.

Horsfield, Peter. *Religious Television: The American Experience.* New York: Longman, 1984.

House, H. Wayne, and Thomas Ice. *Dominion Theology: Blessing or Curse?* Portland, Ore.: Multnomah Press, 1988.

Hudson, Winthrop S., and John Corrigan. *Religion in America.* 5th ed. New York: Macmillan, 1992.

Hutcheson, Richard G. *God in the White House: How Religion Has Changed the Modern Presidency.* New York: Macmillan, 1988.

Ivins, Molly, and Lou Dubose. *Shrub: The Short but Happy Political Life of George W. Bush.* New York: Random House, 2000.

Jorstad, Erling. *The New Christian Right 1981–1988: Prospects for the Post Reagan Decade.* Lewiston, N.Y.: Edwin Mellen Press, 1987.

———. *Evangelicals in the White House: The Cultural Maturation of Born Again Christianity, 1960–1980.* New York: Edwin Mellen Press, 1981.

———. *The Politics of Moralism.* Minneapolis, Minn.: Ausburg, 1981.

Kaplan, Esther. *With God on Their Side: George W. Bush and the Christian Right.* New York: New Press, 2005.

Kazin, Michael. *A Godly Hero: The Life of William Jennings Bryan.* New York: Knopf, 2006.

———. *The Populist Persuasion.* New York: Basic, 1995.

Kelly, Dean M. *Why Conservative Churches Are Growing: A Study in the Sociology of Religion.* New York: Harper & Row, 1972.

Kinchlow, Ben, with Bob Slosser. *Plain Bread.* Waco, Tex.: Word Books, 1985.

Kintz, Linda, and Julia Lesage, eds. *Media, Culture, and the Religious Right.* Minneapolis: University of Minnesota Press, 1998.

Kuo, David. *Tempting Faith: An Inside Story of Political Seduction.* New York: Free Press, 2006.

Leuchtenburg, William E. *In the Shadow of FDR: From Harry Truman to Ronald Reagan.* Ithaca, N.Y.: Cornell University Press, 1993.

Liebman, Robert C., and Robert Wuthnow, eds. *The New Christian Right.* New York: Aldine, 1983.

Lienesch, Michael. *Redeeming America: Piety and Politics in the New Christian Right.* Chapel Hill: University of North Carolina Press, 1993.

Lopatto, Paul. *Religion and the Presidential Election*. New York: Praeger, 1985.

Marley, David John. *To Redeem America: The Use of Politics in the Religion of Martin Luther King, Jr. and Pat Robertson*. Thesis, California State University, Fullerton. 1998.

Marsden, George M. *The Scandal of the Evangelical Mind*. Grand Rapids, Mich.: Eerdmans, 1994.

———. *Understanding Fundamentalism and Evangelicalism*. Grand Rapids, Mich.: Eerdmans, 1991.

———. *Evangelicalism and Modern America*. Grand Rapids, Mich.: Eerdmans, 1984.

———. *Fundamentalism and American Culture*. Oxford: Oxford University Press, 1980.

Martin, William. *With God on Our Side: The Rise of the Religious Right in America*. New York: Broadway Books, 1996.

Marty, Martin E. *Pilgrims in Their Own Land: 500 Years of Religion in America*. New York: Penguin, 1984.

Matalin, Mary, and James Carville. *All's Fair: Love, War, and Running for President*. New York: Random House, 1994.

Matusow, Allen J. *The Unraveling of America*. New York: Harper & Row, 1986.

McGirr, Lisa. *Suburban Warriors: The Origins of the New American Right*. Princeton, N.J.: Princeton University Press, 2001.

Melton, J. Gordon, Phillip C. Lucas, and Jon Stone. *Prime-Time Religion: An Encyclopedia of Religious Broadcasting*. Phoenix, Ariz.: Oryx Press, 1997.

Menendez, Albert J. *Evangelicals at the Ballot Box*. New York: Prometheus, 1996.

Micklethwait, John, and Adrian Woolridge. *The Right Nation: Conservative Power in America*. New York: Penguin, 2004.

Miller, Donald E. *Reinventing American Protestantism*. Berkeley: University of California Press, 1997.

Moen, Matthew C. *The Christian Right and Congress*. Tuscaloosa: University of Alabama Press, 1989.

Moore, R. Laurence. *Selling God: American Religion in the Marketplace of Culture*. New York: Oxford, 1994.

Moore, S. David. *The Shepherding Movement: Controversy and Charismatic Ecclesiology*. London: T&T Clark International, 2003.

Morken, Hubert. *Pat Robertson: Where He Stands*. Grand Rapids, Mich.: Revell Co., 1988.

Neuhaus, Richard John, and Michael Cromartie, eds. *Piety and Politics: Evangelicals and Fundamentalists Confront the World*. Washington, D.C.: Ethics and Public Policy Center, 1987.

Nichols, Bruce J., ed. *In Word and Deed: Evangelism and Social Responsibility*. Grand Rapids, Mich.: Eerdmans, 1985.

Niebuhr, H. Richard. *Christ and Culture*. New York: Harper & Row, 1975.

North, Gary, and Gary DeMar. *Christian Reconstruction: What It Is, What It Isn't*. Tyler, Tex.: Institute for Christian Economics, 1991.

Oldfield, Duane. *The Right and the Righteous: The Christian Right Confronts the Republican Party*. Lanham, Md.: Rowman & Littlefield, 1996.

O'Rourke. P. J. *All the Trouble in the World*. New York: Atlantic Monthly Press, 1995.

Patterson, James. *Grand Expectations: The United States 1945–1974*. New York: Oxford University Press, 1996.

Peck, Janice. *The Gods of Televangelism*. Cresskill, N.J.: Hampton Press, 1993.

Pemberton, William. *Exit with Honor: The Life and Presidency of Ronald Reagan.* London: Sharpe, 1998.

Phillips, Kevin. *American Theocracy: The Peril and Politics of Radical Religion, Oil, and Borrowed Money in the 21st Century.* New York: Viking, 2006.

Pippert, Wesley, ed. *The Spiritual Journey of Jimmy Carter: In His Own Words.* New York: Macmillan, 1978.

Poloma, Margaret. *The Assemblies of God at the Crossroads.* Knoxville: University of Tennessee Press, 1989.

———. *The Charismatic Movement: Is There a New Pentecost?* Boston: Twayne Publishers, 1982.

Pomper, Gerald, et al. *The Election of 1980.* Chatham, N.J.: Chatham House Publishers, 1981.

Pullum, Stephen. *"Foul Demons, Come Out": The Rhetoric of Twentieth-Century American Faith Healers.* Westport, Conn.: Praeger, 1999.

Reed, Ralph. *Active Faith: How Christians Are Changing the Soul of American Politics.* New York: Free Press, 1996.

———. *Politically Incorrect: The Emerging Faith Factor in American Politics.* Dallas, Tex.: Word Publishing, 1994.

Reeves, Thomas C. *The Empty Church: The Suicide of Liberal Christianity.* New York: Free Press, 1996.

Ribuffo, Leo. *Right Center Left: Essays in American History.* New Brunswick, N.J.: Rutgers University Press, 1992.

———. *The Old Christian Right.* Philadelphia: Temple University Press, 1983.

Rifkin, Jeremy, and Ted Howard. *The Emerging Order: God in the Age of Scarcity.* New York: Putnam, 1979.

Riley, Naomi Schaefer. *God on the Quad: How Religious Colleges and the Missionary Generation Are Changing America.* New York: St. Martin's, 2005.

Robbins, John W. *Pat Robertson: A Warning to America.* Jefferson, Md.: Trinity Foundation, 1988.

Robeck, Cecil. *The Azusa Street Mission and Revival.* Nashville, Tenn.: Thomas Nelson, Inc., 2006.

Robertson, Dede, and John Sherrill. *My God Will Supply.* Lincoln, Va.: Chosen Books, 1979.

Robertson, Pat. *Courting Disaster: How the Supreme Court Is Usurping the Power of Congress and the People.* Nashville, Tenn.: Integrity Publishers, 2004.

———. *The Ten Offensives: Reclaiming the Blessings of the Ten Commandments.* Nashville, Tenn.: Integrity Publishers, 2004.

———. *Bring It On: Tough Questions. Candid Answers.* Nashville, Tenn.: W Publishing Group, 2003.

———. *The End of the Age.* Nashville, Tenn.: WestBow Press, 2002.

———. *The Turning Tide: The Fall of Liberalism and the Return of Common Sense.* Dallas, Tex.: Word Publishing, 1993.

———. *The New World Order.* Dallas, Tex.: Word Publishing, 1991.

———. *The New Millennium.* Dallas, Tex.: Word Publishing, 1990.

———. *The Plan.* Nashville, Tenn.: Thomas Nelson Publishing, 1989.

———. *America's Dates with Destiny.* Nashville, Tenn.: Thomas Nelson Publishing, 1986.

————. *Answers to 200 of Life's Most Probing Questions*. New York: Thomas Nelson Publishing, 1984.

————. *The Secret Kingdom*. Dallas, Tex.: Word Publishing, 1982.

————. *Shout It from the Housetops*. Astoria, N.Y.: Logos International, 1972.

————, with William Proctor. *Beyond Reason: How Miracles Can Change Your Life*. New York: Morrow, 1985.

Rozell, Mark, and Clyde Wilcox, eds. *God at the Grass Roots: The Christian Right in the 1994 Elections*. Lanham, Md.: Rowman & Littlefield, 1995.

Rushdoony, Rousas John. *Thy Kingdom Come: Studies in Daniel and Revelation*. Fairfax, Va.: Thoburn Press, 1978.

————. *The Institutes of Biblical Law*. Nutley, N.J.: Craig Press, 1973.

Sabato, Larry, and Glenn Simpson. *Dirty Little Secrets: The Persistence of Corruption in American Politics*. New York: Random House, 1996.

Schaeffer, Francis A. *The Great Evangelical Disaster*. Wheaton, Ill.: Crossway Books, 1984.

Schultze, Quentin. *Televangelism and American Culture*. Grand Rapids, Mich.: Baker Book House, 1991.

————, ed. *American Evangelicals and the Mass Media*. Grand Rapids, Mich.: Academe Books, 1991.

Seaman, Ann Rowe. *Swaggart: The Unauthorized Biography of an American Evangelist*. New York: Continuum Publishing, 1999.

Shepard, Charles. *Forgiven: The Rise and Fall of Jim Bakker and the PTL Ministry*. New York: Atlantic Monthly Press, 1989.

Shibley, Mark A. *Resurgent Evangelicalism in the United States: Mapping Cultural Change since 1970*. Columbia: University of South Carolina Press, 1996.

Sider, Ronald J. *Rich Christians in an Age of Hunger*. Dallas, Tex.: Word, 1990.

Simon, Roger. *Road Show*. New York: Farrar, Straus & Giroux, 1990.

Smith, Christian. *American Evangelicalism: Embattled and Thriving*. Chicago: University of Chicago Press, 1998.

Stout, Harry S. *The Divine Dramatist: George Whitefield and the Rise of Modern Evangelicalism*. Grand Rapids, Mich.: Eerdmans, 1991.

Straub, Gerard Thomas. *Salvation for Sale: An Insider's View of Pat Robertson*. Buffalo, N.Y.: Prometheus Books, 1988.

Synan, Vinson. *The Holiness-Pentecostal Tradition: Charismatic Movements in the Twentieth Century*. Grand Rapids, Mich.: Eerdmans, 1997.

Taylor, Mark Lewis. *Religion, Politics and the Christian Right: Post-9/11 Powers and American Empire*. Minneapolis, Minn.: Fortress Press, 2005.

Thomas, Cal, and Ed Dobson. *Blinded by Might: Can the Religious Right Save America?* Grand Rapids, Mich.: Zondervan, 1999.

Thomas, Evan. *Back from the Dead: How Clinton Survived the Republican Revolution*. New York: Atlantic Monthly Press, 1997.

Viguerie, Richard A. *The New Right: We're Ready to Lead*. Falls Church, Va.: Viguerie Co., 1981.

Wallis, Jim. *Who Speaks for God?* New York: Delta Books, 1996.

————. *The Soul of Politics*. New York: New Press/Orbis Books, 1994.

Walsh, Lawrence. *Firewall: The Iran-Contra Conspiracy and Cover-Up*. New York: Norton, 1997.

Walsh, Shelia. *Honestly*. Grand Rapids, Mich.: Zondervan, 1996.

Watson, Justin. *The Christian Coalition: Dreams of Restoration, Demands for Recognition*. New York: St. Martin's Griffin, 1999.

Watt, David Harrington. *Bible-Carrying Christians: Conservative Protestants and Social Power*. New York: Oxford University Press, 2002.

White, Mel. *Stranger at the Gate: To Be Gay and Christian in America*. New York: Simon & Schuster, 1994.

Wilcox, Clyde. *Onward Christian Soldiers? The Religious Right in American Politics*. New York: Westview, 1996.

———. *God's Warriors: The Christian Right in Twentieth-Century America*. Baltimore, Md.: Johns Hopkins University Press, 1992.

Wilkinson, J. Harvie. *Harry Byrd and the Changing Face of Virginia Politics, 1945–1966*. Charlottesville: University of Virginia Press, 1968.

Willis, Clint, and Nate Hardcastle, eds. *Jesus Is Not a Republican: The Religious Right's War on America*. New York: Thunder's Mouth Press, 2005.

Wills, Garry. *Under God: Religion and American Politics*. New York: Simon & Schuster, 1990.

Wogaman, J. Philip. *Christian Perspectives on Politics*. Philadelphia: Fortress Press, 1988.

Wojcik, Daniel. *The End of the World as We Know It: Faith, Fatalism, and Apocalypse in America*. New York: New York University Press, 1997.

Wolfe, Alan. *The Transformation of American Religion*. New York: Free Press, 2003.

———. *One Nation after All*. New York: Penguin, 1998.

Young, Perry Deane. *God's Bullies: Power Politics and Religious Tyranny*. New York: Holt, Rinehart and Winston, 1982.

Zwier, Robert. *Born Again Politics*. Downers Grove, Ill.: InterVarsity Press, 1982.

Interviews

Boston, Robert, interview by author, tape recording, Washington, D.C., April 14, 1998, and Washington, D.C., November 19, 1999.

Lindvall, Terry, interview by author, tape recording, Costa Mesa, Calif., February 22, 1996, and Virginia Beach, Va., January 11, 2000.

Morken, Hubert, interview by author, Virginia Beach, Va., January 11, 2000.

Robertson, Pat, interview by author, tape recording, Virginia Beach, Va., May 25, 2000.

Titus, Herb, interview by author, written responses to mailed questions, June 19, 2000.

Weyrich, Paul, interview by author, tape recording, Washington, D.C., August 16, 2000.

White, Mel, interview by author, tape recording, Laguna Woods, Calif., September 29, 1999.

Wilcox, Clyde, interview by author, Washington, D.C., September 2000.

⮞ INDEX